Ford GT40
Gold Portfolio
1964~1987

Compiled by
R.M. Clarke

ISBN 1 870642 961

The car featured on our cover is owned by Jim Toensing and was photographed by the compiler at the Cunningham Automotive Museum, Costa Mesa in 1981

Distributed by
Brooklands Book Distribution Ltd.
'Holmerise', Seven Hills Road,
Cobham, Surrey, England

Printed in Hong Kong

BROOKLANDS BOOKS

BROOKLANDS BOOKS SERIES
AC Ace & Aceca 1953-1983
AC Cobra 1962-1969
Alfa Romeo Alfasud 1972-1984
Alfa Romeo Alfetta Coupes GT.GTV.GTV6 1974-1987
Alfa Romeo Giulia Berlinas 1962-1976
Alfa Romeo Giulia Coupés 1963-1976
Alfa Romeo Spider 1966-1987
Allard Gold Portfolio 1937-1958
Alvis Gold Portfolio 1919-1967
Aston Martin Gold Portfolio 1972-1985
Austin Seven 1922-1982
Austin A30 & A35 1951-1962
Austin Healey 3000 1959-1967
Austin Healey 100 & 3000 Collection No. 1
Austin Healey 'Frogeye' Sprite Collection No. 1
Austin Healey Sprite 1958-1971
Avanti 1962-1983
BMW Six Cylinder Coupés 1969-1975
BMW 1600 Collection No. 1
BMW 2002 1968-1976
Bristol Cars Gold Portfolio 1946-1985
Buick Automobiles 1947-1960
Buick Riviera 1963-1978
Cadillac Automobiles 1949-1959
Cadillac Automobiles 1960-1969
Cadillac Eldorado 1967-1978
Camaro 1966-1970
Chevrolet Camaro & Z-28 1973-1981
High Performance Camaros 1982-1988
Chevrolet Camaro Collection No. 1
Chevrolet 1955-1957
Chevrolet Impala & SS 1958-1971
Chevelle & SS 1964-1972
Chevy II Nova & SS 1962-1973
High Performance Corvettes 1983-1989
Chrysler 300 1955-1970
Citroen Traction Avant 1934-1957
Citroen DS & ID 1955-1975
Citroen 2CV 1948-1988
Cobras & Replicas 1962-1983
Cortina 1600E & GT 1967-1970
Corvair 1959-1968
Daimler Dart & V-8 250 1959-1969
Datsun 240Z 1970-1973
Datsun 280Z & ZX 1975-1983
De Tomaso Collection No. 1
Dodge Charger 1966-1974
Excalibur Collection No. 1
Ferrari Cars 1946-1956
Ferrari Dino 1965-1974
Ferrari Dino 308 1974-1979
Ferrari 308 & Mondial 1980-1984
Ferrari Collection No. 1
Fiat-Bertone X1/9 1973-1988
Fiat Pininfarina 124+2000 Spider 1968-1985
Ford Automobiles 1949-1959
Ford Fairlane 1955-1970
Ford Falcon 1960-1970
Ford RS Escort 1968-1980
High Performance Escorts MkI 1968-1974
High Performance Escorts MkII 1975-1980
High Performance Mustangs 1982-1988
Honda CRX 1983-1987
Hudson & Railton Cars 1936-1940
Jaguar Cars 1957-1961
Jaguar Cars 1961-1964
Jaguar XK120 XK140 XK150 Gold Portfolio 1948-1960
Jaguar MK2 1959-1969
Jaguar E-Type Gold Portfolio 1961-1971
Jaguar E-Type 1966-1971
Jaguar E-Type V12 1971-1975
Jaguar XJ6 1968-1972
Jaguar XJ6 Series II 1973-1979
Jaguar XJ6 & XJ12 Series III 1979-1985
Jaguar XJ12 1972-1980
Jaguar XJS Gold Portfolio 1975-1988
Jensen Cars 1946-1967
Jensen Cars 1967-1979
Jensen Interceptor Gold Portfolio 1966-1986
Jensen Healey 1972-1976
Lamborghini Cars 1964-1970
Lamborghini Cars 1970-1975
Lamborghini Countach Collection No. 1
Lamborghini Countach & Urraco 1974-1980
Lamborghini Countach & Jalpa 1980-1985
Lancia Stratos 1972-1985
Land Rover 1948-1973
Land Rover Series II & IIa 1958-1971
Land Rover Series III 1971-1985
Land Rover 90 & 110 1983-1989
Lotus Cortina 1963-1970
Lotus Elan Gold Portfolio 1962-1974
Lotus Elan Collection No. 2
Lotus Elite 1957-1964
Lotus Elite & Eclat 1974-1981
Lotus Turbo Esprit 1980-1986
Lotus Europa 1966-1975
Lotus Europa Collection No. 1
Lotus Seven 1957-1980
Lotus Seven Collection No. 1
Marcos Cars 1960-1988
Maserati 1965-1970
Maserati 1970-1975
Mazda RX-7 Collection No. 1
Mercedes 190 & 300SL 1954-1963
Mercedes 230/250/280SL 1963-1971
Mercedes 350/450SL & SLC 1971-1980
Mercedes Benz Cars 1949-1954
Mercedes Benz Cars 1954-1957
Mercedes Benz Cars 1957-1961
Mercedes Benz Competition Cars 1950-1957
Metropolitan 1954-1962

MG TC 1945-1949
MG TD 1949-1953
MG TF 1953-1955
MG Cars 1957-1959
MG Cars 1959-1962
MG Midget 1961-1980
MGA Collection No. 1
MGA Roadsters 1955-1962
MGB Roadsters 1962-1980
MGB GT 1965-1980
Mini Cooper 1961-1971
Mini Moke 1964-1989
Morgan Cars 1960-1970
The Morgan 3-Wheeler Gold Portfolio 1910-1952
Morgan Cars Gold Portfolio 1968-1989
Morris Minor Collection No. 1
Oldsmobile Automobiles 1955-1963
Old's Cutlass & 4-4-2 1964-1972
Oldsmobile Toronado 1966-1978
Opel GT 1968-1973
Packard Gold Portfolio 1946-1958
Pantera Gold Portfolio 1970-1989
Pantera & Mangusta 1969-1974
Plymouth Barracuda 1964-1974
Pontiac Fiero 1984-1988
Pontiac GTO 1964-1970
Pontiac Firebird 1967-1973
Pontiac Firebird and Trans-Am 1973-1981
High Performance Firebirds 1982-1988
Pontiac Tempest & GTO 1961-1965
Porsche Cars 1960-1964
Porsche Cars 1964-1968
Porsche Cars 1968-1972
Porsche Cars in the Sixties
Porsche Cars 1972-1975
Porsche 356 1952-1965
Porsche 911 1965-1969
Porsche 911 1970-1972
Porsche 911 1973-1977
Porsche 911 Carrera 1973-1977
Porsche 911 SC 1978-1983
Porsche 911 Turbo 1975-1984
Porsche 914 Gold Portfolio 1969-1976
Porsche 914 Collection No. 1
Porsche 924 Gold Portfolio 1975-1988
Porsche 928 1977-1989
Porsche 944 1981-1985
Reliant Scimitar 1964-1986
Riley 1½ & 2½ Litre Gold Portfolio 1945-1955
Rolls Royce Silver Cloud 1955-1965
Rolls Royce Silver Shadow 1965-1980
Range Rover Gold Portfolio 1970-1988
Rover 3 & 3.5 Litre 1958-1973
Rover P4 1949-1959
Rover P4 1955-1964
Rover 2000 + 2200 1963-1977
Rover 3500 1968-1977
Rover 3500 & Vitesse 1976-1986
Saab Sonett Collection No. 1
Saab Turbo 1976-1983
Studebaker Hawks & Larks 1956-1963
Sunbeam Tiger and Alpine Gold Portfolio 1959-1967
Thunderbird 1955-1957
Thunderbird 1958-1963
Thunderbird 1964-1976
Toyota MR2 1984-1988
Triumph 2000-2.5-2500 1963-1977
Triumph Spitfire 1962-1980
Triumph Spitfire Collection No. 1
Triumph Stag 1970-1980
Triumph Stag Collection No. 1
Triumph TR2 & TR3 1952-1960
Triumph TR4.TR5.TR250 1961-1968
Triumph TR6 1969-1976
Triumph TR6 Collection No. 1
Triumph TR7 & TR8 1975-1982
Triumph GT6 1966-1974
Triumph Vitesse & Herald 1959-1971
TVR Gold Portfolio 1959-1988
Volkswagen Cars 1936-1956
VW Beetle 1956-1977
VW Beetle Collection No. 1
VW Golf GTi 1976-1986
VW Karmann Ghia 1955-1982
VW Scirocco 1974-1981
VW Bus-Camper-Van 1954-1967
VW Bus-Camper-Van 1968-1979
VW Bus-Camper-Van 1979-1989
Volvo 1800 1960-1973
Volvo 120 Series 1956-1970

BROOKLANDS MUSCLE CARS SERIES
American Motors Muscle Cars 1966-1970
Buick Muscle Cars 1965-1970
Camaro Muscle Cars 1966-1972
Capri Muscle Cars 1969-1980
Chevrolet Muscle Cars 1966-1972
Dodge Muscle Cars 1967-1970
Mercury Muscle Cars 1966-1971
Mini Muscle Cars 1961-1979
Mopar Muscle Cars 1964-1967
Mopar Muscle Cars 1968-1971
Mustang Muscle Cars 1967-1971
Shelby Mustang Muscle Cars 1965-1970
Oldsmobile Muscle Cars 1964-1970
Plymouth Muscle Cars 1965-1971
Pontiac Muscle Cars 1966-1972

BROOKLANDS ROAD & TRACK SERIES
Road & Track on Alfa Romeo 1949-1963
Road & Track on Alfa Romeo 1964-1970
Road & Track on Alfa Romeo 1971-1976
Road & Track on Alfa Romeo 1977-1989
Road & Track on Aston Martin 1962-1984

Road & Track on Auburn Cord & Duesenberg 1952-1984
Road & Track on Audi 1952-1980
Road & Track on Audi 1980-1986
Road & Track on Austin Healey 1953-1970
Road & Track on BMW Cars 1966-1974
Road & Track on BMW Cars 1975-1978
Road & Track on BMW Cars 1979-1983
Road & Track on Cobra, Shelby &
  Ford GT40 1962-1983
Road & Track on Corvette 1953-1967
Road & Track on Corvette 1968-1982
Road & Track on Corvette 1982-1986
Road & Track on Datsun Z 1970-1983
Road & Track on Ferrari 1950-1968
Road & Track on Ferrari 1968-1974
Road & Track on Ferrari 1975-1981
Road & Track on Ferrari 1981-1984
Road & Track on Fiat Sports Cars 1968-1987
Road & Track on Jaguar 1950-1960
Road & Track on Jaguar 1961-1968
Road & Track on Jaguar 1968-1974
Road & Track on Jaguar 1974-1982
Road & Track on Jaguar 1983-1989
Road & Track on Lamborghini 1964-1985
Road & Track on Lotus 1972-1981
Road & Track on Maserati 1952-1974
Road & Track on Maserati 1975-1983
Road & Track on Mazda RX7 1978-1986
Road & Track on Mercedes 1952-1962
Road & Track on Mercedes 1963-1970
Road & Track on Mercedes 1971-1979
Road & Track on Mercedes 1980-1987
Road & Track on MG Sports Cars 1949-1961
Road & Track on MG Sports Cars 1962-1980
Road & Track on Mustang 1964-1977
Road & Track on Peugeot 1955-1986
Road & Track on Pontiac 1960-1983
Road & Track on Porsche 1951-1967
Road & Track on Porsche 1968-1971
Road & Track on Porsche 1972-1975
Road & Track on Porsche 1975-1978
Road & Track on Porsche 1979-1982
Road & Track on Porsche 1982-1985
Road & Track on Porsche 1985-1988
Road & Track on Rolls Royce & Bentley 1950-1965
Road & Track on Rolls Royce & Bentley 1966-1984
Road & Track on Saab 1955-1985
Road & Track on Toyota Sports & GT Cars 1966-1986
Road & Track on Triumph Sports Cars 1953-1967
Road & Track on Triumph Sports Cars 1967-1974
Road & Track on Triumph Sports Cars 1974-1982
Road & Track on Volkswagen 1951-1968
Road & Track on Volkswagen 1968-1978
Road & Track on Volkswagen 1978-1985
Road & Track on Volvo 1957-1974
Road & Track on Volvo 1975-1985
Road & Track Henry Manney at Large & Abroad

BROOKLANDS CAR AND DRIVER SERIES
Car and Driver on BMW 1955-1977
Car and Driver on BMW 1977-1985
Car and Driver on Cobra, Shelby & Ford GT40
  1963-1984
Car and Driver on Datsun Z 1600 & 2000
  1966-1984
Car and Driver on Corvette 1956-1967
Car and Driver on Corvette 1968-1977
Car and Driver on Corvette 1978-1982
Car and Driver on Corvette 1983-1988
Car and Driver on Ferrari 1955-1962
Car and Driver on Ferrari 1963-1975
Car and Driver on Ferrari 1976-1983
Car and Driver on Mopar 1956-1967
Car and Driver on Mopar 1968-1975
Car and Driver on Mustang 1964-1972
Car and Driver on Pontiac 1961-1975
Car and Driver on Porsche 1955-1962
Car and Driver on Porsche 1963-1970
Car and Driver on Porsche 1970-1976
Car and Driver on Porsche 1977-1981
Car and Driver on Porsche 1982-1986
Car and Driver on Saab 1956-1985
Car and Driver on Volvo 1955-1986

**BROOKLANDS MOTOR & THOROUGHBRED
& CLASSIC CAR SERIES**
Motor & T & CC on Ferrari 1966-1976
Motor & T & CC on Ferrari 1976-1984
Motor & T & CC on Lotus 1979-1983

BROOKLANDS PRACTICAL CLASSICS SERIES
Practical Classics on Austin A 40 Restoration
Practical Classics on Land Rover Restoration
Practical Classics on Metalworking in Restoration
Practical Classics on Midget/Sprite Restoration
Practical Classics on Mini Cooper Restoration
Practical Classics on MGB Restoration
Practical Classics on Morris Minor Restoration
Practical Classics on Triumph Herald/Vitesse
Practical Classics on Triumph Spitfire Restoration
Practical Classics on VW Beetle Restoration
Practical Classics on 1930S Car Restoration

BROOKLANDS MILITARY VEHICLES SERIES
Allied Military Vehicles Collection No. 1
Allied Military Vehicles Collection No. 2
Dodge Military Vehicles Collection No. 1
Military Jeeps 1941-1945
Off Road Jeeps 1944-1971
V W Kubelwagen 1940-1975

CONTENTS

Page	Title	Publication	Date
5	American Challenge	Autosport	April 3 1964
7	The Ford GT	Autosport	April 10 1964
8	200 MPH at Le Mans	Motor	April 11 1964
10	Ford GT Racing Coupé	Autocar	April 10 1964
15	Ford's 200 Mph Le Mans Challenger	Motor Racing	May 1964
16	Ford Enters Three GT Cars	Australian Motor Sports	May 1964
18	New Ford GT for Le Mans!	Sports Car Graphic	June 1964
21	Ford GT	Road & Track	June 1964
23	Ford GT	Car and Driver	June 1964
28	A Look at the Daytona Winner Ford GT40	Road & Track	May 1965
34	The Ford in Carroll Shelby's Future	Car and Driver	June 1965
43	Meanest Car in Town	Car Life	July 1965
48	GT40 on the Production Line	Car Life	July 1965
52	The Ford GT40	Motor Sport	Sept. 1965
54	Ford GT40 Track Test	Motor Racing	Nov. 1965
57	Ford GT Mark III	Road & Track	April 1966
58	Ford GT40 Track Test	Sports Car Graphic	Oct. 1965
61	The Super Street-Car	Autocar	April 29 1966
65	The Challenge to Ferrari	Road & Track	May 1965
70	Ford GT40	Sports Car Graphic	May 1966
74	Daytona Continental 24-Hour	Sports Car Graphic	May 1966
78	Le Mans 24 Hours	Car and Driver	Sept. 1966
87	Ford GT40	Motor Sport	Dec. 1966
90	Portrait of the Le Mans Winner Technical Analysis	Road & Track	Oct. 1966
99	Ford GT40 Performance Test	Canada Track and Traffic	Nov. 1966
101	Easy Victory	Motor	April 15 1967
104	Ford GT40 "Super/Street" Road Test	Car Life	Nov. 1966
110	Ford Mark III Road Test	Car and Driver	June 1967
115	Ford Mk. II	Car Life	June 1967
120	Ford Fantastic	Motor	June 17 1967
128	The Only Way to Fly Road Test	Cars	July 1967
134	Racing History of the Ford GT Prototypes	Road & Track	Jan. 1968
142	A Streetcar Named Desire	Autosport	March 1 1968
145	Lone JW Ford Outlasts Porsches	Autosport	Oct. 4 1968
153	'This Magnificent Machine…'	Motor	Oct. 26 1968
157	24 Heures Du Mans 1969	Road & Track	Sept. 1969
162	Australia's Roaring Fordy	Australian Motor Manual	June 1969
166	Ford's Greatest Racer Reborn	Autocar	Sept. 29 1984
168	GT40 MkV	Automobile Magazine	June 1986
176	GT Forte	Classic and Sportscar	March 1987

ACKNOWLEDGEMENTS

The Ford GT was first shown to the public 25 years ago in early 1964. It was a successful combination of British technical expertise and US money that went on to win Le Mans on four separate occasions.

Initially the car suffered reliability problems most of which were centred around the Italian gearbox. Ford worked hard on its deficiencies during 1965 and improved it to such an extent that in June 1966 they secured a one-two-three win at Le Mans with the Mk II version.

The following year started well for the GT40's with a win at Sebring for the seven litre MK IV car. Ford entered four cars for Le Mans. Gurney and Foyts car succeeded in taking first place at the French circuit at an average speed of 135 mph and pushed the distance record to 3,250 miles.

The GT40 went on to even greater glory in 1968 with the JW Automotive car No. 9 driven by Rodriguez and Bianchi taking first place. This success was repeated again in 1969 when Ickx and Oliver finished a few lengths ahead of the Herrmann/Larrousse Porsche 908.

For those that would like a more detailed report on the GT40s progress we would suggest that you turn to Jonathan Thompsons excellent article from Road & Track 'Racing History of the Ford GT Prototypes' that can be found on page 134.

We are indebted to the publishers of the worlds leading motoring journals for allowing us to include their copyright stories in this anthology. Our thanks in this instance go to the management of Autocar, Automobile Magazine, Autosport, Australian Motor Sports, Classic and Sportscar, Canada Track and Traffic, Car and Driver, Car Life, Cars, Motor, Motor Manual, Motor Racing, Motor Sport, Road & Track, and Sports Car Graphic for their ongoing support.

R.M. Clarke

THE FORD G.T. Just prior to fitting the windscreen, head lamps and windows, the challenger from U.S.A. looks very potent.

In the summer of 1962, Henry Ford got tired of the semi-secret participation in racing that was widespread and decided that the existing ban should be broken. "Let's go racing," said he, and much saloon car dicing was the result, plus the supply of engines for the Carroll Shelby Cobras and the Indianapolis exercise with Lotus. Wishing to go still further into racing, principally with the object of improving the production cars, it was considered that a Grand Prix programme would fail in the latter respect, while to produce a Grand Touring car and compete with it would be just what was required.

It was decided that the design team which developed the Mustang should form the basis of a small group with freedom from the main Company, and that it should

AMERICAN CHALLENGE

A Lola-Designed and Developed Ford G.T. Car for European Racing

By JOHN BOLSTER   Photography by GEORGE PHILLIPS

TAIL VIEW—which Ford hope will be a familiar one to their rivals, although we hear Enzo Ferrari does not care much for this idea.

operate in England to be in the midst of the suppliers of specialist products. Because he had already raced a car of the same size as the team were producing, Eric Broadley was approached and agreed to give up a year of his time to design and development. His two existing prototype Lolas were bought as guinea pigs, their various components being gradually replaced by the parts of the Ford G.T. Richie Ginther carried out the tests at Goodwood, and later Bruce McLaren and Roy Salvadori assisted, other circuits also being used. Simultaneously, a theoretical appraisal of the Lola design was made in America, theory and practice teaching very much the same lessons.

The most important research was in the aerodynamic department. It was found, in $\frac{3}{8}$-scale model testing in the University of Maryland wind tunnel, that the proposed car would just about take off and fly at 200 m.p.h. The usual rear "spoiler" was ineffective with a car of this shape, but a spoiler some way back *underneath* the nose could be arranged to reduce front lift greatly and rear lift quite considerably. A fairing behind the spoiler actually allowed the total drag figure to be reduced below that of a "clean" car. Enough air could not be collected for a rear radiator, however

large the scoops, so a front radiator was adopted, lying forward almost horizontally. An air intake in a high-pressure area beneath the nose exhausted into a low-pressure area above it. Air for engine breathing was collected from two high-pressure areas near the back of the tail and ducted forward. This aerodynamic cooling, when transplanted to one of the guinea pig cars, at once dropped the temperature by 20 deg. C. These results were checked by full-scale testing at Dearborn.

It was found to be important that the car should not change its attitude by diving in front or lifting at the rear while braking, for this could cause serious aerodynamic instability at very high speeds. However, it was also discovered that to have 100 per cent. anti-dive and anti-lift angles could cause the suspension to be extremely harsh, all shocks being transmitted into the structure. This work, and the angle of geometric rise and fall of the wheels, needed an infinity of calculations. Accordingly, a computer was programmed and the results incorporated in the suspension geometry, the resulting assemblies being tried on the guinea-pig car.

Much work has been done on driver environment, air for the cockpit being collected in a high-pressure area ahead of the screen and exhausted through a line of ports around the roll bar fairing. Pump-up air bags, incorporated in the backs of the bucket seats, allow a change of posture during a driving spell. The seats are part of the structure and have air extraction to avoid driver perspiration, the pedal assemblies being adjustable. The windscreen wiper problem has yet to be solved.

The main stress-bearing structure is of 0.28 in. steel, the two large longitudinal members forming hollow receptacles for the Goodyear plastic petrol bags. The superficial body parts are of glassfibre. Abbey Panels of Coventry are responsible for the panels and P. Jackson for the specialized mouldings. The brakes are Girling $11\frac{1}{2}$ ins. discs with C.R. callipers in front, B.R. rear and separate reservoirs.

It was found that magnesium wheels obstructed the flow of air round the brakes and there were mounting problems. Accordingly, Borrani 15 ins. wire wheels with light alloy rims have been chosen. These rims are extremely wide, 6.5 ins. in front for 5.50 ins. tyres and 8 ins. at the rear for 7.25 ins. tyres, which are being specially made by Dunlops. The rack and pinion

THIS VIEW shows the four-speed Type 37 Colotti gearbox, and the special exhaust system devized by Derrington.

steering by Cam Gears has a 15 to 1 ratio and incorporates an hydraulic damper. Helical springs, with adjustable telescopic dampers by Armstrong, form the suspension medium. Elaborate aircraft-type double-row roller bearings are used for the suspension pivots.

The hub carrier housings are of magnesium, front and rear. A double wishbone geometry is used in front, double trailing links, with a transverse top arm and an inverted A at the bottom, forming the rear suspension layout. The drive shafts have Hookes joints outboard and Metalastic joints inboard. The Colotti Type 37 four-speed gearbox will be used, though an

DRIVING COMPARTMENT ready for final fitting of instruments, steering wheel and seats (right).

BILL PINK and John Etteridge fitting the facia panel after connecting up the wiring on the very low Ford G.T. developed by Lola.

Salvadori, Dan Gurney, Phil Hill, Richard Attwood, and Jo Schlesser.

BRIEF SPECIFICATION

Engine: Ford V8, 3.76 ins. × 2.87 ins. (4.2-litres). Four twin-choke 48 mm. Weber carburetters. 350 b.h.p. at 7,200 r.p.m. Maximum torque, 280 lbs./ft. at 5,600 r.p.m.
Transmission: Colotti four-speed dog-change box. Gearbox ratios 2.50, 1.70, 1.29 and 1 to 1. Final drive ratios available between 3.09 and 3.55 to 1.
Dimensions: Wheelbase 7 ft. 11 ins. Track 4 ft. 6 ins. Overall length 13 ft. 3 ins. Width (maximum) 5 ft. 10 ins. Height 3 ft. 4½ ins. Ground clearance 4.8 ins. Weight 1,980 lbs.
Theoretical Speed: 215 m.p.h. (approx.).

all-synchromesh five-speed box may emerge from Fords later on. The engine will be the pushrod-type Ford V8 at first with the Indianapolis twin-cam unit in the offing. Dry sump lubrication is used and the 36 amps. alternator and transistor ignition are both by Ford. The carburetters are four double-choke downdraught Webers.

The production is under the wing of Don Fry, Assistant General Manager of Ford of America. Frank Zimmerman is in charge of Special Vehicle Activities, with Roy Lunn as Advanced Concepts Manager and John Wyer as Resident European Manager (Special Vehicle Activities). Ford of Dagenham have taken over interior styling and purchasing activities. Eric Broadley we have already mentioned, and the design team are Leonard Bailey (head), Chuck Mountain, and Ron Martin.

The cars are billed to run at the Le Mans practice session, 17th-18th April, Nürburgring, 31st May, and Le Mans, 20th June. The drivers will be Bruce McLaren, Roy

REAR SUSPENSION utilizes Metalastic universal joints and is typically Grand Prix in conception (left). OIL AND WATER radiator, oil tank for the dry sump system, hydraulic supply tanks and rack-and-pinion steering can be seen in this view (right). THE POWERFUL V8 engine with deflector plate removed to show the four twin-choke downdraught Weber carburetters (above, right).

THE FORD G.T.

America's Challenge to the Might of Maranello

Ford's fabulous G.T. was given wide acclaim by the Press, both technical and national daily. However, one question went unanswered, and will remain unanswered, until it makes its racing début: Will this Anglo-American creation cause Enzo Ferrari any lost sleep?

Certainly few cars have caused such widespread speculation. Certainly, too, it has the potential and, most definitely, Ford have signed some fine pilots—Bruce McLaren, Roy Salvadori, Dan Gurney, Phil Hill, Richard Attwood, and Jo Schlesser. The G.T. championship is at present led by the Cobras of Carroll Shelby, who had several fingers in the Ford G.T. pie. He, at least, has shown that Maranello is not invincible, as, up until recently, they had appeared.

The Grand Touring category is now hotting up. It needed further challengers to supplant some of the lost enthusiasm that is so often associated with one-make domination. Shelby did a fine job and was well rewarded. He carved an opening that the go-ahead Ford manufacturers have been quick to follow. The result is the ultra-sleek, 4.2-litre V8-engined G.T. prototype that is the subject of this week's cutaway drawing by Theo Page.

FASTEST EVER FORD. Less than a year's design and development went into the promising Ford G.T., which was exclusively revealed in last week's AUTOSPORT. The low-line (40 ins.) and close resemblance to the Lola G.T. can be seen in the picture of the completed monocoque-constructed car. The Ford G.T. is scheduled to make its first racing appearance at the Nürburgring 1,000 kms. on 31st May.

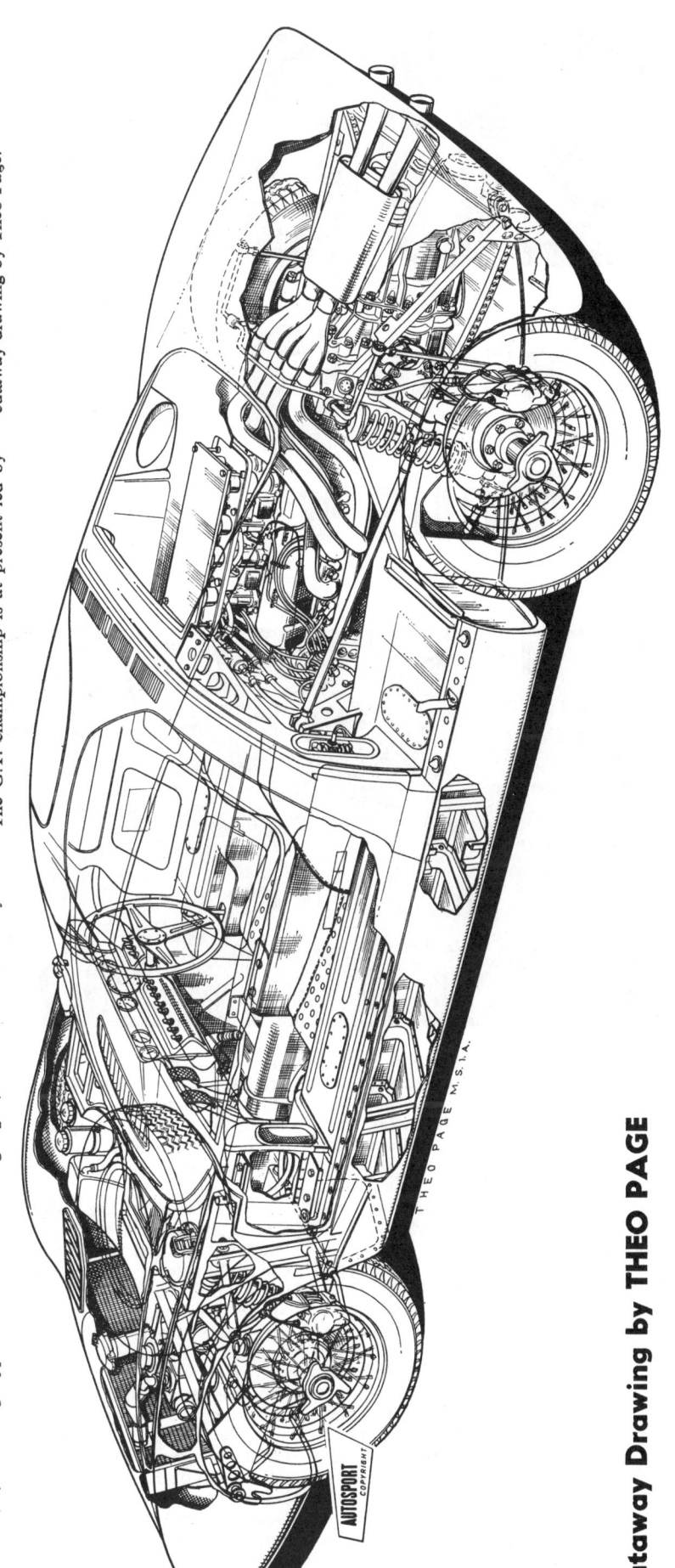

Cutaway Drawing by THEO PAGE

200 MPH at Le Mans?

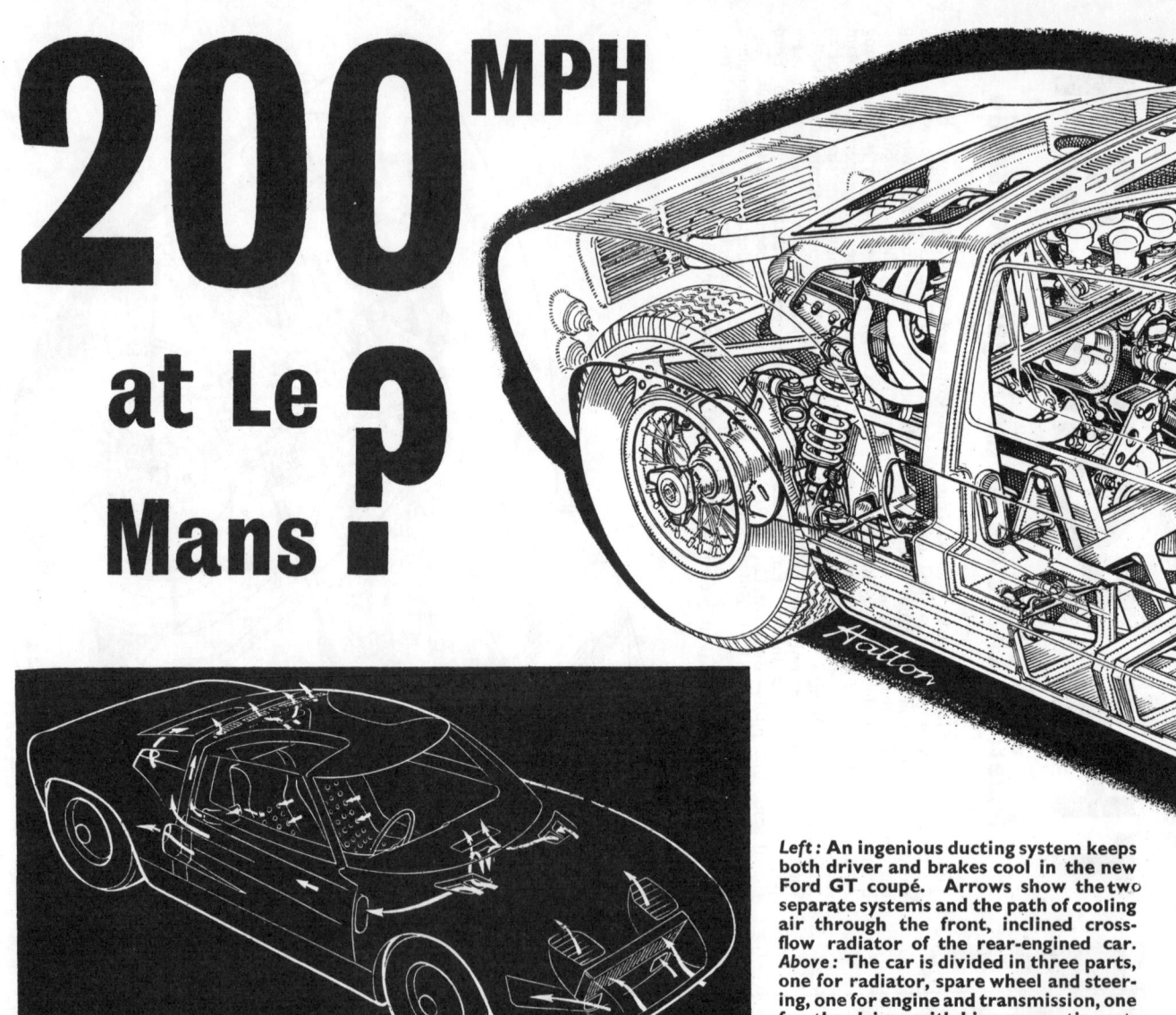

Left: An ingenious ducting system keeps both driver and brakes cool in the new Ford GT coupé. Arrows show the two separate systems and the path of cooling air through the front, inclined cross-flow radiator of the rear-engined car. *Above:* The car is divided in three parts, one for radiator, spare wheel and steering, one for engine and transmission, one for the driver with his pneumatic seat.

THREE low, compact, rear-engined cars now nearing completion (the first one went to the New York Show last week) may break Ferrari's four-year domination at Le Mans. The Ford Motor Company of America has staked its computers, its wind tunnels, engineering and styling talent and a great deal of money on doing just that.

The new Ford GT cars are of joint Anglo-American parentage. In Dearborn, Detroit, one-time Aston Martin designer Roy Lunn built the little rear-engined Ford Mustang, then in the early months of 1963 led a small team that produced a design study of a Le Mans winning Ford. In Bromley, Kent, Eric Broadley designed and built the Ford V-8 powered Lola GT car. Ford decided to go ahead with the Le Mans plans and to build the cars in Europe, so Roy Lunn came back to England and contacted Broadley, who agreed to construct the new vehicles. To do it on the Ford scale, Broadley moved his organization from Bromley to a new building on the Slough Trading Estate. John Wyer, ex-Aston Martin director and team manager, joined the team as European Manager of the Special Vehicles Activities of Ford Division, which is responsible for the project.

Early in August the two Lola GT cars began their careers as test beds for the new cars, and from then until the end of November covered hundreds of miles at Goodwood, Snetterton and Monza. During the test programme, they were progressively modified by changes to the front and rear suspension, the cooling systems, the brakes and other details to bring them as close as possible to the specification of the new Ford GT cars. While this circuit testing was going on, ⅜ scale and full size models of the new body shape were being tested in wind tunnels at Dearborn and Maryland. Alarming early tests showed that at around 200 m.p.h. the body was developing so much lift that only the slightest encouragement—such as striking a bump in the road—would be needed for the car to take off and fly. Eventually, it was found that a spoiler placed below the nose at the front of the car cured this tendency, and the final body shape was shipped to England in November to be used for the manufacture of moulds and forms for the actual race bodies.

These are of 23 gauge (0·028 in.) steel monocoque construction—unlike the Lola GT of mixed steel and light alloy. Pontoon sections form the body sills and are the basic structural members although the roof skin is also used as a stressed member. The engine and the front and rear suspensions were carried by tubular structures on the Lola, but these elements are built up largely from steel sheet in the Ford GT cars. The hinged nose and tail sections and the two doors are of reinforced glass fibre. The crash bar and fixed seats form an integral part of the structure being inherited, together with the adjustable pedals, from the little Mustang.

Ford roll out the big guns to challenge Ferrari at last

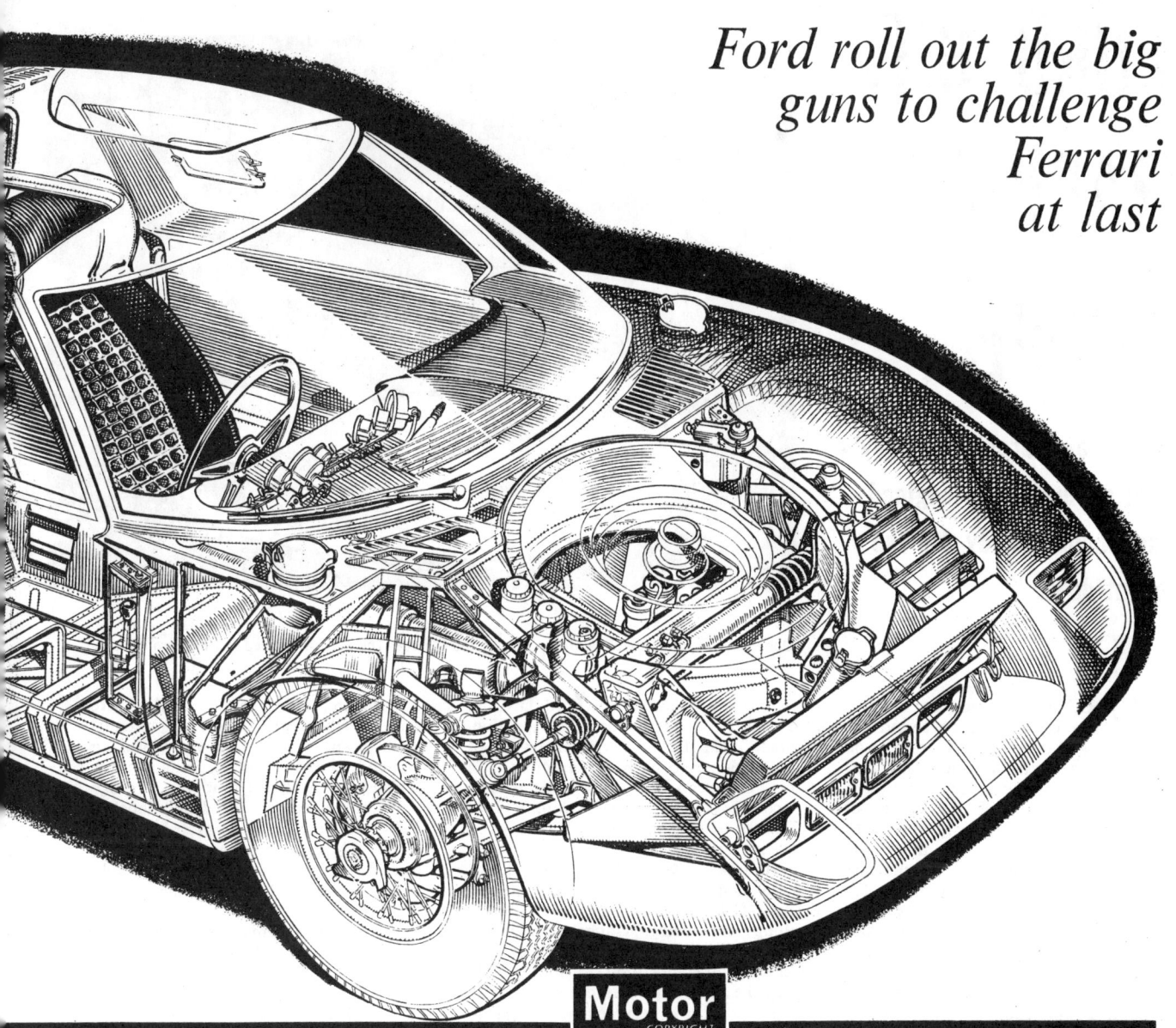

The front suspension by upper and lower wishbone links and Armstrong adjustable damper and coil spring units is fairly orthodox, but the rear suspension bears a closer resemblance to the Lola Formula 1 car than to the Lola GT, with the usual Formula 1 layout of a single upper link, a reversed wishbone lower link and twin radius arms. Computers in Ford Engineering Research at Dearborn made it possible to study mathematically the geometric behaviour of the wheels.

Initially, the cars will be powered by lightweight versions of the 4·2-litre Fairlane engines developed originally for the 1963 Indianapolis Lotus 29s. Later, however, new twin overhead camshaft Ford V-8s may give the cars some 420 b.h.p. The Colotti 37 four-speed gearbox and final drive unit—also designed for the Indianapolis Lotus 29s—will be used this year, but other units are being developed by Ford in Dearborn and a five-speed synchronized transmission is being built by ZF in Germany for 1965.

Anyone who saw a part-cooked red-faced Moss extracting himself from the confines of his 4½-litre Maserati coupé at Le Mans a few years ago will realize that installing a big engine in a small car brings enormous driver-cooling problems. As the accompanying drawing shows, this problem has been tackled with ingenuity by the Ford engineers.

An unusual feature of the driver's seat is the inclusion of a small inflatable bag in the lumbar region of the rear squab. By inflating or deflating the bag the driver can alter his seating position and so relieve any aching back muscles.

Such attention to detail distinguishes these low white and blue coupés. Drivers at Le Mans will be Bruce McLaren, Roy Salvadori, Dan Gurney, Phil Hill, Jo Schlesser and Dick Attwood. Whatever else happens, if they do not cover the timed stretch of the Mulsanne Straight at over 200 m.p.h. there will be disappointment at Slough and at Dearborn.

FORD GT SPECIFICATION

ENGINE. V-8, 95.25 × 72.89mm., 4,183.6 c.c. o.h.v. (pushrods); four dual choke Weber carburetters; comp. ratio, 12.5/1; max. power 376 b.h.p. at 7,200 r.p.m.; max. torque 299 lb. ft. at 5,200 r.p.m. Alternative twin overhead camshaft version of this engine may be fitted for Le Mans.

TRANSMISSION. Borg and Beck 8½ in. twin plate clutch. Colotti four-speed non-synchronized gearbox and final drive unit incorporating a limited slip differential.

RUNNING GEAR. 11½ in. Girling disc brakes outboard mounted at front and rear with dual master cylinders; rack and pinion steering with hydraulic damper; coil spring and double wishbone link i.f.s.; single strut upper arm, inverted A lower arm and twin radius rod i.r.s.; wire wheels with Rudge hubs carrying 7.25-15 in. Dunlop tyres at the rear and 5.50-15 in. Dunlop tyres at the front.

DIMENSIONS. Wheelbase, 7 ft. 11 in.; length, 13 ft. 2.6 in.; track (front and rear), 4 ft. 6 in.; width (over scoops), 5 ft. 10 in.; height, 3 ft. 4.5 in.; ground clearance, 4.8 in.

FORD G.T. RACING COUPÉ

American parent company's British made mid-engined monocoque ready for the count-down

Open Day, before a quick publicity visit to the U.S.A. The nose is painted matt to avoid glare

WHEN the starter's flag falls for the 1,000-km race round the Nürburgring in Germany on 31 May, a team of American and British design engineers and constructors, backed by all the brass of Dearborn, will be touching wood with fingers crossed. It will mark the maiden performance in competition (apart from Le Mans practice on 17-18 April) of an intriguing new G.T. contender. With all the dollars and engineering resources of Ford behind it, plus the skill and experience of Eric Broadley (designer-constructor of Lola competition cars, whose services have been acquired on a short-term contract) and the co-operation of component suppliers in this country, France, Italy and Germany, its potential looks truly formidable.

It was back in the summer of '62 that Henry Ford II took the epic decision to involve his American Ford Division directly in international competition. Since then factory-prepared teams of production saloons have participated in big European rallies (a Falcon was second overall in this year's Monte Carlo Rally), in track races and drag-strip events; and special engines were developed to power Colin Chapman's Indianapolis Lotus entries and Carroll Shelby's A.C. Cobra sports-racer. But greater things were being planned meanwhile.

Early in 1963 it was decided to construct a full competition car from scratch, and the G.T. type was chosen as bearing the closest relationship to "main line" products. Thus it would provide a sort of development platform for features of function and safety that would benefit the everyday Ford. Most of the problems of Le Mans, for instance—such as mechanical endurance, driver comfort, braking efficiency from perhaps 200 m.p.h., aerodynamic stability—are those of the highway, greatly accentuated. The idea of buying a leading contender (Ferrari, in this instance) was seriously considered, but the prestige value of this move seemed questionable. Public opinion would probably have attributed any success mostly to Ferrari, and if the project failed Ford would have been blamed for dragging a great name through the dust.

In June 1963 a small branch organization was formed to go ahead on its own, operating in freedom but with everything Dearborn could offer to support it. Its chief is Roy Lunn, a Briton who was with A.C. and Aston Martin before becoming chief designer for Jowett, at the age of 24, in 1949; he joined Ford at Dagenham in 1954, shifted to Dearborn in 1958 and has progressed to the status of manager, Advance Concepts Department of the Ford Division.

Without its moulded nose and tail shells, the monocoque skeleton looks remarkably small and simple. Here only the doors and sill panels have been added

The Ford G.T. is only waist-high to (left to right) John Wyer, Eric Broadley and Roy Lunn. In addition to rectangular Cibié headlamps with iodine vapour bulbs, there are two pass-lamps set in the aerodynamic 'spoiler' beneath

Among his mechanical offspring have been Dagenham's 105E, the German Taunus 12M with vee-four engine and front-wheel drive, and the little Mustang open sports car with the Taunus engine. Key U.S. men in his team are Len Bailey as top design engineer, assisted by Chuck Mountain and Ron Martin, who are now at work in one of two adjacent small factories in the Slough Trading Estate, where the G.T.s are being built. The main reason for constructing them in this country was because so many component manufacturers vital to the project, with ready-made products and long competition experience, are close at hand.

Apparently the new car's elements were laid out before the move to Slough, and it can be likened to a Mustang with a roof. In many respects it seems to bear an even closer resemblance to Eric Broadley's Lola G.T., which was the sensation of the Racing Car Show in London early in 1963. For this reason, and also because he was willing to set aside 12 months for 100 per cent participation in the project, Broadley was co-opted. Two of his cars were bought by Ford, and last August a programme of appraisal began, first with Richie Ginther to drive them, later with Bruce McLaren and Roy Salvadori. In the meantime Broadley's drawings were analysed in the U.S., and theory was found to coincide with practice, as recorded by the development drivers.

One by one, various Ford-designed parts were substituted for individual appraisal—an aerodynamic cooling system and modified suspensions, for instance—and the Indianapolis engine was installed. By the end of last November the development hybrids had been tested at Snetterton, Brands Hatch, Goodwood and Monza. A month later the basic design of the thoroughbred was virtually complete.

Meanwhile extensive wind-tunnel research had been undertaken in the U.S.A. to determine the best aerodynamic form for the body. A full-scale mock-up was used at Dearborn to check high and low pressure areas around the body surface at very high speeds, so that the inlets and outlets of cooling ducts for the radiator, brakes, spring dampers, carburettor area and driver compartment could be established. A scheme to fit small side radiators just ahead of the rear wheel arches was quickly abandoned because air flow in those regions was insufficient within acceptable limits of intake area.

The so-called aerodynamic cooling arrangement adopted—which dropped

Left: Behind the tilted cross-flow radiator is the engine oil tank, and the spare wheel sits in the recess above. Right: Air for eight hungry throats enters through nostrils in the roof-cum-bonnet. The radiator header tank is visible just above two of the four Bendix fuel pumps

FORD G.T. RACING COUPÉ...

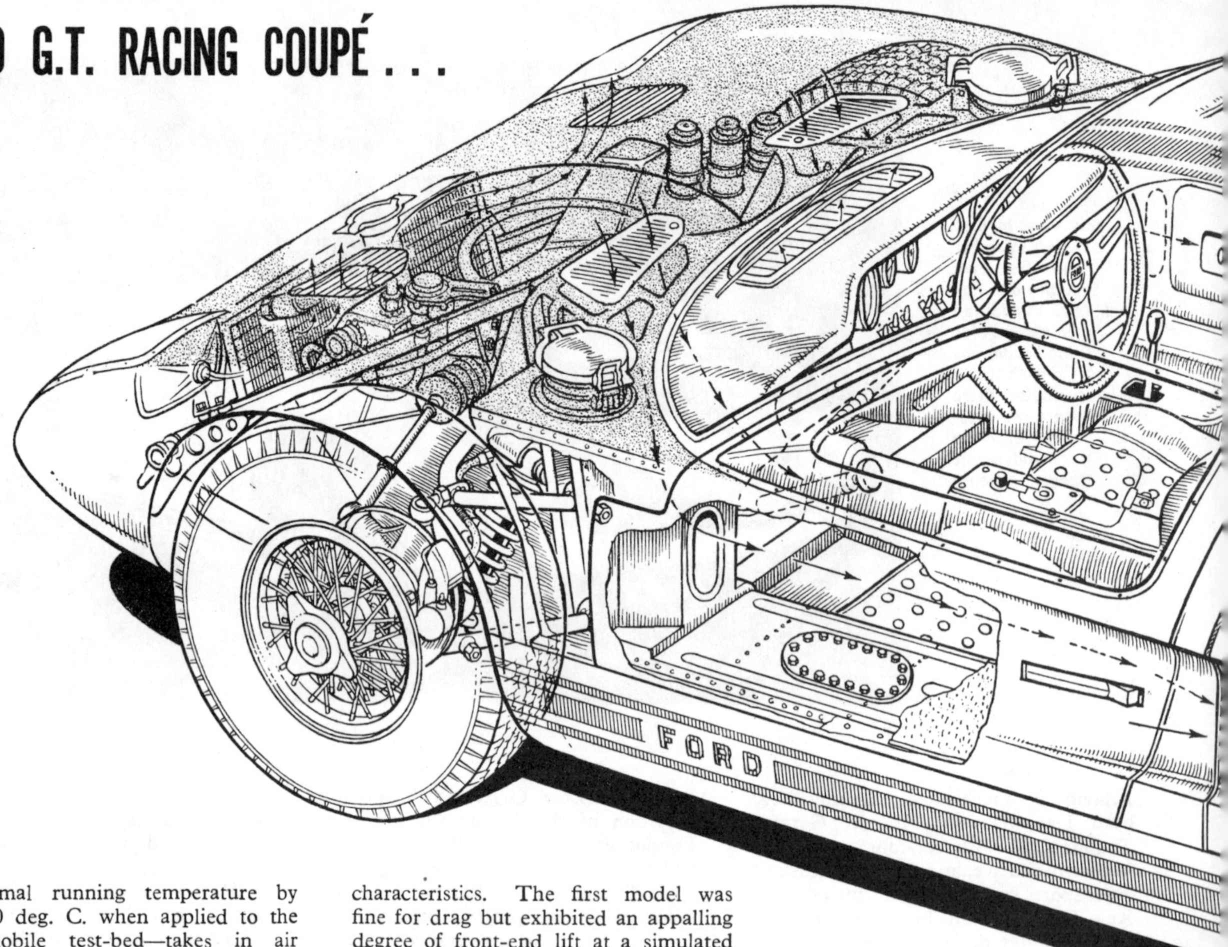

the normal running temperature by about 20 deg. C. when applied to the Lola mobile test-bed—takes in air beneath the nose, feeds it up through the forward-inclined radiator and exhausts through twin outlets on a low-pressure area of the upper nose surface, and in such a position that the warmed air should not get drawn into the interior ventilation system.

A three-eighth-scale model was tunnel-tested (76 times) by the University of Maryland to check drag and lift characteristics. The first model was fine for drag but exhibited an appalling degree of front-end lift at a simulated 200 m.p.h. Modified forms of nose shell were tried, but the ultimate answer was a "spoiler" beneath the nose; the 3·5in. deep type adopted not only reduces front-end lift (evening out its proportion to that at the rear) to an entirely acceptable figure but also—quite fortuitously—reduces drag. Incidentally, anti-dive (braking) geometry has been incorporated in the front suspension, to keep the car's "trim" and stability as near constant as possible.

A phrase that keeps recurring in discussion with Roy Lunn is "driver environment." During a long-distance race his comfort is extremely important. Such factors as noise—particularly wind roar—fumes, heat, lack of fresh air and indifferent seating must each have an adverse effect. A concerted attempt has been made to render the Ford G.T. properly habitable, and its ventilation system is particularly ingenious. Air enters the car through apertures in the usual high-pressure area just ahead of the screen, and a proportion of it can be admitted to the interior of the seats which, incidentally, are fixed. They are trimmed in a lightweight plastic material liberally studded with small circular outlets, the intention being that this cool air flow will evaporate perspiration, one of a driver's major discomforts. The driving seat has an inflatable lumbar pad in the backrest, which can be adjusted by a hand pump and pressure release valve within the driver's reach. This enables him to avoid backache during long stints by altering the "set" of his spine.

By exhausting air from the interior at a low-pressure area in the roof, a powerful through-flow is achieved. Some of the air entering the car is diverted to pass through tunnels in the doors and carried to the 'midships engine compartment. In addition, there

Interior features include fixed, ventilated seats and movable pedals. Instruments are the simplest possible

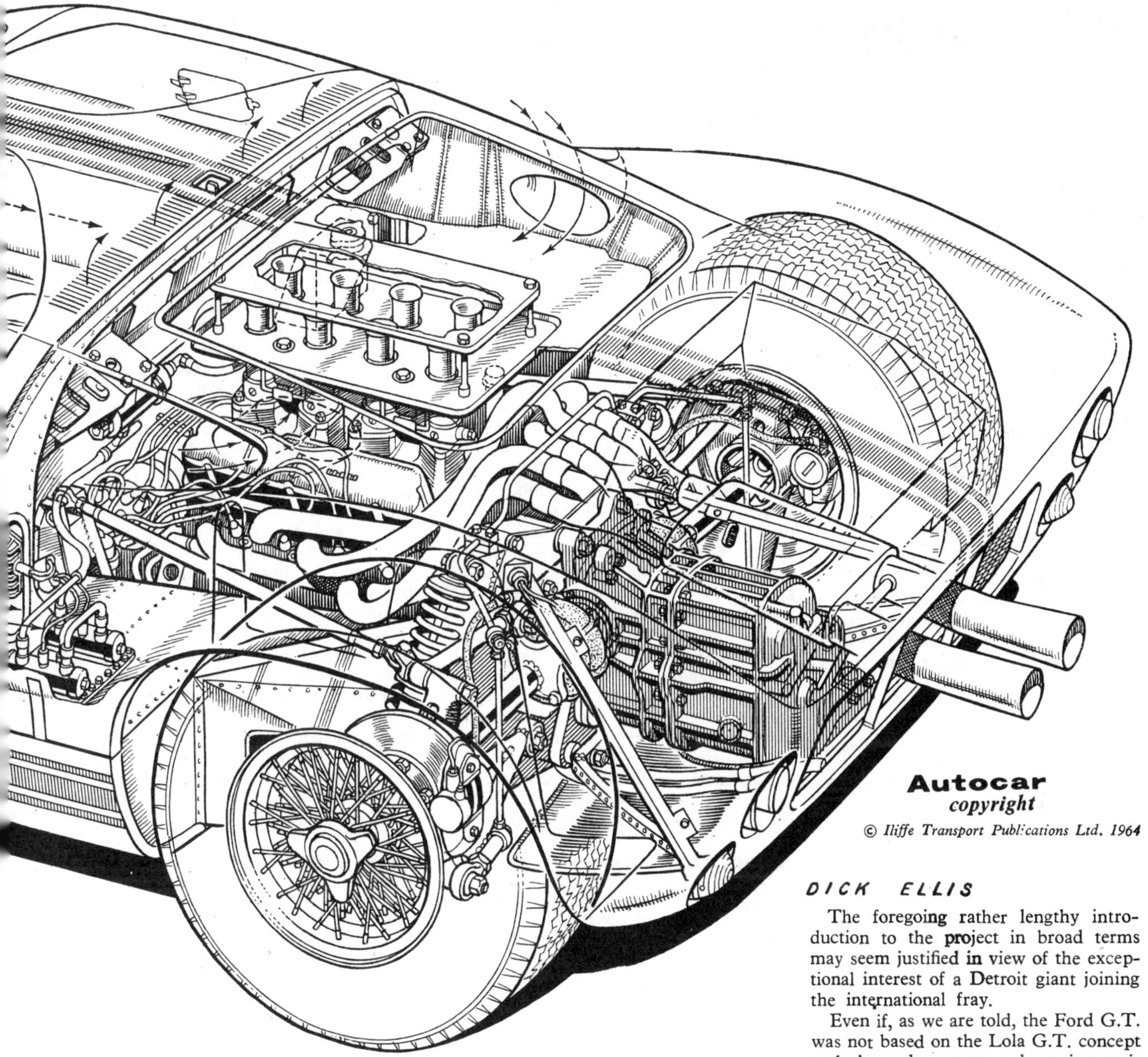

Autocar copyright
© Iliffe Transport Publications Ltd. 1964

DICK ELLIS

are scoops just ahead of the wheel arches leading to the brakes, dampers and engine, and extra ones above these leading to the carburettor area. More air for the engine room is picked up beneath the car, and all of it leaves through two large rectangular exits in the blunt tail.

Maybe this is the first competition car which has had some of its problems fed into an electronic computer. For instance, given a few basic data, the magic box quickly disgorged masses of information on wheel attitudes in relation to progressive deflections of the suspension that might have taken human brains weeks to calculate.

Three cars are being built to start with, of which one is complete but had not been run at the time of writing. There should be two at the Le Mans practice session, one is entered for the Nürburgring (Bruce McLaren and Phil Hill) on 31 May, and three for Le Mans proper on 20 June. John Wyer, ex-competition chief and more recently director and general manager of Aston-Martin, is styled European resident manager for the Ford G.T. project, and with the first car complete takes over responsibility for the building of the remainder and executing the racing programmes. Drivers for Le Mans are to be McLaren, Gurney, Phil Hill, Salvadori, Attwood and Schlesser.

The foregoing rather lengthy introduction to the project in broad terms may seem justified in view of the exceptional interest of a Detroit giant joining the international fray.

Even if, as we are told, the Ford G.T. was not based on the Lola G.T. concept and the only common denominator is the 'midships engine layout, the similarities in configuration, dimensions and disposition of the main components are remarkably close, so comparisons are inevitable.

There is, however, a fundamental difference in that, whereas the Lola structure was composed of a short,

Some 350 b.h.p. are packed into only 13ft x 5ft 10in. x 3ft 4in. of motor-car. With Le Mans gearing, it should be good for over 200 m.p.h.

FORD G.T. RACING COUPÉ...

monocoque centre section fabricated from riveted sheet steel and duralumin, with multi-tube frames attached to each end, the Ford is almost entirely of spot-welded sheet steel supplemented at the front by two square-tube stiffeners from the top of the scuttle down to the nose, and at the back by a light, detachable framework supporting the tail shell. The sheet steel work has been undertaken with speed and precision by Abbey Panels Ltd. of Coventry.

Particularly interesting features are that the seats are fixed and contribute to the structure (pedal reach being adjustable), that the long side sills below the doors contain flexible, bag-type fuel tanks, and that a substantial protective roll-over member divides the living compartment from the engine room.

Plastic Body Panels

Body panels are glass-reinforced plastic mouldings by Specialised Mouldings Ltd., of Upper Norwood, and were painted by Harold Radford Ltd. of London, who also made the air-conditioned seats. These and the interior trim, instrument panel and layout generally were planned by Ford at Dagenham, who also did much of the component purchasing and other donkey-work. Great care has been taken to blend the screen, side and rear windows smoothly into the body form to defeat air drag, and the flush screen is secured by an adhesive.

As with the Lola, the spare wheel is carried in the nose, where part of it sits over an oddly shaped reservoir for the engine's oil supply, a dry sump system being employed. Front suspension is orthodox by coil springs and welded tubular wishbones, the upper ones rather short because of the bulk of the spare wheel between them, the lower ones with very widely spaced trunnions. Magnesium hub carriers are ball-jointed to the wishbones, and steering is by a simple rack-and-pinion gear.

At the back each magnesium hub carrier is located fore-and-aft by long radius arms, the upper one forming a triangle with a short transverse strut. Below is a narrow A-frame with the peak of the A inboard. Coil springs encircling Armstrong adjustable dampers, similar to those up front, are used. The rear suspension linkage incorporates anti-lift and anti-squat geometry.

Girling outboard discs of 11.5in. diameter and with aluminium calipers are used at each wheel, no servo assistance being provided. Front and rear circuits are independent. A figure quoted was slowing repeatedly from 130 to 30 m.p.h. in 6sec on the Snetterton circuit. As the Ford is expected to reach 200 m.p.h. down the Mulsanne straight at Le Mans, and has to be braked to about 45 m.p.h. for the right-hander at the end, brakes are important.

Italian Borrani wire-spoked wheels with light alloy rims and Rudge centre-lock hubs have been chosen in preference to cast wheels to allow plenty of air around the brake discs, and because the secure fastening of the cast type seems less certain. Dunlop tyres have been chosen, those at the rear sitting on massive 8in. wide rims. Tyre dimensions are 7.25-15in. at this end; at the front 5.50-15in. on 6.5in. wide rims.

While there is a possibility that one of the cars at Le Mans might have the new vee-8 Ford engine (as described by Roger Huntington on 10 January) with twin overhead camshafts to each block, the units now being fitted are slightly derated versions of last year's Indianapolis type. These are based on the production Fairlane, but the main castings are of aluminium. As the Colotti gearbox has only four speeds, the useful torque range for road racing circuits has to be vastly wider than for the "Brickyard," and the choke sizes for the four twin-barrel Weber carburettors are reduced—in fact, to 48mm diameter.

Individual exhausts are bunched in two groups of four, each group culminating in a tuning chamber and single outlet. Net power output is given as 350 b.h.p. at 7,200 r.p.m., maximum torque occurring at 5,600 r.p.m. The rev counter dial is hatched in red between 7,000 and 8,000 r.p.m. and above this the red is unadulterated.

Transmission begins with a three-plate Borg and Beck racing clutch, and passes through a Colotti Type 37 four-speed gearbox, without synchromesh, to a straight-cut bevel final drive incorporating a limited-slip differential. The drive shafts have Metalastik Rotaflex couplings inboard and B.R.D. needle-roller universals outboard.

The limitations of the present gearbox have been accepted for its known ability to transmit high power with reliability, but this is obviously a temporary compromise. Various designs of automatic transmission are being considered closely, and it seems justifiable to prophesy that the Ford G.T. will have such a one in time, bearing in mind the U.S. industry's tremendous experience with automatics of many types.

Although so much of this fascinating projectile has been tried out and developed independently, the fact remains that as an entity it is brand-new. Thus Roy Lunn, John Wyer and their henchmen dare not anticipate immediate full success. Yet no competition car can have had more concentrated effort poured into it, and the project deserves to succeed.

Specification

ENGINE

No. of cylinders	8 in 90 deg vee
Bore	95.5mm (3.76in.)
Stroke	72.9mm (2.87in.)
Displacement	4,195 c.c. (256 cu. in.)
Valve position and operation	Overhead, pushrods and rockers
Compression ratio	Not quoted
Max b.h.p. (net)	350 at 7,200 r.p.m.
Max b.m.e.p. (net)	162 p.s.i. at 5,600 r.p.m.
Max torque (net)	275 lb. ft. (approx) at 5,600 r.p.m.
Carburettors	4 twin-barrel Weber 54mm downdraughts, 48mm chokes
Fuel pumps	3 Bendix electric
Tank capacity	37 Imp. gallons (168 litres) x
Lubrication system	Dry sump
Cooling system	Serck cross-flow radiator, with oil cooler in unit
Electrics	12 volt, 52 amp. hr. battery, with Ford 42 amp alternator. Ford transistorized ignition

TRANSMISSION (Transaxle)

Clutch	Borg and Beck dry 3-plate, 7.25in. dia, hydraulic operation
Gearbox	Colotti 4-speed, no synchromesh
Gearbox ratios	Top 1 to 1; third 1.29; second 1.70; first 2.50
Final drive	Straight-cut bevel, ratio (for Le Mans) 3.09 to 1, limited slip differential

CHASSIS

Brakes	Girling discs, independent hydraulic circuits front and rear, no servo. Disc dia. 11.5in. F and R
Suspension: front	Double wishbone with anti-dive geometry, coil springs and Armstrong co-axial telescopic dampers, anti-roll bar
rear	Magnesium hub carrier located by upper and lower trailing arms, transverse upper strut and reversed lower wishbone. Coil springs and Armstrong co-axial telescpoic dampers, anti-roll bar
Wheels	Borrani wire-spoked centre-lock, with light alloy rims. Rim width 6.5in. front, 8.0in. rear
Tyres	Dunlop Racing. Front, 5.50—15in.; Rear, 7.25—15in.
Steering	Cam gears rack-and-pinion, ratio 14 to 1
Steering wheel	15in. dia

DIMENSIONS

Wheelbase	7ft 11in. (241.3cm)
Track: front and rear	4ft 6in. (137.2cm)
Overall length	13ft. 2.6in. (402.8cm)
Overall width	5ft 10in. (177.8cm)
Overall height (unladen)	3ft 4.5in. (103cm)
Ground clearance (laden)	4.8in. (12.2cm)
Kerb weight	Approx. 17 cwt—1,900 lb (862 kg)

PERFORMANCE DATA

Top gear m.p.h. per 1,000 r.p.m.	(3.09 axle) 28.9
Weight distribution	F. 43 per cent R. 57 per cent

FORD'S 200 MPH Le Mans Challenger

Right: *A lot of rubber to take a lot of power. Dunlop 7.25s are on the rear of the Ford GT, to be spun by a 350 horsepower V8 via a Colotti Type 37 gearbox.*

Below: *The look that spells power—and there's more of it to come, later this year, from the twin-cam Ford V8 Indy engine.*

FORD's answer to the Ferrari GTO and 250LM—a 4.2 litre Grand Touring coupé known simply as the Ford GT—is back in Europe after making a spectacular public debut at the New York Motor Show. Its next assignment is at Le Mans for the practice days on April 18 and 19, and its first competitive appearance will be on May 31, when Bruce McLaren and Phil Hill will share it in the Nurburgring 1,000 Kilometres race. Then comes the big test—the Le Mans 24 Hours—when the first car will be joined by another Ford GT as a part of the American company's determined effort to break the Italian domination in this much publicised classic.

The Ford GT is very much an international

project. The original design was carried out in the United States, and scale models were wind tunnel tested at speeds up to 150 mph. These tests disclosed a tendency for the car to lift, a fault which was cured by modifying the air intakes and attaching a 'spoiler' to the underside of the car at the front.

With the aerodynamics sorted out, the design team, headed by 39-years-old Roy Lunn, came across to Europe and engine transmission and suspension components were developed during track tests at Brands Hatch, Goodwood, Snetterton and Monza, using two 1962 Lola GTs as mobile testbeds.

As we recorded in the December issue of MOTOR RACING, data collected from these tests was fed into the Ford engineering computer back in America and analysed, and this enabled the car's development time to be cut by several months.

By the end of last year, the design and development work had been almost completed, and Dagenham's engineers, stylists and purchase experts were brought in to complete the final design. It has been an impressive example of a case where too many cooks have not spoiled the broth, or let it cook too slowly —the whole project has taken only one year from its inception.

The Ford GT naturally reveals considerable evidence of Eric Broadley's thinking (Eric having joined the project during 1963), but from the purely styling point of view there are also traces of ATS GT in the body shape.

The car is built up on a steel monocoque structure, to which the glass-fibre body outer panels are attached. The dashboard unit is also in glass-fibre. No less than 76 tests were carried out in the Maryland University wind tunnel with the ⅜-scale model before the final body shape was developed, and these were supplemented by further tests on a full-size model at Ford's own wind tunnel at Dearborn. The result is a car 13 feet long and 3 feet 4 inches high.

The centre engine location was chosen because it allowed the use of a low silhouette and a clean front end, and anti-dive and lift characteristics were built into the suspension, mainly to stabilise the car during the heavy braking from high speeds.

Many of the tests were directed towards using the natural air flow and forces round the body to determine cooling system air flow, engine intake supply, engine compartment ventilation, interior ventilation, and brake and shock absorber cooling air supply. The cooling air is taken in at a pressure area under the nose and exhausted into a negative area on the top body panel. Roy Lunn calls this an aerodynamic cooling system because it allows the air to flow naturally because of the air flow effects.

Air for interior ventilation enters through the dash panel, and allows full ventilation without opening the side windows, thereby reducing drag and wind buffeting. A lot of thought has been given to driver comfort, and in fact even the seat is air conditioned. The cooling air circulates into the back of the seat to evaporate any perspiration that may accumulate during a long race.

The independent wheel suspension is by double wishbones and coil-spring-damper units at the front and twin trailing arms, lower reversed wishbones and single top arms at the rear, the coil-spring-damper units being located ahead of the drive shafts.

Steering is by rack and pinion, and 11½ inch Girling disc brakes are mounted outboard all round. The 15 inch aluminium wheels carry 5.50 Dunlop tyres at the front and 7.25s at the rear.

The 4.2 litre power unit is similar to the pushrod Ford Indianapolis engine, and as fitted to the Ford GT it produces 350 horsepower for a car which weighs 1,820 pounds dry, of which 57 per cent is carried on the rear wheels.

The drive is taken through a 7½ inch diameter three-plate clutch to a Colotti Type 37 four-speed gearbox-final-drive unit, and then through 'doughnut' couplings to the one-piece final drive shafts.

Fuel for the Weber 48 mm twin-choke downdraught carburettors is fed by three Bendix pumps from plastic containers housed in the main frame side members, which have a capacity of 37 Imperial gallons. Quite a complicated system of exhaust pipes is necessary, but they terminate in a single neat expansion box above the transmission with twin outlets.

Roy Lunn, who was designing cars for AC, Aston Martin, Jowett and Ford of Great Britain before moving across to the Ford Division in America in 1958, has completed his part of the Ford GT project. John Wyer, as European Manager of Ford's Special Vehicles Activity, and his staff have the responsibility for building further team cars, preparing them and racing them. It is a fascinating assignment, spiced by the knowledge that provision is being made to drop in the Indianapolis twin-cam 4.2 litre engine later in the year. No wonder Enzo Ferrari is dubious of his chances this year in the GT field!

The drivers for Le Mans will be chosen from Phil Hill, Dan Gurney, Roy Salvadori, Bruce McLaren, Jo Schlesser and Richard Attwood—a formidable combination which underlines the importance which Ford are placing in these fastest Fords of all time.

An American manufacturer enters big-time motor racing

The first of the Ford GT cars, capable of 200 mph, which the AMS New York office staff saw at a special preview early in April.

Ford enters three GT cars

AMS'S New York office and British correspondent, Alan Brinton, combine to give you the first full story on the most exciting news in motor racing since Mercedes Benz withdrew its works teams from competition.

FORD'S answer to the Ferrari GTO and 250LM —a 4.2-litre grand touring coupe known simply as the Ford GT — was flown from Britain to America at the beginning of April to make a surprise appearance at the New York Motor Show.

It was soon back in Britain for its first testing before going to Le Mans for the practice days on April 18 and 19. First race appearance is scheduled for May 31, when Bruce McLaren and Phil Hill are due to share it in the Nurburgring 1000 kilometres race.

Then comes the big test — the Le Mans 24 Hours— when the first car will be joined by two others, as part of the American company's determined effort to break the Italian domination in this much-publicised class. Drivers at Le Mans will be Phil Hill, Dan Gurney, Bruce McLaren, Roy Salvadori, Jo Schlesser and Richard Attwood.

International project

The Ford GT is very much an international project. Original design was carried out in the United States, and scale models were tested in a wind tunnel at up to 150 mph. These tests revealed a tendency for the car to lift, and this was cured by modifying the air intakes and attaching a "spoiler" to the underside at the front.

With the aerodynamics sorted out, the design team, headed by 39-year-old Roy Lunn, came to Europe, and engine, transmission and suspension components were developed using two 1962 Lola GTs as mobile test beds.

Data collected from these tests was fed into a Ford engineering computer back in America, and the analysis enabled the car's development time to be cut by several months.

There is evidence of a great deal of Eric Broadley's thinking in the design, Broadley, of course, being the designer of the Lola GT.

Many wind tunnel tests

The car is built up on a steel monocoque structure, to which the glass-fibre body outer panels are attached. No less than 76 tests were carried out in the Maryland University wind tunnel before the final body shape was evolved, and these were supplemented by further tests on a full-size model at Ford's own wind tunnel at Dearborn.

The result is quite breathtaking, with a car 13ft. long and only 40in. high. A centre engine location was chosen because it produced a low silhouette and clean front end.

A lot of attention has been directed towards using the natural air flow and forces round the body to determine cooling system air flow, engine intake supply, engine compartment ventilation, and the supply of cooling air to brakes and shock absorbers. Air for interior ventilation enters through the dash panel and allows full ventilation without opening the side windows. Even the seat is air-conditioned, with cooling air circulating into the back of the seat to evaporate any perspiration.

Suspension is by double wishbones and coil-spring-damper units at the front and twin trailing arms, lower reversed wishbones and single top arms at the rear (the coil-spring-damper units are ahead of the drive shafts).

Steering is by rack and pinion, and 11½in. Girling disc brakes are mounted outboard all round. The 15in. aluminium wheels carry 5.50 Dunlop tyres at the front and 7.25s at the rear.

350 bhp engine

The 4.2-litre power unit is similar to the pushrod Ford Indianapolis engine and produces 350 horsepower for a car which is said to weigh 1820lb. dry (of which 57 per cent is carried on the rear wheels).

The drive is taken through a 7½in. diameter three-plate clutch to a Colotti Type 37 four-speed gearbox-final-drive unit, and then through "doughnut" couplings to the one-piece final drive shafts.

Fuel for the Weber 48 mm twin-choke downdraught carburettors is fed by three Bendix pumps from plastic containers housed in the main frame side members, which have a capacity of 37 gallons. The complicated exhaust pipe system terminates in a single neat expansion box above the transmission with twin outlets.

Roy Lunn, who was designing cars for AC, Aston Martin, Jowett and Ford of Britain before moving across to the Ford Division in America in 1958, has completed

for Le Mans

his part of the Ford GT project. John Wyer, who became known as one of the world's finest team managers when with Aston Martin, is now European manager of Ford's Special Vehicles Activity; his staff have the responsibility for building further team cars, preparing them and racing them.

11 Ford-powered cars will race at Le Mans

It is a fascinating assignment, spiced by the knowledge that provision is being made to drop in the Indianapolis twin-cam 4.2-litre engine later in the year.

With three Ford GTs, plus eight more cars with big Ford V8 power units, ranged against 10 large Ferraris, this year's Le Mans looks like being one of the best in the race's long history.

Ford Vice-President's statement

Describing GT cars as "highly advanced highway vehicles", Ford Motor Company vice-president Mr. Lee Iacocca said in New York the Ford GT has been built "to run and not just to show . . . it has been built to test advanced Ford vehicle concepts and to challenge foreign car supremacy at leading road racing courses in this country and abroad.

"Ford regards grand touring (GT) category racing as the toughest form of motor sports," Mr. Iacocca said, adding that "it may be significant that some of our Detroit competitors describe their fanciest offerings as 'GT' models."

Noting that GT races are run on road courses which test everything on the car — engine, brakes, transmission, suspension — Mr. Iacocca also emphasised that GT cars face an endurance test ranging up to 24 hours in the Le Mans event. "A GT is a special kind of all-round car that

Continued on Page 53

FORD GT — VEHICLE SPECIFICATIONS

GENERAL

Wheelbase .. .. 95in.
Tread
  Front .. .. 54in.
  Rear .. .. 54in.
Overall
  Length .. .. 158.6in.
  Width .. .. 70in. (over scoops)
  Height .. .. 40.5in.
Miscellaneous Heights
  Cowl .. .. 28.25in.
  Windshield .. .. 39.2in.
  Steering Wheel Top .. .. 31.35in.
Minimum Ground Clearance .. .. .. 4.8in.
Weights
  Basic (no fuel) .. .. 1825lb.
  Front Distribution .. .. 745lb.
  Front Distribution 42%

BODY

The GT car employs semi-monocoque construction of .025 steel. Hinged front and rear panel sections and doors are of reinforced fibreglass.

ENGINE

Cylinders
  Number 8
  Bore .. .. 3.76in.
  Stroke .. .. 2.87in.
  Displacement .. .. 255.3 cu. in.
  Compression Ratio .. .. .. 12.5 to 1
Power Output (Dynamometer)
  Maximum BHP .. .. 350 at 7200 rpm
  Maximum Torque .. .. .. 294 at 5600 rpm
Carburettors .. .. 4 Dual Barrel
                                48 mm Webers
Lubrication System
  Capacity .. .. 15 qt. — dry sump

TRANSMISSION

Colotti
  First Gear, 2.50; Second Gear, 1.70; Third Gear, 1.29; Fourth Gear, 1.00; Reverse, 2.50.

CLUTCH

Two Discs
  Diameter .. .. 8.5in.

BRAKES

Front Brake
  Disc Diameter .. .. 11.5in.
Rear Brake
  Disc Diameter .. .. 11.5in.

STEERING SYSTEM

Steering Ratio .. .. 14.0 (overall)
Turns (lock-to-lock) 2.8
Turning Circle Diameter 40ft
Steering Wheel Diameter .. .. .. 15in.
Steering Wheel Adjustment .. .. .. 2.0in.

WHEELS

Front .. .. 6.50 RIM x 15
Rear .. .. 8.00 RIM x 15
Tyres—size
  Front .. .. 5.50 x 15
  Rear .. .. 7.25 x 15

FUEL SYSTEM

Tank Capacity .. .. 37 gallons

NEW FORD GT for LE MANS!

IN LAST MONTH'S SCG we brought you the first details of the sensational new Ford GT Coupe, that will be racing the best the world has to offer this year in Europe and in the United States. Although we had two drawings and a cutaway of the car with last month's report, no photographs of the completed car were available, for the very simple reason that the car wasn't completed at press time. After a real round-the-clock last-minute rush, the first coupe was finished in time to be flown to the New York Auto Show in April. To tie in with last month's technical report, and to further familiarize you with the car's many interesting details, these photos were rushed to us by Ford. Some of their strongest racing enthusiasts are in their Public Relations office!

1. The perforated seats shown here through which air is circulated. Gear shift is directly to the right of driver seat. Pedals are floor mounted, horn button is Ford's GT emblem.
2. Rear suspension with reverse lower A-arm, extra light hub carrier, single upper arm, short drive shaft using rubber joint to compensate for length replacing normal splines.
3. Front suspension details include cast alloy spindle support, ball joint top and bottom, outboard disc brakes, leading steering arm that is actually integral with spindle support.
4. Rear section details include trans-axle, Indianapolis-type headers with silencer incorporated. Visible is the overflow radiator tank on right of fire wall with dual Bendix pumps.

NEW FORD GT for LE MANS!

1. Cross flow radiator is made integral with oil cooler. Dam below it houses running lights and air scoops but main purpose is to assure adequate air flow through grill opening. Note large single windshield wiper, gas filler caps at corner of windshield.

2. Oil reservoir and rack and pinion steering repose directly behind large cross flow radiator, spare tire fits directly above these.

3. Wire wheels were used instead of latest magnesium disc wheels to speed brake cooling.

Forty inches high, 350 horses strong, 200 mph fast—in other words, Total Performance!

FORD GT

Out of Dagenham and Detroit, on a Broadley-to-Wyer-to-Lunn triple play, a new racing car

WHEN THE FORD MOTOR Company returned to motor racing, it did so on a scale that is only possible for a vast corporation with an almost unlimited budget. So far, we have seen Ford powering Lotuses at Indianapolis, Ford at road races powering AC Cobras, and Ford at stock car races powering Fords. However, because it is an international company, Ford is now planning to contest international events, and the latest addition to its stable is the Ford GT.

The Ford GT looks suspiciously like last year's Lola and it is in fact a Lola derivative because most of the work was carried out at the Lola facilities in England under the direction of Eric Broadley. However, the car is called the Ford GT and the Lola name has been dropped. Others connected with the GT include Roy Lunn, the project manager, and John Wyer, previously a director of Aston Martin and now in charge of the racing program.

This is a strong team, particularly when one remembers that all the might of FoMoCo is behind it. However, it will need all the strength it can muster, because its intention is to oppose Ferrari in the prototype class of the Manufacturer's Championship. At the same time, the AC Cobras will be contesting the GT class against the Ferrari GTOs.

The GT was completed in a period of 12 months since its inception, and the whole project appears to have been carried out with an exceptionally high degree of planning and development work, utilizing all available resources such as wind tunnels and computers, and nothing seems to have been left to chance.

The whole conception of the GT is quite radical, the most striking feature of the car being its low height of 40 in. Other dimensions are: wheelbase 95 in., length 159 in. and track 54 in. The weight of the car less driver and fuel is 1820 lb and the distribution front and rear is 43-57%, which at first might seem to be an undue rearward bias. However, weight distribution of this nature is not uncommon in race cars, and can be compensated for by tires and suspension.

The main body section is a semi-monocoque structure and all the unstressed parts (such as the doors) are thin fiberglass fabrications. Much attention has been given the aerodynamics because the car is expected to approach 200 mph on the Mulsanne straight et Le Mans. Not only did this involve extensive wind tunnel testing of the body shape itself, but also the air flow to the various components requiring cooling,

The three parents—John Wyer, Eric Broadley and Roy Lunn.

Weber carbs and bundle-of-snakes exhaust on '63 Indy engine.

Ford GT resembles Broadley-designed Lola GT but is aerodynamically cleaner.   *Businesslike driver's compartment.*

FORD GT

including the driver. Cockpit ventilation is always a problem with GT cars, and this has been solved by ducting air from the pressure area under the nose to a position above the instrument panel so that the necessity for opening the side windows is eliminated. At the same time air is ducted to an "air conditioned" driver's seat, which is perforated with a series of holes so that perspiration is evaporated.

Another interesting feature of the seat is that the back is inflated, and this can be adjusted to suit various drivers by a hand pump in the cockpit. Deflation is taken care of by a push button on top of the pump. Another feature designed to improve driver comfort is the pedal layout, which is adjustable in the manner of the original Ford Mustang sports car while the seat is a permanent part of the main structure.

The car was designed to take the Ford 4.2-liter Indianapolis engine, which develops 350 bhp, but the eventual power unit is likely to be the Ford twin-cam·Indy engine. The engine is mounted in the middle behind the driver. The drive is taken to the transmission by an English Borg & Beck multi-plate clutch of 7.5-in. diameter, and the transmission itself it a Type 37 Colotti. This transmission has the disadvantage of only four speeds, but at the time it was the only proven transmission available which would withstand the torque of the engine.

The front suspension is conventional with upper and lower A-arms, and the rear suspension uses lower inverted A-arms with transverse links at the top and long trailing links from the main bulkhead. The inboard universal joints on the axles are Metalastic units which eliminate the need for splines. The Girling disc brakes are mounted inboard both front and rear and 11.5-in. discs are used, cooled by air ducted from the front intake and two additional intakes, one on each side of the body.

It is difficult to predict how the Ford GT will perform under actual racing conditions, but it is evident that is is an extremely well-engineered car constructed with all the resources of the Ford Motor Company and using some of the best brains in the racing business. GT racing is a fiercely competitive branch of the sport, with an enormous spectator following in Europe, and, in consequence, the effect on sales of a win is considerable. Obviously, this is what Ford has in mind.

However, when all is said and done, Ford must be complimented for having the courage to put its reputation on the line against the full might of Ferrari, and it will certainly be interesting to see the outcome of its efforts during the 1964 season.

"Spoiler" with lights and scoops improved aerodynamics.

FORD G.T.
AN AERODYNAMIC FERRARI-CATCHER

BY DAVID PHIPPS

The key to its aerodynamics is found in the front spoiler, which reduces front end lift.

These views show the steel (below) and fiberglass (above) parts of Ford's GT machine.

As the shout "Ford has changed" is echoed around the nation by radio and TV networks well in advance of the expected changes for 1965, it's becoming increasingly obvious that Ford's other favorite slogan "Total Performance" was launched somewhat prematurely.

While Ford's successes in various forms of racing have been resounding, it's questionable if the results are commensurate with the investment. Ford's essay into GT racing is particularly weird. Shelby's AC-Cobras have generally acquitted themselves very respectively, but we all remember how John Mecom's Chevy-powered Lola GT beat the Shelby équipe at Nassau. Ford's own Lola development work had not resulted in as much as a running prototype by Sebring-time (although Broadley's original Lola was conceived, designed and raced during a 100-day period a year ago). The Grand Touring category class win at Sebring regained much prestige for Shelby, but when the new Ford GT appears, it will be in direct competition with the Cobras, giving a new slant to the theme of "Total Performance."

It was in the summer of 1962 that Ford Motor Company let it be known that it was going to renew participation in automobile competition. Initially this took the form of increased interest in stock car racing and drag racing, quickly followed by a venture into European-style rallying and a decision to collaborate with Lotus in running a team of cars at Indianapolis. Engines and "technical assistance" were also supplied to a number of other outside concerns—notably the Shelby firm.

All this was only a start, however, and in the spring of 1963, attention was turned to GT racing, which offered obvious rewards in the sphere of image building and could also do a lot towards the improvement of the company's normal products; after all, conditions experienced at Le Mans or the Nürburgring resemble ordinary roads, but are much accentuated.

From this point of view GT racing has much more to offer than Indianapolis or Daytona, though stock car racing on road circuits should yield the same sort of results. Before the GT even ran, Ford had learned a great deal which is directly applicable to road cars as a result of aerodynamic tests on a model in a wind tunnel. If they had not been going into GT racing they would never have built that model.

Initially, the simplest way to achieve the desired end appeared to be the well-established American

FORD GT

practice of going out and buying the strongest contender, and in the GT sphere we all know who that is. Subsequently, having failed to buy Ferrari, the people concerned realized that any success they might have achieved would have been attributed to Ferrari, and every failure would have been blamed on Ford. Heaving a sigh of relief, they sat down to work out just exactly what they wanted to do, and this, in essence, was to make a car which would beat the Ferrari. (If you can't join 'em, beat 'em.)

Then followed talks with Colin Chapman about the GT project; later John Cooper was called in to discuss it. Finally Ford came to an agreement with Eric Broadley who had a Ford-engined GT car running.

In theory, it should be quite easy for Ford to design and build an all-out competition car. Eric Broadley had done it with a staff of 10 and no resources whatsoever. The problem was, that for all its many ramifications, Ford had no department set aside to design and build such machinery. The nearest thing was Advanced Concepts, which already had some experience from building the Mustang I. Even so, it is one thing to make a show car which is never liable to be called upon to prove itself in competition, and another to produce a vehicle which must face up to—and beat—the best opposition the world can provide.

Many major manufacturers don't race simply because they are afraid of being beaten. If they win—so what, they damn well should. If they lose, especially to a smaller concern, then what the hell are they playing at? Ford decided that the risk was worth taking, and went ahead. Using Advanced Concepts as a starting point, but one not sufficiently experienced to jump headfirst into European-style racing, they wisely looked around for someone to help with the development and racing of their new toy. Eric Broadley proved "extremely co-operative." They also brought in John Wyer, formerly of Aston Martin as technical director and team manager. The scientific approach to racing employed by Wyer and Aston Martin (with varying degrees of success) will combine naturally with Ford's scientific approach to the design of the car.

The man in charge of the whole project is Roy Lunn, who worked on the design of the chassis of the Jowett Jupiter R-4, the Aston Martin DB-2 and the Ford Anglia 105-E before moving to Dearborn, where he eventually became head of Ad-

SPECIFICATIONS FORD GT

ENGINE:
Water-cooled V-8, aluminum block, 5 main bearings
Bore x stroke ... 3.76 x 2.87 in, 95.6 x 73 mm
Displacement .... 255.3 cu in, 4195 cc
Compression ratio .... 12.5 to one
Carburetion .. Four dual-throat Weber 48-mm
Valve gear .... Pushrod-operated overhead valves
Power (SAE) .... 350 bhp @ 7200 rpm
Torque .... 294 lbs-ft @ 5600 rpm
Specific power output 1.37 bhp per cu in, 83.8 bhp per liter

DRIVE TRAIN:
Clutch .... 8.5-in dry twin-disc
Transmission .... 4-speed GSD (Colotti) non-synchro

Gear	Ratio	Over-all	mph/1000 rpm	Max mph
Rev	2.50	7.72	—12.7	95
1st	2.50	7.72	12.7	95
2nd	1.70	5.25	18.8	141
3rd	1.29	3.98	24.7	186
4th	1.00	3.09	31.8	200+

Final drive ratio .... 3.09 to one (3.55 to one optional).

CHASSIS:
Steel platform with steel framework for fiber-glass body
Wheelbase .... 95 in
Track .... 54 in F & R
Length .... 158.6 in
Width .... 70 in
Height .... 40.5 in
Ground clearance .... 4.8 in
Dry weight .... 1825 lbs
Weight distribution F/R 42/58%

Suspension
  F Ind., unequal-length wishbones and coil springs, anti-roll bar.
  R Ind., inverted lower wishbone, top transverse link, double trailing arms, coil springs, anti-roll bar.

Brakes .... Girling 11.5-in discs F & R
Steering . Rack and pinion (14.0 to one ratio)
Turns lock to lock 2.8
Turning circle .... 40 ft
Tires .... 5.50 x 15 F, 7.25 x 15 R
Revs per mile 672

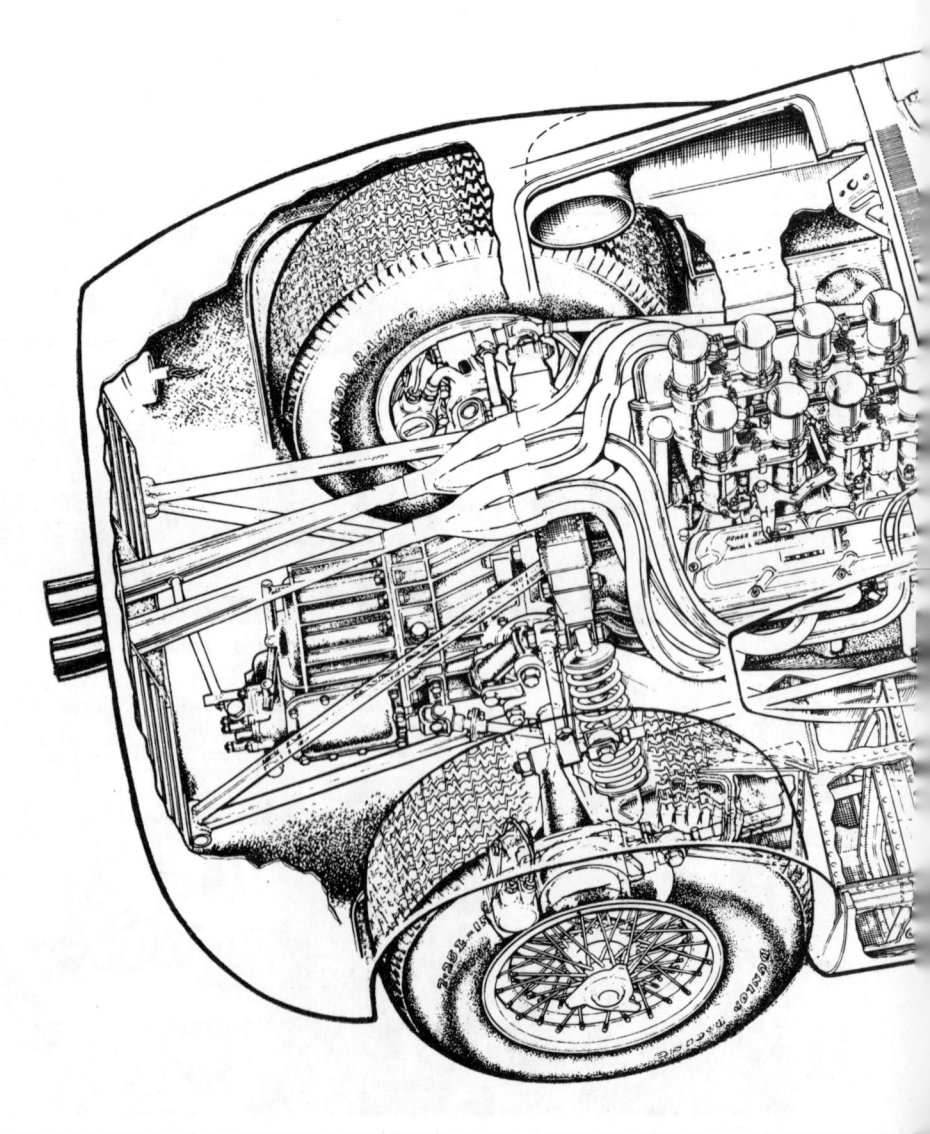

vanced Concepts, Ford Division.

The tiny Lola workshop at Bromley was clearly neither adequate for its new task nor in keeping with the image which the new car was intended to create, and thus in November 1963 the whole operation was transferred to a new factory at Slough, about 22 miles west of London and 3500 miles east of Dearborn. The object of all this was to combine the obvious advantages of a small specialist firm with the resources of a large corporation—and at the same time make it a little difficult for all the frustrated engineers in Ford Division to pop 'round and make "a few helpful suggestions" every other day.

The original Lola GT was described and illustrated in C/D July 1963. Subsequently it ran at Le Mans (C/D September 1963) and went very well between rebuilding stops before getting itself overturned. It clearly needed a lot of development, particularly in the aerodynamics sphere, but was a wonderful effort for such a small concern. And for Ford it was obviously a useful mobile testbed.

Having enlisted Broadley's assistance (for an undisclosed number of dollars, and an unspecified period) Ford employed Richie Ginther to carry out appraisal tests of the Lola GT at Goodwood and at the same time sent all Broadley's drawings back to Dearborn for analysis; the resultant findings tallied remarkably well with Ginther's report. After this the Lola was progressively developed, the main changes being to the cooling system and suspension. The original intention was to use twin side radiators, mounted in the engine compartment, in the 1964 car, but extensive tests on a full-scale model showed that it was impossible to get adequate air flow through them via the intake ducts on the sides of the body (the minimum requirement is 8000 cubic feet per minute). Furthermore, a conventionally mounted radiator, with front intake and outlets beneath the car, proved little or no better. The solution was a conventional system with a very low frontal air intake in a high-pressure area, with outlets on top of the hood, in a low-pressure area.

The results of the suspension changes were rather less conclusive, particularly as testing was hampered by a variety of mechanical problems, but sufficient for the so-called "computer-designed" suspension to be chosen for the new car; in fact the computer is not used to design the suspension but to work out the wheel angles obtained with a variety of linkages and mounting points, a

FORD GT CONTINUED

task which would take a prohibitive amount of time by normal methods.

At the end of November 1963 the modified Lola was put to bed and all attention was focused on the new Ford. The engine was to be the Indianapolis Fairlane unit, with pushrods initially and twin cams later; its capacity kept down to 4.2 liters in view of the FIA's sliding scale of minimum weights for GT prototypes (1818 lbs in this case). In respect of the engine, and of the transmission (Colotti 37, as used in the Lola GT and the Indianapolis Lotus), Roy Lunn's men are in much the same position as the British firms which rely on outside sources for such items; they just bolt them in and hope for the best—though in this case they will probably have Ford engine mechanics under their feet once the racing begins.

The chassis, a massive sheet steel structure which weighs over 300 lbs and is incredibly stiff (over 10,000 lbs-ft per degree), is very similar to that of the Lola, consisting of two deep D-section side members linked by a stressed floor and four transverse bulkheads. Rubber fuel tanks are fitted in both side members.

As already intimated, the biggest single step forward on the new car comes in the sphere of aerodynamics. The Lola had a total drag of 503 lbs at 200 mph and a lift of 528 lbs at the front and 168 lbs at the rear. The lift became acute if a crosswind was blowing, and a mere 15° yaw would raise the front lift to 786 lbs and the rear to 384 lbs. In extreme conditions the lift on the front wheels became greater than the load on them and they would actually become airborne.

Experiments with a high nose shape accentuated the problem. Total drag at 200 mph was 519 lbs, front lift 540 lbs and rear lift 108 lbs. At 15° yaw the figures went up to 614 lbs drag, 844 lbs front lift and 362 lbs rear lift. Then they went to a low nose shape, which reduced straight-line drag to 507 lbs, front lift to 445 lbs and raised rear lift to 199 lbs. At 15° yaw, however, total drag was still 596 lbs, front lift 704 lbs and rear lift 422 lbs. At this stage a front end spoiler was introduced, mounted below the nose and located just behind the air intake, pointed slightly forward. With a spoiler depth of 2.67 in, front lift was down to 326 lbs and rear lift up to 266 lbs, with an insignificant increase in total drag (513 lbs). A further reduction in lift was obtained by doubling the spoiler depth, but this increased the total drag of the

body to 531 lbs at 200 mph as well as proving impractical as regards ground clearance, so a happy medium was struck with a faired 3½-in spoiler which reduced both drag and lift to very acceptable levels. In straight-line motion at 200 mph, total drag is 488 lbs, front lift is 236 lbs and rear lift 272 lbs. A 15° yaw angle only increases total drag to 591 lbs (almost identical with the Lola) but keeps lift down to 309 lbs front and 343 lbs rear. Experiments were also carried out with the retractable headlights in their extended position, and the increase in both drag and front end lift was quite marked. Nevertheless, this type of headlamp will be used, at least on some of the cars, as it provides better illumination than a fixed lamp behind a plastic fairing; in addition, Ford feels that there is a big future for retractable lamps in passenger cars.

In general, the final body shape is surprisingly similar to that of the Lola, but rather more stylish, especially at the rear end. The doors, cut away into the roof, are the same, the angles of windscreen and rear window are much the same, and overall height is up half an inch. Major Ford innovations are the ducts behind the doors, originally intended as radiator intakes and now used for cooling the rear brakes, plus, of course, the aerodynamic cooling system and the front-end spoiler. A great deal of attention has also been paid to air-flow within the body, for the cooling of things like the suspension units, the gearbox and—most important of all—the driver. Far too little attention is paid to driver environment on many cars, both competition and commuting, but pretty well everything possible has been done on the Ford GT. Through-flow ventilation is provided without the need to open windows (with a consequent increase in noise, buffeting and drag) air coming in just ahead of the windscreen and going out above the rear window. The seats (fixed, as on the Mustang I, with adjustable pedals) are ventilated to evaporate perspiration, and are equipped with small, push-button operated inflatable rubber bags which provide support for the small of the back and can be inflated or deflated at will to vary the position of the spine during long driving stints.

Front suspension, by unequal-length wishbones and co-axial coil/shock absorber units, is straightforward and similar to that of both the Lola GT and Mustang I. At the rear, where the Lola had a wide-based leading lower wishbone, a top transverse link and a single trailing radius arm, the Ford has an inverted lower wishbone, a top transverse link and twin trailing radius arms. Spring rates used during tests of the Lola varied from 90 lb/in to 150 lb/in at the front and 120 lb/in to 185 lb/in at the rear, so it seems reasonable to suggest that the springs on the Ford will come somewhere between the two extremes—probably towards the higher end, as the roll centers are relatively low at 4.1 inches front, 4.64 inches rear, and the proposed front and rear anti-roll bars are fairly slender. As on most current Formula One cars, the suspension linkages are designed to combat nose-dive under braking and nose-lift (or rear end squat) under acceleration, the loads being taken out into the chassis structure rather than the suspension springs. A notable innovation is the use of self-aligning roller bearings as bushings for the suspension linkages.

Braking is by 11.5-inch discs, outboard all around, with massive Girling CR calipers at the front and BR calipers at the rear. The wheels, rather surprisingly, are spoked Borrani with aluminum rims, the main reason for this choice being ease of attachment. (Lola had some trouble on this score last year.) Wire wheels are also said to improve brake ventilation, but it is doubtful whether much air gets through the spokes at really high speed. Dunlop tires are used, sizes being 5.50 x 15 on 6½-inch rims at the front, and 7.25 x 15 on 8-inch rims at the rear.

After being shown at New York's International Auto Show, the Ford GT made its first track appearance at the Le Mans trials on April 18/19. It may make its competition debut in the 1000-Kilometer Race at Nürburgring and will definitely race at Le Mans in June. Three Ford GT entries have been accepted for the great French classic, and Ford is building a fourth spare car for practicing and development. The car's first appearance in the USA will probably be at Bridgehampton in September. The question of homologation has not yet been raised; Ford prefers to see how the car goes first, rather than to adopt a Cassius Clay approach. The team drivers are Dan Gurney, Phil Hill, Roy Salvadori, Bruce McLaren, Richard Attwood (who drove for Lola at Le Mans last year) and Jo Schlesser.

The main objective, of course, is Le Mans, and by mid-June the Ford team should be in good shape. One car may even have a twin-cam engine by then, though this could hardly be regarded as the first line of attack. Roy Lunn's modest ambition is for the cars to show potential this year and perhaps win in 1965, but everyone else is going to expect them to win first time out. With their Mercedes-Benz-like approach they could well do it, though it won't be at all easy; the serried ranks of Ferrari will take a lot of beating. **C/D**

Triumvirate in charge of Ford GT project are Eric Broadley, John Wyer and Roy Lunn.

Final product is extremely well finished and looks rather like a series-produced example.

ALICE BIXLER PHOTO

A Look at the Daytona Winner FORD GT-40

BY TONY HOGG

UNFORTUNATELY, the inner sanctums of Detroit, where top level decisions are made, are barred to members of the fourth estate, and even to the staff of *Road & Track*. It is therefore impossible to tell when, why, and by whom the decision was made at Ford to project an image of "Total Performance," and engage in a comprehensive and systematic program of racing to include such events as Le Mans, Sebring and similar international races in the prototype class.

At one time there was some speculation that Ford would buy out Ferrari lock, stock and barrel, and nasty-minded people felt that this was based on the theory that "if you can't beat 'em, buy 'em." Apart from any difficulties that undoubtedly arose during the negotiations, it is much more likely that Ford's decision was based on the fact that the resulting cars would be nothing much more than Ferraris bearing the Ford nameplate, which would have done little or nothing for the Ford image.

One of the reasons for the negotiations with Ferrari was to accelerate the program by taking over an existing enterprise, rather than starting completely from scratch. But when the deal fell through Ford began looking about for someone to build cars for its project, finally picking Englishman Eric Broadley, whose Lola GT coupe was very similar to designs on the boards at Ford, but was already in the testing stages.

Broadley is a construction engineer by training, who got into race car building as an avocation. Quiet and unassuming by nature, he is probably quite the equal of Colin Chapman as an engineer and, although he has received little credit for the project, he is the father of the Ford GT.

The next step was to undertake an extensive program of testing and research on the existing Lolas. This was conducted at various English circuits and at Monza, using drivers such as Roy Salvadori and Bruce McLaren. Meanwhile, John Wyer, who had managed the Aston Martin racing team for a number of years, was put in charge of development in England, and Englishman Roy Lunn, who has been with Ford of Dearborn for several years, was appointed chief designer.

The new car was officially presented to the press for the first time at the 1964 New York Automobile Show, where it was introduced by Ford vice president Lee Iacocca. During the course of his speech, Iacocca referred to it as "an American Manufacturer's car," which is one way of describing it, although, apart from the engine and one or two very minor items, it would appear to have been built in England by Englishmen and designed in America by Americans led by an Englishman.

The 1964 season was not particularly successful and the car did not win any races. However, it created great interest and a very favorable impression wherever it appeared. A lot was learned by the team, and Richie Ginther was timed officially at 207 mph on the Mulsanne straight at Le Mans. During 1964, Carroll Shelby was also campaigning his Cobras at the same events so, in fact, Ford was competing against itself with two totally different teams.

In order to unify the road racing project and bring everything under one roof, a decision was made to hand the GT project over to Shelby American for 1965, but to continue construction of the cars at Ford Advanced Vehicles, at Slough, England. Phil Remington, Carroll Shelby's chief

In the latest version of the Ford GT, a Cobra-modified Ford 289-cu-in. engine is used. The engine oil and differential oil coolers are placed on either side of the Type 37 Colotti transmission and fed by ducted air.

FORD GT-40

engineer, had been closely associated with the project since its inception so he has been able to continue development work without the necessity of commuting to Dearborn or London.

At this time, some 15 GTs have been built, and present plans call for a total of 50, some of which will be open cars, some coupes, and some will be set up for street use. Work is also under way on a 427-cu-in. prototype. For those people who are in the market for this type of fast transportation, the price has not yet been fixed, but it is rumored to be in the region of $15,000.

When the cars were received by Shelby, they were put through a series of exhaustive tests at Riverside and Willow Springs. From these tests it was apparent that several problems existed, and the major ones related to the engine temperature, the transmission, the brakes, the weight, and the road-holding at very high speeds.

Fortunately for the Shelby organization, the Aeronutronic division of FoMoCo (in Newport Beach, Calif.) numbers among its employees several racing enthusiasts who are also experts in the instrumentation and aerodynamics of missiles. By enlisting their aid and equipment, a lot of progress was made on these problems in a comparatively short time.

The engineers from Aeronutronics were amazed at how little was known about what they referred to as "low speed aerodynamics," as applied to 200-mph race cars. This term would seem reasonable enough for people engaged in the 18,000-mph nose cone business. In fact, aerospace techniques have proved very successful when applied to race cars and it is likely we will see considerably more progress in this particular area in the future.

When the Ford GT was in the development stage, a good deal of reliance was placed on wind tunnel testing for air flow over the body and also through the various ducts. Although a large amount of data was obtained from these tests, the car didn't respond as the tests indicated it should.

It would appear that there are several reasons for this state of affairs, and the main one is that background data concerning the wind tunnel testing of cars are very limited. Second, little is known about reproducing ground effect in a wind tunnel, because it is not a factor in aircraft design, and third, scaling down a car to model size is relatively much more critical than with aircraft if the resulting car is to behave on the road as the model does in the wind tunnel.

With the assistance of Herbert L. Karsch, Loyle E. Baltz and Bob L. Pons, among others from Aeronutronics who donated their time, two different systems of testing were used, although both are basically the same. In the first, telemetry was employed so that information from instruments in the car was transmitted to a truck parked by the circuit, where data could be either read instantaneously from instruments in the truck or, alternatively, checked later from tape.

The second method was to mount an oscillograph recorder in the car to record data on paper with the car in motion. In each case, such information as the air pressures and temperatures in the ducts, the engine revolutions and, by coupling potentiometers to the suspension, the exact movement of the suspension at any point on the course could be recorded with the car being driven at racing speeds.

The advantages of using aerospace techniques are that time is saved, there is no hit-and-miss involved, and an

Rear suspension has outboard brakes; Metalastik joints inboard.

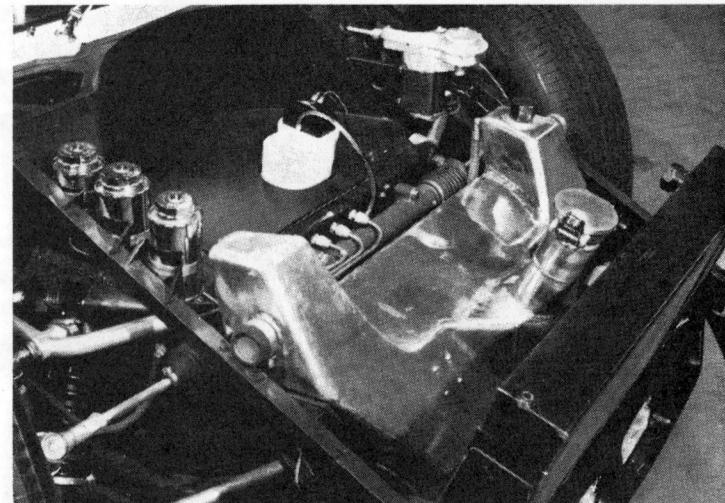

In the car's original form, four gallons of oil were carried in a tank mounted in the nose for the dry sump system.

Cockpit was engineered for maximum driver comfort. Sound level is low and interior remains cool.

exact record of the car's behavior under racing conditions can be compiled. On the other hand, the equipment is expensive and it requires skilled operators. However, it is ideally suited for the purpose because it is exceptionally light and compact, it will withstand all the shocks and vibration of a race car, and it can be run off the car's power supply because the oscillograph draws only about 8-10 amps.

Apart from the very sophisticated methods of testing introduced by Aeronutronics, much time was spent driving the car with tufts of wool attached to the body, and then following its progress around the circuit in a chase car carrying a passenger with a Polaroid camera.

With the experience gained during the 1964 season, and as a result of tests conducted by Shelby American, a number of changes have been made to the Ford GT. To overcome the water temperature problem, the nose has been redesigned and the ducting altered. In its original form, the engine was dry-sumped and four gallons of oil were carried in a front-mounted tank. By reverting to a wet sump, and eliminating the tank and its associated plumbing, about 75 lb were saved. At the same time, this left more room in the nose for a redesigned cooling system.

As far as the wet sump is concerned, it has to be extremely shallow and the capacity is nine quarts, but no oil temperature problems have occurred. An additional advantage of removing the oil tank from the nose was to permit the designer more latitude, because the original nose was found to be a near perfect air foil which caused the front of the car to lift at very high speeds. This has been corrected and the high speed stability has improved considerably.

The car was originally powered by the 4.2-liter pushrod Indy engine, but this has been replaced by the competition Cobra version of the Ford Fairlane 289-cu-in. unit. Although heavier, the 289 is cheaper and its 13% greater displacement provides more torque at a lower speed, which is an advantage because there are only four forward speeds in the Type 37 Colotti transmission. At the same time, the Shelby organization has had a vast amount of experience with the 289, so that the mechanics can set up an engine for a particular circuit and race distance.

During the 1964 season, trouble was experienced with the Colotti transmission-cum-differential. New, Ford-made ring and pinion gears gave a partial cure, and a more recent change is the adoption of involute splines for the four dog clutches which are used to effect gear changes. These changes are expected to cure most of their troubles, pending the arrival of all-new units from ZF in Germany. These will have five forward speeds, by the way. There is an oil cooler on each side of the transmission, with air supplied by special ducts. One cooler is for engine oil, the other for the transaxle lubricant.

The clutch is an English Borg & Beck 7.25-in. unit containing three driven plates. Its capacity is sufficient to handle the power output of the 289-cu-in. engine, although it would become marginal if the torque were increased by an appreciable extent. In order to reduce shock on the transmission, the inboard universal joints are Metalastik. These are a potentially weak point in the car (rubber) and they have been redesigned for longer life.

On circuits which place a premium on brakes, the Girling system on the GT has come very close to its limit on several occasions. The car was originally equipped with wire wheels in order to assist in brake cooling, but these did not help so a switch has been made to magnesium wheels, which are both lighter and more rigid.

At present, solid brake discs of 11.563-in. diameter are

Front suspension is extremely rugged.

FORD GT-40

used front and rear, with one piston on each side of the caliper operating one pad on each side. To improve cooling, the ducts to the brakes have been modified, and the next step is to switch to Kelsey-Hayes ventilated discs, which not only present a bigger surface area for heat dissipation, but also tend to draw air into the center of the disc and expel it at the periphery. Another modification to the braking system involves the use of Teflon lines covered with steel braid to prevent expansion due to the very high hydraulic pressure.

The rear brakes are mounted outboard, and whether this is from choice is not known but apparently there is insufficient clearance for inboard mounting. Aggravating the brake cooling problem is the size of the rear tires. Carroll Shelby has always favored getting plenty of rubber on the ground, so 9.00-15s are used at the rear mounted on 9.5-in. rims and the maximum section of these tires is approximately 12 in.

Since Shelby American took over the cars, the suspension has remained basically unchanged. Its chief characteristics are that it incorporates a considerable amount of anti-dive at the front and anti-squat at the rear, and it also appears to be abnormally heavy so that unsprung weight is greater than necessary. In fact, the whole car is probably about 200 lb above design weight, although wet-sumping the engine and eliminating the wire wheels have cut this to some extent.

From conversations with the drivers and after riding as a passenger in the car, we observed that the GT gets an awful lot of power to the ground as soon as the power is needed. In a slow turn, it tends to understeer slightly and, when entering a fast turn on a trailing throttle, it gets a bit twitchy. However, these are merely characteristics rather than faults. The absence of dive and squat are distinctly noticeable under conditions of heavy braking and acceleration.

In direct contrast to some other competition cars, driver comfort was obviously a concern of the designer, so that the GT can be driven for long periods without making undue demands on the stamina of the driver. The noise level is comparatively low inside the car, and the flow of fresh cool air through the driving compartment is carefully controlled. These two factors alone can make a big difference in a long race such as Le Mans (for which the car was designed).

In its original form, the car was equipped with inflatable seats which could be adjusted to suit the requirements of any driver. These have now been discarded on the grounds of undue complication rather than from fear of a blow-out, and the present seats are not adjustable but the pedals can be moved instead.

It is apparent that the Ford GT is one of the most sophisticated competition cars ever built. Admittedly, Parkinson's Law has been applied to some extent, as one would expect in such a big corporation, with everyone from the styling department to the janitor wanting to get in on the act. However, the basic design shows great potential and one cannot help feeling that Ford made a wise decision in electing to run during 1965 under the Shelby American banner.

"My inflating seat's gone stark, staring bonkers!"

The Ford in Carroll Shelby's Future

"Shucks," says Carroll Shelby, "I'm not an engineer. I'm not even very smart. The only thing I understand is human nature. I just like to bring the right people together and see what happens. I think I've put the right people at Shelby American; they're getting the job done." Yes. At least the Ford Motor Company thinks Shelby has the right combination—they recently entrusted him with the care and feeding of their very special baby, the Ford GT.

Shelby American has come a long way. Less than three years ago it consisted of Shelby and an answering service. Then Carroll conceived the Cobra. All he needed was a few of the "right people" and a couple of engines on the cuff. He approached Ford, just then committing itself to the performance image, and they gambled on the Texan's venture (though he still owns Shelby American in its entirety).

Obviously, it was going to take more than money, good engineering and a lot of promise to make the Ford GT a success. Ol' Shel seemed to be the man most likely to make it happen, both for Ford and the GT

BY STEVE SMITH

The Cobra was an instant success on the race tracks and orders poured in. Shelby moved from a back room in Dean Moon's speed shop to larger quarters, the ex-Reventlow "works" in Venice, California. As his business mushroomed, Cobras won four SCCA championships in two years and came within a whisker's breadth of prying the World Manufacturer's Championship loose from arch-rival Ferrari.

Today, Shelby American is a budding empire, doing a $15 million annual business and capable of producing 6000 cars a year. They just moved into a new facility adjoining Los Angeles International Airport: two huge hangars—North American Aviation used to assemble Sabreliners there—with about 96,000 square feet of working space on a 12½-acre plot. One building will house the administration and racing departments and the other will be devoted to the manufacturing assembly lines. The space between the two hangers is already blackening with wild tire marks.

Shelby American employs about 200 people now, more than half of whom are the sexiest collection of feminine beauty we've ever seen. Shelby's personal secretary, for instance, is Thayer Beyer, whom many of you will remember as the statuesque Irving in "Breakfast at Tiffany's." Yes. Shelby American is big business and getting bigger all the time. And Carroll is no longer just another one of racing's colorful characters; the boom-or-bust nature of his career seems to have taken a permanent upward swing.

Shelby was doing all right by Ford. And Ford was doing all right by Shelby. The two companies, drawing closer together, signed an iron-clad five-year contract that could keep Shelby American operating on a profitable basis, even if Ford pulled completely out of racing. Success! Ford designed a new all-coil, all-independent suspension for the Cobra. Shelby turned Ford's Mustang into a winning race car. Finally, under a "reciprocal technical and marketing assistance arrangement," Ford handed their GT over to Shelby, lock, stock and barrel. Leo Beebe, Ford Division's special vehicles activities manager, said, "We are taking this move to consolidate the construction and racing of all our GT-type vehicles within the same specialist organization," or, in effect, "here—we'll design 'em, you build 'em and race 'em."

For two years Ford had tried to build and race their car, hopefully named the "Ford GT," despite the fact that it's still a prototype in the eyes of racing's lawmakers. (The project name of the car is "GT 40" because it's 40 inches high; this was to distinguish it from another proposed GT prototype—somewhat taller—that never got beyond the drawing board stage).

In Ford's hands, the little coupe had a checkered career but never saw

FORD GT

a checkered flag. The first year of its existence was consumed with getting it built. In '64 it was entered in four races—the Nürburgring, Le Mans, Reims and Nassau—and failed to finish each time, though it had led for two glory-filled hours at Le Mans and set a new lap record there. Less than two months after being delivered to Shelby, the Ford GT made its competition debut in the 1243-mile, 12½-hour Daytona Continental (*Racing*, May *C/D*). Two GTs were entered and two finished, in first and third place (a Shelby Cobra was second).

Shelby's two GT 40s will be joined by two more at Le Mans, where Ford would—and may have to—spend a million to win. But whether or not Shelby races the Ford GT elsewhere on the GT prototype championship circuit depends on how well it does at Sebring, a week from the time of this writing. Much of the interest at Sebring (see race report, this issue) will have been focused on Shelby and the Ford GT. This is the story of the car to date.

The origins of the Ford GT—basically a sleek little two-seater man-guided missile, as long as a Volkswagen, as tall as a tall dog, capable of 100 mph in reverse and twice that pointed the right way—the origins of this car had nothing to do with Shelby. Two nearly-twin concepts sprung from two sources separated by the width of the Atlantic.

Late in 1962, Eric Broadley, a talented young designer/constructor of racing cars called Lolas, turned his hand to what seemed a promising idea—a GT coupe with a big engine just ahead of the rear wheels. The so-called "midship" placement of the engine offered two main advantages—better aerodynamics and better handling. Broadley rushed a Ford-engined version to completion in time for the London Racing Car Show. It was a sensation, and carefully noted by some of the boys in Ford's Advanced Concepts Department who had been thinking along similar lines. Roy Lunn, a displaced Englishman who manages this exotic, Dearborn-based group, had designed the midship-engined Mustang I in 1962. It was a nice car, but its little Taunus engine didn't pack much of a wallop and Lunn was toying with the idea of building something like it, only with the Fairlane V-8. Shades of Shelby! The coupe idea was attractive too, GT cars and 200 mph being all the vogue.

So Ford contracted Broadley's services for a year, hired away John Wyer from Aston Martin (where he had been racing manager, then general manager) and set out to build a GT car. Progress was excruciatingly slow. The basic design was quickly mapped out, but minor errors nagged the effort.

First, Broadley's tiny shop in Bromley was much too small and the operation had to be transferred to new facilities at Slough (rhymes with "plow"), 22 miles west of London. In Dearborn, it quickly became apparent that the side-mounted radiators that had worked so well with the Mustang I's 1.5-liter V-4 couldn't get enough air to cool the big American V-8.

The GT 40's chassis is similar to the Lola's, with a monocoque center section welded up (mostly by penetration welding; it's terribly intricate) of innumerable pieces of sheet steel. It weighs close to 300 lbs. and is one of the stiffest chassis ever built—about 12,500 lbs/ft per degree (the Ferrari 300/P/2 would be lucky to check out at 3000). It's also one of the strongest; two cars have crashed from extremely high speeds and in both cases the cockpit area has remained intact.

A very advanced suspension was designed and the wheel angles for given wheel deflections "read out" on a computer—giving rise to the story that the computer did the designing. Basically, the front suspension is an unequal length wishbone system; the rear consists of two trailing arms, an upper lateral link and a reversed lower wishbone. Healthy doses of anti-dive, anti-squat and anti-lift have been designed into both ends. The first engine was a 4.2-liter (252 cu. in.), 350-horsepower version of the alloy-block, pushrod Ford Indy engine, re-tuned for road racing. (For a complete technical description of the car as it was first publicly shown, see June '64 *C/D*). Once into the hardware stage, the chassis, suspension and engine

Clockwise, from the #72 GT at the top that Richie Ginther and Bob Bondurant drove to

third place at Daytona: Ford's Roy Lunn and European team manager John Wyer, mother-henning; Ken Miles, team driver and co-winner at Daytona with Lloyd Ruby; Richie Ginther, Ford's most experienced test driver; Phil Remington, mechanical inspiration of Shelby-American.

FORD GT

have never given much trouble, but almost everything else did.

A basic body and several alternative body sections were put through a series of 76 runs at the University of Maryland's wind-tunnel. Everything seemed fine, so the car was hauled off to last year's mid-April Le Mans testing day. The aerodynamics proved too hairy for test driver Jo Schlesser, who got out of shape at 150 mph on the Mulsanne straight in the wet and crashed, writing off the car (but not, luckily, Schlesser). A spoiler was added to the tail and the problem seemed once again in hand. Next came the GT 40's maiden race at the 1000-kilometers of the Nürburgring, where it went out with transmission failure. Failure of one part or another of the Colotti transmission put the cars out at Le Mans and Reims. Fire eliminated one of the three GTs at Le Mans, another was written off at Monza during a test session, and "the human element", i.e., faulty assembly, shot both cars down at Nassau.

By the end of '64, 10 cars had been built or were on the stocks. Number 1 was the car flown to New York for a press showing and wrecked two weeks later at Le Mans. Numbers 2 through 5 are in existence (except the one that crashed at Monza). Numbers 6, 7 and 10 were being built; 8 and 9 were just being completed. A packet of money had been spent—though not nearly as much as everyone imagines—with nothing to show for it except a lot of promise. Less than a month after the Nassau debacle, the project was handed over to Shelby.

This raised eyebrows in some quarters. John Wyer was thought by many to be a team manager *par excellence*. Shelby's Cobra team in Europe last year, on the other hand, had been obviously ill-prepared to do battle with Ferrari and bad team management may have been the largest single factor between the Cobra and the World Championship. Ford's official reason for the transfer, as mentioned, was to put all the road-racing cars in one basket. Ford officials privately talked about the year-round balmy climate in Southern California being better for testing, plus the fact that Riverside—unlike Monza—isn't right in Ferrari's back yard under the *Commendatore's* nose. But, in truth, Lunn's group had gone about as far as they could go, and Wyer's group wasn't getting the job done. At least, they weren't producing the desired results.

In any case, Shelby looked more attractive. After all, '64 was the Shelby operation's first year of racing in Europe. His organization seemed to be shaping up. "It's like a dragster," said a Shelby spokesman. "We were spinning our wheels, but we've got traction now." Sure enough, both the overseas racing team and the home front pulled together during the second half of the year and got some pretty impressive results. The fast-growing company could learn fast, too.

So Shelby American took over the Ford GT project. We inspected the cars and the new facilities soon after the two team cars had arrived back from their victorious Daytona outing. To find out exactly how Shelby had done it, we interviewed Ken Miles, another displaced Britisher, who is Shelby's competition advisor and a regular team driver. "We have several advantages over most of the other people who have played with the car," said Miles. "Ford Advanced Vehicles in England haven't had the skilled personnel to do the work. Ford Advanced Vehicles in Dearborn—whilst they have the facilities—can't react as quickly to a situation as we can. We can react to a suggestion—we can do something—right *now*. We don't have to go through elaborate procedures of putting through formal design changes. If we decide we don't like something, we take a hacksaw and cut it off.

"We still have the core of the original Shelby American organization," Miles said: "Carroll himself, Phil Remington, and some extremely good craftsmen who are used to this sort of panic operation. Practically everything we do is a panic operation. But, if anybody can do it, we can."

The "can-do" atmosphere pervades the original nucleus. "It's been a real team effort," said Ginther, who has driven the GT 40 for both Ford and Shelby. "It's *(Continued on page 40)*

Clockwise, from the front suspension with the Shelby ducting: the new—and hitherto un-

tested GT 40 roadster: the Shelby-modified nose ducting: the 1964 version (compare this with the radiator air entry and inlets above): the engine bay of the Shelby Daytona car with transaxle oil cooler (right), engine oil cooler (left), 289 cu. in. engine and reworked suspension.

a really big difference... things are happening rather than just being discussed. There's a sense of urgency and necessity that's rubbing off on everybody."

Miles added, "One of the things that is so gratifying about our Ford GT program is that we took on a challenge which others had tried to meet and had failed. The boys in the shop rose to the occasion and did a hell of a good job. Let's face it, Daytona was no fluke—it was a team effort."

Mechanically, Shelby American's chief engineer, Phil Remington, is the key to the success of the GTs at Daytona, as well as being responsible for the performance of the Cobras for the past several years. He's the one man who seems to know everything. He makes all the little bits and pieces come together to function as a working machine. It's said that he laid out the last of the Scarabs, the rear-engined Mk IV sports/racing car, on the floor of Reventlow's shop... without so much as a blueprint. Miles says of Remington: "He's an inspiration. He's not only a brilliant cut-and-try engineer, he also has a personality that instills confidence in the people working for him."

Thus imbued with the spirit of Shelby American, we went to watch the cars being reassembled for Sebring. Dismantled, they looked like stripped down fighter planes being overhauled. The first thing Shelby had done when he received the two GTs in January was to repaint them in his team's colors: a deep, royal blue with twin white stripes. Then the cars were taken to Riverside for a shake-down run. Surprisingly, "the handling was atrocious," said Miles. "They had been taken apart and put back together so many times that the design settings had gotten lost. It's a highly sophisticated and extremely complicated piece of machinery, and because of that, it's extremely susceptible to minor errors in assembly. So, when we re-set the suspension to the original specifications, the cars improved enormously. This was our first job—to get the car back where it had started from."

This done, three more interrelated problems raised their heads and begged for solution: aerodynamics, weight and brakes.

"The aerodynamics," both internal and external, reported Miles, "were excruciatingly bad." Aerodynamically, the car had been rather too imaginatively engineered from the beginning. First there had been the misguided attempt to draw radiator air in from the sides of the car. Then there had been the little problem of 1100 lbs. of lift at the front end of the car when running flat-out at a 15° yaw angle. Then the lack of a spoiler that sent Schlesser off the road at Le Mans. On paper, or standing still, the aerodynamics looked great. There was very fancy ductwork running all through the car, supposedly delivering the right quantity of air wherever it was needed. Even the backs of the seats were "air conditioned" with ducts leading to the inside of the upholstery. Unfortunately, little or none of it worked very well.

The Ford Advanced Vehicles crew kept fiddling with the nose shape, trying to find a configuration that would stabilize the car but still have a low drag factor. The wind tunnel tests had not incorporated internal aerodynamic ducting, and it was only later discovered that 76 horsepower were being burnt up just trying to ram air through the car.

"The aerodynamic problems we've had with the car," Miles told us, "were essentially ones of air flow within the car being affected by external details. For example, we were getting very little air flow to the brakes, although they had huge ducts ostensibly directing vast quantities of air at them. In fact, the brakes were overheating badly. The engine was getting too hot. The engine compartment itself was getting too hot. The cooling water was getting too hot. The engine and gearbox oil was getting too hot. All this in spite of a large number of apertures which should have supplied them with more than enough air. We discovered that what was happening was that—due to design changes that had been made over a period of time, probably without reference to the original specifications—practically all of the ductwork was at a 'stall' condition," i. e., no air was moving in the ducts.

The GT has two pairs of air inlets at the rear; one right behind the door and another higher up and farther back, beside the rear window. Originally, the upper ducts were supposed to admit air for the carburetors and the side ducts were to pick up air for the rear brakes. Remington decided to split off both pairs. The inboard side of the upper ducts now goes to the carbs, the outboard side goes to the rear brakes. The lower halves of the side ducts now direct air to the exhaust system, the right upper half feeds air to the transmission oil cooler, and the upper left leads to the engine oil cooler (both coolers are Shelby additions). Engine compartment air was originally picked up at grilles in front of the windshield and ducted through the doors. Ford found out that the grilles were in a near-zero pressure area and put a small louvred grille over the engine compartment behind the rear window. Remington enlarged the louvres by about 100%.

At the front, not enough air was getting to the brakes or through the radiator. Relatively minor alterations sufficed to get air to the brakes, but the radiator was a Gordian knot. Ford Advanced Vehicles had been convinced that a dry-sump lubrication system was necessary. Remington didn't think so. It required a separate oil tank, overflow tank, oil radiator, oil lines and 15 quarts of oil to be circulated by a second, power-consuming scavenger pump—all of which added unwanted weight. Moreover, the oil tank and radiator were up in the already-crowded nose. "We'd congested the whole front end of the car," apologized Lunn; "in future approaches we'll allow more space."

Remington couldn't wait. He'd gambled on a conventional wet sump for the Cooper-Ford "King Cobras" and it had worked well enough. The distance from the crank centerline to the ground was the same as the Ford GT's, so out went the dry sump system. This left more front aperture area available for air flow to the radiator, and allowed the exit flow to be cleaned up. Adding a small spoiler on the forward lip of the air exit on top of the hood dropped the water temperature 40°.

"We now have a condition where the engine runs excessively cool," reported Miles. "This happy state of affairs means that we can redesign the nose, cutting down on the air flow through the radiator and thus improve the top speed of the car with no increase in horsepower." Lunn's group is already at work on a new nose that is longer and lower. It will make its first appearance at Le Mans, June 19.

The next problem was weight. Close to 60 lbs. had been saved by abandoning the dry sump, but the car was still overweight. Ready to go, less fuel, it had never weighed less than 2200 lbs. The design target had been 1800 lbs. Originally, the GT 40 used the aluminum block, pushrod Indy engine, but this was discontinued when the "production line" started making the four-cam Indy engines. The GT 40 is now powered by the stock 289 cu. in., 385-hp cast-iron Cobra engine—just like the ones in the Daytona coupes except for the one-inch shallower oil pan and a smaller diameter 3-plate clutch. The minimum allowable weight for a GT prototype of this engine size is 2035 lbs, so only 100 or so more pounds can be saved from the Shelby cars before they have to start ballasting.

Although there has been talk of welding up a chassis center-section out of aluminum sheet (which would save about 100 lbs.), the first approach will probably be to lighten the fiberglass body parts. The present nose and tail sections are, "typical European fiberglass," according to Miles. "What we need are some body sections laid up using fiberglass linen in very thin sections, which will give the rigidity and strength we need—without the weight."

The Borrani center-lock wire wheels have already been scrapped. "The wire wheels were originally fitted in the belief that you would get some air flow through the wheels, which would result in the brakes running cooler. This is a fallacy; you don't get any air flow through wire wheels when they're spinning —they're just like a solid disc," said Miles. Specifications were drawn up for magnesium wheels and sent to Ted Halibrand. He couldn't have the mag wheels ready for Daytona, so the GTs ran with cast aluminum wheels. Mag wheels will be on the cars at Sebring and after.

The mag wheels were not only stronger and lighter, but also gave Remington the opportunity to increase the rim widths from six inches in front and eight in the rear to eight in the front and nine-and-a-half in the rear. Nobody was very comfortable with the Dunlop R6 tires and they were replaced by Goodyear Indy tires. The wider rims necessitated widening the rear body section about two inches increasing the spare tire area, and reworking some of the chassis paneling near the forward end of the pannier gas tanks in the door sills to get enough steering lock.

So, finally, to the brakes. Part of the problem was solved with improved ducting and by the mag wheels (which tend to draw heat away from the discs). At Daytona, the "g" loads on the banking were so high that the wheels were pressed up into the wheel wells and squashed the ends of the ducts; this will be remedied by Sebring. Kelsey-Hayes, which works very closely with Ford on disc brakes, made up a set of radially-ventilated discs from Meehanite for Shelby American. These were put on the cars for practice at Daytona and the drivers were ecstatic about the way they worked . . . until the discs cracked. Remington said that Kelsey-Hayes would make the next set of vented discs from high nickel content cast iron. "The vented disc," said Miles, "is definitely the answer."

Final touches to the car before Daytona included replacing the four Bendix fuel pumps with three Stewart-Warner adjustable pumps, adding a hatch on the right side of the engine compartment to get at the oil filler pipe and dip stick, and installing a pressure filling system for the radiator, like NASCAR stockers.

Having taken care of these primary considerations, the Shelby organization found they had come full circle: the weak point on the car was once again the gearbox. Until now, it has been a Colotti Type 37, a four-speed non-synchro transaxle unit. For Daytona, Ford cut their own helical ring and pinion sets, with a 10° helix angle, to replace the Colotti straightcut gears. Ford also made 20 other changes and supplied tubular halfshafts to eliminate the Metalastik couplings.

During the race, the team drivers babied the transmission. Ginther and Bondurant used low gear in their car; Miles and Ruby did not. Miles said the transmission in his GT, "could have gone another 12 hours," but low gear in the other car had been chewed up and the pieces were clogging up the rest of the gears.

Obviously, the Colotti will be retired as soon as a substitute can be found. The best bet for now is the new ZF 5-speed. A ZF is being fitted to the car Wyer will manage in Europe and should have its first public outing at the Le Mans test day in mid-April. The "Zed-F" box has had trouble with the needle bearings on the mainshaft in bench tests, which has held up delivery while it was being corrected. Assuming all goes well, one of Shelby's cars should have a ZF for the 24-hour race.

Handily enough, this brings us to a discussion of the future of the GT 40, and of the new components being designed for it—transmissions, engines, bodies, et cetera.

The first order of business is, of course, the automatic transmission. "There's no question about it," says Miles, "the automatic box—with manual override—is the way to go. What you need is a small torque converter, efficient at high revs, but inefficient at low engine speeds where torsional vibrations are rather high. This sort of fluid coupling would take some of the load-unload shock out of the drive." Ginther agrees: "It would be the smartest thing anybody could do—especially for long distance races."

Ford will doubtlessly want to list the automatic as an option for the GT car on the homologation papers, thus the specifications for it may be announced at the same time production plans are announced—hopefully by June—whether or not the car has actually raced with the new transmission.

It's also probable that new engines will be offered to take advantage of the stronger gearbox. As powerful as the car is now, Shelby would like to see it still more so. So would Ginther: "It could use more power. Definitely. The four-cam Ferrari could just run past us on the straight at Daytona. For endurance racing, it wouldn't be necessary to have more power throughout the range—just at the top. If we could 'cruise' comfortably at over 200 mph on the Mulsanne straight at Le Mans, for example, we could be very careful with the car elsewhere around the circuit and still have lap times that would win the race." Some of that speed may be found in new nose shapes, but more likely it will come from hotter engines.

The current engine puts out 385 bhp at 7000 rpm and 312 lbs/ft. of torque at 5000 rpm. There's also a "high-torque" engine with less peak power but 342 lbs/ft. of torque (also at 5000 rpm) that's used for circuits like Sebring and the Targa.

"The 289 is by no means at the end of its tether," said Miles. "We're working on a couple of projects that will bring the power up another 30 or 40 horses, still with 4.7-liters displacement. It's no secret that we're working on aluminum heads for the engine." These heads, being developed in England and Italy, feature much improved breathing, though still incorporate rocker shafts, not the bathtub rocker arrangement used in the "porcupine head" Chevy 396. "There are other engines in the offing—out and out racing engines—but nothing has been finalized as of now."

Apparently the four-cam Ford Indy engine is no longer being considered, although it will fit in the GT 40 if the heads are reversed and the sill modified to clear the exhaust pipes. Equipped with Webers, a

FORD GT CONTINUED

four-cam engine was in the car at one time, in England, but Ford called up and said they needed their engine back. Since then, interest in using the four-cam has waned. For one thing, it costs a mint ($15,000). For another, as Lunn points out, there is no displacement limit on GT cars or GT prototypes, while the Indy engine was developed against a 4.2-liter maximum. "We feel we can do better by using volume to get horsepower than by squeezing a lot of horsepower out of a small displacement engine."

Using a ⅜-inch stroker crank, the 289 can be taken out to 327 cubic inches—about the limit for the Fairlane block. At that, the short connecting rods (5.155 inches center-to-center, vs. the Chevy 327's 5.7 inches) have such a high angularity that they tend to drive the piston into the cylinder wall. Some new pistons are being made up, with the wrist pin practically sitting in the dome, so that rods with a longer center-to-center distance can be used, giving less angularity. Gurney went flat-out for eight hours with a Cobra 327 (called the "325" or "325/327", presumably to avoid sounding like a Chevy), so its reliability is improving each time out. Shelby told us, "We'll probably settle on the 325—that seems to be about the kind of horsepower we're looking for, the kind of power we can apply with our present chassis development and tire configurations." The production GT 40, using this engine with aluminum heads, would have over 450 horsepower on tap, which ought to hold off the Ferraris for a year or so.

For the future, there is the 427 cu. in. pushrod engine (the single cam 427 won't fit without major alterations and probably isn't needed). With the aluminum heads from the Cobra 427, the big engine weighs only about 100-125 lbs. more than the cast-iron 289. The minimum weight for a 7-liter GT prototype is 2310 lbs., or 285 lbs. more than the maximum weight for a 4.2-liter prototype. The minimum weight for a 325 cu. in. prototype is 2123 lbs. (Oddly enough, there is no minimum weight for homologated GT cars.) A 427 is being shoe-horned into a GT 40 in Dearborn as this is being written, incidentally, but probably won't be ready for Le Mans.

Presumably, the only thing holding down the engine size at this point is the lack of a suitable transmission. As Shelby is impressed by the quality of Hewland gearboxes, we asked Remington about the new Hewland LG 500, designed to withstand the torque of 7-liter V-8s. "Physically, the LG 500 is a little too big for the present package." It's pretty safe to infer that the 427-engined GT 40 will be experimental until the second generation for Ford GTs. But could the GT 40 chassis take it? "There is no doubt in my mind," said Miles, "that the basic chassis configuration could cope with the kind of power we could get from the 427." Shelby commented that they were, "sitting better with this chassis than any chassis that's been built in the history of auto racing."

As to body changes, there is already the roadster variation, with a new tail. No one seems to know who wanted the roadsters in the first place, though. By consensus, the only place the drivers would prefer it would be the Targa Florio. Elsewhere, they wouldn't want to give away the aerodynamic advantages of the coupe, not even on the Nürburgring's roller-coaster track. The roadster hasn't saved much weight because the absence of a stressed roof meant the chassis had to be beefed up to maintain rigidity.

One of the two roadsters arrived at Shelby's just as we were leaving. We asked Remington what he was going to do with it. He scratched his head. "I dunno—use it for evaluating new components, I guess. Like if we want to try out a ZF; brake tests; the new nose; see what we can't do to clean up the back end."

Otherwise, no major body changes are planned, although, as Remington said, "the body is still bad, dragwise." Shelby was more optimistic: "We're working in much smaller degrees than most other companies in this field because we have so much experience behind us. We probably know more about aerodynamics than anybody."

Naturally, improvements aren't going to go on *ad infinitum*. At some point it will be more sensible to "freeze" the design and start producing it in a series. A Ford official indicated that it would be "competitively" priced with comparable Ferrari models. This means about $16,000, a price Lunn opines people will pay *if* the car is a winner. The financial wheels at Ford aren't out to make a big profit, but they wouldn't like to take a bath, either. So the actual production dates, figures and prices are largely contingent on the car's race record.

Immediately after Sebring, Shelby's two GTs will be shipped to England where they will be readied for the Le Mans test day in April. Then they'll be brought back to Ford Advanced Vehicle's Slough facility and prepared for the race itself. For the all-out assault on Le Mans, Shelby's GT 40s will be joined by the one being managed by Wyer and one from Ford of France. Where else Shelby's cars will appear depends on how they do at Sebring and Le Mans. The schedule is being planned one race at a time and played by ear.

Eventually, Shelby would like to stop fielding a team of factory cars —let the customers do the racing with his support—and turn Shelby American into a manufacturing and marketing company, leaving research, development and racing to other organizations like All-American Racers, Inc., in which Shelby is Dan Gurney's partner.

When the GT 40 goes into production, Shelby American will be listed as the official manufacturer, though in fact they will be welded up in England and finished by Shelby in California. The Slough "factory" consists of three little buildings with a total area of about 1000 square feet. It's really just a collection and assembly center for all the pieces made on the outside. Ford will be the "vendor" of raw GTs to Shelby, just as Ford is the vendor of raw Mustangs to Shelby for the Mustang GT 350.

Shelby plans to build 100 cars— 50 "strictly for racing" and the other 50 as street cars. The GT 40s will be marketed in the U.S. through a group of about 50 high-performance Ford dealers set up around the country who will specialize in stock cars, sports cars, drag racing cars and engines, speed equipment, Cobra kits and the like.

Eventually, actual manufacture of Ford's GT-type cars will be transferred to Shelby American, but probably not until Ford Advanced Vehicles comes up with a successor to the GT 40 that is both competitive on the race track and more adaptable to series-production techniques. This could point toward plastic, as has been rumored, because it's light and easy to work with. By all rights, it should be a worthy successor. "We now have a basic car," says Lunn, "from which to develop better products." Can it be true that racing improves the breed? You better believe it, Henry.

c/D

MEANEST CAR IN TOWN

The GT-40 is "Ultimate Performance"

BY JAMES T. CROW **ILLUSTRATIONS BY GENE GARFINKLE**

BLUE AND white are the international racing colors of the United States. They have had little enough use, goodness knows, because the U.S.-built cars that have participated in international racing have been few. There was Jimmy Murphy's Duesenberg which won the French Grand Prix in 1922, the Chrysler-powered Cunningham sports cars of the early 1950s, Lance Reventlow's unsuccessful Scarab grand prix cars of 1960 and precious few others. In the past few months, however, a new blue-and-white racing car has appeared in the winner's circle at two long-distance international races and has been widely hailed as the harbinger of a great new era where American cars will meet and beat the best the world has to offer. This is the Ford GT-40.

It is an exciting car to look at. A coupe. Low. Squat. Mean looking. In physical dimension it is small. Only 40.5 in. high, its roof-line is more than a foot closer to the ground than the average American sedan. It's about the height of your appendix scar. In overall length it is 158.6 in., roughly 4 ft. shorter than the bumper-to-bumper length of a typical U.S. compact.

It's difficult to understand how anything so small could come out so mean and nasty looking. If the lines were all smooth and uncluttered, as they appear in the double-page Ford ads, it would be a sweet and sleek machine, on a par, for appearance, with the pleasantly smooth lines of the Porsche GTs. But in the "as-raced" condition, there are ducts and scoops and vents all over, great odd-shaped air outlets atop the front deck and rectangular little Judas windows cut into the plastic side screens. In addition, there are spoiler tabs tacked on in front of the front tires and a built-in, slightly upswept ducktail on the top edge of the chopped-off rear. It reminds you, somehow, of one of the great middleweight fighters of the past. Experienced. Rough. Lumpy. But marvelously efficient.

Under that nasty-looking aluminum hide, there lie suspension and running gear which also are determined to get the job done. The engine is located behind the driver and ahead of the rear wheels in the now-accepted (for racing cars) amidships position. The engine used in the car's two successful U.S. races has been the all-out competition version of the Ford 289-cu. in. pushrod engine developed by Shelby-American for the Cobra. Power figures on this engine, which is equipped with a nest of four double-throat 48 mm Weber carburetors, show it to have about 380 bhp at 7000 rpm and 315 lb.-ft. of torque.

Behind the engine is a 4-speed all-synchromesh Italian-built Colotti gearbox and transaxle. The rear wheels are driven through double-jointed half-axles which have Metalastik rubber coupling joints next to the gearbox and constant-velocity universal joints outboard at the hub-carrier.

The front suspension is straightforward independent with unequal length A-arms, coil springs, tubular shock absorbers and an anti-roll bar. At the rear there is a lower A-arm, a single upper arm, trailing links, coil springs, tubular shock absorbers and an anti-roll bar. Girling disc brakes, mounted outboard, are used all around.

The chassis of the GT-40 is typical of the contemporary trend in racing car chassis design. Down each side of the car there is a hollow rectangular box and these are the main structural members. They do double duty by also housing flexible fuel bags. Joined to these boxes and the reinforced floor pan are the sheet metal bulkheads. It is an example of the now popular semi-monocoque construction and,

FORD GT-40

though it is not particularly light as racing car chassis go, it is very strong and rigid.

All the GT-40s are right-hand drive and the seats are semi-reclining and extremely comfortable. These seats are solidly fixed in place, but the pedals can be adjusted fore and aft to accommodate drivers of different leg length. Much attention has been given to personal comfort, which is especially important if the drivers are to operate at maximum efficiency in long-distance racing.

The performance of the GT-40, to put it mildly, is brisk. If set up for dragstrip performance, which it obviously is not, the power-to-weight should result in elapsed time of just under 11 sec. and a velocity of roughly 130 mph for the quarter-mile. For top speed, it is capable of more than 200 mph. Indeed, a car driven at Le Mans last year by Richie Ginther was clocked at over 207 mph on the Mulsanne straight. It is, in short, a special kind of Ford and, if you can overlook the redundancy, is the "ultimate Total Performance Ford," just as they say in the advertisements.

THE TWO races won by the GT-40 took place in Florida last spring. First was the Daytona Continental, a 2000-km. (1243 miles) race around the road circuit at Daytona Speedway. This course, which incorporates about two-thirds of the famous banked tri-oval plus some wiggly bits on the flat infield, is 3.81 miles long. It is regarded as a fast circuit and the quicker machines, such as the GT-40, lap it at averages over 110 mph. There were two GT-40s entries, one for Ken Miles and Lloyd Ruby, the other for Richie Ginther and Bob Bondurant. The Miles/Ruby car was five laps ahead by the end, the second-place car was a Cobra coupe, and the other Ford GT-40, which had led earlier but dropped back after having ignition troubles during a pit stop, finished third.

This victory gave Ford no points toward the Prototype championship as the Continental is not one of the seven races counting toward the trophy this year, but it gave the GT-40 backers a tremendous boost in morale and prestige.

This win was a comparatively easy one. There were faster cars in the race, but these, Dan Gurney's 325-cu. in. Ford-powered Lotus 19 and John Surtees' 4-liter (242 cu. in.) Ferrari, eliminated themselves with mechanical troubles and the Ford strategy of lapping at a comfortable speed paid off.

At Sebring a month later, the Ford GT-40 placed second overall, but did win the Prototype class. The overall winner was the all-out sports/racing car of Jim Hall and Hap Sharp, a Chevrolet-powered Chaparral, which led the GT-40 by four laps at the end.

This GT-40, driven by Miles and New Zealander Bruce McLaren, ran with the same dependability it displayed at Daytona, having no major problems at all as it circulated around the 5.2-mile airport circuit for 12 hours. Its nearest competition in the Prototype category finished third overall, two laps behind. This was a 3.3-liter (200 cu. in.) Ferrari 275-LM driven by Britisher David Piper and South African Tony Maggs.

The GT-40's victory in the Prototype class at Sebring was in some ways easier and in other ways more difficult than at Daytona. There were none of the latest Ferraris at Sebring, thus the Fords had the edge on overall speed. Throughout the early hours of the race the Miles/McLaren Ford GT-40 simply stayed within catching distance of the quickest Ferrari. Then the Ferrari, a 3.3-liter driven by Graham Hill and Pedro Rodriguez, suffered a broken rear end in the eighth hour and the point was never brought to issue. This Ferrari, by the way, was entered in the sports/racing class, not the Prototype class, but there's no reason to suppose that the Ford people would have been content to finish behind it.

Ford also scored other victories at these two races as Ford-powered Cobra "Daytona" coupes handily won the Grand Touring class at both events. In fact it now appears that Ferrari is not going to seriously contest the GT championship this year.

UNLESS YOU have kept up with them, the rules that govern the various kinds of cars and the several kinds of championships in international competition are incomprehensible. These regulations are established by the *Commission Sportive Internationale* of the *Federation Internationale de l' Automobile*. This CSI, made up of delegates from the interested nations is, in effect, the Contest Board of the international sanctioning body, FIA. Through the years there have been many mutations in the regulations governing the cars and the championships, but they have never been less realistic than now.

This loss of touch with reality results primarily from the multitude of pressures that are inflicted upon the CSI. These pressures come from the automobile manufacturers, who are, as a whole, more interested in production automobiles than in specialized racing cars; from the race organizers who clamor for cars that are capable of more "spectacle" to please the crowds; and the CSI delegates are also very sensitive to what they believe is "public opinion" which may, they fear, result in legislation against motor racing of all kinds.

In the recent past and extending into the present, the CSI has heavily favored Grand Touring cars, capital G capital T. By CSI's definition these are cars "built in small numbers for customers who are interested in better performance . . . and who are not particularly concerned about economy." The rules also stipulate that these must be produced at the rate of at least 100 identical units per year but then go on to add so many exceptions as to result in approval of a machine that is nothing much less than a racing car based on a production model.

Oversimplifying it a bit, it can be said that the emphasis on Grand Touring cars by the CSI came about for two reasons. First, after the Le Mans accident in 1955, where nearly a hundred people were killed, there was great political noise made in France and Switzerland about legislation against racing. Concurrently, manufacturers were applying pressure to the international body to give greater prominence to cars that were closer to those the majority of manufacturers were building for sale.

The CSI found what it believed to be a solution to both pressures; first it would reduce the displacement limit for sports cars eligible for the much-prized Manufacturers Championship and, at the same time, convince both the legislators and the manufacturers of its good intentions by putting more emphasis on GT cars. Having gone this far, the CSI was eventually pressured into taking the next step and giving the Manufacturers Championship to GT cars and into making an even further de-emphasis of the traditional sports/racing car. At its lowest ebb, the CSI even fragmented the Manufacturers Championship by dividing and sub-dividing the GT cars by displacement. This assured that almost any manufacturer who was serious about it could win something. However, it also resulted in a distinct lack of enthusiasm among the spectators and press. The spectators and press wanted to see exciting racing and exciting racing cars, not a parade of comparatively tame machines they could see on the highway every day.

Attempting to counteract the effect of the CSI and bring some glamor and excitement back into sports car racing, the organizers of four major races got together to offer a special award, called the *Challenge Mondial,* for a new class they defined as GT Prototypes. Unable to block this, the CSI made it an official FIA class and attempted to emasculate it by carving out a set of rules that required the prototypes to comply with the GT regulations so far as dimensions and physical requirements were concerned. To this, the CSI also added a table of minimum weights based on displacement.

Thus the Prototype is neither a GT car nor a sports/racing car. Taking the GT-40 as an example, it is, first of all, much heavier than a racing car needs to be. With the 289-cu. in. Ford engine, the GT-40s must weigh at least 2044 lb., which is probably at least 500 lb. more than the sports/racing Chaparral.

This additional weight may assure that the car is not of flimsy construction and that the seat padding hasn't been skimped on, but it puts an almost insurmountable handicap on a Prototype when it is required to race against a sports/racing car. For example, given two cars having 385 bhp, one with a racing weight of 2200 lb., the other 1650 lb., the heavier car can leave the starting line and a quarter-mile later be going about 128 mph while the lighter car will have gotten there 0.8 sec. sooner and achieved about 141 mph. No amount of driving skill can overcome disparities of that order.

So the GT-40s are typical of an unrealistic breed of car called GT Prototypes; they are designed to win those long-distance races which lead to the international championship in that class. They can't enjoy much success in open road racing competition where the present trend is toward super-sophisticated design, lightweight construction and even bigger engines.

THE DEVELOPMENT of the Ford GT-40 is in many ways typical of what is required when one wishes to start with a clean sheet of paper and end up with a race winner. The first version of the car was built by a small British firm outside London called Lola Cars Ltd. The Lola coupe was designed by a young Englishman, Eric Broadley, who, along with Colin Chapman of Lotus, is one of the world's great designers of road racing cars. This was more than three years ago.

Three cars were built by Lola and all were powered by Ford engines. The coupes were very exciting machines and attracted much attention because they looked so "right," which has been a characteristic of Broadley's work ever since his first commercial success, the front-engined Lola 1100 which achieved fame by consistently beating the Chapman-designed Lotus XI.

A Lola coupe was entered in the 1963 Le Mans 24-hour race, its most serious effort that year, and though it was obviously very fast it had a number of bugs to be worked out; it ultimately crashed.

The slender resources of Lola Cars were exhausted by the end of the 1963 season. One Lola coupe (later crashed at Riverside) had been delivered to the Texas oilman and racing team patron, John Mecom, and Broadley and the other two cars were available when Ford made its offer.

In 1964, with the car campaigned by Ford Advanced Vehicles, it was more of a public relations success than a racing triumph. Still, it did have that great promise which convinced Ford that victory was within its grasp if only the final few development problems could be solved.

The cars were obviously fast enough in the 1964 Le Mans race but there were serious problems with stability as they approached maximum speed. Also, there were gearbox troubles, which caused the retirement of both cars at Le Mans and again at Reims. There was a tendency toward engine overheating, which resulted in running very high oil temperatures, and continuous worries about brake cooling. What was required, obviously, was a concentrated development program where these problems could be sorted out.

The decision by Ford to turn the campaigning of the cars over to Shelby-American was a logical one.

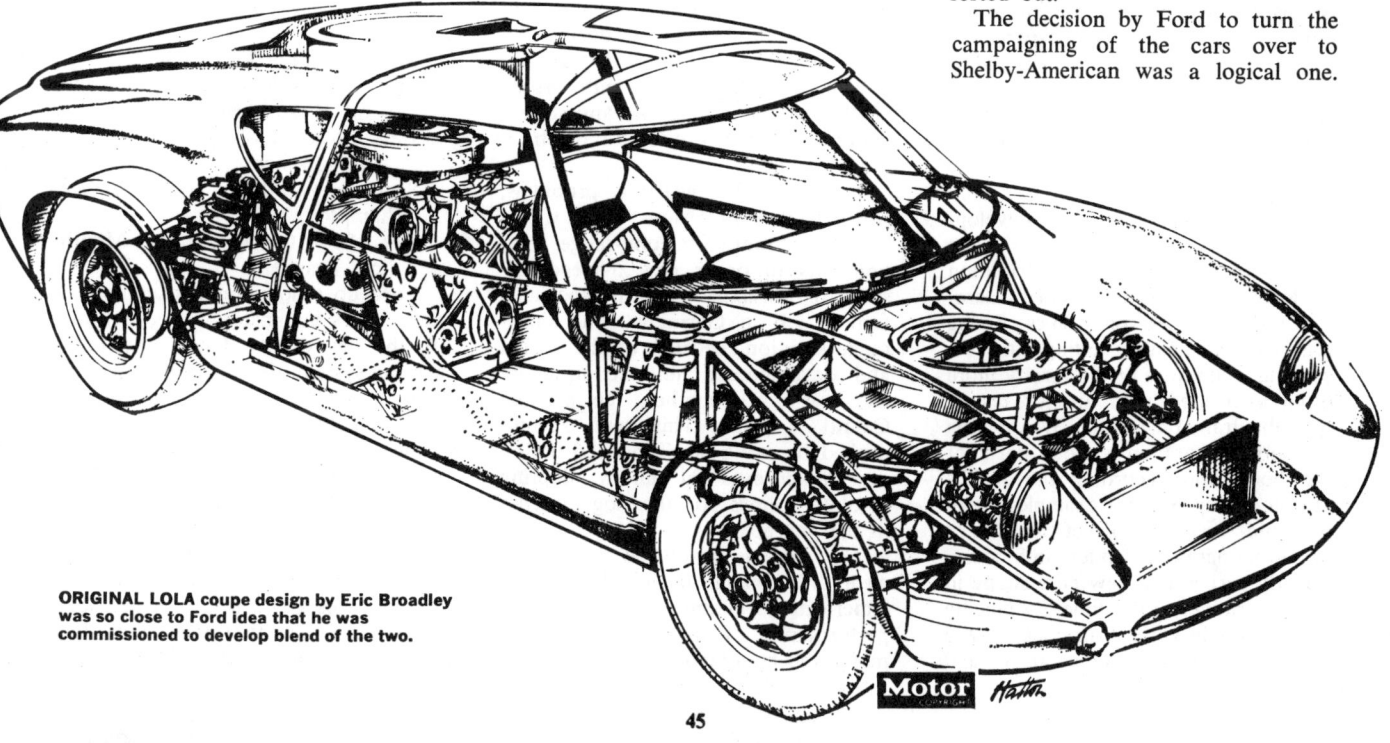

ORIGINAL LOLA coupe design by Eric Broadley was so close to Ford idea that he was commissioned to develop blend of the two.

LOLA PROTOTYPE had cooking version of Ford 289 with scant exhaust system. From this version, development progressed (see right).

BY LE MANS in 1964, the GT-40 had gotten the bundle-of-snakes exhaust, Weber carburetors, reversed suspension arms, and a lot more rubber.

FORD GT-40

The S-A organization had already shown itself capable of maintaining a major offensive with its successful campaign of the Cobra. This project, which combined a 10-year-old AC chassis design with a good medium-size American engine, the Ford 289, resulted in complete domination of U.S. production car racing and came within a wink of wresting the Manufacturers Championship away from Ferrari in 1964. In effect, it drove Ferrari from the field of GT racing in 1965.

The track-testing and development of the GT-40 is a story in itself. There were several problems to be solved, as noted earlier, and most of these were complicated by the very high performance of the car.

High-speed stability, for instance, is not a characteristic to be fooled with. Not only does the car have to be operating at near maximum, it must also have a driver capable of obtaining this full performance and at the same time of making intelligent observations about the car's behavior. These are the qualities of a good test driver and Shelby-American has several of these available.

Also very important in the development of the GT-40 after its arrival at Shelby-American was the contribution made by personnel from Ford's aerospace division, Aeronutronics. Using highly sophisticated testing and recording techniques of the variety more often associated with aircraft testing brought dramatic results. By applying pressure sensors on various parts of the body and recording the results at different speeds, for example, Aeronutronics was able to plot the pattern of aerodynamic behavior and consequently arrive at a new nose shape in a comparatively short time. By placing transducers in various air ducts, it was possible to measure temperatures and pressures and accurately assess the efficiency of the ducting. In redesigning the nose and changing the ducting in line with what had been learned, stability was not only improved but there was also an immediate drop in engine temperature. This reduction in engine temperature had a further bonus as it made it possible to change from the 16-qt. dry sump oil system to a 9-qt. wet sump and the saving of about 75 lb.

The program to improve the aerodynamic characteristics utilized yet another technique from aircraft testing: Tufts of woolen cord were attached all over the car. By using a chase car and photographing the behavior of these tufts while the car was in motion, it was possible to study and improve the flow of air around the car.

Other important changes made during the Shelby-American development included replacing the 255-cu. in. pushrod engine, which Ford developed primarily for Indianapolis and had been used in the GT-40 during the 1964 season. Replacing it was the 289-cu. in. Cobra engine with which Shelby-American had had much experience and which offered more mid-range torque.

To solve the gearbox problems, which were very serious, there was a 2-part program. The long-range solution was to order new 5-speed all-synchro transaxles from the specialist firm of ZF in Germany. The short-range solution, because of the design and development time required by ZF, was to strengthen the existing Colotti 4-speed. This was accomplished by using new ring and pinion gears made by Ford and by adopting involute splines for the dog clutches in the gearbox.

The suspension of the car underwent little change during the Shelby-American development program. The performance of the suspension was monitored by attaching potentiometers to various members so that their action could be studied, but no changes outside of adjustments were required.

A Shelby trademark, big fat Goodyear tires, replaced the narrower Dunlop tires previously used. The car is equipped with cast-magnesium wheels instead of wire wheels, too. Wire wheels had been used in an attempt to obtain better brake cooling but actual measurement of brake temperatures (plus the improved ducting from monitoring air flow) indicated that the stronger alloy wheels could be used without reducing brake efficiency.

THAT THE development program has been a successful one is attested to by the GT-40's victories at Daytona and Sebring. It must be remembered, however, that the Prototype championship is based on the best performance in four of the seven events on this year's calendar. The seven events are:

March 27—Sebring 12-hour race.
April 25—1000-km. race, Monza, Italy.
May 9—Targa Florio, Sicily
May 23—1000-km. race, Nurburg Ring, West Germany
June 19-20—24-hour race, Le Mans, France
Sept. 19—500-km. race, Bridgehampton, N.Y.
Oct. 10—1000-km. race, Monthlery, France.

Ford does not intend to contest all these races but instead to concentrate on the key events. Under the FIA's scoring system, the longer the race, the more points are awarded. The 500-km. race at Bridgehampton, N.Y., for instance, will award 11.7 points to the winner, while at Sebring, a 12-hour race, the winner received 14.4 points. For the Le Mans 24-hour race, the longest race on the calendar, the winning car will get 18.0 points. Though Ford's plans aren't firm, it seems logical to speculate that after contesting the Targa Florio and Le Mans it will be able to better judge which future races will be best to enter.

Ford's only competition for the Prototype Championship this year will come from Ferrari as neither of Britain's potential challengers, Jaguar and Aston Martin, has a car that will run within miles of the latest Fords or Ferraris. The ability of the Ferraris, however, should not be underestimated. Although the Fords finished far ahead of the nearest Ferrari at Daytona and Sebring, this does not necessarily indicate that they are going to do so in future races—particularly at Le Mans.

L<small>E</small> M<small>ANS</small> is the critical race. A win at Le Mans could make up for almost any other failure. Even winning the championship would be hollow if it did not include victory in that famous 24-hour race. And this philosophy applies to Ferrari as well as Ford. Thus we can expect that both teams will make an all-out effort to win.

Le Mans is probably the world's most famous race outside of Indianapolis. Located southwest of Paris in the province of Sarthe, the 13.5-km. (8.3-mile) circuit is made up of smooth, well maintained public roads that are closed off for the occasion. The course itself is a comparatively easy one, as there are few turns and little that is tricky. However, the extended duration of the race makes heavy demands on both machinery and personnel. Tire wear is not especially high at Le Mans because of the smooth surface but, as the cars are limited as to the amounts of gasoline they can carry, the GT-40s will be making pit stops every 90 to 120 min. At Sebring, the pit stop pattern seemed to be to take on fuel only at one stop, then fuel, tires and brake pads at the next. These stops required about 2 min. for fuel alone and an average of 7 min. for the full servicing. Drivers were changing at every stop at Sebring, but this will probably be increased to every other stop at Le Mans to give the drivers longer periods of rest.

The opposition by Ferrari at Le Mans will be formidable. Fourteen Ferraris have been entered, six by the factory and the balance by semi-factory teams such as the U.S.-based North American Racing Team. The brunt of the Ferrari effort will be carried by the new 330-P2 models which have 4-liter, 4-cam, 12-cyl., engines reported to develop 430 bhp. In the only two appearances thus far where the performance of the P2s could be compared with the GT-40s, the new Ferraris have been faster.

At Daytona, where John Surtees and Pedro Rodriguez shared a P2, the Ferrari not only had the fastest practice lap, but was running within sight of Dan Gurney's Ford-powered Lotus 19 sports/racing car until the Ferrari's tires began coming apart on the high-speed banking. No P2s participated at Sebring, but at the Le Mans trials in early April there were four P2s faster than the fastest of the GT-40s. The quickest of these Ferraris was driven by John Surtees who lapped at 3:35.1, or 139.98 mph. The fastest lap during the race last year was by Phil Hill in a GT-40 at 3:49.2, 131.37 mph. The quickest of the GT-40s in the April trials, one driven by Dickie Attwood, lapped at 3:40.9, more than 5 sec. slower than Surtees' Ferrari.

These lap times are indicative rather than conclusive, however, as the Fords were all using the 289-cu. in. engines. They may use the stroker version of the 289, the new 325-cu. in. Ford, in the race. In addition, there was much experimenting going on, as could be expected, and two of the cars were the Sebring cars which had not been refurbished since that race. A roadster version of the GT-40 was also tried but it was found to suffer in top speed from the reduced aerodynamic efficiency.

There is no doubt at all that the GT-40s will be well-managed and well-driven. The boss at Shelby-American, Carroll Shelby, is innately shrewd and in addition to his own racing experience (which includes winning the 1959 Le Mans in an Aston Martin) is one of the great masters of practical psychology. For drivers he will have a superb line-up—experienced drivers who specialize in Le Mans, like Phil Hill who has won there twice in Ferraris, Richie Ginther, Dan Gurney and Bruce McLaren. And he can team these with his lesser-known but highly capable men, Bob Bondurant, Dickie Attwood and Sir John Whitmore.

It is possible, however, that the fully developed GT-40 will arrive at Le Mans just one year too late. In 1964, the GT-40s were the fastest cars on the circuit by a comfortable margin. This year they may not be. This year they may be completely reliable and simply not fast enough.

Finally, even if the GT-40s don't win at Le Mans, or even if they don't win the Prototype championship this year, they are going to be in an excellent position next year. In 1966, thanks to another new set of rules formulated by the CSI, there will be a new class introduced which will fit the GT-40 exactly. This class (Category A, Group 4, Appendix J) is called "sportscars" (one word) in the official translation and requires a minimum production of 50 cars within a 12-month period. The Ford Advanced Vehicles shop near London is already busy building toward the required number. ■

FORD GT-40 SPECIFICATIONS

List price	$16,250
Curb weight, lb., approx.	2100
distribution, %	42/58
Tire size, front	6.00-15
rear	9.00-15
make	Goodyear
Brakes, disc dia., in.	11.5
make	Girling
Engine make & type	Ford V-8, ohv
Bore x stroke, in.	4.00 x 2.87
Displacement, cu. in.	289
equivalent cc.	4726
Compression ratio	11.5:1
Carburetion	4x2, Weber
Bhp @ rpm	385 @ 6900
Torque, lb.-ft. @ rpm	315 @ 5000

DIMENSIONS

Wheelbase, in.	95
Tread, front/rear	54/54
Overall length	158.6
width	70.0
height	40.5
equivalent vol., cu. ft.	260.0
Frontal area, sq. ft.	15.7
Ground clearance, in.	4.8
Steering ratio	14:1
turns, lock to lock	2.8
turning circle, ft.	40.0

CLUTCH & TRANSAXLE

Gearbox ratios, 4th	1.00:1
3rd	1.29:1
2nd	1.70:1
1st	2.50:1
Final drive ratios	3.09–3.55:1
Clutch type	3-plate, dry
dia., in.	7.25

AT SEBRING last spring, car had progressed to meanest appearance yet, with ducts and airflow spoilers added to increase efficiency. Only a lighter Chevrolet-engined sports racer beat it.

GT-40 ON THE PRODUCTION LINE

BY JOSEPH LOWREY

BEHIND A modest signboard which says *Ford Advanced Vehicles Ltd.*, on a British industrial estate, there is a new plant in which a unique international operation is coming to fruition. At Slough, 25 miles west of London, but less than a 10-min. drive from that city's international airport, the Ford GT-40 coupe is being developed and built in small numbers.

To the world, the Ford GT-40 which notched up its first big victory at Daytona is an American car, planned by an American corporation, powered by an American engine, built with American money and raced in American colors. But it is being built in Europe because the newest ideas on international road racing "spark" and are learned first on the continent where the sport is based. Also, this is because vital racing car components can be obtained, modified and serviced more quickly close to the British, Dutch, French, German and Italian factories which build them, than in Detroit, 3000 miles away.

Ford Advanced Vehicles Ltd., where I spent a fascinated afternoon recently, is quite a small company and has a total staff of only 45. Its two plants total 16,000 sq. ft. of floor area. The company's job is to produce Ford GT cars with which Shelby-American Inc. can win motor races. Facilities which have been established at Slough should be ample for development and for assembly of the 50 cars currently planned, and the team there can call upon the resources of specialized plants all over Europe as well as upon the know-how and facilities of Ford Division at Dearborn.

Technically, Ford Advanced Vehicles Ltd. is a British company, its ownership by the British Ford Motor Company (all shares in which are held by Ford of USA) simplifies international taxation and other administrative problems. On the 5-man board of directors are two executives of Ford of Britain, two executives of Ford Division, and John Wyer as the full-time Managing Director. Roy Lunn, as Ford Division's Manager of Advanced Concepts, launched the Ford GT project and remains on the board of directors, although he is again based in Dearborn. Like Len Bailey, who is Chief Engineer at Slough, Lunn was born in Britain and later emigrated to America. John Wyer, who was apprenticed in the Sunbeam car plant and came to Ford from a job as Technical Director of Aston Martin-Lagonda Ltd., has run racing teams and sports car factories with equal success.

When the idea of Ford building its own GT cars for international road racing was studied, there were obviously two alternative ways in which the job could be started. Ford could design its own car from scratch, or it could take over an existing project which offered the right scope for development. In the 1963 Le Mans 24-hour race, a Lola coupe powered by a Ford V-8 engine had performed very promisingly, so it was decided that Ford should take over this car design,

STARTING CONSTRUCTION on the 50-car batch of Ford GT-40 coupes, workmen build up the rear suspension of one car while another body shell awaits.

which Eric Broadley had been developing on very slender resources. John Wyer's estimate that in this way Ford got results about six months sooner than would have been possible by designing a new car from scratch probably errs toward optimism about how quickly an all-new design would have been raceworthy.

Initially, Ford bought the two existing Lola GT coupes and signed a contract with designer Broadley to develop from this basis a car called the Ford GT. Wyer, who had by then been hired as Ford Division's European Manager, Special Vehicles, had an office in the new plant which Eric Broadley acquired with Ford backing. At the end of a year, when Eric Broadley's contract expired, a new company called Ford Advanced Vehicles Ltd. was formed, with premises next door to Lola Cars Ltd. and also on another street a quarter mile away. The Ford plant at Slough looks roomy rather than being tightly packed with equipment. It offers good working conditions for designers and office staff as well as for the men in the workshops.

At the time when work on the Ford GT began, Aston Martin-Lagonda Ltd. was moving its experimental and racing departments from west London to a new factory 50 miles away at Newport Pagnell, so a good many of its former mechanics now work either for Lola Cars Ltd., or for their former boss at Ford Advanced Vehicles Ltd.

In buying the two Lola GT coupes and putting their designer under contract, Ford acquired brilliantly conceived cars in running order. No changes in the basic concept of the 1963 Lola were needed to turn it into a 1964 Ford, although it has since

STEEL BODY structure of GT-40 is shown to a visitor by John Wyer (dark hair), managing director of Ford Advanced Vehicles Ltd. The hull is extremely rigid.

FRONT-ON view of the steel hull, with the radiator and air ducts in place. Ducts behind radiator exhaust the cooling air, those flanking radiator direct airstream at the front disc brakes.

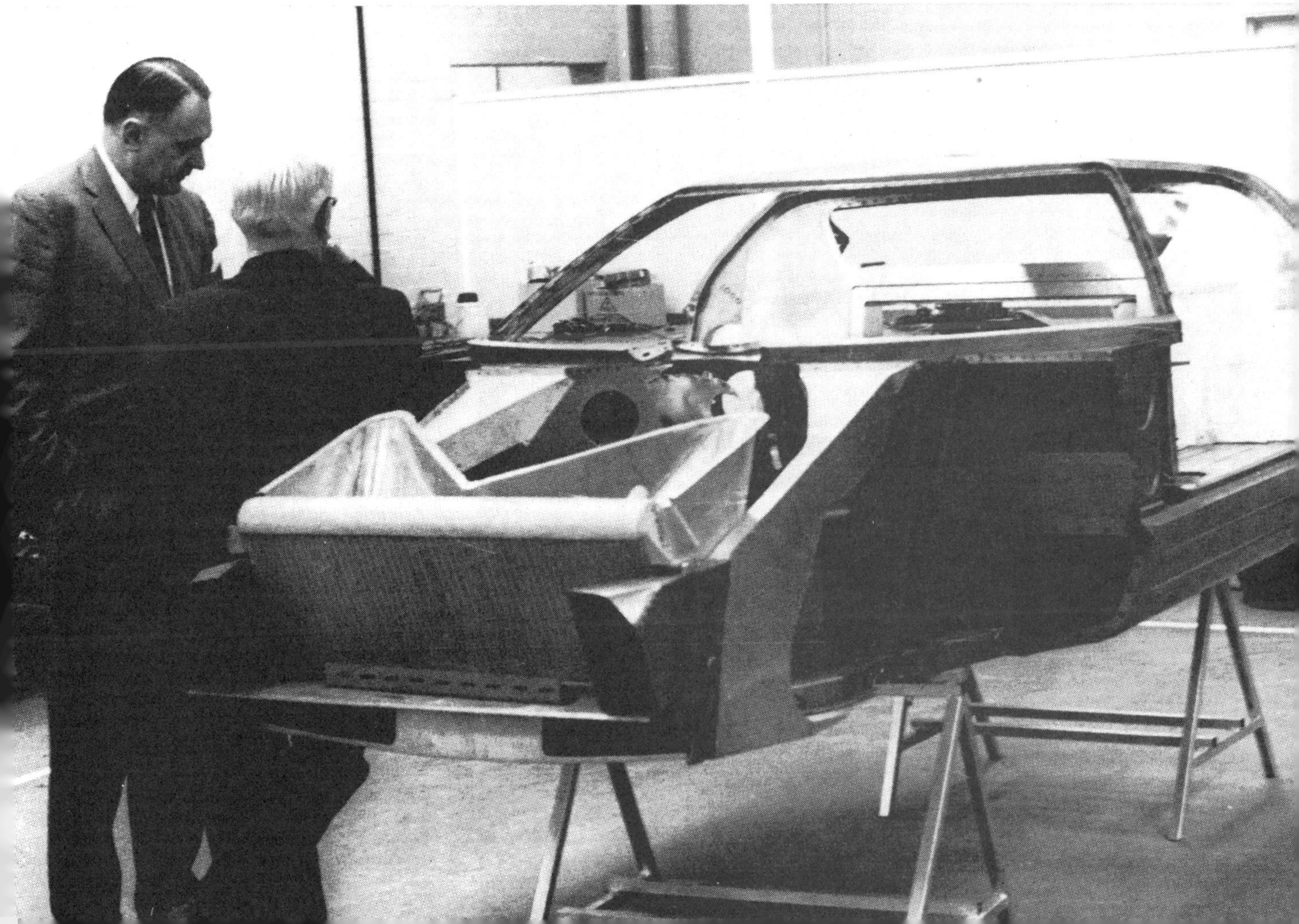

GT-40

been a case of devoting money and man-hours to perfecting every component of a design which had originally been built with virtually amateur resources.

Structurally, the Lola-based Ford GT-40 is a masterpiece. Broadley, and his slightly longer-established rival, Colin Chapman of Lotus (who is also building "powered-by-Ford" cars), are the two best chassis designers in the road racing game today. There is an inspired simplicity about the way in which strength has been provided just where it is needed, the designer having been able to think 3-dimensionally, whereas so many cars are obviously planned 2-dimensionally on paper. For example, long fore-and-aft radius arms for the independent rear wheel suspension are neatly organized to run up inside hollow box-sections of the car's main frame; and, the roof frame is formed as an elegantly simple pyramid. The strength of the GT-40 was well-proved, before aerodynamic stability problems were satisfactorily solved, by a couple of 170 mph crashes from which drivers Jo Schlesser and Sir John Whitmore walked away. Dearborn's wind tunnel experiments had suggested that the car needed a lift spoiler under its nose, whereas practical trials on the fast racing circuits showed that an upturned spoiler above the tail, which gave 150 lb. of downthrust, was the feature which really stabilized the car. This "spoiler" also reduced the drag instead of increasing it.

Two huge box-section longerons of sheet steel are the basis of the GT-40 chassis, and completely enclose the two flexible-bag fuel tanks. Reinforcement comes from the roof frame of the coupe body, which is also a steel box-section where the tops of two big doors almost meet one another, and from a bolted-in box member above the transaxle which helps to brace the main one-piece structure. The complete production-line hulls are being built by Abbey Panels Ltd. of Coventry, which built all the integral hulls for Jaguar racing models. The fiberglass moldings for the body come from a factory at Southampton.

The dimensions of the GT-40 have been planned around the Fairlane series of engines, but can also accommodate their double overhead camshaft variants. John Wyer is happy about the power which present and future versions of this engine can provide, but is not convinced that a car scaled up to use the larger Galaxie series engines would be any faster in road races over long distances which involve pit stops for fuel and tires.

Victory at Daytona was scored with the Italian-made Colotti 4-speed gearbox, but now a German Zahnradfabrik Friedrichshafen (ZF) 5-speed synchromesh gearbox is available and this is expected to make the cars more reliable for slightly less weight. As a rule, Ford Advanced Vehicles Ltd. does very little work on the engines, which are built up for racing by Shelby-American Inc. In the manner of all present race-winning cars, the GT-40 has its engine directly ahead of the rear transaxle, a remote radiator in the nose of the car.

Perfected in detail by Ford research work (which used analyses by electronic computer in parallel with track tests by such veteran race drivers as Roy Salvadori) the Lola front suspension is a classic layout of ball-jointed wishbones, swept forward for the sake of a slightly lighter and neater layout. Rear suspension is independent and follows the much-copied layout which Eric Broadley pioneered on a 2-seat car with a 67-cu. in. Coventry Climax engine. It is a layout of elegant simplicity, using wishbones with inward-pointing tips and two fore-and-aft links to secure exact control over wheel alignment at all times.

As the line production for Ford GT-40 coupes, at the rate of one car every few days is established, very high standards of finish are being set. This model's primary objective is to win races, but it is furnished so that people who love to own the fastest GT cars for street use will be keen to buy any examples available, even though the V-8 engine with its four twin-barrel Weber carburetors, two seats, two fuel tanks and a spare tire do not leave much luggage space in a car of 95-in. wheelbase and 40.5-in. roof height.

To speculate about the long-term future of this unique example of trans-Atlantic cooperation: Ford now has on its payroll a first-class development team under strong management, but has taken a risk in allowing the "idea man," on whose designs the GT-40 is based, to re-establish himself as an independent builder of race cars in the plant next door. With luck, this may work out excellently. Eric Broadley's creative genius may be at its most productive when he is his own boss, and as he will no doubt be glad to call on Ford for parts and other help, successors to the GT may get the benefit of future Lola ideas anyway! ∎

PROTOTYPE IN foreground is stripped for replacement of transaxle and further modification, while in rear is one of the molded fiberglass tail sections.

JOSEPH LOWREY PHOTOS

THE FORD GT 40

WHEN Eric Broadley produced his Lola coupé at the Racing Car Show at the beginning of 1963 there was no inkling then of what it was going to lead to. It is now a matter of history that the Ford Motor Company, having failed to buy the Ferrari firm "lock, stock and vee 12-cylinder barrels," shopped around for another likely basis on which to start building up a GT Prototype racing programme with the main intention of winning the 24-hour race at Le Mans. The object of this move was to short-cut their way to success by buying "experience" rather than earning it the hard way, like everyone else. The Lola coupé looked a likely proposition, in fact it was one of the most advanced and exciting cars produced in recent times, and the mighty Ford Empire bought the Lola and Broadley and his men. A new factory was built on the Slough Trading Estate, to the West of London, and the firm of Ford Advanced Vehicles Ltd. was established as an English base from which to operate in European racing. Broadley was retained for 1964 and John Wyer was in charge, while there was close co-operation with the Dearborn experimental department, although at times it would have been best to have left the job to Broadley.

Using the prototype Lola coupé, with Ford V8 engine and Colotti gearbox, as a basis, the Ford GT coupé was evolved, although to be more accurate it was a Lola-Ford GT coupé, for Broadley had his own staff with him, and the cars were made and built in England by British craftsmen and mechanics. Altogether some twelve experimental cars were built, of which two were open version, but they were all basically to the original design, Ford supplying the money and engines. All of these experimental cars were kept within the Ford Empire, two going to Carroll Shelby, whose Shelby Cobra organisation was working closely with Ford Advanced Concepts at Dearborn, while another went to Ford's own Experimental department, for testing and evaluation. Two were destroyed in crashes while testing, and another has been a "works hack," suffering all manner of experimental alterations.

During 1964 Ford entered GT Prototype racing with a singular lack of success, and bearing in mind the potential of the original Lola coupé which Broadley ran at Le Mans in 1963, driven by Hobbs and Attwood, it seemed that they had redesigned the prototype and improved it to such an extent that it had less potential than when it started. After many trials and tribulations the Ford GT Prototype looked as though it was going to challenge Ferrari's supremacy in this category of racing, and it was the first car that we had seen for some years that was able to keep up with the works Ferraris. Knowing the money and effort that was going into this GT project in various organisations all supported by Dearborn, it looked as though they might be very successful in 1965. The Slough factory was still doing development and experimental work, though Broadley had now left and re-formed his Lola Cars firm, making sports cars and Formula Two cars, so that Wyer was in charge of F.A.V. and in California the Shelby

The Lola coupé at the 1963 Racing Car Show.

organisation was making strides in turning the GT 40 into a raceable proposition, rather than an experimental car. In addition Ford France were given a car to run in races, thus swelling the number of Ford entries. With Broadley and all Lola design influence gone from the Slough factory one was justified in referring to the cars purely as Ford GT Prototypes, although there were three separate teams running them, and an indication of the lack of a concerted effort could be seen in the fact that they appeared to be three separate entities, the Slough cars being painted pale green, the Shelby cars blue with white stripes, and the Ford France car was left in the original colours of white with blue stripes. Nor was there any continuity over such things as wheels and tyres, some using wire wheels, others using alloy wheels, some being on Goodyear tyres, others being on Dunlop tyres. Presumably all the results of these variations were collected and compiled to provide useful data, but I should have thought that this could have been done in pre-race testing.

With Ferrari producing his new P.2 car for 1965, with 4 o.h.c. V12 engine, the old push-rod Ford V8 engines, developed from the Fairlane looked a bit agricultural and lacking in power. It was reasonable to suppose that a test car would appear at Le Mans for the practice weekend fitted with an Indianapolis Ford V8 engine, the 4 o.h.c. fuel-injected racing engine, if only to worry Ferrari, but the only cars to turn up were fitted with very ordinary push-rod engines. For the race the Shelby team arrived with two GT 40 coupés fitted with 7-litre Galaxie engines, but while very fast they were also very heavy on fuel and destroyed themselves very early in the race. The other Ford entries were the 4.7-litre versions, though 5.3-litre engines were tried in practice, but the whole effort was a disaster for various mechanical reasons not necessarily connected with the basic design of the car. Le Mans was a costly effort, for in the garage in the town were ten Ford-engined cars and when it was suggested that they represented £100,000 the Ford people laughed.

With the new F.I.A. rules coming into force next January, in which there will be three categories of GT racing, Ford decided to go into limited production with the GT 40 coupé. The new classes for GT racing are (a) one-off Prototypes (b) Competition GT cars, of which 50 must have been built within 12 consecutive months, and (c) GT cars, of which 1,000 must have been built within 12 months. The Ford project is to build 50 by the end of the year and thus get Homologated in category (b). As a result of knowledge gained through racing and testing, a finalised design has been settled upon and a production line is already well under way at Slough, the first few cars having been delivered, while at the time of a recent visit another seven were in various stages of assembly. The aim is to produce two a week until the end of the year, which should not be beyond the bounds of possibility. From the experimental cars the production ones differ in a few ways, such as the use of a 5-speed Z.F. gearbox built in Germany, the adoption of the wet-sump 4.7-litre Ford V8 engine as used in the Shelby Cobras, and a longer and smoother nose cowling, which has entailed a different sub-frame of square-section tubing ahead of the main bulkhead, and this also permits the carrying of a larger spare wheel and tyre.

The main body/chassis unit is fabricated from sheet steel and is of welded construction, this unit starting just behind the front wheels and finishing just ahead of the rear wheels, the majority

The first production GT 40 at Silverstone in May 1965.

of the weight being within the wheel base; only the radiators being forward and the gearbox being to rear beyond the axle centre-lines. This steel chassis/body unit is made by Abbey Panels Ltd., of Coventry and it arrives at Slough in a bare and unpainted form. Front and rear sub-frames are fitted, for carrying body panels etc. and the unit then goes to Harold Radford Ltd., where the fibreglass doors, rear engine-hatch which forms the complete tail, and front nosepiece, which is a single moulding, are cut-and-shut to fit the chassis/body unit, these panels then being marked and retained for the car in question. The fibreglass components are made by Glass Fibre Engineering, of Farnham, Surrey and delivered to Slough in the bare unpainted state. When the chassis/body unit is returned from Radfords the factory at Slough then assembles all the suspension parts, steering, wiring, engine, gearbox and so on and the nearly completed car then goes back to Radfords for final trimming of the interior, seats, glass and so on, the final car being painted in the particular colour required by the customer. Borrani wire wheels and Goodyear tyres are fitted as standard, but Halibrand alloy wheels are an optional extra and other makes of tyre can be supplied on request.

The 4.7-litre Ford engine comes from America as a bare unit and at Slough are fitted the four double-choke downdraught Weber carburetters, modified valve covers, alternator and exhaust manifolding and pipes. The engine is rated at 380 b.h.p. at 6,500 r.p.m. with a maximum torque of 330 lb./ft. at 5,500 r.p.m. The total weight of the car is 2,000 lb. (17.85 cwt.) and to stop all this from anything up to 180 m.p.h. there are 11½ in. Girling Disc brakes on each wheel.

Realising that there are not 50 drivers in GT racing capable of handling a GT 40 coupé, let alone 50 that are prepared to buy such a car, part of the production will be turned out in detuned form as a fully equipped road car. A single 4-choke Holley carburetter will be used instead of the Webers, large silencers

---

FORD GT 40 SPECIFICATION

Engine: Ford V8, 101.6 × 72.9 mm. (4,736 c.c.), push rod o.h.v. Compression ratio 10:1.
Gearbox: Z.F. 5-speed and reverse. Final drive 4.22:1 or 3.33:1.
Wheels and Tyres: Borrani wire spoke, alloy rim with 5.50 × 15 in. front and 7.00 × 15 in. rear, Goodyear.
Steering: Rack and Pinion.
Wheelbase: 7 ft. 11 in.
Track: 4 ft. 7 in.
Dimensions: 3 ft. 4½ in. high × 5 ft. 10 in. wide.
Brakes: Girling Disc 11½ in. diameter.
Chassis/Body: Welded steel sheet semi-monocoque. Fibreglass doors and front and rear hinged sections.
Electrical System: 12 volt transistorised ignition. 57 amp. hour battery.
Suspension: Double wishbones and coil spring/damper units, front. Lower wishbones, top transverse links, double radius arms and coil spring/damper units, rear.

---

and more legal exhaust systems will be fitted and the cockpit will be more lavishly trimmed with numerous home-comforts and a great deal of sound deadening knowledge applied. It is anticipated that about 20 such versions will be built, and they should become prized acquisitions. The price of the complete car ready to race, or fully fitted out for road use will be £5,200, plus £1,300 purchase tax in this country. At a total of £6,500 it becomes an expensive toy, but what an exciting one, and surely the most advanced and fastest GT car, when it is homologated, unless Ferrari nips in with a production P.2. and gets it homologated.—D. S. J.

Ford GT for Le Mans

Continued from Page 17

must perform like a decathlon champion," he asserted. "At Ford, we read that as 'total performance'."

Mr. Iacocca said Ford decided to enter GT racing because "we believe that GT racing explores the ultimate in highway driving. It not only tests total performance today, but also points the direction of total performance tomorrow in the car you and your families and your neighbors will drive.

"GT car has taught us plenty"

"In a little over a year — without even entering a race — the Ford GT car has taught us plenty."

With its 200-mile-an-hour speed, Mr. Iacocca said the Ford GT has taught engineers lessons in three areas: achieving minimum vehicle drag, equalising pressure front and rear to keep the car on the ground, and using the natural high and low pressure areas which exist around the car to get air in and out.

As a result of tests, for example, cooling air has been ducted through outlets in the top of the hood at a natural low-pressure area rather than simply into the engine compartment. This development not only reduces the air temperature of the car when in motion, but also permits air to circulate naturally to aid cooling when the car is stopped.

Noting developments in suspensions and brakes, Mr. Iacocca told newsmen that "I could cite many more examples, but, frankly, we're working right now to incorporate many of them in our Ford passenger cars of the future. That's the real pay-off," he said. "We're meeting and solving problems today that we might not otherwise have faced for another 10 or 20 years in the course of normal passenger-car development and design.

"The Ford GT is more than a car. It's a test of Ford engineering skill and ability. In going into GT racing, we feel we are accepting the toughest challenge presently available to the minds and talents of motor-car builders."

THERE was a big sigh of relief from our photographer when it was all over. You see, he is a firm believer in the idea that 'things' always happen in threes. The track test of the Ford GT had got off to a bad start when the rear half of the body flew off at about 100 mph in front of the pits on the first lap. (There was a good enough reason for this—it hadn't been clipped on! Fortunately, apart from a few grazes and a broken rear screen, it was still in good shape, and was promptly replaced.)

The next incident occurred during a pit stop to change a plug (we had had to start it up from cold on hard plugs, and one of them had objected). Starting up again, there was a very impressive ball of fire from the Webers, and as I simultaneously switched off, floored the throttle and fumbled for the extinguisher, our intrepid cameraman, who had been taking one of his scintillating close-ups of the car's back end, performed an equally impressive backwards-facing standing-start high jump!

After that he was convinced the whole affair was doomed, but when we packed up the only other thing which had become bent (unofficially, of course) was the GT lap record for the short circuit. This was, perhaps, the best compliment that could be paid to this outstanding car, the performance of which puts quite a drain on superlatives.

Let's make it quite plain that this was no

Exclusive

TRACK TEST
JB John Blunsden

FORD GT 40

fully race-sorted car. It was exactly as it had left the Slough workshops of Ford Advanced Vehicles, since when it had been brought down to Brands Hatch for a few exploratory laps of the short circuit by Sir John Whitmore, then used as a showroom exhibit. John had lapped the car in 56 seconds, and says that with a few 'tweaks', and if he really steeled himself, he could probably get it round in 55 seconds dead. (Current GT record, 57 seconds.) The best I could manage was 56.8 seconds, running the Goodyears at about 35 psi. Talking to John later, he was of the opinion that the pressures should have been a minimum of 40 psi, and that the difference was probably worth a good half-second. If anyone can name an 'off the shelf' GT car to match these times, first time out, I'd like to hear of it!

The GT 40, as the competition version is designated, comes with a 380 bhp at 6,500 rpm version of the 289 cubic inch (4,736 cc) Ford V8 engine, running with four Weber 48 IDA carburettors and a compression ratio of 10 to 1. Maximum torque is 330 pounds/feet at 5,500 rpm.

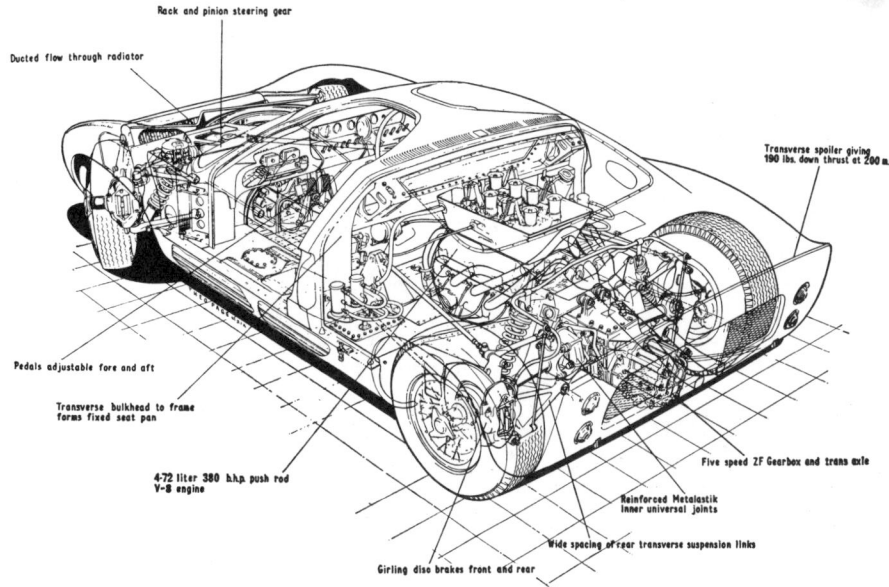

SUPERB ZF GEARBOX

Transmission is through a Borg and Beck 7¼ inch triple-plate clutch, with quite a light action and a moderate pedal travel, to a superb ZF five-speed all-synchromesh gearbox, with a right-hand shift. There is a sliding lock which makes it impossible to by-pass the second-and-third sector when shifting up from first or down from fourth, plus a flick-down guard protecting reverse position, forward of first. The standard ratios are 2.42, 1.47, 1.09, 0.96 and 0.85 to 1 (3.75 to 1 reverse), with a choice of 4.22 and 3.33 to 1 final-drive ratios. With the lower final drive installed, Brands Hatch became a second, third and fourth circuit, 7,000 rpm coming up in third in front of the pits (120 mph), and 6,500 rpm in fourth (127 mph) being reached at the braking point for Paddock.

The Borrani wire-spoke 15 inch wheels have light alloy rims, and carry 5.50 tyres at the front and 7.00s at the rear, with 11½ inch diameter Girling brake discs immediately inboard of them carrying CR and BR calipers, front and rear, respectively. The rack-and-pinion steering is geared to 2.8 turns, lock to lock, and this feels just about the ideal compromise between responsiveness and lightness.

There is a very robust-looking double-wishbone front suspension system, and the now-conventional rear-end layout incorporating lower wishbones, upper transverse links and parallel radius arms, fully adjustable, of course. The dampers fitted inside the coil springs are also of the adjustable type.

One of the most difficult jobs in driving this car is climbing in or out! It calls for quite a technique—especially climbing out—because the driving seat is well inboard of the outer edge of the body, and the gap between steering wheel and seat cushion, though quite adequate for driving, is a bit marginal for body contortions. If you happen to be tall, you also have to remember to duck your head when closing the door over you, because the roofline is a bare 40½ inches above the ground.

But once you are installed behind the wheel, the GT 40 approaches the ultimate in racing-car comfort. The ventilated seat, which offers a very reclining driving position, is a fixture, any adjustment necessary being taken up at the pedals. (In fact, things were just about ideal as the car arrived.)

The black decor is most attractive, and the detail finish of a considerably higher standard than might be expected from what is essentially a competition car. The instrument and control layout (white markings on black-faced dials, and matching flick switches, all clearly marked) has been well thought out, and although there are no less than seven dials and 12 switches, you soon learn where to look or feel for the essential ones.

The rev counter, immediately behind the steering wheel, is flanked by the oil pressure gauge on the right, and the water temperature gauge on the left. Then, running further left, we have oil temperature, fuel pressure and ammeter gauges, with, on the extreme left, a large speedometer, angled towards the driver. The switches, lined up below, are in four groups. Running from the left are the sidelights, headlights and pass lights tabs, then come the washers and wiper tabs, and in a third group the dipper and overriding rear light tabs. (This last control is to illuminate a pair of rear lights permanently if the car's normal lights circuit packs up.) The fourth switch group, to the right of the steering column, comprises flashers, left-hand fuel pump, right-hand fuel pump and ignition controls, and there is a separate panel-light switch above, to the right of the oil-pressure gauge.

Two cockpit features became apparent very early on in the test. The first was that it takes a little time to get used to the relatively restricted rear vision—I just didn't see the going of that engine cover! The second was the effectiveness of the cockpit ventilation equipment. In the fairly high ambient temperature of the test, I was very comfortable when travelling fast, but noticed the considerable temperature build-up immediately I slowed down in the pit road.

The next outstanding impression came from the gear shift. Once I had remembered that the shift from second to third calls for a very slight pull to the right, instead of straight back (which lands you in neutral!), it became a dream of a box. It really is a wonderful mechanism, and you can bang that lever around as though you are pre-selecting gears in an automatic transmission. This is a big help coming out of Clearways, because it means that the shift from second to third, which occurs when you've still got quite a bit of sideways 'G' on, calls for the minimum change of torque at the back wheels, and therefore helps to keep the car that much more stable.

HARD WORK FOR BRAKES

The brakes called for quite a firm pedal, and there was quite a lot of squealing from the discs, but presumably this would have died down as the pads became fully bedded in. Travelling at the speeds of which the GT 40 is capable, even on the short circuit, the brakes have to be used quite hard, and once or twice I detected what I thought was either too much, or uneven braking at the back, causing rear-end steering going into Paddock. But on reflection, this was probably the result of too-soft damper settings causing tail lightness over the 'hump' at this point, and upsetting the brake balance. Certainly, after we had screwed up the dampers several clicks all round the trouble virtually disappeared, although I still felt it wise to apply the brakes very progressively at this point.

Being essentially a fast-circuit car, it came as no surprise to find that the GT 40 had been given a fair measure of built-in understeer, and that if one were to set the car up specifically for the short Brands circuit, rather less understeer would have been chosen. Nevertheless, the only place where it became noticeably time-consuming was up at the hairpin, where about a half-second lift-off just before coming out

Left: Wide and low. The 4.7 litre V8, giving 380 horsepower, snuggles comfortably between the broad track. The roof is only just over 40 inches from the ground.

Below: Snug and functional. Says Blunsden: 'The black decor is most attractive, and the detail finish of a considerably higher standard than might be expected from what is essentially a competition car.'

Exclusive

proved necessary to keep it on a reasonably tight cornering radius.

The comparatively low tyre pressures probably contributed towards a momentary feeling of understeer half-way through Paddock, but this always neutralised itself going into the dip. Otherwise, the car cornered most impressively, and although quite a lot of arm work was necessary to get the best results over the top of Clearways, it was reassuring to find that considerable liberties could be taken with the power to unstick the rear wheels into a very controllable slide. Indeed, standard technique coming out of Clearways seemed to be to provoke a gentle rear-end breakaway and hold the car's attitude on the accelerator rather than by the steering. John Whitmore later suggested to me that with this car we have the best of both worlds—the inherent stability and ease of control of a front-engined design, coupled with the greater competitiveness of a mid-engine layout. This seems to sum it up very well, for though it may not have outstanding 'feel' at the back end, it is most kind to newcomers, and allows them to lap competitively without a long and anxious gestation period—that, surely, is the hallmark of a great design.

This is quite a wide-tracked car (55 inches front and rear, with a 95 inch wheelbase) and there seems to be ample rubber on the road. The ride comfort—probably emphasised by the seat design—deserves the highest praise, and the GT 40 proved completely stable over the notorious rough patch on the apex of the right-hand kink between Kidney and Clearways.

As supplied in the GT 40, the 289 Ford engine is moderately top-endy, with an exhaust note which smoothes out perceptibly above about 4,000 rpm, and sounds quite delightful above 6,000. It probably guzzles petrol at an impressive rate from its 30½ gallon fuel cells, but who cares? The cooling system seemed to work well, and despite losing a drop of water through the lack of a sealing ring on the filler cap (someone had 'borrowed' it!) the temperature gauge steadied itself between 75 and 80 degrees F.

I am lucky enough to be offered many interesting and exciting cars for MOTOR RACING track tests, but I can honestly say that not one of them has given me more genuine driving pleasure than this beautiful-looking pale green Ford GT 40. And I'm glad to say that 'things' do *not* always happen in threes!

FORD GT MARK II

A 7-liter weapon aimed at winning the Sports-Prototype championship in 1966

BY RON WAKEFIELD

ALTHOUGH THE "all-new" Ford GTP sports car prototype pictured in last month's "Miscellaneous Ramblings" will be fielded by FoMoCo at Le Mans, the 7-liter Ford GT in Mark II form will constitute Ford's main prototype effort in 1966. Several significant changes are evident in the new version of the GT and there are myriad small changes of a development nature, most of which are aimed at improving the car's durability inasmuch as there's really no question about its being fast enough. Development work is being done primarily by Shelby American and carried out under the supervision of acknowledged development expert Phil Remington.

Most obvious of the changes are the new body contours front and rear. The new nose is essentially the same as the "production" GT-40, which means that the Mark II is about 9 in. shorter than the previous 7-liter car. The rear end is also new and Ford hopes the various fins and spoilers cobbled up for use at Le Mans last year won't be necessary now. Tests at the Ford proving ground track at Kingman, Ariz., have indicated good stability at 200 mph.

A few pounds have been saved here and there in the body panels by the use of thinner material and there are many structural changes. For instance, there are new jack pads at the front so the same jack can be used front and rear; reinforcing has been added around suspension mounting points at the front; the rear control arm pivot-point studs are now supported on both ends rather than being cantilevered—a small change but apparently an important one. Suspension uprights at both front and rear have been modified for more strength and the new double-adjusting Koni shocks described in February R&T (page 16) are used.

It is fairly well known that the vented rotors used for the disc brakes last year were cracking regularly. To eliminate this problem, the Shelby people have designed a new rotor with the internal ribs curved instead of radially straight. The rotors are also finished by a new process developed by Kelsey-Hayes called "Die Pac"—a coating of 98% copper and 2% carbide which is claimed to give a better coefficient of friction and better heat transfer.

The gearbox, always a problem with this car, now has a single oil pump instead of the double ones used before and is now being made by the Transmission and Chassis Division of Ford rather than Kar Kraft. The engine is pretty much the same as last year, with modifications made to the dry sump lubrication system for better de-aeration of oil returning to the supply tank and a stronger sump for better support of the bell housing. The radiator is larger—now 11.5 x 25.0 x 4.0 in.—and has a new header tank, mounted higher on the front bulkhead than before and equipped with a 21-psi cap.

Engine output will be 460-470 bhp at 6500 rpm and the cars are expected to weigh about 2475 lb full of fuel and ready to race. The Shelby team will campaign these Mark IIs and they will be backed up by a team of lightweight 4.7-liter GT-40s managed by Alan Mann, and the GTP, which will probably be run by Roy Lunn.

TRACK TEST: Ford GT 40

BY JERRY TITUS

PHOTOS: DARRYL NORENBERG

High-angle shot of the roadster reveals its very clean and efficient lines as it smokes down Riverside's back straight at over 150 mph.

FOR OVER A YEAR AND A HALF SPORTS CAR GRAPHIC MAGAZINE has been reporting the development and campaigning of the Ford GT. Now it is approaching the time when these fabulous machines will be offered to the public. We started badgering Shelby-American's general manager, Jim MacLean, for a track test of the Ford GT just before LeMans. With the various cars being shuttled between Los Angeles, Dearborn, England and the Continent, it took a few months to arrange. The particular model we tested is called the roadster. It's identical to the coupe, but without the roof. It was equipped with a relatively tame version of the 289-inch high-performance V-8, and a Colotti four-speed transaxle. Ken Miles had it out at Riverside as a development car in a program that will determine in what final form it will be delivered to customers.

We'd sat in the GT a couple of times before, but were still impressed by the comfortable seats and driver-positioning. Even though you sit deep between the stressed side sections housing some 39 gallons of gas and the narrow center tunnel, there still is an impression of considerable roominess due to the flat instrument panel and the relative lowness of the tunnel and tanks. The brake and clutch pedals are short, floor-mounted affairs with the gas pedal hanging; the ideal setup for efficient heal-and-toe work. The steering wheel is leather bound, flat, and of moderate size, placed nicely for optimum control.

Equipped with downdraft Webers and the "bundle-of-snakes" exhaust system, the Ford produces that same wild snarl with which the Indy cars chilled everyone. Only the sound of a sports/racing Ferrari at full chat is equal to it in sheer, savage noise. The engine

Tuned-length exhaust system uses a resonator in secondary stage atop the four-speed Colotti. Note that inner U-joints are metalastic type.

Ford GT40

fired up and even idles with unexpected docility. The multi-disc clutch was something else; either IN or OUT with very little between. Getting a heavy car off the line with this kind of setup is a ticklish job, and certainly nothing to have for around-town driving. It can be accomplished, but the clutch would not stand up to such abuse very long. Contained in a tight and positive pattern, the short gearshift lever is located on the right. It was connected to the first of the big Colotti gearboxes we've driven. It's non-synchro and takes more than a little practice to engage without grinding, unless you're going flat out. Engine rpms MUST be matched with those of the gear shifts. Everything else is very easy to adapt to.

Underway, the heaviness (some 2200 pounds) is immediately apparent and accented by both the soft suspension and the general solidness of the vehicle. Taking it through Riverside's Esses, we found it extremely simple and dependable to control from the first lap onward. Steering pressure is slightly on the high side, and the general attitude definitely understeering. Tire bite and the ability to keep the tire on the ground over surface deviations was exceptionally good. By the time we got on the track, workmen were replacing the guardrail at Turn One, following installation of a new underpass. A full timed lap was impossible, but Ken had been out earlier and was cutting 1:36's; certainly not a top Modified time, but quicker than the best a competition Cobra could hack. It's rather hard to evaluate in this instance, as the test unit was neither fish nor foul, neither full-race nor tame enough for the street. There wasn't quite enough power for racing and the tires weren't the hot setup for that application, but the car got around the course like a thoroughbred. Aside from some judder that may have been an imperfect disc or an out-of-balance tire, stopping power was excellent, with the good anti-dive characteristics making it deceptive as far as weight was concerned. The streamlining was evident from a stability standpoint, holding the roadster rock-steady on the straight.

The Ford GT, in all, is quite a machine. A week after our test, Shelby shipped the test unit up to San Francisco to use as a pace car with Lew Spencer at the wheel. Lew started out slow but, by the time the ABC-Production event rolled around, we were really hard-pressed to keep up with him. "I can't help it," he said later, "that thing is such a ball to drive!"

This, we feel, sums it up nicely.

At right is one of the most comfortable and efficient "offices" we've ever sat in. Gearshift is just to right of flat, leather-bound wheels. Pedals are on rack that can be adjusted to suit individual driver's needs. Red-line on this engine was 6500 rpm, but some 289's go higher.

In which Innes Ireland introduces Ronald Barker to one of the lowest forms of motoring

The Super Street-Car

That's the GT40—that was... Produced by Ford Advanced Vehicles of Slough, with 335 b.h.p. V-8 engine amidships and 5-speed transaxle. Hinged nose and tail sections are of moulded glass fibre, but the cockpit is steel framed with a tough roll-over member

I DIDN'T see it at first: "There, idiot!" they said, "you're practically tripping over it!" I mean to say, just how low can you get? At three feet four this capsule-on-wheels scarcely comes up to your belly button, and you have to get right down to see any daylight at all between its belly button and the road. According to the spec. there's 4in. clearance, but at a casual glance it looks as though the Ford would have as much difficulty passing over a door-stop as a dachshund with middle-age droop in its centre-section.

Whichever way you look at it the whole concept of this package is astonishing. It's only 14ft long despite the considerable nose overhang, 5ft 10in. wide and, to be exact, 3ft 4½in. high, the base of the screen just over 2ft 4in. above ground level. Yet is contains two people stretched out comfortably almost to full length, a 4.7-litre 335 b.h.p. engine with 5-speed gearbox and 31 gallons of fuel. As a road car it is "out of this world" as most people know it.

When you have to step into something like this for the first time there are always people watching. Is it because they're sadists and know some part of your anatomy is in for a rude shock on the way down? You feel much more self-conscious, surely, than Grissom and Shepard & Co., who at least had practised it lots of times before TV viewers saw them.

Actually I said "Ow!", settling finally on the safety harness buckle just when it seemed I'd made it unharmed. Heave up an inch or two to pull it free, and my head in turn hits the screen, the rear-view mirror, the door frame where it tongues into the roof, and even the inner back window. A steadying hand in the door for support and it begins to swing to, the horizontal blade of its top going for my neck like Mme. Guillotine. What *does* one do with a Big Head in a small car?

Times have changed since the very rich wanted only cars with bodies so high they could walk right through without removing headgear. Inevitably some of those who buy a Ford GT 40 (for £6,647 7s 11d) will do so mainly for social distinction, and will be content to enjoy this from what Stanley Holloway might describe as a semi-recumbent posture; yet there is room even for a crash helmet.

They have provided me with a very experienced chauffeur named Ireland; having practised it for Le Mans starts, he knows just how to slither into place behind the wheel, with legs stiff and his right trouser end kept well clear of the gear lever on that side. But what with his Gannex and my Padded Hopkirk, stop-watches, crash-helmets, camera box and a packet of After Eights, there simply isn't room for us, too. So the crash-helmets are stuffed into one of the two luggage tins under the (rear) bonnet, the camera is slung out.

The seats are rather close together, since the wide sills below the doors not only contribute to the hull's strength but also carry our fuel supply in Goodyear flexible cells. They are form-fitting seats without aggressive humps and bumps, and extremely comfortable. But they're not for fidgets; once you've dropped into place they embrace you as intimately as a jelly in its mould.

To some extent the seating can be arranged to suit the individual customer. Since the pan is a fixture, the pedal assembly is adjustable for reach,

Super Street Car...

and a loose cushion to lay over the backrest would overcome the large husband-little wife (or vice versa) problem. John Wyer, Managing Director of Ford Advanced Vehicles, says that customers will be asked to come to the Slough factory for a "fitting"!

In such a snug cockpit, and with that vast, steeply raked screen inviting the sun to fry the occupants, thorough ventilation is imperative. So there's the famous Ford Aeroflow system, with big adjustable vents at each end of the facia, and the black p.v.c. seat trim is perforated to allow cool air to pass through it.

In wet weather one huge blade with a strong spring pressure and powerful motor sweeps the screen, its spindle offset to give the driver the fullest benefit. It is said to keep working properly up to the car's maximum—and that's around 160 m.p.h. in this standard "street" form. In the padded facia some of the strictly functional instruments are angled to face the driver; left to right are a 200 m.p.h. speedometer, ammeter, gauges for fuel pressure, oil and water temperatures, rev counter (with red sector covering 6,500-7,000 r.p.m.) and oil pressure gauge. No fuel level gauge in this prototype. A multi-purpose lever to the right of the steering-wheel serves the direction indicators, headlamp beams and horns. An automatic cigarette lighter is rather clever—you simply stick the weed in and after a few seconds it's ready for smoking.

Among the production luxuries are an electrically heated screen and tinted safety glass for the doors and back window; the doors in our car, though, have Perspex windows with little hinged panels. Right behind your neck is a small, vertical glass window; and between this and the outside moulded window that lies flush with the roof line is the induction room, so to speak. Grouped in the middle of this are the eight mouths of four double Weber carburettors, like a nest full of hungry fledglings concealed beneath a big air cleaner-silencer. Adding hush subtracts power, and this probably absorbs from the vee-8 engine as many horses as it takes to drive a standard Mini at top speed.

Rearward view is not too bright but adequate through this double glazing, and otherwise one can see splendidly. Looking forward over the short, sloping nose one is reminded of a Porsche, but lowered and widened. Perhaps it is because of the depth of the front and side windows that one suffers no claustrophobic repressions.

Innes presses the starter button above the central backbone and the mid-engine springs to life, with a fairly throaty Dearborn beat rhythm that evens out as the revs rise. We glide away smoothly on the fairly low first gear, and he is up into fifth speed of the Colotti box while we are still dawdling through the soulless Subtopia of Betjeman's favourite town. Although the motor is a fairly hot one it remains tractable enough to pull to less than 1,000 r.p.m. (25 m.p.h.) in fifth.

From this level one has a dwarf's eye view of the world rushing by, and I thought of this the following evening when David Frost, commenting on freak April weather that suddenly laid a thick carpet of snow over much of the country, gave this solemn warning to 3ft dwarfs living in the Pennines: that there were 4ft drifts! The GT 40 would not take long to bury, either. Familiar dips in the road become that much deeper relative to one's line of sight and hedges acquire added stature. Nor, of course, does one have any view of what lies ahead through other vehicles' back windows. But the human brain quickly adapts to new circumstances, and the GT 40's electrifying acceleration gives opportunities denied to other traffic.

To ride with a Grand Prix professional of Innes Ireland's calibre gives the competent normal driver a quite new perspective on the art. Only someone like he can show just what such a car can do, and how. It must be infinitely galling for those who design and assemble the GT 40s that very few owners will ever discover and enjoy their full potential.

It isn't only a matter of superior judgment and super-rapid reactions, but there is a complete absence of drama from one's progress. Innes never once took the engine up to high revs in the indirects, never jerked his passenger's neck during a quick upward change, nor took any chances. Yet however hard he may be driving he misses nothing going on around him, and several times his wildfowling instincts were aroused by spotting mallard lifting off a small lake, or some other species of duck doing a full-flap touchdown. Over lunch, incidentally, we learnt something of the subtle art of trout-tickling and other country pursuits. Not all racing drivers, you see, have one-track minds, and the Ireland field of knowledge and experience means never a dull moment for his travelling companion.

It would be irrational to describe the "street" GT 40 as an ideal touring car, although one owner is having his fitted with TV, radio telephone, and air conditioning. Sounds to me a bit like how many students can you cram into a telephone kiosk —until finally there isn't room to make a call. And with the engine pushing out all that power just behind the cockpit and precious little space for silencers, the voice strings sometimes have to fight rather hard to tickle the eardrums. Perhaps one could install a drivie-talkie intercom set like rally drivers use, with throat amplifiers.

Yet it remains a very fine road car, more docile and practical than might be imagined. The suspension is sur-

Innes Ireland—super chauffeur. A crash helmet (for Silverstone), you see, but no gloves and a radio in the door

prisingly resilient, and a complete freedom from roll combines with the seating's lateral support at high cornering speeds to relieve the body muscles of any conscious demands.

It's almost relaxing even, and in no time one is in such close harmony with the car that the prospect of a quick trip to Edinburgh or the Côte d'Azur would be irresistible. What a nonsense such a vehicle makes of the current 70-limit—even in 2nd of the 5 gears, this speed is within its happy cruising revs!

We have booked the main circuit at Silverstone for a brief dice and to enable Michael Cooper to get busy with his cameras. Whenever one is about to be the non-combatant partner of a man and machine tried near to the limit the instinct for self-preservation has a little inside battle with the will to be stimulated by danger. Every time I am swept off the runway or back to *terra firma* in a modern commerical jet, a little inner voice tells me that this could be the moment of truth, that my life depends on very delicate human and mechanical threads. These are really the only kicks that remain for an air passenger today. I am ready for kicks now, and looking forward to being frightened a little. But, please, not too much.

It is a cold, blustery day, so how splendid to find our crash-helmets cooked to a friendly warmth in the engine compartment—my shiny, little-used one in Napier green looking very sprog beside Innes' famous black-and-white checkerboard job. I carry a small tape recorder, a more logical means of gathering information than to try to write notes during high-speed lapping.

Although I had never before been hustled round that circuit by a top-flight driver, the air of unconcern in that recording is unbearably blasé, as though we were taking one of those advanced driving courses and thinking out loud in the approved manner. The fact is that the Ford never seems to be going fast, and one longs for the extra urge of the competition version to liven things up. But we were approaching Stowe at almost 140 m.p.h., changing down twice to 3rd, reducing speed to about 80 and passing the apex at 90-odd; accelerating to 120 before Club, down to 3rd again and up to 115 or so through the gentle left-hander called Abbey. We attacked Woodcote at about 95-100 in 4th, had gathered speed to 110 or so by the apex and changed up to 5th under the *Motor* bridge at 120.

When I had asked Innes beforehand how fast he took the next right-hander (Copse) he had no idea. It's a nice turn that opens out as you emerge from it; we dropped to 3rd and a true 80 m.p.h. (I had guessed nearer 70) and were doing 120 by the time we reached the left-hand curve called Maggotts. Tricky Becketts —sharper than 90 deg to the right —brought us down momentarily to about 70 (in 3rd), then there was a super full-throttle blast through Chapel, using the road's full width, and up to 140 again before Stowe.

The rev counter never rose above

"Don't you ever get baked in your jacket?"—at the Green Man, Brackley Hatch (near Silverstone)

Super Street Car...

5,500 even in the indirects, we had no apparent slides or other excitements, and the process assumed an exact rhythm devoid of drama but constantly thrilling—so much so that I quite forgot to take out a stop-watch to check lap times. By the standards most of us know, the cornering power of that Ford is phenomenal, but from

Mine's a Ford GT too! It cost £5,860 less, but has more headroom

such a low altitude one's sense of speed is completely upset. After a few laps it doesn't even feel particularly fast any more.

Next we set off for the M.I.R.A. proving grounds near Nuneaton, to take acceleration times over the quarter-mile and kilometre, probably marred slightly by an excess fuel pressure and consequent over-richness. The best runs were in 14·2 and 26·2 sec respectively, well over 130 m.p.h. being reached by the end of the kilometre. Compare these, though, with some astonishing figures John Wyer gave me for the competition version during practice on the Mulsanne straight at Le Mans last year:—

0–100 m.p.h. 8·8 sec
0–150 m.p.h. 18·5 sec
0–168 m.p.h. 24·1 sec

Innes had never visited M.I.R.A. before, so just for the hell of it we hared round the 2·8-mile outer circuit for a few laps, where the car's supreme stability made 130 or so m.p.h. round the narrow banked curves and over 150 on the straights seem arrogantly prosaic.

For the return journey Innes settled back into the passenger seat, metaphorically crossed his heart—and soon fell fast asleep. For the driver this is one of those rare machines with which he feels completely at ease within the first few miles, that flatters his modest skill without ever putting him in his place with a subversive trick. There is instant, almost animal response from the high-geared steering, the small leather-covered wheel an almost telepathic link between his brain and the road.

No one had said: "*Watch it, chum, if you have to lift your foot halfway through a corner*" or anything like that, because no warnings are needed. No oversteer, understeer, no sudden breakaways, no allergy to cross-winds or wavy road surfaces—no excuses for dragging out the familiar dicer's clichés for another airing. The gear-change is fun: on the way down you have to run through the lot because an interlock mechanism prevents short-cuts. Probably other drivers think you are just being exhibitionist as you reduce speed before, say, a traffic signal—whang! down to 4th; whang! 3rd; whang! 2nd; whang! 1st. Well, let's be honest—you have to do it, but you rather like it.

It's the same on the way up, although John Horsman did tell me afterwards that one could get 5th direct from 3rd. Whereas there's quite a gap between 1 and 2, some of the other ratios seem needlessly close; for instance, the step up from 4 to 5 is only 11½ per cent. The ratios are 2·42, 1·47, 1·09, 0·96 and 0·85. With the 4·22 to 1 final drive fitted, the overall top gear ratio is 3·59, but one has the option of 3·33 final drive gears.

I have a suspicion that one would go on playing with that gearbox even after living with the car for a time, though there's enough engine torque to deal summarily with most traffic situations most of the time in top gear. You don't need a ballerina's foot control or muscles for the clutch, the brakes are all you expect, the minor controls are simple and easily found, and the only sad disillusion comes when you find yourself, all too soon . . . back in Slough! The Ball is over, the glass slipper is lost, and there's no prospect of a handsome Prince to bring it back.

THE CHALLENGE TO FERRARI

Porsche Carrera 6/Ford GT Mark II

PHOTOS ALICE BIXLER

THE INTERNATIONAL CHAMPIONSHIP that is being battled over by the greatest names in road racing is this year known as the "International Trophies for Prototype Sports Cars." This is the big one, the one that Ferrari, Ford and Porsche will be contesting in 1966.

The regulations for this championship specify that there will be two displacement classes— over and under 2 liters. Last year Ferrari won the over-2-liter championship, humiliating Ford at Le Mans and winning where it was necessary at the other championship races. In the under-2-liter class, Porsche had it pretty much its own way.

This year, however, Ferrari is preparing a serious challenger for the smaller division as well (see page ?.) and to meet this threat, Porsche has introduced its new Carrera 6. This car is all new, not a development of the Porsche 904 which will now run in the Sports 50 class for the other major championship, the International Championship of Sports Car Manufacturers.

The Carrera 6 has a space type tubular frame, fiberglass body and gull-wing-style doors. Typical of Porsche's appreciation of the necessity for driver comfort in long-distance events, the driving compartment is comfortably outfitted and both the steering wheel and the seat are adjustable.

The Carrera 6 has a flat-6 aircooled engine with a bore and stroke of 66 x 80 mm, for a total displacement of 1991 cc. More than 230 bhp is being developed by this engine (the factory gives the figure as 210 DIN hp at 8000 rpm) and there is usable power available between about 3500 and 8200 rpm, a usefully wide power band. A 5-speed gearbox is used and the top speed of the Carrera 6 is given by the manufacturer as 280 kph, roughly 175 mph. The weight of the car without fuel but with oil is about 1275 lb.

The Carrera 6 was very impressive in its first competition appearance, the Daytona 24-hr race. Driven by factory pros Hans Herrmann and Herbert Linge, the Carrera 6 won the 2-liter Sports-Prototype class and finished 6th overall. At Daytona, however, there were none of the new Ferrari Dino 206/S on hand and when these meet in future races, the struggle should be a classic one.

In the big-engined class, Ferrari's number one challenger is the Ford GT Mark II. This has been developed from the 427-cu-in Ford GT that was rushed to completion for last year's Le Mans race and failed after leading impressively

THE CHALLENGE TO FERRARI

during the opening hours. The Mark II, powered by the huge 7-liter pushrod Ford engine, has been de-tuned slightly to give "only" about 465-475 bhp. This power, combined with the aerodynamic shape, should propel it along Mulsanne straight at Le Mans at something over 200 mph. Last year's version, less clean aerodynamically, was clocked at 185 consistently and was reported to have touched 210 on occasion. The 427 GTs went out with gearbox trouble last year but this component has been thoroughly tested in the interim and should be ready to go the distance.

There will be a total of eight events counting toward the Sports Prototype championship in 1966. By definition of the Federation Internationale de l'Automobile, races counting toward the over-2-liter championship can be no shorter than 1000 km (621 mi) long or 6 hours duration. Under-2-liter championship races can be half that distance, but as most of the races are for both divisions, the smaller engined cars will be covering roughly the same distance as their larger-engined counterparts.

Counting toward the championships in 1966 are the following races:

Feb. 5-6 24-hr Daytona Continental
March 26 12-hr race, Sebring, Fla.
April 25 1000 kms, Monza Italy
May 8 Targa Florio, Sicily
May 22 Spa GP, Belgium
June 5 1000-km race, Nurburgring, Germany
June 18-19 24-hr race, Le Mans, France
Aug. 14 Hockenheim GP, Germany (2-liter division)
Oct. 2 12-hr race, Reims, France

It is not yet known which of the European races, besides Le Mans, will be entered by Ford. Having already won at Daytona, and expected to make a strong show at Sebring, Ford will have to run (and win) at least three European races in addition to Le Mans if it expects to wrest the championship away from Ferrari. There is little doubt, however, that there is more publicity benefit to be gained by a victory at Le Mans than by backing into the championship by piling up points from lesser wins and there is no doubt at all that Ford's major effort in 1966 will be to win at Le Mans.

ILLUSTRATIONS BY
WERNER BÜHRER

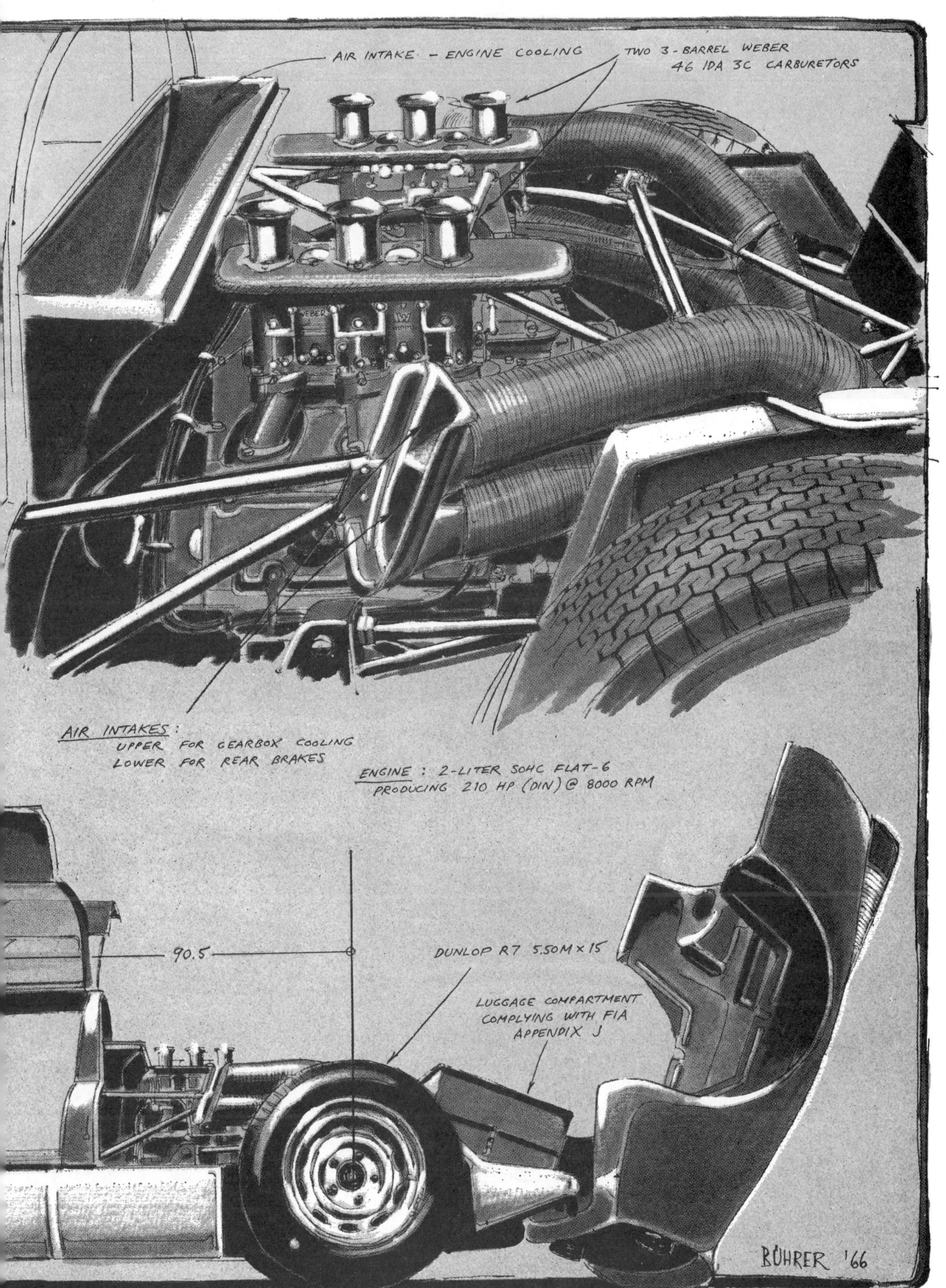

REVISED RADIATOR AIR OUTLETS

40.5

FORD 427 GT - MK II

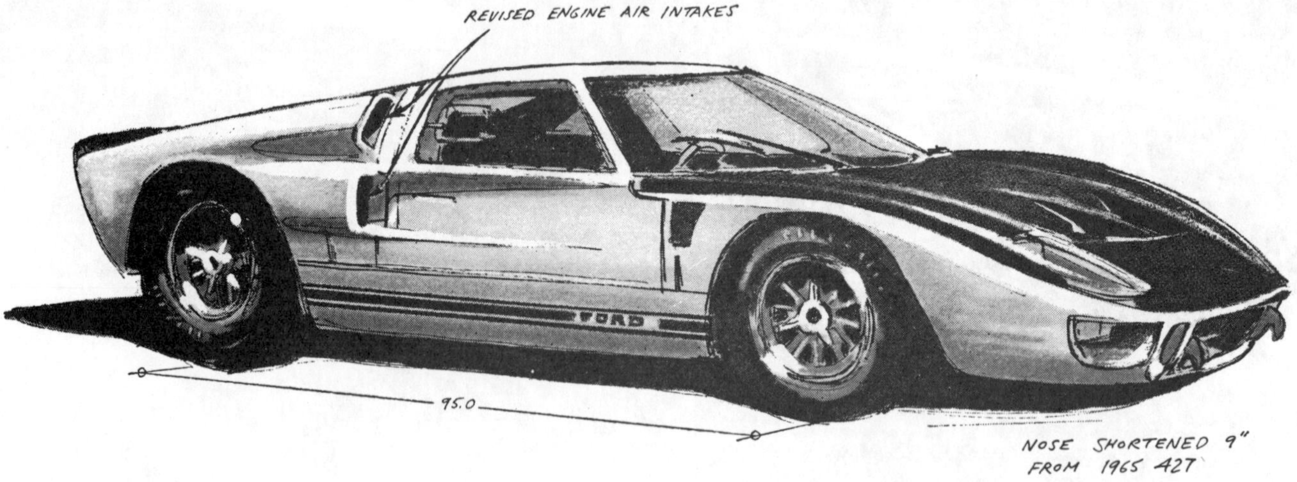

REVISED ENGINE AIR INTAKES

95.0

NOSE SHORTENED 9" FROM 1965 427

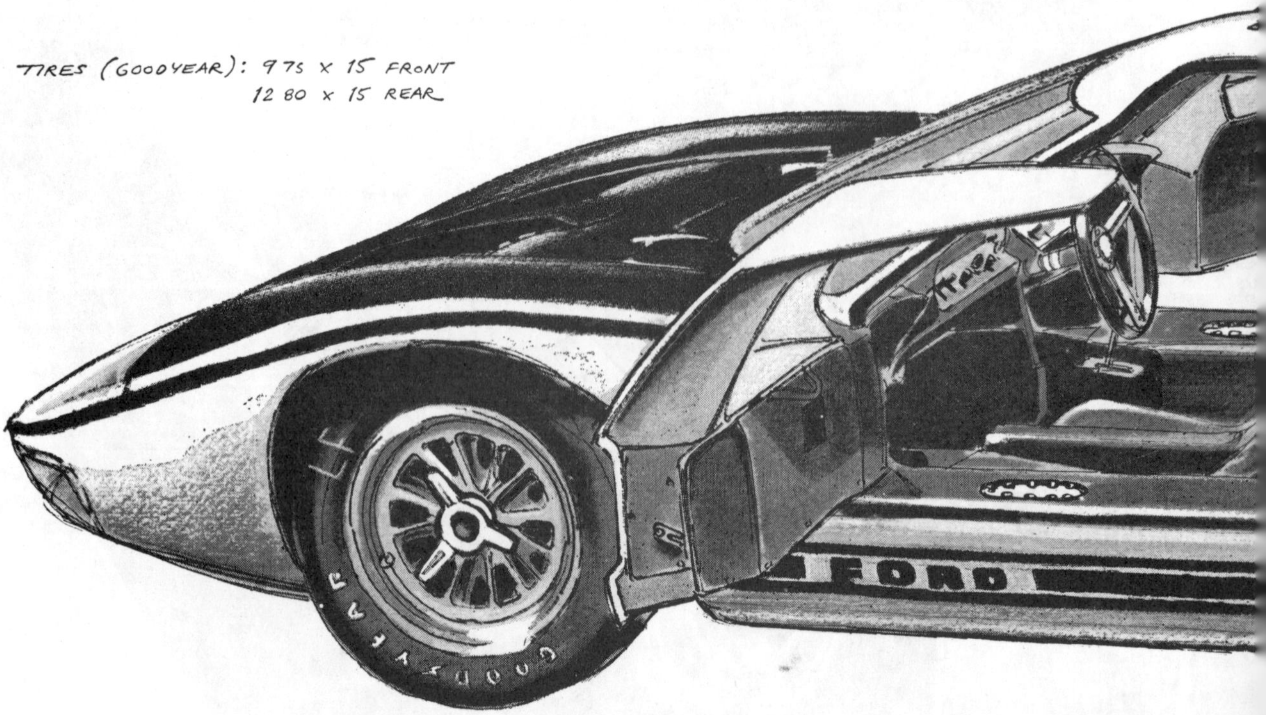

TIRES (GOODYEAR): 9.75 x 15 FRONT
                  12.80 x 15 REAR

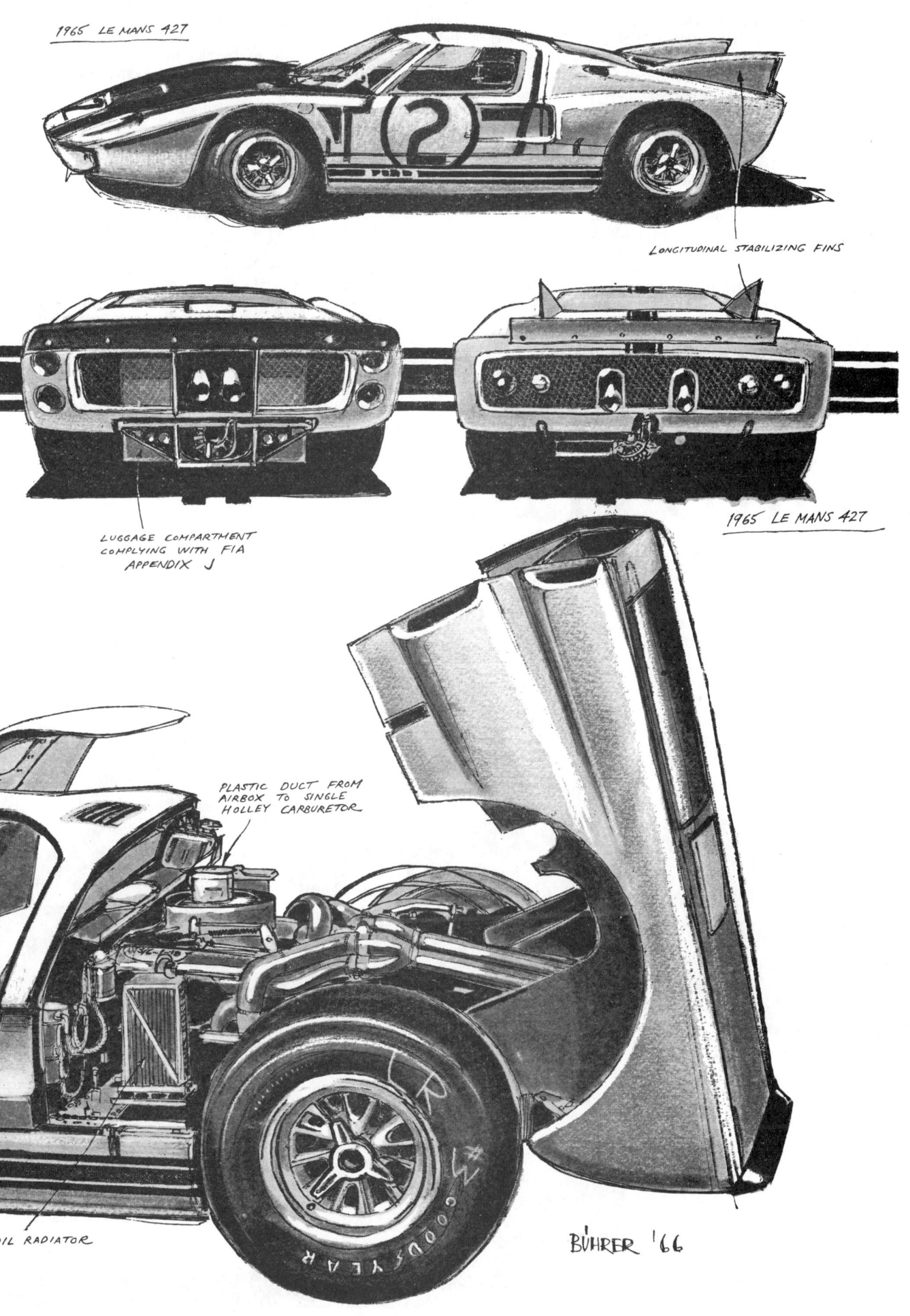

IN OUR AFFLUENT SOCIETY, THE SEARCH FOR A STATUS SYMBOL BECOMES DAILY MORE DIFFICULT. A few years ago you could impress the neighbors with a set of hi-fi equipment, color television in every bedroom, or a high-speed power boat in the back of the garage. Now, unless you have all these things, you're getting close to the Administration's under-privileged classification, and more important, you'll cut no ice at all with the folks next door!

What's left? Well, you could buy a new bed, and have it delivered nice and slow so that everyone in the street can read the inscription on the headboard, "As used by Elizabeth Taylor and...." Or you could install a pint-size computer in the kitchen and invite all your fat friends in for a computerized diet of low-calorie foods (a hidden electronic brain will photograph and weigh them as they step over the threshold, the news will be fed through the computer, which will then supply the appropriate diet). On second thoughts, this will probably win you more enemies than friends.

No, better go back to that perennial status symbol, the motor car, though with Cadillacs becoming as prolific as Cortinas, and Ferraris as numerous as Fiats (at least, that's the way it's beginning to look), it's a nightmare trying to find something to really ring the bell.

And so, a hearty vote of thanks to the Ford Motor Company, through whose good offices (especially the one in Slough, Buckinghamshire, England, with 'Ford Advanced Vehicles' on the front door) the status-seeker shall seek and he shall find.

Knock on the door, ask to see John Wyer, and if you happen to have £5,500 in your hand (the equivalent of $15,500 U.S. dollars will do — indeed, in view of Britain's balance-of-payments difficulties, will probably be more acceptable!) he'll build you a road-going version of the car that's twice broken the Le Mans' lap record, and which, with a bit of luck and a few million dollars, might even win the race there this year. In short, you can become a member of the ultra-exclusive 'GT40 Set.'

Now, as Mr. Wyer will be anxious to tell you, they don't sell GT40s to just anyone, in the same way that beatniks are not exactly encouraged in Saville Row. And, just as they have never even heard of the term 'off the racks' in that palace of master tailoring, so, at Slough, they wouldn't dream of issuing you with a GT40 for which you had not been given a personal fitting. (Don't mention it to your friends, but the reason for

FORD GT40

If you're looking for the ultimate in status symbols, a personally-fitted Ford GT40 for everyday use is it!

BY JOHN BLUNSDEN

PHOTOS: JOHN BLUNSDEN AND FORD OF ENGLAND

FORD GT40

this is that, as on all Ford GTs, the seats are fixtures, a part of the basic body structure, and variations in leg room are made through adjustable pedals. It's far better for the image if you just casually mention that it was built around you, and leave it at that!)

Another thing it's worth keeping quiet about is the power unit. Don't, whatever you do, say it's based on the Ford 289 that close-on half the world seems to be using, with a bit of 'Weber carb tune' to give it 335 bhp at 6,250 rpm. Far better to say that it's the specially developed Ford race engine, very slightly detuned to give it that unfussy boulevard performance which makes the GT40 such a natural for expeditions to the supermarket. Apart from helping to maintain the image again, it also happens to be Broadley (sorry, I meant broadly!) true.

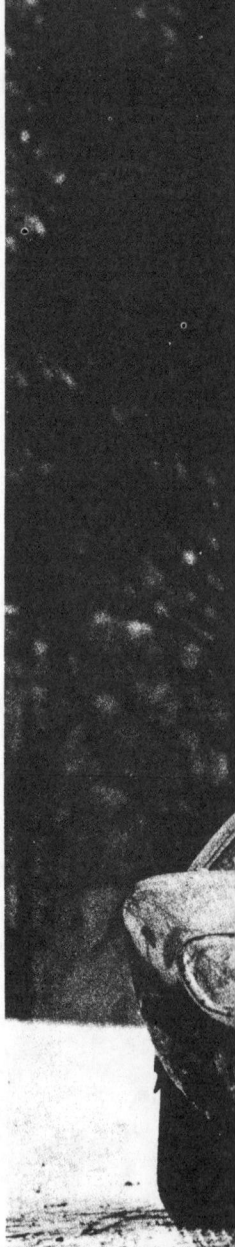

If you find that the neighbors are not too impressed with this detuning business, steer the conversation around to the point where they've just got to ask, "What'll she do?" This is where you say, "Well, it depends upon the gear-box and final-drive ratios." (If you'll accept a spot of advice, you'll take the standard set, even though you can specify a whole load of alternatives. At least you'll then be able to remember exactly what your maximum speeds in the gears are, and trot out the telling figures with a carefully rehearsed air of casualness.)

"With the gearing I've chosen as being the most suitable for my own personal needs (ha ha!), it gives me 58 mph in first, 90 mph in second, and 127 mph in third." (Pause for the inevitable, "But what's so marvelous with 127, why I can get nearly...") Then interrupt with "...142 mph in fourth and, just in case I'm really on form, I've got a fifth gear that'll give me a cool 160 mph before I reach the red line." Don't whatever you do, admit that you'll likely never be brave enough to get the needle over 120 or 130, because he's certainly not going to admit that he's never done over 90 in his Caddy, especially now that he's on the defensive! Oh yes, you might as well mention that the trans-

mission's by ZF, and that they also turn out some good sets of gears for Jim Clark's Lotuses, as well.

Even in a world of 'the bigger the better,' the motor car is becoming the exception, and anything that stands only 40 inches high is impressive, so keep mentioning the height, and the fact that like all good Grand Prix drivers, you drive it lying down. And when the girls chorus, "Lying down?!", you explain away the wide center tunnel which divides the two seats by pointing out that occasionally there are moments in life so precarious that even sex has to take a back seat (of which there is none), and that the GT40 is the ultimate expression of a sport of another type, which can also be highly enjoyable... "Why don't you climb in, and find out?"

The getting-in process, she will find, calls for considerable athletic prowess, mainly in the broad jump — no pun intended — and either a pair of slacks or a tight skirt and a do-it-yourself instant repair kit. It's all on account of those side side cells, which between them swallow up 31 Imperial gallons of fuel (the very best, of course!), which should be sufficient to let you give her a 400-mile test run.

(continued on page 77)

DAYTONA CONTINENTAL 24-HOUR

BY WALLY KORB

The First Round was between Ford, Ferrari and the Chaparral-Chevrolet!

THE SUCCESS STORY OF DAYTONA INTERNATIONAL SPEEDWAY'S OPERATION IN GENERAL, and their 'Continental' in particular, is at least impressive enough to make the old Horatio Alger rags-to-riches stories turn green with pure envy.

Remember back to 1962? That first Continental was a three-hour affair with a rather mixed bag of machinery — sports, GT and semi-stocker. And although Dan Gurney blew the engine of his Lotus 19 on the last lap of the race, he was able to win (see May 1962 SCG) by cranking over the finish line on the starter motor.

Two years later the Continental was enlarged to 2000 kilometers (about 13 hours of running on the 3.81-mile course), the field of cars was much more impressive, and the race was won by Pedro Rodriguez/Phil Hill in a Ferrari.

Last year the race was largely unchanged except that the field was still more competitive (see May 1965 SCG), largely because the Shelby Cobra/Ford GT threat was so strong. In fact, they swept the Ferrari field embarrassingly clear of the finish line as they took the first six places, with the exception of a fifth-place Porsche 904.

Well, then, where do you go from there? Why, to a 24-hour race, of course, with a still bigger, more competitive field and all the hoopla of 'the biggest and best.' Not too bad for five years of growth, hey? Next year, perhaps there will be a longer infield portion of track, resulting in a smaller percentage of the course run on the high bank but a greater overall length, enabling a still larger starting field.

Actually the enlargement of this year's race to 24 hours was probably of less importance than the extremely competitive field of cars which was entered, and the fact that both Ford and Chaparral teams looked on it as a pre-Le Mans test. Taking a quick look at the overall entry picture, 60 cars qualified to start the race. Of that total, 30 of the cars were capable of lapping the course at 100 mph or better, and were then only about 15 seconds apart in their lap times. Fifteen of the total entries were Ford-powered, while Ferrari had twelve cars, Porsche had eight and Chevrolet had four.

Of the Ford-powered cars, five were the new Ford Mk. II (427-inch) variety, driven by Miles/Ruby, Hansgen/Donahue, Bucknum/Ginther, McLaren/Amon and Gurney/Grant and qualified first, third, sixth, seventh and eleventh in the order listed. Ferrari was represented by two P2's driven by Rodriguez/Andretti (NART entry) and Bianchi/Langlois (Ecurie Francorchamps entry) and qualified fourth and fifth, and no less than eight 275 LM's, of which the fastest three were driven by Follmer/Wester (qualified eighth), Wilson/Hulme (ninth) and Piper/Attwood (twelfth).

Porsche had the strongest entry ever brought to the Continental, with a brand new six-cylinder 'Carrera 6' coupe driven by Herrmann/Linge and five 904's, two of which were factory-sponsored and driven by Mitter/Buzzetta and Klass/Schuetz.

Two of the Chevy-powered cars were outstanding, notably the new Chaparral 2-D (see last month's SCG), a coupe of much cleaner lines than the older cars, driven by Phil Hill/Bonnier and qualified second, only 0.2 second slower than the Miles/Ruby leading time of 1:57.8. Fastest qualifier of the GT vehicles was the Penske-entered Corvette 427, driven by Guldstrand/Moore/Wintersteen and qualified at 2:10.6.

It was a tremendously thrilling sight to see this fine field of cars parade around the banked track, but there were misgivings in some minds about cutting loose the pace car on the far side of the track, thereby giving the field only a scant half lap of sorting-out time before turning onto the infield. (Last year's race allowed a complete lap for this sorting-out to take place.) Fortunately all drivers put on a fine display of skill and intelligence, and the first turn was negotiated without any unpleasant incidents.

Bonnier jumped into first-lap lead, followed closely by Ken Miles. Miles tired of waiting around on the second lap and promptly blew by the Chaparral on the back straight, where the

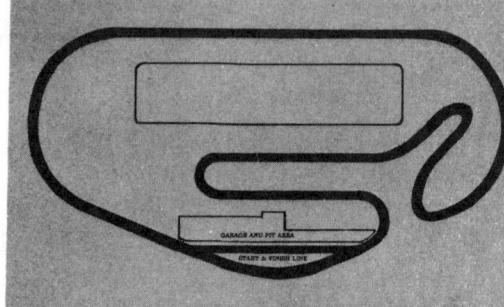

Sent out to play "rabbit" for the Ford team, Ken Miles, above, was able to hold an infallible pace once the Chaparral, lower right. was out of contention with unexpected ills. Winner in the GT category, top right, was the Penske-entered 427 Sting Ray, despite necessity of replacing radiator and repairing headlights as a result of two shunts. Center, the Carrera 6's debut was completely successful as, even with a slipping clutch, it stayed well up among the leaders throughout the entire 24-hour event.

Mk. II Fords were reportedly capable of 183 mph and the Chaparral some 12 mph slower. For the next 24 hours, the "Hawk" and his co-driver, Lloyd Ruby, would relinquish this lead only 15 more times in 678 go-arounds. In two laps, the pace was established and it was quick — only five seconds off best qualifying time. Bonnier shocked everyone — including Hall's crew — by pulling in on

DAYTONA CONTINENTAL 24-HOUR

the seventh lap and complaining of strange noises directly aft of his derriére. This was finally traced to fuel-slosh in the reserve tank that is actually built into the seat. Jo had never driven the car with the reserve in service, and he figured it best to find out early what malady was setting in. But it cost precious minutes and removed the immediate

Gurney leads the Ferraris of Rodriguez and Rindt through the tight, infield section of the Daytona course. It's not an impressive road circuit.
PHOTOS: JERRY TITUS AND JACK BRADY ASSOCIATES

The Maxwell/Martin Volvo and Vega/Byrne TR4 are lapped on the bank by Ireland's 250LM. Volvo finished 21st, the TR4 24th, but Ferrari DNF'd.

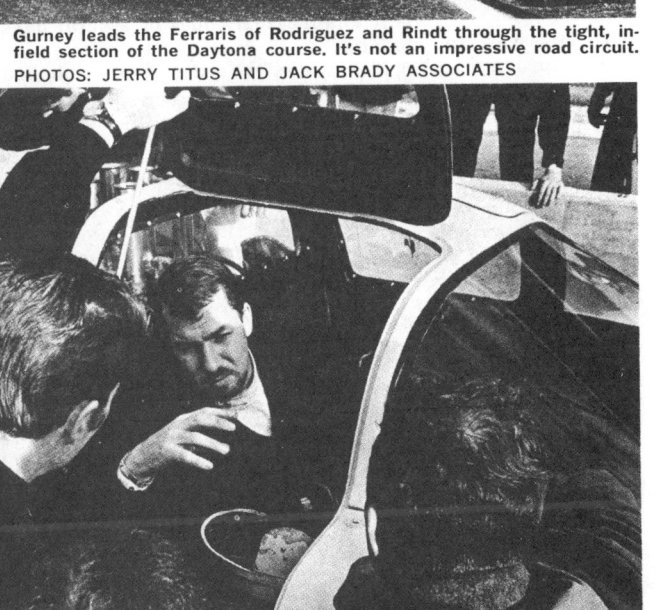
Bonnier tries to describe strange noise to Hall and Hill that caused him to pit on fifth lap. It turned out to be gas sloshing in the reserve tank.

Ford's two-speed automatic transaxle is huge as compared to Chaparral's but has to handle the torque of the 427-in. engine. Overheat put it out.

FIA suitcase compartments (two required now) were, as shown on this P2 Ferrari, located in the tail, behind wheels, on most prototypes.

DAYTONA

Chaparral threat from the leaders.

The Miles/Ruby car, fielded by Shelby, and the Hansgen/Donahue entry of Holman/Moody were obviously Ford's "rabbits," out to set as near a killing pace as they dared. Gurney and Grant in the other Shelby entry laid back a ways, holding a firm and confident pace. The two quickest Ferrari P2's — Rodriguez/Andretti and Bianchi/Langlois — were holding their own, but not bringing pressure on the leaders.

But the real break in the race came at 3:45 PM when the Chaparral pulled into the pits with steering trouble. After extensive investigation, the trouble was traced to a binding pinion gear and it was repaired as rapidly as possible. But the blow of losing almost exactly one hour so early in the race was a most serious one. Certainly, at this stage of the race, 25 laps were not impossible to catch up, but the fact remains that it put a great deal more of the burden of the chasing and catching on the backs of the Ferrari's.

Actually, the P2 Ferrari's did indeed put on a good show of pressuring the leaders, running strongly in places just off the pace during the first hours of the race. But the additional effort seemed to work adversely on some of their fellows, as the Wilson/Hulme, Dernier/Ickx and Ireland/Hailwood Ferrari's all went out with transmission failures before four hours had been run.

Meanwhile, Phil Hill had the Chaparral moving at beautiful speed and proceeded to rip off a bundle of laps around 2:01-2:02. But very shortly after five hours another minor but time-consuming problem struck in the form of a broken exhaust manifold. After it had been repaired the car was nearly an hour and a half back of the leaders, an almost insurmountable liability to overcome, even in a 24-hour race.

At six hours there were at least three Ferrari's which were motoring in contention, the P2's mentioned earlier and the Rindt/Bondurant 275 LM. But on Lap 171 the most serious blow to Ferrari hopes was suffered when the Bianchi/Langlois P2 was retired. Actually, Ferrari hopes rested primarily on the remaining P2, which at this point and throughout the race was driven smoothly and flawlessly by Pedro Rodriguez and Mario Andretti. This is particularly noteworthy in the light of the reputation that both have for being hard chargers. If either had really pushed too hard during this stage of the race, the car would surely have been eliminated. Instead, they both drove a smart race, and although the car was never placed higher than third, it was most definitely in contention.

One of the Ford Mk. II's was an experimental automatic transmission car, driven by Bucknum/Ginther in a most capable manner, but some several seconds a lap slower than the leading Fords. Ginther had to pit on the second lap. The emergency brake had been left partially on and this boiled the brake fluid. Shortly after midnight the car pitted with almost exactly the same exhaust malady the Chaparral had suffered earlier. Still more of a coincidence, both cars retired shortly after 300 laps, although with different ailments this time. The Ford went out with transmission difficulties, while the Chaparral suffered some sort of gradual upper A-arm failure which caused the right rear suspension to give way partially and send Bonnier looping through the infield. The car was officially retired some unlucky thirteen hours after race start.

In spite of the fact that the Chaparral had been out of any serious contention ever since its long stop for steering adjustment, it was a popular favorite with many spectators, and its actual retirement saddened them. Hill and Bonnier had given the car a whale of a drive even when it did not appear to have much of a winning chance, and consistently turned the fastest laps of the middle period of the race. During the twelfth hour Bonnier blasted it around the course to a new competition lap time of 115.8 mph, very close to the best qualification times of several days before.

Meanwhile, the same Fords that had

dominated the lead for so long were continuing to do just that; but in the early morning hours, Rodriguez began bettering his earlier lap times by two to four seconds, in an all-out attempt to pressure the leaders into some serious errors.

The leading Miles/Ruby car was in the admirable position of not even needing to adjust their lap times at all, since they were protected by a buffer zone of two other cars. So it was that the Fords of Hansgen/Donahue and Gurney/Grant took up the Rodriguez challenge with a vengeance. So much so, in fact, that Gurney broke not only the competition lap record, but the qualification one as well with a sizzling 116.5 mph.

Many more hours remained to be run, and quite a few heartbreaking retirements, coming after even longer hours of racing, were still forthcoming. The Guldstrand/Moore/Wintersteen 427 Corvette was nearly eliminated when it ran afoul of cars and wall late in the race, but it was able to remain in the race (sans most of its nose and requiring eventual radiator replacement) and win the GT class over the Roan/Coleman/Bencker Porsche 911. But the little Sebring Sprite which had moved up as high as 22nd place blew spectacularly with only about an hour to run, thereby eliminating the fine drives of Paul Richards and Ray Cuomo.

Long before dawn everyone was taking a long look at the Porsche contingent as a real threat. Herrmann and Linge had been circulating the 'Carrera 6' at a fantastic pace for an under-two-liter machine, and the Mitter/Buzzetta 904S was not far behind. Two sedans, a Barracuda and a Rambler Marlin, were trying to go the distance. The Barracuda was turning respectable lap times but the Marlin, looking for all the world like a pregnant skateboard, was a rolling course hazard. It finally lost a wheel and retired, but the wheel bounced off the Gurney/Grant Ford, giving Grant a few bad moments. The Barracuda went on to finish 36th overall.

Two Mustang GT350's were very much in the race, one running as high as 16th overall at one point, then dropping back to finish 26th. This was the Kearney/Reina entry. The other, driven by West and Macon, retired in the predawn hours. Yet the night had not taken the toll many had predicted. At six in the morning there were still 41 cars circulating, most of them fairly healthy.

Of major consequence in the outcome of the race was an anticipated brake-*disc* change on the leading Ford GT's. To improve wear, they were using an impacted copper/iron surface on the discs, and tests had shown this had a probable life of some 13 hours under maximum use. The discs had been modified to slip off the hubs — more or less quick-change — but still required that the calipers be unbolted. Holman-Moody made their change to the Hansgen/Donahue car just after daylight. The stop took approximately 15 minutes. At seven o'clock Miles pitted and the Shelby crew made the swap in under five minutes, taking the pressure completely off the leaders.

As far as the overall race outcome was concerned, little of consequence happened in the last six hours. When it became obvious to Rodriguez that his car would not be able to force three faster cars into anything unpleasant, he dropped his pace back to normal and held on to a sure Fourth.

The liveliest bit of business which transpired during the closing hours was that the Ford Mk. II's of Hansgen/Donahue and Gurney/Grant continued their remarkably close duel for second place. The Gurney/Grant car was part of the Shelby American operation and was running on Goodyear tires, while the Hansgen/Donahue car was Holman-Moody prepared and running on Firestone's. Hmmm, see the internal politics at work? Or, can you imagine what would happen if the two cars should engage in a big duel for Second which would force both to retire?

Well, gosh, actually the whole tempest subsided when, at the last pit stop, the Hansgen/Donahue car required at least as much time to get back on the course as the Gurney/Grant, and the minute and a half margin which separated them was just too much to shoot at. Oh, well, it would have been interesting.

So the three Ford cars took the first three places, followed by the P2 Ferrari and still another Ford. The really impressive part of the Ford operation was their tremendous durability. For example, three of last year's GT 40's suffered many problems, particularly the Essex Wire entries, both of which lost various cogs in their transmissions. But the new cars, the Mk. II's looked and sounded tremendously strong, and actually rivalled the Porsche's in this department, although the Porsche's ran like trains and placed their six-cylinder 'Carrera 6' in sixth place, and their 904's in the first four places in the Sports class.

Daytona being the first in the series of World's Manufacturer's Championship events, it must be examined to determine the potential of entries in the forthcoming Sebring and Le Mans endurance races. Obviously, the big inches of the Ford Mk. II's will make them the car to beat at Le Mans, with its long straights. But the Fords are heavy — reportedly 2300 pounds — and will be at a big disadvantage at Sebring, where the high-adhesion concrete and tight corners make for hellish braking rates, and the lighter Chaparral will have an initial acceleration as well as a stopping advantage. Enzo Ferrari will definitely have his more powerful P3's sorted out to run Le Mans, possibly at Sebring, and they may well be able to chase the Fords down the straights. The Daytona race was the maiden voyage for the 'Carrera 6.' It was completely successful and Porsche will undoubtedly have a strong contingent at both Sebring and Le Mans, chewing at the big fellows and waiting for them to sicken or break. So it's still anyone's fight. Daytona was an impressive first round, even though many top drivers felt that we need a second 24-hour race like we need World War III.

FORD GT40
continued from page 73

This should give her time to soak up all the 'bull' you give her about the equipment. The instruments she'll be able to see for herself, so just mention, as a throw-away line, "Of course, you'll have already noticed that it's got every instrument in the book," and concentrate on some of the other stuff. But don't make it too obvious — the subtle way is usually the most effective. Like:

"Do make yourself comfortable, Honey, and relax on that gentle cushion of air that's flowing through the perforated seat covers, and by all means adjust the outlet of the Aeroflow fresh-air system so that the volume, temperature and direction of the air is entirely to your liking. And if you tire of the view through the electrically heated windshield, by all means glance through the tinted glass of the side and rear windows if you find the color more restful," and all that jazz.

You might also mention that it's the special exhaust that makes it so easy to listen to the radio at high speed, or to converse in such a seductive voice, and that it's the 25-percent reduction in shock stiffness that's making for such a smooth ride... that and the softer brake pads. Let her play around with the heater-demister or air conditioning equipment, and tell her that even the engine's cooled by a thermostatically controlled fan (she won't understand, but it sounds good).

Tell her that she looks great against the black decor of the interior, and that your choice of exterior color from the 150 options offered to you, is so obviously 'hers.' By now, if you've been doing your job properly, she'll be in a 'Let's get away from it all' mood, and she'll be understanding when you say, with just a hint of apology, that the specially heat-resistant boxes astride the engine will only accommodate two medium-size suitcases, and that you're still awaiting the latest 'U' shaped box, which will carry three.

If she doesn't slide further down in her seat, and say, "We'll make do with two," turn the car 'round and head for home. It'll mean that either she's thumbed a lift under false pretenses, or else you've got no right to own a GT40 in the first place.

As I said, Mr. Wyer and his chums don't sell them to just anyone!

"We had to tamper with your design just a little, I'm afraid!"

Le Mans 24 hours

BY BROCK YATES

At four o'clock, somewhere out on the circuit, Ken Miles was the undisputed winner of the 24 Hours of Le Mans. At four hours plus two minutes, he had lost to Bruce McLaren and Chris Amon. Miles lost a race that would really have put him in the books because a few fellows from the Ford Motor Company couldn't resist driving home their point with a photo finish. The photo finish backfired and left everybody feeling sour and uneasy.

It was nearly perfect until the end. The Ford Motor Company's third annual assault on Le Mans was as classically executed as a von Clausewitz campaign until those final, rain-soaked moments when an otherwise flawless system broke down and left the race blighted with mysterious anti-climax and corporate confusion.

The difficulty began as the two protagonists, Ken Miles and Bruce McLaren, climbed into the cockpits of their Ford GT Mk. IIs to complete the final hour of the world's most prestigious road race. Miles, the superbly conditioned, 47-year-old test driver for Shelby American, took the wheel from his teammate, Denis Hulme, and headed for the finish with nearly 40 seconds' advantage over McLaren, who had in turn relieved fellow New Zealander Chris Amon. Though both cars were on the same lap, and had exchanged the lead several times during pit stops, the powder-blue Miles/Hulme car had commanded a major portion of the race ever since the team of Dan Gurney and Jerry Grant had retired after 18 hours of leadership. The pace had slackened radically—as it does near the end of all Le Mans races—and Miles was puttering around the eight-mile circuit in slightly over four minutes—30 seconds slower than he was capable of running. But McLaren was going faster, and a buzz of excitement passed through the bleary crowd along pit row. Within three laps McLaren had gobbled up Miles' lead and his car was cruising dead astern like a great black shark waiting for the kill. Only 15 cars were still circulating the giant track, and the long minutes when the main straight was empty and silent only heightened the tension.

"We were told to finish neck-and-neck," said Ken Miles following the race, "and that's what we did. If they'd let Bruce and me race for it, we wouldn't have had all this nonsense." Miles was a bitter man. He had obediently slowed down in a last-minute rain squall and permitted Bruce McLaren to pull alongside. Joining them was third-place

PHOTOGRAPHY: PETE BIRO

Le Mans 24 hours

Ken Miles and Denis Hulme, in a 7-liter Ford Mk. II (above), dominated the final six hours of the race, but were aced out by 24 feet. The Jo Siffert/Colin Davis Porsche Carrera 6 (below) led a fourth-through-seventh Porsche sweep.

Ronnie Bucknum—12 laps behind—and the three Fords splashed sedately across the finish line with Miles the apparent winner. He returned to his pit, picked up Hulme and proceeded toward the cluster of officials and dignitaries, fully confident that he had become the first man in history to win three major endurance races (Daytona, Sebring and Le Mans) in a single year.

Miles and Hulme were within a few paces of the victory bouquets held by race official Henry Ford II when the loudspeaker crackled with a "correction." Due to a recalculation by the scorers, the announcer said in French, McLaren and Amon had been declared the winners because their car had traveled the greater distance. The greater distance referred to was the 8-or-so meters (about 24 feet) farther down the starting grid from which the McLaren/Amon car had started the race. And therefore, according to mind-bending Gallic logic, they had traveled that much farther during the 24 hours than had Miles and Hulme. Additionally, McLaren had been clocked fractionally faster than Miles on the final lap—another factor in the insanely complicated, hair-splitting rules for deciding dead heats. The fact that Miles and Hulme had maintained a consistently higher position during the race and had qualified nearly a second faster was not relevant, and a diffident McLaren and Amon were herded onto the victory platform in place of their more deserving cohorts.

As at Sebring, when a last-lap breakdown had taken the victory away from Dan Gurney and Jerry Grant and handed it to Miles and Ruby, McLaren and Amon were far from jubilant over their good fortune. Being great competitors and highly conscientious men, clearly-established victories are important factors in their careers, and it was obvious that neither of them felt comfortable wreathed in garlands on that drizzly afternoon in Le Mans. But that was the way it was to be, according to the canon law of the Automobile Club de l'Ouest, and only one bald question remained—why had the Ford Motor Company permitted an otherwise perfectly maintained operation to degenerate at the conclusion of such an important race?

Apparently, the men responsible for Ford's assault on Le Mans had meticulously prepared for every eventuality except a tight finish. The

The Matra-BRMs easily outran the Porsches, but weren't as reliable. Above, a Matra leads the Phil Hill/Jo Bonnier Chaparral, which got to sixth before retiring with a dead battery.

The first overall 7-liter Ford Mk. II (below) was driven by Bruce McLaren and Chris Amon. Definitely uncomfortable in the winner's circle, their contractual obligations cost Ford a bundle.

Le Mans 24 hours

At 2 A.M., Carroll Shelby (above) had cars running 1-2-3; but there were still 14 dreary hours to go, and brake troubles were developing. The morning sun highlights the leading Gurney/Grant Ford Mk. II (right) which had been setting an incredible pace for 18 hours when it succumbed with a blown radiator gasket.

Le Mans 24 hours

A serious threat, the Ginther/Rodriguez Ferrari 330/P3 above went out during the night with a broken gearbox. Below, the Ford team: l. to r., Amon, McLaren, Roy Lunn Miles and Hulme, making smiles after race.

Ferrari threat had evaporated in the small hours of the night, with better than 12 hours to go. All the Fords were slowed down and ordered to maintain their relative positions. It all seemed neat and orderly—the Gurney/Grant car would win, followed by the Miles/Hulme and McLaren/Amon cars; a 1-2-3 finish for the Shelby American Fords. Even when Gurney's car retired with a blown gasket (a radiator hose had worked itself loose), Fords were still running 1-2-3 as the Bucknum/Hutcherson Holman-Moody-Stroppe entry moved into third. There wasn't much to do but keep the cars alive for the last six hours.

Then the Ford officials had the bright idea of arranging a dead heat. It seemed like a good idea at the time; Miles and McLaren would cross the finish line abreast of the Bucknum/Hutcherson car to make a pretty photo finish. During the last pit stops, each driver was told what to do and was sent on his way for the final slow laps. Only then did someone discover the odd rule: in a dead heat, the slower-qualifying car, having started farther down the line and thus having traveled a greater distance, would automatically be given first place.

It was at this point that the magnificent Ford organization fell apart. If Miles was signalled to stand on it, McLaren might get sore, might try to race him, and surely the photograph would be ruined. After flapping ineffectually for awhile, the Ford men lapsed into silence. No action was taken. McLaren caught up with Miles, and in a sudden burst of eagerness, even led him across the finish line by a car-length. Shelby was later to say wistfully; "I would have given fifty thousand dollars to have Ken win." All it would have taken was a pit signal.

Few people were aware of this situation. An American TV announcer babbled ignorant speculation, suggesting that no one connected with the race knew what was going on, until his adviser, Phil Hill, finally exploded, "Look, let's face it. They know *exactly* what's going on down there; *we're* the ones who are confused!"

Ironically, Kiwi teammates McLaren and Amon had contracts with British Petroleum and Firestone, but their car was shod with Goodyears (after starting the race on Firestone rain tires) and fueled by Shell. Ford had to buy up the BP contract, to the tune of over $40,000, and the Goodyear ads won't mention McLaren and Amon, only the fact that

LE MANS 24 HOURS

the race was won by a Ford on Goodyears (the second year in a row).

In any case, the finish of Ford's greatest victory was drowned in confusion, contradiction and ill-feelings, which in turn flawed a grand strategy that made Ford the deserving and obvious victors from the moment the race began.

Critics of Ford accused them of overwhelming the race by sheer weight of numbers, but the fact remains that only eight of the 13 Fords entered had top-level corporate help. They were, of course, the 220-mph 7-liter Mk. IIs, possibly the most costly and complicated racing cars in history. Thousands of miles of testing—most of it by Ken Miles—had proven every component over a 24-hour span, and there was no fear that the Le Mans program would degenerate into panicked, last-second bumbling as it had the year before. The corporation had split the responsibility for maintaining the cars between Shelby American and Holman-Moody-Stroppe, who were given three cars each, and British Alan Mann, who had two of the heavy (2685 lbs.) 470-hp coupes.

For awhile it appeared that Ford might be aced out of winning the race by a driver shortage, which would have added a final note of irony to their frustrating struggle for supremacy at Le Mans. First, old pro Walt Hansgen was killed during the April Le Mans trials, and his spot as co-driver with Mark Donahue in a Holman-Moody-Stroppe entry was filled by Australian Paul Hawkins. A.J. Foyt's place in another H-M-S car (with Ronnie Bucknum) was reluctantly accepted by stock car pro Dick Hutcherson after Foyt burned his hands at Milwaukee. Jack Sears retired rather suddenly and Frank Gardner was called up to share the driving with Sir John Whitmore on one of Alan Mann's machines. Probably the biggest blow to the Ford driving line-up occurred when Miles' Sebring and Daytona teammate, Lloyd Ruby, suffered a back injury in a light-plane crash several weeks before the race. His place in the Shelby American operation was quickly filled by Denis Hulme, though Alan Mann's search to find a co-driver for Graham Hill went on almost until race time. First Jackie Stewart was injured at Spa, and Mann appointed American Dick Thompson as a substitute. During practice Thompson was involved in a crash that also wrote off an independent American GT 40 (driven by Dick Holquist and M.R.J. Wylie) and he was disqualified as a result. The crash occurred at the exit of White House corner, at the head of the main straightaway, and Thompson drove to the pits and reported the incident to a marshal. The marshal said nothing and Thompson was thrown out for committing a "moral offense" by "failing to show proper concern for a driver in an accident." Ford's point was that the race organizers should be responsible for knowing about accidents and attending to the injured. The officials, who had tried to disqualify the car as well, made a deal, and Thompson was sacrificed to save one Ford. Thus, a search was undertaken for another driver experienced with big cars, one who could drive endurance races and who was not contracted to other manufacturers. This was harder than expected, and finally, after official practice was closed, Australian sedan driver Brian Muir was signed for the job. In a rare gesture of rule-bending for Americans, the officials opened the track on race morning so that Muir could take *one* familiarization lap.

Ford wasn't the only team with driver problems. The Ferrari effort was also gravely handicapped at Le Mans. After bluffing about not giving Le Mans his full attention, Enzo predictably appeared with a very strong team of three 4-liter 330/P3s, four modified 4.4-liter 365/P2s and three 2-liter Dinos—plus a quantity of slower, independent machinery that made the "weight of numbers" accusation against Ford seem a trifle silly (Ferrari actually had 14 cars to Ford's 13). Ferrari fortunes proceeded smoothly until three days before the race when star John Surtees suddenly quit, leaving Mike Parkes without a co-driver in the P3 coupe. Though SEFAC Ferrari representatives weren't saying much, it appeared that Surtees quit in a huff when the Ferrari management told him they were adding Lodovico Scarfiotti to share the driving with himself and Parkes. The rules specifically forbid a third driver, unless one of the two original starters is declared medically unfit to carry on, and the Ferrari people allegedly decided to say that Surtees was not in physical condition to run 24 hours. This led to a grand, arm-waving argument which ended with Surtees stalking out of the Ferrari pits and flying back home to England. Ferrari bounced back brilliantly—thanks mainly to the rock-steady 4-liter P3s. Although Dan Gurney's Ford turned in the best practice lap at a record-breaking 3:30.6 (Phil Hill ran a 3:33.0 in practice last year), the Ginther/Rodriguez 330/P3 was fifth fastest and highly competitive at 3:33.0. As an indication of the tremendous speeds being registered at Le Mans this year, all of the major contenders, including the three top Ferraris and the Chaparral, easily bettered Phil Hill's race lap record of 3:37.5 and Gurney finally lowered that mark (which is the official record) to 3:30.6, or 143 mph, during the early race's stages.

From the opening day of practice, the Chaparral 2D was the darling of the crowds. Whether it was its rather French-sounding name, or the fact that it was the only car capable of competing on even terms with the Ferraris and Fords, the white car, complete with its periscope air intake and its Texas license plate, brought cheers from the fans whenever it appeared on the track. A converted Chaparral 2, the coupe was derived from the same plastic hull that carried Hap Sharp to victory last year at Nassau, Riverside and Las Vegas. Powered by a 327

---

24 HEURES DU MANS
LE MANS, FRANCE, JUNE 18-19, 1966

Position	Drivers	Car	Class	Distance
1.	Bruce McLaren/Chris Amon	7.0 Ford Mk. II	SP	359 laps
2.	Ken Miles/Denis Hulme	7.0 Ford Mk. II	SP	359
3.	Ron Bucknum/Dick Hutcherson	7.0 Ford Mk. II	SP	347
4.	Jo Siffert/Colin Davis	2.0 Porsche Carrera 6	SP	338*
5.	Herbert Linge/Hans Herrmann	2.0 Porsche Carrera 6	SP	337
6.	Peter de Klerk/Udo Schütz	2.0 Porsche Carrera 6	SP	336
7.	Gunther Klass/Rolf Stommelen	2.0 Porsche Carrera 6	S	320
8.	Piers Courage/Roy Pike	3.3 Ferrari 275/GTB	GT	312
9.	Henri Grandsire/Leo Cella	1.3 Renault Alpine	SP	310
10.	Pierre Noblet/Leon Dernier	3.3 Ferrari 275/GTB	GT	309
11.	Robert de Lageneste/Jacques Chienisse	1.3 Renault Alpine	SP	306
12.	Guy Verrier/Robert Bouharde	1.3 Renault Alpine	SP	306
13.	Mauro Bianchi/Jean Vinatier	1.3 Renault Alpine	SP	305
14.	"Franc"/Jean Kerguen	2.0 Porsche 911	GT	283
15.	Jean-Louis Marnat/Claude Ballot-Lena	1.3 Mini-Marcos	SP	257

Race Distance: 3000.2 miles, **Average Speed:** 125.38 mph (new records)
Fastest Lap: Dan Gurney (7.0 Ford Mk. II) 3:30.6, 142.9 mph (new record)

cubic inch Chevrolet engine, the car weighed in at 1792 lbs.—which gave it a clear advantage in braking and acceleration over the heavier Fords and Ferraris, though it was appreciably slower on the straights.

Had it not been for a combination of poor planning and plain, dumb luck, the crowd's beloved Chaparral might have finished very high in the final standings. The team's problems began during a heavy rain squall that buffeted the track half-an-hour before the start. Because of the threatening weather, Firestone rain tires were fitted—a time-consuming operation on the Chaparral because the car has bolt-on wheels, rather than the more convenient knock-on variety. But no sooner had the change been made than the sun returned and Jo Bonnier was forced to run the opening stint of the race on the wrong rubber. It took nearly 10 minutes to remount the dry tires. It rained later, and the Chaparral lost more ground when a second switch was undertaken. To make matters worse, the leading Fords and Ferraris were blithely rolling through the wet and the dry on a new Goodyear "intermediate" compound that provides adequate roadholding and wear in all weather conditions—an ideal compromise for Le Mans' capricious climate.

As the flag dropped at four o'clock Saturday afternoon, Pennsylvanian Skip Scott was the first man across the track and he gunned his Essex Wire Ford GT 40 out of sight around the Dunlop bend with a substantial lead. But it was a different story on the long Mulsanne, where he was swallowed up by a determined herd of big Fords and Ferraris, and the leader on the first lap was Graham Hill in his gun-metal gray Alan Mann Mk. II. Bonnier was running fifth at the start and managed to stay within tactical striking distance of the leaders until his first pit stop.

Phil Hill's shifts at the wheel of the Chaparral gave the car its best moments at Le Mans. As night fell, the veteran cranked off steady 3:37 laps in an effort to regain the time lost changing tires. Slowly he struggled back into the top ten, finally reaching sixth place before a minor electrical failure put the Chaparral out of the race. A power drain, possibly from a faulty starter motor, ran the battery dead shortly before midnight and the Texans watched helplessly as the race officials thumbed the car off the track. According to the rules, a new battery may not be fitted, and push starts are not allowed, so an otherwise perfect Chaparral was rolled silently down the pit lane with the deafening cheers of the crowd following it through the gloom.

Dan Gurney and Jerry Grant were in firm command by this time after taking the lead on the second lap and never being seriously threatened thereafter. Ken Miles was running with his customary verve, having battled his way into second place after stopping on the first lap to latch his door. There had been some unexpected attrition among the Ford forces, beginning on the first lap when Paul Hawkins arrived at the Holman-Moody pit with a broken half-shaft. This was repaired, but a series of ailments, including the loss of the tail section on the Mulsanne straight and a growling differential, retired the car early. The Gardner/Whitmore car was out before nightfall with brake and clutch troubles, leaving six Fords to face three smooth-running Ferraris, led by the Ginther/Rodriguez P3, riding solidly in fourth.

Ferrari's bad luck had been restricted exclusively to the three Dinos, which were out of the race practically before the crowd had settled into their seats. This left the French Matra-BRMs a clear field in the under two-liter class because they were able to outrun the lighter but less-powerful Porsche Carrera 6s with ease. But outrunning the Porsches is one thing; outlasting them is quite another, and the beautifully disciplined factory team refused to be rattled by the quicker French cars and plowed teutonically ahead like ships in convoy. Through the night they went, lap on lap, hour on hour, waiting patiently for the Matras to break. The Matras obliged and the factory Porsches, led by the Jo Siffert/Colin Davis car, ran onward, robot-like, to finish fourth, fifth, sixth and seventh overall—a resounding Porsche victory.

Midnight brought a heavy drizzle from the black sky and frowning, silent Ford men paced the dimly-lit corridor behind the pits like expectant fathers in a hospital waiting room. The noise of the cars on one side, and the milling, rain-soaked carnival crowd on the other, was distant and muffled. "The Old Man is really runnin' in that rain," said Carroll Shelby with obvious concern. He was referring to Miles, whose pace seemed well within the limits of the car, but was faster than the strategy called for. During the entire race, the "Old Man"—whose driving becomes more masterful with each passing year—was given harshly-worded signals to slow down. Chris Amon came out of his pit to report quietly that his car was having brake troubles and the frowns grew deeper. This was not a new problem—other Fords were coming in with cracked discs, probably caused by over-cooling down the long straight followed by a searing heat build-up while braking for the Mulsanne corner. Jerry Grant, who had run only three laps of practice but was now lapping at the same speed as his partner, brought the unsettling news that he and Gurney were having trouble steering their car in the wet.

Then word came that the Mario Andretti/Lucien Bianchi Ford was out with a blown head gasket. Though not among the leaders, they had been circulating steadily in a back-up role and now there were only five Fords, including the one driven by Dick Hutcherson, who was getting his introduction to night racing at 200 mph over the rainy, fog-smattered Sarthe terrain. Graham Hill arrived in the Ford pit to tell how a front suspension upright on his car had broken, forcing him to abandon it out in the dark hinterlands of the track. Now there were only four Fords left and suddenly the nauseating prospect of defeat came over the Ford leadership. But there was nothing to do except stand there in that dank cavern, hollow-eyed and helpless, and listen to the cars roar past.

First it was a rumor. There had been a crash. A Ferrari was involved. Names were mentioned, but nobody knew until someone returned with the official word: Scarfiotti had piled into two smaller cars in the darkness and had destroyed his P3. He was bruised and shaken and would be alright, but most important to the Ford men, his car was out. Less than an hour later, the big race was over. The gearbox had broken on the Ginther/Rodriguez Ferrari—the same trouble that had retired the Masten Gregory/Bob Bondurant modified 365/P2 earlier—and now there was no one running with a prayer of threatening the Fords.

Morning light came with Gurney and Grant well on their way to victory, until cooling trouble ended their fine drive. That left Ken Miles and Bruce McLaren to act out their climactic drama and to send Ford away from Le Mans with the one checkered flag that they had sought with more determination, more poor luck, more frivolous waste, and more exhausting work by a small group of dedicated men than any other single project in the history of automobile racing. c/d

On the road with the FORD GT40

The shape of things that must come

HOW LOW?—The writer normally only permits photographs of himself doing something interesting, but he has permitted this one of himself " about to do something interesting," in order to show the low overall height of the Ford GT40. "D.S.J." is but 5ft. 2½in. tall, yet he dwarfs the 4.7-litre coupé Ford.

WHEN Eric Broadley's Lola coupé, with Ford V8 engine mounted amidships behind the cockpit, appeared at the 1963 Racing Car Show I was very excited, as were most people who saw it. The whole conception of the car looked so right, and I remember thinking how I would dearly like a ride in it some time, but did not contemplate driving it as it seemed way out beyond my capabilities. This was January, 1963, and now just under four years later I have been using a production version of this original prototype car on the road for a week as my normal motoring machine, temporarily replacing the 4.2-litre Jaguar E-type.

As is well known, the mighty Ford empire bought Broadley and the Lola coupé, set them up in a factory at Slough and developed that first car into a Ford GT as a racing car and started three years of serious motor racing, culminating in victory at Le Mans, apart from many other events. From the first factory in Slough developed "Ford Advanced Vehicles" who were in charge of the mid-engined coupé project, and as the racing versions progressed so did the idea of production versions to be sold to the public and used as road cars. The first racing coupés were very much Lola-Fords, but gradually the Ford engineers took over completely so that the name Lola could justifiably be dropped, and Broadley ended his contract and returned to Lola Cars to work on the design of sports cars. The mid-engined coupé gradually became completely Ford and was designated the GT40, but to Eric Broadley must go all the credit for the original conception and early development of what has become the most outstanding car of the day and very much a leader for the car of tomorrow. When I talk about "car" I mean the specialised competition or GT car, not bread-and-butter stuff for Mr. Everyman. At the end of 1965 the GT40 was well into production (hand-built) and chassis GT40P/1013 was finished off as a road car rather than a competition car. Mechanically the specification was not changed, nor was the shape, but there was a lot of attention to "home-comforts," such as interior trim, door pockets, radio, heaters, silencers, heavier flywheel and a less-fierce clutch. The 4.7-litre Ford engine was not tuned to such a high degree and the maximum speed was modestly quoted as 164 m.p.h. In racing trim and depending on axle ratio, tyre size and so on, these Ford coupés were capable of 190 m.p.h. down the Mulsanne straight at Le Mans, and given a long enough "run-in" they could probably touch 200 m.p.h. as a freak maximum. A quoted road maximum of 164 m.p.h. was not out of the way, and this would mean an easy 150-160 m.p.h. on a Motorway straight.

During 1966 the GT40 was produced in increasing numbers, all the chassis/body units for Le Mans emanating from F.A.V. at Slough, so that a proper production line of 6-8 cars at a time was set up. Having started at chassis GT40P/1001, the P denoting the finalised production series for homologation as Group 4 sports cars, a mixed array of cars to GT40P/1052 was completed by the end of the summer. I say mixed as some were to Group 4 specification and sold for racing, such as GT40P/1009 to Peter utcliffe, 1014 to Karl Richardson, 1021 to Nic Cussons and so on, others went to Shelby and Alan Mann as body/chassis units for building the 7-litre Mk. II cars for Le Mans, and some were built as road cars, such as 1033 to Switzerland, 1034 to Gloucestershire, 1043 to America and so on, altogether eight road versions being built. By the end of the year twenty more road versions, numbers 1053 to 1072, will be completed and shipped to Dearborn for customers in the U.S.A. These 72 cars are all in the production series, there having been numerous experimental and prototype cars built during 1965.

Car number GT40P/1013 was retained by Ford Advanced Vehicles of Slough as a "demonstrator" and it was this one that John Wyer and John Horsman kindly lent me for a week, with the advice "have fun." It does not need much imagination to appreciate that the GT40 is a very fast car, though how fast and how safe you cannot appreciate to the full until you have driven it, or been driven in it by a very competent driver. At the end of 1965 I had a few quiet laps of the Goodwood circuit at the wheel of a GT40 (actually GT40P/1008) owned by Ford of Dagenham, and was staggered at the ease with which it could be driven at the standard of a mediocre "club-driver." Everything on the car worked beautifully and efficiently and you felt you could do no wrong. After my few laps I got Sir John Whitmore to show me how it should really be driven and he set out to frighten me, not realising that providing I have confidence in the driver I have never yet been frightened in the passenger seat of a racing/sports car. He threw that GT40 about with all the Whitmore abandon that one used to associate with him on BMC-Mini racers. Not only were the road-clinging qualities of the GT40 outstanding, but its manners were impeccable when he overcooked it and we got all sideways, usually done deliberately by him.

As the GT40 has been developed various people have expressed strong opinions about it, one of these being Carroll Shelby, and I had long discussions with him about the GT40 concept as applied to an everyday GT car, he being of the opinion that it could never come about due to heat, noise, space and comfort. He was pushing the Shelby-Mustang and the Shelby-Cobra at the time, so was probably biased. Having been an avid Porsche fan for years, and enthusiast for the 904 and Carrera Six as the type of GT car that must come, I was all in favour of the GT40, with 350 b.h.p. amidships.

I have been using a 4.2-litre E-type Jaguar for all-round motoring for two years now, and consequently have become pretty used to speeds between 100 and 140 m.p.h. with acceleration to match, so when I left the E-type at Slough and set off in the Ford GT40 I did not feel I was moving into a new world, as far as performance was concerned, and no doubt Wyer and Horsman felt a lot happier than if my normal motoring was all done in a Viva or Anglia. My short trip at Goodwood had confirmed my ideas about the handling and performance of the GT40 so what I was really interested in now was its

87

ability to be used as a replacement for the E-type. I am not suggesting that either car is suitable for everyday motoring of the town-bred commuter, the parking enthusiast or the domestic man. I am fortunate in that practically all my motoring can be open-road type sports car motoring, so that considerations of number of seats, luggage space, tractability, parking ability, use by all members of the household and so forth do not enter into my life. One friend actually had the audacity to look at the Ford GT40 and say " What's it like for parking in London? " I told him I wouldn't want to take it to London, let alone park it there, and that I had it for motoring with a capital " M " not for parking (in fact this particular car is often driven in London by F.A.V. staff men on demonstration duties). Another friend who was taken for a " demo " said " not for me, but just what you want, as your motoring is competitive even if you are only going down to the village." Two more friends who were given rides, one making a journey of over 40 miles just for the opportunity, asked what were the snags. The only one I could think of at that moment was the limited luggage space, so I said that I could not even take a tooth-brush and pyjamas. Almost in unison they chorused " Who cares about sleeping in your clothes when you can motor in a car like that." I mention these examples in passing as they indicate the reaction of motoring enthusiasts to what must be the most outstanding car on the road today. Another friend who is a scientist/engineer accompanied me on a fairly long and fast cross country trip and was absolutely staggered at the smooth ride and ability of the wheels to stay on the ground not only over undulations and round bumpy corners, but over long brows at 120 m.p.h. or more and over short humps at half that speed. He knew all about the theories of low polar moments, central mass weight, seats at the C of G and so on, but had never had an opportunity to experience such things in practice. He smiled serenely in technical satisfaction. With an all-up weight of just under a ton, a power output of at least 335 b.h.p., the straight-line performance does not need measuring, it must be impressive. The outstanding thing about the GT40 is not " what it does " but the " way that it does it."

The seating position is very reclining, like a modern Grand Prix car, but so good is the visibility through the large raked screen with its pillars wrapped around the sides, that even in heavy traffic there are no problems. The windscreen pillars are cleverly placed so that the thickest part is on a radial line from the driver's eye, which means that he is presented with the smallest possible obstruction to his vision, unlike some family cars that suffer from the widest section of the windscreen pillar being transverse to the radial sight line. The nose of the car falls away in front of you, containing as does only the radiator, with thermostatically controlled fan, spare wheel, steering gear and bulkhead for the front wishbone suspension. Sitting in the car gives no impression of how low it is because of this superb visibility and you wonder why people stand and stare and drivers ahead look anxiously into their mirrors. The steering wheel is vertical and at arms' length so that you point the car rather than steer it, and there is more than enough room for the passenger, even when the driver boobs and gets a bit crossed-up! An inch or two from the steering wheel rim, on the right, is the very solid gearlever that controls the 5-speed ZF gearbox down at the very tail of the car. There is a purposeful wooden knob on the gearlever, with the letters GT on the top. Just above it is an " all-purpose " lever; up and down operates direction winkers, press and it blows the horns, move it left and it flashes the headlights, move it right (with the lights on) and it dips the headlights. There are all the usual instruments, including 8,000 r.p.m. indicator in front of the driver, and 200 m.p.h. (!) speedometer on the passenger side, while at each end of the instrument panel is a spherical air vent. Under the dash is a horizontal hand-brake looking suspiciously like a standard Anglia component. Between the seats is a padded bulkhead to keep the occupants apart under cornering forces and on this is an ashtray and a starter button.

Power comes from a pushrod 4.7-litre Ford V8 engine running on four double-choke downdraught Weber carburetters, with a Climax-type cross-over exhaust system feeding into a large silencer on top of the gearbox and with two large-diameter tail pipes sticking out of the tail like a pair of cannon. At tickover and low speeds the V8 engine sounds a bit like a tractor, but a touch of the accelerator pedal and the r.p.m. shoot up and everything goes smooth. For all normal purposes 5,000 r.p.m. in the gears was adequate, while 5,500 r.p.m. in top (25 m.p.h. per 1,000 r.p.m.) was reached on any old road. A short length of Motorway had 5,800 r.p.m. showing with acceleration showing no sign of tailing off. There was no opportunity (Monday traffic) to reach 6,000 in top gear, but at anything over 5,000 the engine was impressively smooth. There were a number of occasions to settle down to some cruising on undulating open roads at 5,500 in 5th gear and at this speed everything was working with the sort of smoothness that convinced me that the GT40 would do this all day without any strain. Ford quotes a maximum of 6,250 r.p.m. at which 335 b.h.p. is claimed.

I have a very short list of desirable gearboxes, this part of a car being one of my essentials for enjoyable motoring, and on this list are things like Porsche 911 and Alfa Romeo. At the top of the list is now the ZF box of the GT40. Reverse and first are on the left, first being back towards you, second and third are in the centre and fourth and fifth across to the right, the movement across the gate being infinitesimal. There is a very clever and foolproof interlock mechanism that only allows two segments of the " gate " to be open at any one time. Thanks to this you can push the lever across from 1st to 2nd, or 3rd to 4th with no possibility of getting the wrong gear. Similarly when changing down you pull the lever diagonally across towards you from 4th to 3rd with no fear of going into 1st for bottom gear is not available until the lever goes into second gear and opens the interlock. The only drawback to this system is that if you do a crash-stop in 5th you cannot snick the lever into 2nd or 1st for getting away again, you must go down through the sequence, 4th, 3rd, 2nd, 1st. The movement of the lever is so small that you get used to this

ADVANCED VEHICLE.—Outwardly the road-equipped Ford GT40 is identical to the competition version as regards shape, but Borrani wire wheels are fitted as standard. The air intake at the rear of the door feeds to an oil cooler, while the one above the rear wheel takes air to the carburetters. In spite of the lowness no problems as regards ground clearance were encountered.

UNUSUAL.—*From any angle the Ford GT40 is unusual and intriguing. This view shows to advantage the large wrap-round windscreen that affords such superb visibility. The two large ducts on the nose cowling allow the escape of hot air from the radiator, and the three N.A.C.A. ducts take cold air into the interior. The headlamps are behind transparent covers, while below them are passlights and winkers.*

manoeuvre and you can do it quicker than you can say it. With gearbox ratios of 2.42, 1.47, 1.09, 0.96 and 0.85 the speed of the change can be easily envisaged and all ratios are synchronised. There is one little peculiarity about the GT40 as far as gearchanging is concerned and that is when you are driving quietly about the place (which isn't often) and making leisurely changes with small throttle openings after each change. As the clutch bites there is the squeak of protesting tyres from behind you. The drive shafts to the independently sprung rear wheels, shod with 7.00 x 15 in. Goodyear tyres, have large rubber "doughnut" universal joints at their inboard end. As you accelerate, even gently, they "wind-up" and a leisurely gearchange allows them to "unwind" just as the clutch takes up again, so you get a split second of wheel-lock and the wide Goodyears give a little squeak of protest. Driving the GT40 in the way that is meant, and the way that it really enjoys, this does not occur, for the fast gearchange and wide throttle openings do not allow time for any "unwind" on the dough-nuts.

Acceleration, apart from sprint bikes and dragsters, now has a new meaning for me, for the GT40 is doing 100 m.p.h. before you can say Barbara Castle, and it feels constant right up to 150 m.p.h. I thought the E-type Jaguar had acceleration from 80-130 m.p.h. but I now have to alter my sense of values, and the handling of Ford makes it all so safe. Known local bends that the Jaguar can accelerate round in the upper 80s were taken easily at 120 and still accelerating. One of my prerequisites for high-speed motoring is to have enough reserve of horsepower and torque at 100 m.p.h. to be able to stamp on the accelerator and surge forward so that you are quickly past an impending change of road traffic conditions. I have put the Porsche 911 and 911S aside because they do not reach my requirements, as exemplified by the E-type, and I have felt the Jaguar to be adequate in this respect (here I am talking about a full day's motoring on the Autostrada from Turin to Naples, not a blind up the M1). The Ford makes the Jaguar seem dull and woolly, even in the 5th gear, while you can do this "urge at 100 m.p.h." test in 3rd or 4th if you want to, the estimated maxima being 127 and 142 m.p.h.

Getting this sort of performance is no great problem these days, but getting it as safely, smoothly and confidently as the Ford GT40 does is a new conception of motoring, and it makes you really appreciate the modern racing car, for in all mechanical respects, as regards ride, suspension control, cornering power, steering and braking this road equipped GT40 was identical to the Group 4 racing versions. When you drive it fast over winding undulating roads at speeds in excess of 110 m.p.h. the suspension and shock-absorbers are working superbly, the engine is smooth, the steering light and unbelievably accurate, so that it is easy to see why so many racing drivers have rushed to get on the Ford payroll, it was obviously not money alone that attracted them. The steering characteristics at all normal fast speeds is essentially neutral, but on high speed corners, with low cornering forces, over exuberance is scrubbed out by understeer and a very gentlemanly characteristic of the front running out a little wide. On slow corners with a high cornering force being generated the rear end will slide, but is instantly corrected by the high-geared steering. The wide track and low centre of gravity make noticeable roll non-existent and the car remains well balanced and well mannered at all extremes, as Whitmore demonstrated very ably at Goodwood last year.

Fuel is carried in two sidetanks that run under the door sills and contain Goodyear Fuel Cells and hold 20 gallons between them. They are filled by enormous quick action fillers on each side just by the screen pillars; the average pump attendant seemed very suspicious of squirting the tiny nozzle of his Gilbarco pump into the gaping orifice, as though afraid a hand was going to come up the filler neck and grab the nozzle. On a measured 10 gallons of Esso Golden the Ford did 137 miles (13.7 m.p.g.) driven hard, giving short sharp demonstration runs and on fast (a very relative term after a week with the GT40) open roads. I was not prepared to waste this week of glory on doing an economy run, but it would not be difficult to achieve 15 m.p.g. and still not be overtaken, while a single Carter or Holley carburetter would no doubt give 18-20 m.p.g. with E-type Jaguar performance.

During nearly 900 miles of ridiculously fast motoring I became so enamoured of the Ford driving position and road manners that I felt I was getting into a "vintage" car when I got back into the Jaguar. I have yet to find adjectives good enough to describe the way the GT40 motors about the place, and can only sum it up by saying that it is an entirely new conception of motoring. One that Grand Prix drivers and certain other racing drivers have known for some time in racing circles, but here it was in a usable road car. The mid-engine layout for a GT coupé is so obviously right from the performance, road holding and handling point of view, that it is now up to designers to think of ways of overcoming the little snags that come in its train when using the car for everyday motoring. With such a low roof line doors present a problem and though I was able to slide in and out easily, it is more difficult for the average-sized driver and almost impossible for the tall driver. Thinking on the lines of sliding or roll-top doors seems the obvious trend. Three-quarter rear vision is another problem, for those who worry about things behind them. At the moment this is overcome by sticking Les Leston-type "goody" mirrors on each side, but this seems too archaic for such an advanced vehicle as the GT40. Also the carrying of spare wheel in the nose should be a thing of the past and then you could use the space for luggage. Some form of inbuilt emergency castor or roller to get you to the next service station would seem suggested here. The great holes in the fibreglass body work for the fuel fillers, right on points of critical air-flow over the body must surely be a temporary measure, and the road dirt that is swirled up behind the car so that it covers the rear vertical surface, including the lamps and number plate, is such that improvements will have to be made if the police force are going to remain calm.

At the moment the GT40 is such an unknown quantity to the world at large that it generates respect and admiration at all times. It was truly amazing how often drivers in front would look in their mirrors and give a couple of flashes on the left-hand winker to say they were ready to be overtaken (a practice used widely on the Continent, and which I am pleased to see is gaining use over here). The E-type Jaguar, with its distinctive front aided by excellent publicity has instilled this sort of respect in the average motorist, but the GT40 made it almost embarrassing at times. To wave pedestrians over crossings, or drivers of ordinary cars in front of you at intersections, through the steeply-raked Ford windscreen was to generate confusion and incredulity. It was not so long ago that Cisitalia staggered the sporting world with their 1,100-c.c. coupé that was *only* 49 inches high. The 4,700-c.c. Ford GT40 is 40½ inches high. This, I feel, is progress, as is the fact that you can now travel the Mulsanne straight in a production GT car that would not be embarrassed by the traffic in Le Mans or Tours, at speeds in excess of the maximum of the Le Mans winning cars of 1952/53. After driving the GT40 about on the ordinary roads it is not difficult to visualise cruising the Mulsanne straight at 190 m.p.h. in a few years' time.

Some people have described the GT40 as a crude American monster doing everything by brute force and lacking the

CONTINUED ON PAGE 143

TECHNICAL ANALYSIS
PORTRAIT OF THE LE MANS WINNER

BY RON WAKEFIELD

PHOTOS BY SCOTT MALCOLM

There's a lot of cheer in the Ford racing organization, from Ford general manager Don Frey right on out to the errand boys in the three racing teams. After three years of trying, Ford became the first outfit to win the Le Mans 24-hr race with an American car. And win they did, in grand style with a 1-2-3, even if the finishing order of the three wasn't quite what Mr. Beebe had planned.

Why was the Ford performance so much better this year than in the two years past? Why did Ford campaign the big Mark II, rather than the lighter GT-40 with the 289 engine or the more advanced "J" car? Why a slow-turning 7-liter engine instead of a lighter, high-output unit such as the Indianapolis dohc engine? Or even the 7-liter single overhead cam?

Toward the end of 1964, Roy Lunn, Ford's chief design engineer on the GT project, began to have doubts about the development possibilities of the basic 4.7-liter GT-40. About that time Ford set up Kar Kraft—a wholly owned subsidiary intended to be small enough to get things done with dispatch appropriate to racing ways but close enough to the parent company to draw on its resources.

With Kar Kraft set up and Lunn its head, the first project of the small company was to design a new transmission. The original Colotti had been modified in 20 ways to cope with the relatively large 4.7 engine but its reliability was still marginal; Lunn felt it had to be replaced as transmission failures were still the most common difficulty.

Kar Kraft's next project was to chop up two GT-40 chassis to accommodate the hulking 7-liter Ford Galaxie engine.

Work on these two cars was started in March 1965 with no real thought of running them at Le Mans that year. But tire developments made decent handling possible and with the first running car Ken Miles lapped Ford's 5-mi oval track at Romeo, Mich., at 201 mph. Whereupon somebody up high said this is the car we are going to race!

If Ford people had been experienced at Le Mans, they wouldn't have tried it. They missed the April practice altogether with the 427 cars and actually finished building the second one at Le Mans just before the race, but nevertheless started both cars. What happened is well known now. Hasty preparation resulted in a gear that was intended for scrap being put into one gearbox and dirt on a bearing surface of the other gearbox, putting both the new KK transmissions out of commission. However, from the amount of development work that has been done since then, it seems unlikely that the cars would have finished anyway in 1965.

Lunn says he learned one big thing from the 1965 experience: that the big engine, loafing around at 6000 rpm, was the way to go.

The New Racing Approach

John Cowley, in charge of managing the racing effort from Dearborn, wisely realized the value of intramural competition. Thus he decided to put *three* racing teams on the job of preparing and racing the cars for the 1966 effort. He stayed at the helm of the operation, coordinating the three teams' work and feeding information back and forth so that

THE Ford-Ferrari / Ferrari-Ford DEAL

What happened when Ford sent Don Frey to Italy to negotiate the purchase of the Ferrari company

IT IS FAIRLY well known that in 1963 Ford Motor Co. set out to buy Ferrari. Until now, however, the details of the story, and even official confirmation of the negotiations, have remained obscure. Here's the story of what happened.

In January 1963, Henry Ford II and Lee Iacocca came up with the idea of buying the Ferrari company. What they had in mind, mainly, was to get into international racing—especially the GT variety. They reasoned rightly that if they wanted a quick start it meant buying brains, experience and facilities. And the best example of all these was Ferrari.

About the same time, word somehow got to Ford of Germany that Ferrari was interested in a merger with Ford. Probably it was one of those periods when Ferrari was short of money. But the important fact is that both parties were interested—and apparently independently so.

In April the Ford people made up their minds. Phil Paradise, head of Ford Italiano, was chosen to make the advance. He did this in May, approaching Mr. Ferrari with the ⟶

---

each team could benefit from the findings of the others. Previously the teams had gone their own way without much central supervision. Cowley and his two aides—Homer Perry and Chuck Folger, both development engineers—pulled the efforts together while still allowing the initiative and competitive spirits of the separate teams to motivate their work. These three men supervised most of the vehicle tests, which required a staggering amount of travel as tests were run at Daytona, Sebring, Kingman (Arizona, Ford's desert proving ground) and Riverside.

Besides the good coordination, bringing in the Holman-Moody outfit was a major factor in this year's organization. Cowley says that there was a bit of skepticism about a stock-car team's ability to do the job; but H-M certainly proved their own ability at it as well as putting Shelby American even more on its toes. Furthermore, at least one highly significant engineering development that came out of Holman-Moody.

In addition to the new team structure, there was simply greater experience throughout the Ford Dearborn group. By this time the Ford people had gained a good feel for racing. There was a Le Mans Committee, made up of top personnel from the participating divisions of the company—(Engine & Foundry, Transmission & Chassis, and Ford Division) meeting regularly to discuss mutual problems and courses of correction. It all added up to a properly concentrated operation focused on one thing—winning at Le Mans. A brief outline of the people, groups and their functions:

–Donald Frey: VP and general manager of Ford Division.
–Leo Beebe: public relations & promotion, director of racing activity.
–Le Mans Committee: coordinate entire Le Mans activity.
–Jack Passino: manager, Special Vehicles Activity (all GT cars).
–John Cowley: race manager.
–Kar Kraft: design and build original prototypes. Headed by Roy Lunn, with Chuck Mountain, Ed Hull and Bob Negstad on staff, and various "moonlighting" Ford engineers.
–Race teams: Shelby American, Holman-Moody, Alan Mann Racing, Ltd.—prepare, develop and race cars.

The Mark II and its Development

AFTER LE MANS 1965, Ford people were sure that they had in the Mark II (as all 7-liter GTs are called) a car fast enough to be competitive in 1966. If it could last.

The Mark II was basically the same car as the original GT, which had been conceived by Eric Broadley in 1962-63 and refined extensively by Lunn's team of designers. The 7-liter engine and various strengthening components required with it added several hundred pounds of weight; it had a longer nose to accommodate more radiator and ducting, and cast alloy wheels rather than the wire ones of the original GT-40s, now called the Mark I. Conventional in layout for a contemporary GT racing car—a midship engine driving the rear wheels, semi-monocoque chassis construction, short-and- ⟶

THE Ford-Ferrari / Ferrari-Ford DEAL

idea of forming two companies out of a merger:

FORD-FERRARI: With Ford as the majority stockholder, this company would build and sell the kind of luxurious sports and GT cars Ferrari was already building.

FERRARI-FORD: The racing company. Ferrari would be the majority stockholder and basically in control but Ford would want to make use of publicity and engineering developments from the racing activities. Also, Ford wanted the option to purchase Ferrari's equity in this company upon the Commendatore's death.

This arrangement seemed essentially satisfactory to both sides, so Ford sent over Donald Frey, Ford Division's general manager, with a team that included an assets-determination specialist, a manufacturing expert and two lawyers to begin the official negotiations. The talks began in mid-May.

Frey says that Mr. Ferrari was sincerely interested in making the deal. Frey stayed in Modena, driving out to Maranello each day to work on details with Ferrari. Ferrari himself rarely arrived before 10 AM and it was usually after lunch before anything was accomplished. Enzo Ferrari is one of those night people, with a late metabolism cycle. Thus work often continued until late at night.

There was little difficulty in agreeing on terms for the Ford-Ferrari part of the deal. Though Ferrari takes great pride in his passenger cars, he has always been closer to his racing. He demonstrated this by being relatively amenable about the passenger car business while having great reservations about the arrangements for the racing organization.

The negotiations got as far as even discussing the emblems to be used on the various cars. Ferrari would sketch out possibilities, with combinations of crests and prancing horses and/or the two names on them. Ferrari placed a figure of $16 million on what Ford would purchase, and at the time negotiations ended, the Ford group had arrived at a figure of $10 million. But there was room for bargaining on both sides.

Frey discussed details of possible racing activities with Ferrari. They talked at length about Indianapolis, and Ferrari surprised Frey somewhat by showing a lot of interest in the Indianapolis 500-mi race and even having a couple of engines he had designed with that race in mind.

But when the talk got down to brass tacks about the racing company—who ran what, who got the publicity and so on, Ferrari began to have doubts about the whole thing. For one thing, he wanted Ford to sever its relations with Shelby-American. Ford, on the other hand, felt an obligation to Shelby and this upset Ferrari. He felt, understandably, that there would be a serious conflict here. Another question from Ford, "What if we wanted to campaign GT cars at Le Mans, promoted by Ford?" brought a significant pause.

Ford's lack of interest in Formula 1 was also off-putting to Ferrari. This was during the time of the 1.5-liter formula, remember. Perhaps if the negotiations had taken place later—when the 3-liter formula was looming ahead—this might not have been a problem.

Why was Ferrari interested in merging with Ford? Frey says that Ferrari admired the elder Henry Ford greatly as a person and respected Ford as a company. He envisioned a happy combination of the large, reputable mass-market car builder combined with his own small-volume artistic approach. He was not interested, definitely, in adapting mass production methods to his passenger cars.

Don Frey recalls some amusing incidents during the ten days he spent in Italy at that time. One evening after a very late-starting day, dinner with Ferrari lasted until 1:00 AM. And for a Ford executive whose regular business day starts around 9:00 AM and winds up about 6:30 PM, this was going a bit far.

On another day, Ferrari drove Frey in one of his latest production models to a favorite inn up in the mountains near Maranello—*Il Gatto Verde,* the Green Cat—and on the way back gave a demonstration of the driving verve for which he's well known. He managed to hang the passenger's side out over the edges of the cliffs and to get Frey's side close enough to the solid walls that Don was more than a little impressed. But Frey was determined to be stoic and rode it out

FORD GT MARK II

long-arm independent suspension front and rear—it was unorthodox in but one area—the large, heavy, slow-turning V-8. Lunn and his people, but not necessarily all the racing teams, were convinced that the big engine was the way to go: it was relatively cheap, well proven (in NASCAR racing) and so related to production engines as to offer maximum advertising potential. There wasn't room, by the way, for the more bulky sohc 427. And a complete development program would have been necessary to make the Indy dohc engine suitable for a 24-hr race.

But with the big torquer came new problems. Most directly related were power transmission components, but most perplexing was the problem of stopping a 2800-lb plus machine

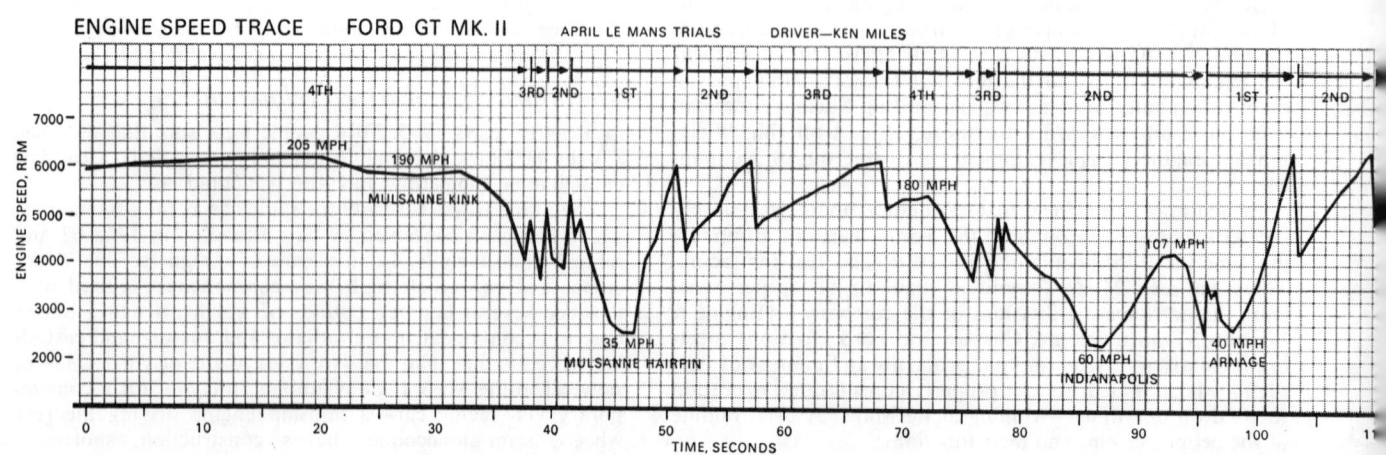

without a word. Frey also adds that Ferrari's driving was flawless.

Frey was impressed with Ferrari's warmth and volatility. Often described as tyrannical and unapproachable, Ferrari insisted throughout the talks that his loyal employees must be taken care of and was explicit in his proposed arrangements for members of his family.

The talks ended abruptly on Saturday morning after ten days of negotiations. Frey received a phone call from one of Ferrari's lawyers, informing him that there would be no further discussion and that there would be no deal. Disappointed but not really surprised, considering the difficulties the talks had brought to light, Frey and his team packed up.

In June of the same year, Frey journeyed to England where he made the arrangements with John Wyer and Eric Broadley that led to the formation of Ford Advanced Vehicles and subsequently the racing effort that finally led to victory at Le Mans. That's how it all began. —RW

Don Frey, for Ford   *Enzo Ferrari, for Ferrari*

(with driver) from 200 mph! The added weight meant harder pounding on suspension pieces at courses like Daytona. The long nose brought on new aerodynamic problems, in the form of poor rear end stability—witness the plethora of fins, tabs and the like on the 1965 Le Mans Mk IIs. However, now there was time to think, to test systematically, to do it right this time . . .

The development program went methodically forward.

A Year of Improvement

ENGINE: After it was apparent that the 7-liter pushrod engine was going to be used, Passino and Shelby asked for all possible weight reduction in the engine. Gus Scussel, engineer at Ford's E & F (Engine & Foundry Division) in charge of the project, achieved it with aluminum heads, an aluminum hub on the vibration damper and a water pump of the same light alloy. This comparison of engine weights is enlightening:

    7-liter, NASCAR version.....................602 lb
    7-liter, Le Mans version....................550 lb
    4.7-liter GT Mk I...........................432 lb
    4.2-liter Indianapolis......................428 lb
(all weights dry, less exhaust manifold, air cleaner, clutch)

The nice thing about using this engine, says Scussel, is that he knew at the outset that it had the durability to go 24 hours, providing the rpm range could be controlled. Thus all it needed was refinement, and to keep the speed range where he wanted it, Scussel issued a firm edict to all drivers that 6200 rpm was the limit. No exceptions, even though the engine had a safe limit of 7400 rpm for short-term use. To this end, each car's tach was accurately calibrated and a calibration chart taped in the driver's side door jamb.

Aluminum heads meant a small reduction in valve size from the NASCAR version: gauge diameter of intakes was reduced from 2.16 in. to 2.06, exhausts 1.70 to 1.625. Otherwise head design remained the same, but compression ratio was reduced from 12.5 to 10.5:1 because Le Mans fuel is only 101 octane (research method) vs. the 102.8 allowed in stock car racing. As far as octane requirement is concerned, the 10.5:1 aluminum head is about equivalent to a 10.0:1 iron head because it conducts heat faster. The regular "hi-riser" intake manifold was retained.

Aside from the aluminum heads, the most important change for GT use was a dry sump. This was completely redesigned this year by E & F and has two scavenge pumps driven by an internal chain from the crankshaft, replacing last year's one pump driven by an external, toothed belt. The pressure pump is gear driven from the camshaft and produces 65-70 psi at 6000 rpm. The oil cooler is a NASCAR item also; cooling is so effective that in cool weather it's necessary to blank off parts of it. Maximum oil temperature under any conditions encountered so far has been 250° F.

Tailoring the engine for the GT also included devising a suitable exhaust system, and carburetion. With the exhaust it was simply a matter of getting the required length of pipe for every cylinder and fitting the resulting bundle into the small space available. Not so simple, after all—there are many (trial and) error bundles lying around the buildup shops!

Somewhat surprisingly, the carburetion settled upon was a single 4-barrel Holley unit, rated at 780 cu ft/min flow. This

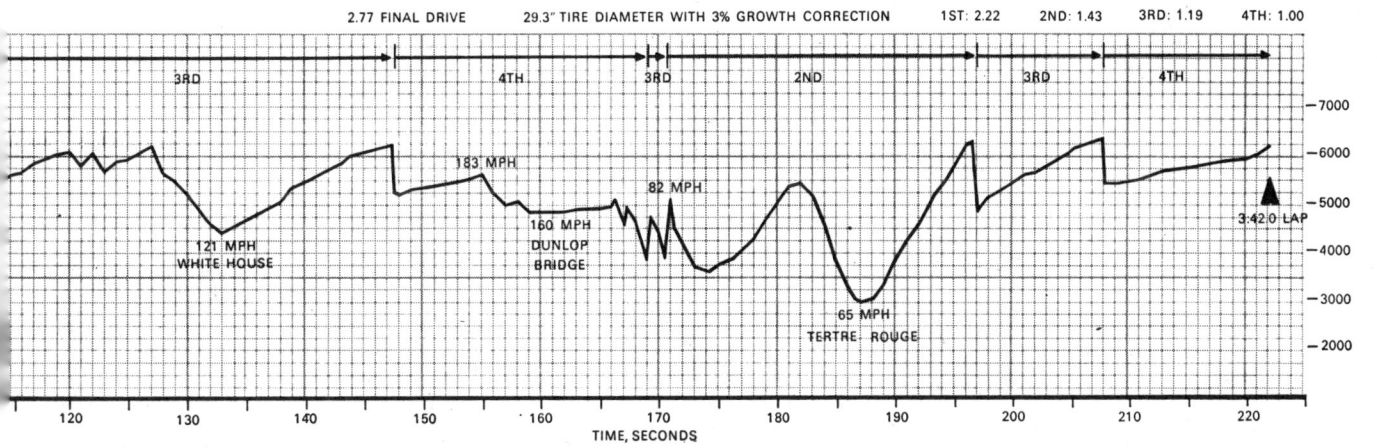

93

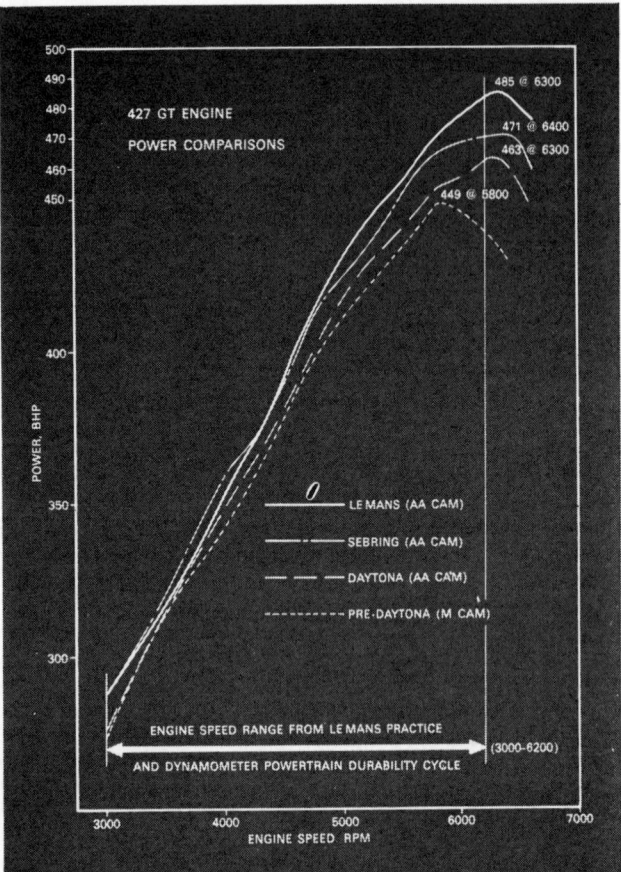

Four power curves for the GT 427 engine show the progress made up to Le Mans time by detail refining of engine.

The 427 GT engine, as installed in the Le Mans cars. Dry sump and exhaust bundle are most obvious features of GT version.

The Holley 4-barrel carburetor with its cam for secondaries.

FORD GT MARK II

looks odd among the multiple Webers of competing cars, but apparently does the job well. E&F wanted vacuum-operated secondary throttles opening, but Ken Miles won out and got mechanical opening. This is accomplished by a cam-and-rod arrangement designed for equal opening, primary and secondary.

Durability testing was thorough in the usual Ford way. Ford dynamometer facilities are extensive and comprehensive, able to accurately duplicate any driving pattern through computer-programmed changes of speed, load, and throttle opening. After preliminary test runs by drivers in an elaborately instrumented car (measuring and recording on an oscillograph such things as engine speed, manifold vacuum, rear wheel speed, throttle plate angle and axle shaft torque) it was comparatively simple for Ford dynamometer people to reproduce the track conditions on an engine test stand. The dynamometer cycle allowed 6800 rpm in 1st and 2nd gears, 6250 in 3rd and top, and was run for 48 hours—as compared to the 6200 limit for drivers and about 38 hours normally put on a given engine (4-hour break-in, 4-hr vehicle sort-out, 6-hr practice, 24-hr race). Thus at race time durability wasn't a question mark in any sense.

In its Le Mans form, the engine is anything but a high-output unit. At 485 bhp (the NASCAR version produces 520 bhp) it produces only 69 bhp/liter, far below the 100 bhp/liter now achieved almost routinely in high performance engines. It runs about 2000 rpm slower than competing engines and will pull smoothly from 1000 in top gear! It is inexpensive to boot, and it is a great achievement to have taken a basic sedan engine and won Le Mans. Complete specifications will be found in accompanying tables.

TRANSMISSION: Getting the tremendous torque of the 427 engine to the ground has been a real challenge for the Ford engineers. However, the problems have been solved and transmission failures are no longer a problem with Ford GTs. Kar Kraft conceived the present transaxle assembly; it is a light-alloy encased unit making maximum use of available heavy-duty Ford gears and shafts.

A Long 2-dry-plate clutch, each plate 10.0 in. in diameter, transmits torque to the input shaft of the gearbox; a production 4-speed synchronized gearset takes over from there, and finally a set of transfer gears takes the torque to the output shaft. It is the transfer gearset that is varied to give different final drive ratios: the differential ring gear and pinion are always the same at 3.09 (34/11). In the case of the Le Mans Mk II, the transfer gearset is 0.899:1 for a final drive ratio of 2.77:1. The four gearbox ratios are 2.22, 1.43, 1.19 and 1.00:1.

Kar Kraft is busy with automatic transmission design and development, now that the manual is working so well. There are two types currently under study. Both are 2-speed plus torque converter with manual shifting. The simpler of the two, lighter than the 4-speed manual, is similar to the Chaparral unit with a dog-clutch synchronized spur gear box. This type requires lifting the throttle foot for upshifts and ju-

Above, front cover assembly, exploded to show chain drive from crankshaft and gears for the two scavenge pumps. Below, front view of sump showing passages and scavenge pickups.

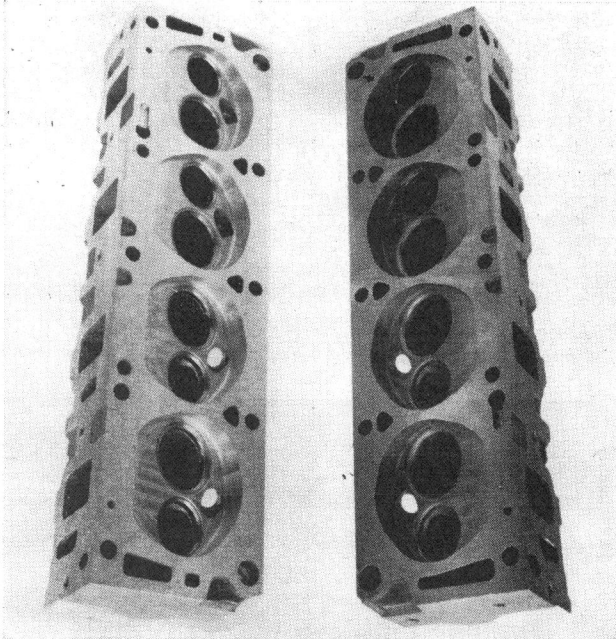

Left, GT aluminum head and right, Galaxie cast iron head.

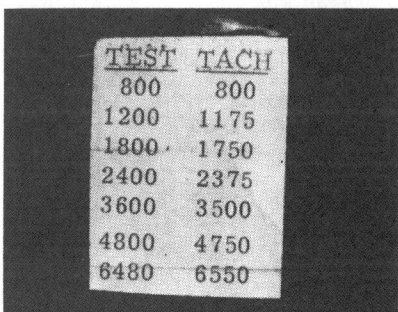

Drivers used tach calibration charts.

Transaxle has its own oil cooler.

dicious coordination for downshifts—allowing some room for error on the driver's part. The other is a "power-shift" type, which is bulkier and heavier but allows upshifting and downshifting under full power. Again, this is a constant-mesh spur gear box but is shifted hydraulically by oil pressure and disc clutches; the driver's lever operates valves only. It was this unit that was used in one car at Daytona (ran 14 hrs) and Sebring (finished). The torque converter in either transmission is from a Falcon Six, with strengthened vanes, has a stall speed of about 4200 rpm and a maximum multiplication of 1.9:1. For a race like Le Mans, first gear would be about 1.45:1 for an upshift speed of 135 mph. But neither of the automatic boxes is up to Lunn's expectations yet, and development work continues. He is hoping for a maximum power loss of 3-4%, rather low for a torque converter. The typical loss for a modern passenger car automatic, which includes a larger hydraulic circuit for automatic shifting of planetary gearsets, is about 8%.

CHASSIS & SUSPENSION: Changes to the chassis structure have been for convenience and strength. New jacking points at the rear are now the same as those at the front—made possible by the new body shape at the rear. Daytona tests produced cracks in engine mounts and in the structure around the front A-arm pivots, so gussets were added in appropriate places. A-arms up front were increased in diameter, and new front upright castings were designed with greater wall thickness and bearing area, and some internal ribs. The pivot point for the rear upper control arm is now supported at both ends instead of being cantilevered, and the control arm length now can be adjusted without removal. New wheels also resulted from the Daytona tests—they have heavily reinforced spiders. Modifications to date bring the chassis' torsional rigidity to 10,000 lb-ft/degree corrected to the usual 100-in. wheelbase. Most of this development work was carried out by Shelby American.

Roy Lunn says that Ford has stolen the lead in handling and aerodynamics—"If Chaparral and Ferrari had mastered these, we wouldn't have seen them, with their drastically better power/weight ratios!" Again, these achievements have been made possible by Ford's vast engineering resources. For instance, suspension geometry doesn't have to be plotted out on paper time after time until the desired combination is obtained; rather, the computer in effect does this work thousands of times faster than human beings can. Aerodynamics have been studied in the Ford wind tunnel, capable of 130 mph, and checked out on Ford proving grounds under 200-mph steady running. Impressive though Chaparral facilities are for a small outfit, they can't be equated with the vast resources of Ford even if GM help is coming in.

Rather than any revolutionary suspension improvement, then, we must say that suspension geometry of the Ford has been refined to the teeth by the fast trial-and-error of the computer, and as usual fine-tuned by the driver's seat-of-pants. Koni double-adjusting (separate adjustment for jounce and rebound) shocks replace the Armstrong units formerly used.

The original Ford GT as it emerged from Ford Styling in early 1964. Lines were clean and smooth but many lessons in aerodynamics loomed ahead. High front end was problem.

The first Mk II, with its greatly extended nose for the additional cooling the 427 engine requires. Cast wheels, air outlets and tail with spoiler were also new.

The latest Mk II, ready to race. New front end brought length back down; revised rear end has smoother taper, new scoops. Only roof scoops were added for Le Mans.

Instrument layout exhibits legibility, a bit of misspelling and a sense of humor.

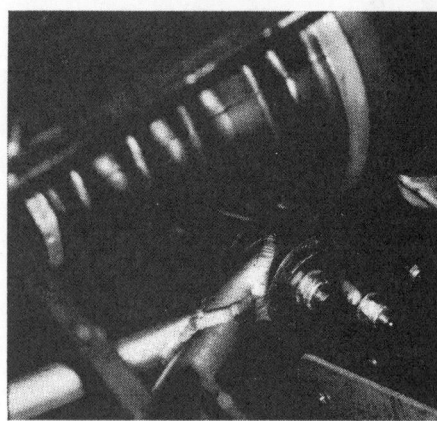
Rear support for lower rear A-arm is new; arm was formerly cantilevered from front side of pivot point.

High side scoops are split: upper part to carburetor, lower to brakes. Roof scoops for brakes were added at Sebring

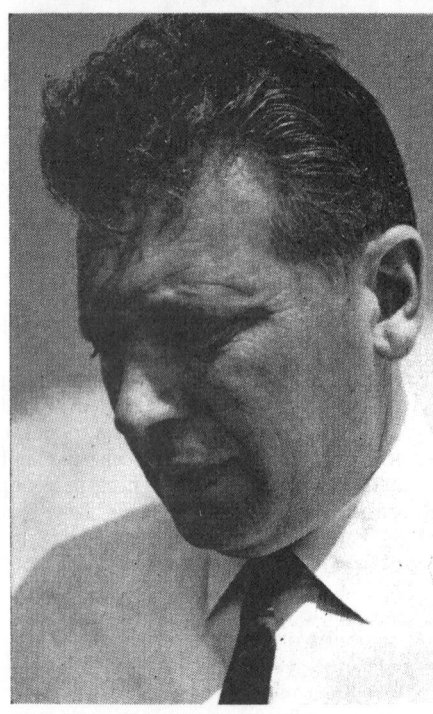
Phil Remington, Shelby's chief engineer.

FORD GT MARK II

Wheelbase remains the same as the Mk I at 95 in., tread is increased 1 in. to 57 at the front and remains 56 in. at the rear.

BRAKES: As noted before, brakes have been a sticky problem. Nobody at Ford or Shelby American will say that the brakes are adequate yet—but rather that the driver must be careful with them. Last year the radial-spoked rotors (vented discs) cracked regularly. Curved spokes this year have reduced failures somewhat but not completely, and metal coatings tried earlier failed to live up to expectations. With 653 sq in. of swept area, there is no room for larger discs or pads. What happens in use is that the rotors get tremendously hot during braking and then cool very rapidly as speed builds.

A Shelby-American mechanic prepares to mate the Kar Kraft transaxle to the engine of the winning car.

Phil Remington demonstrates the ease with which the brake discs are removed. Two bolts hold caliper in place, and wheel itself locates the disc's hat section axially.

FORD GT MARK II SPECIFICATIONS

ENGINE

No. cyl & type .... V8, ohv
Bore x stroke, mm ...... 108 x 96
   In .... 4.24 x 3.78
Displacement, cc/sq in ... 6997/427
Compression ratio 10.5:1
Bhp @ rpm .... 485 @ 6200
   Equivalent mph 205
Torque @ rpm, lb-ft .. 475 @ 4000
   Equivalent mph 128
Carburetors ...... 1 Holley 780 cfm
   No. barrels, dia ...... 4 x 1.688
Type fuel required .... premium
Lubrication system: dry sump; 1 pressure, 2 scavenge pumps
Ignition system .... transistor
Max spark advance 38° @ 4000 rpm
Alternator capacity, amp 52
Camshaft timing:
  Opening at 0.100 cam lift:
    Intake .... 8°30' ATC
    Exhaust .... 39°30' BBC
  Closing at 0.100 cam lift:
    Intake .... 36°30' ABC
    Exhaust .... 11°30' BTC
Camshaft drive .... silent chain

DRIVE TRAIN

Clutch type .... 2-dry plate (Long)
   Diameter, in 10.0
Transaxle: Ford T-44, designed by Kar Kraft, built by Ford T&C Div. Galaxie 4-speed gearset; transfer gears and T&C limited-slip differential; aluminum case.
Gear ratios: 4th (1.00) 2.77:1
   3rd (1.19) 3.30:1
   2nd (1.43) 3.96:1
   1st (2.22) 6.18:1
Synchromesh .... on all 4
Differential ratio 3.09:1
Transfer gear ratio 0.899:1

CHASSIS & SUSPENSION

Frame type: semi-monocoque, 0.024–0.049 sheet steel.
Brake type: vented disc, single caliper.
   Swept area, sq in 653
Tire size, front 9.75-15
   Rear 12.80-15
   Make .... Goodyear "A"
Steering type ...... rack & pinion
   Ratio 16.0:1
   Turns, lock-to-lock 2.25
   Turning circle, ft 34
Front suspension: independent with unequal length A-arms, coil springs, tube shocks, anti-roll bar.
Rear suspension: independent with trailing arms, unequal length lateral arms, coil springs, tube shocks, anti-roll bar.

ACCOMMODATION

Normal capacity, persons 1
   Occasional capacity 2
Seat width, in .... 2 x 15.5
Head room 37.0
Seat back adjustment, deg: variable to driver's preference.
Entrance height, in 39.0
Step-over height 15.6
Door width 33.0

GENERAL

Race weight, lb (tanks full) ... 2682
   With 150-lb driver 2832
Weight distribution (with driver), front/rear, % 38/62
Wheelbase, in 95.0
Track, front/rear 57.0/56.0
Overall length 163.0
   Width (over scoops) 70.0
   Height 40.5
Frontal area, sq ft 15.8
Ground clearance, in 3.9
Overhang, front/rear 39.0/29.0
Usable luggage space, cu ft 3.5
Fuel tank capacity, gal 42

INSTRUMENTATION

Instruments: 7000 rpm tachometer, oil temperature, oil pressure, water temperature, fuel pressure, ammeter, gearbox oil temperature.
Warning lights: differential oil pressure, engine oil pressure.

CALCULATED DATA

Lb/hp (race weight) 5.8
Mph/1000 rpm (4th gear) 31.5
Engine revs/mi (60 mph) 1905
Piston travel, ft/mi 1200
Rpm @ 2500 ft/min 3965
   Equivalent mph 127
Cu ft/ton mi 166
R&T wear index 21.0

SPEED IN GEARS

4th (6200), mph 205
3rd (6200) 170
2nd (6200) 140
1st (6200) 89

Because pad wear and rotor cracking were insoluble, at least for this year, it seemed that methods had to be found for replacing brake parts quickly. Two neat solutions along this line came forth from the racing teams. Shelby American head Phil Remington devised quick-change brake pad retainers which allow rapid removal and replacement of the pads. A remarkable new feature was conceived by John Holman of Holman-Moody during the year's development: quick-change discs! This is a first, and surely will start a trend. The disc hats are outboard of the hub flange and held in place by the wheel studs, the caliper and the wheel itself. Thus when the wheel is removed, and the caliper swung away (which requires only the loosening of two bolts), the disc may be snatched off and a new one slipped on in seconds. Design details and development work on this item were carried out by Ford and Shelby American engineers. Disc diameters

FORD GT MARK II

remain 11.6 in front and rear, and Girling BR single calipers are used at both ends of the car.

BODY: Only the midsection of the Mk I body remains the same in this year's Mk II. Front and rear sections are completely new and it is a tribute to their designers that absolutely no add-on tabs, fins or the like were needed this year. Only the adjustable spoiler at the rear was needed, and this was set at heights from 1.5 to 3 in. to suit different drivers.

The most striking body change is the front end. It is 9 in. shorter than last year's nose and is actually a "production" GT-40 nose with slightly higher fender humps for more wheel travel. Wind tunnel work, and Phil Remington's engineering intuition, said that the nose had to be as low as possible. And the shorter length gets the center of pressure back toward where it should be. The front end, therefore, is responsible for the lack of fins on the rear. It also saves 19 lb.

The rear end is higher, for clearance of the new vertical suitcase bins, by about 2 in. at its extremity. The wind tunnel

was used to develop new ducting for improved engine, transaxle and brake cooling, and the new duct disposition is thus:
- Side scoops—low, right side: transaxle
  - —low, left side: engine oil
  - —high, both sides, upper 2/3: carburetor
    lower 1/3: brakes
- Top deck scoops—added at Sebring: brakes

Louvers in the center of the rear deck direct air over the exhaust pipes and get that hot air out. The new tail weighs 37.5 lb vs 80 for the old one.

Other body improvements have been for convenience, such as a new access panel in the nose for getting at the spare tire and oil tank. Before, the whole nose had to be lifted.

Mark II Driving Impressions, by Ken Miles

"WHEN PROPERLY set up," Ken Miles says, "this is the easiest car in the world to drive. If not, it's awful—but then, this is typical of any really modern racing car. Small changes in chassis tune produce large changes in handling. The suspension is designed for a particular ride attitude; as speed goes up this attitude changes. We spent two days getting the car to handle right at Le Mans, found that the spoiler setting needed to be 2 in., not 1. Most critical thing is precise control of rear suspension geometry with 4-link arrangement used today—tires are still an area of much ignorance—even after arriving at basic suspension geometry with help of IBM, I have to get it adjusted on the track.

"It's a cooking engine. I can lug it down to 1000 rpm in 4th. When does it come 'on the cam'?—oh, about 3000 rpm! We babied them. The thing's safe for 7400 rpm, but we never exceeded 6200 in the race.

"It's a bloody oven inside! It takes a fair amount of physical effort to drive—steering is heavy—you brace yourself in banked turns so you can hold onto the controls. This is due largely to the fact that the car has been developed so far past its original state. The steering feeds back quite a lot, and I get big blisters...

"Cornering is pretty neutral, takes severe provocation to hang the tail out, and then it's only briefly. She really wants to stay put. I say neutral, but that's my car. Ron Bucknum likes a little noseplow, Lloyd Ruby wants the tail hanging out—we get three different patterns of tire wear.

"The gearbox is easy to shift after broken in and has completely unbeatable synchro. It could be lighter if it weren't built around Galaxie internals, has an extra shaft to bring drive back through.

"Brakes are high-effort. Can't possibly lock wheels. They are our Achilles heel; there's just not room for a brake big enough. Running 1650° F, there's too much variation in temperature—I planned my driving so only one disc change would be necessary. Unfortunately, one of the new discs was bad and I had to stop again. At the end of the race, this set was in good condition, ready for another go.

"The seating is very comfortable, yes. Hard to get into, but no aches at all after the race. For rear vision, pick the mirror glass off the floor and hold it in your hand. The wipers work well at high speeds, but the washer hardly works at all.

"Throttle linkage is very important. It must achieve two things: it must be smooth, and progressive—slow at first opening, getting faster. I have these qualities, but I don't like the suspended pedal. Not natural.

Riding with Ken, I found that indeed the Mk II is a flexible car. It isn't quiet, of course, but with the big noises going out the back it's not horrendous; the ride is about that of a street Cobra. There's a realization of great structural strength, but there are rattles all over. And it IS possible to lug from 1000 in 4th. Acceleration in the indirect gears, once past 3000 rpm, is simply indescribable.

Summary

THE FORD GT Mk II, though its beginning was in England, has evolved into a distinctly American car. Contrasted to its contemporaries, it compares with them just as an American sports car does with European ones—the big point of difference being that the American car has a relatively heavy, large-displacement and slow-revving engine with unsophisticated valve gear. For the first time it proved that this power concept can be fully competitive with the light, high-output European engines in a long distance race like Le Mans.

If Ford is to continue racing, and it appears fairly likely that the company will, it is the new "J" car that will be campaigned as the prototype car. It is the logical evolutionary step from the Mk II, but having been drawn up on a clean piece of tracing paper, with the 427 engine designed in, it embodies all the Ford people have learned in their three years' experience with the GTs.

Miles and Ruby drove an open car at Sebring that was a prototype for the J car: it had a single-sheet aluminum underbody, which wasn't quite satisfactory but which pointed the way toward using the honeycomb aluminum structure the J car now uses. As a result of the use of this material in bulkheads (as well as other new structural efficiencies) the weight of the J car's underbody is only 169 lb, versus 360 for the Mk II's single-sheet unitized steel underbody.

Back at Ford Dearborn, out there at Shelby American, over there at Alan Mann and down there at Holman-Moody, everybody has crossed fingers. At this writing it was budget time in Dearborn. We all hope the budget says "go".

BY PETER BONE

□ In making a street version of the highly successful Group 4 car, little has been done to disguise its racing origins. This became apparent as soon as we requested a place to stow a camera case during the journey out to Mosport Park. Paul Cooke, Comstock crew chief in charge of the car for FoMoCo while it was in the Toronto area, lifted the rear bodywork and there, nestling against the biggest muffler we have seen in many a year, were two large metal boxes. These, he informed me, were for luggage. Despite his claim that these were heat resistant, the whole area felt warm enough after only a few miles of city driving for us to decline to risk cooking the photo equipment, although they may be alright for the man with a fireproof toothbrush and asbestos pyjamas.

Happily, luggage accommodation is probably the last thing on the mind of the prospective GT40 customer, and in most other areas this is an exciting automobile. Just getting in is different for the seat pans are an integral and load-carrying part of the hull structure into which the hammock-style seating pads fit. This is non-adjustable but the back rake gives a semi-reclining position, and the padding comes high enough to act as a headrest. Buckled in with the shoulder and lap straps, there is not only comfort, but a tremendous feeling of security, despite being on a door handle level with most of the surrounding traffic. Head room isn't much, about 1½ inches for me (under six feet), so the tall man would just have to slide further down in the seat, hence the value of shoulder straps if the car is to be used on very bumpy roads. Both the pedals and wheel are adjustable to give a tailored driving position, and we feel that this style of seating arrangement will appear on production cars in the years to come.

Noise level in the cockpit is high, another legacy of the racing car, for the 289 CID, 335 hp V-8 sits directly behind the seat-cum-bulkhead and despite insulation and massive silencing equipment, makes itself known. On bumpy roads, the suspension thumps and bangs, while there is considerable tire noise on any surface, as there is no rubber cushioning in the system. Again, this sort of thing is unlikely to deter a prospective customer, although it is a little unnerving at first. We would note that the noise level is much the same at 100 mph as it is at 30, the aerodynamics of the car being such that wind noise is not evident at any speed. This, plus the sure-footed security of the car and its tremendous acceleration capabilities make speed judging a difficult task for the passenger, and it was astonishing how quickly it could be hustled over the rough back roads around Mosport.

Once at the track there was time to examine the mechanical aspects of the car. The basic structure is of .024 inch steel with wide section "pontoons" either side of the car providing much of the chassis stiffness, and doubling as gas tank space (15 Imperial gallons on either side in neoprene cells).

T&T FORD GT40 PERFORMANCE TEST

These pontoons are joined by the floor panels, and sturdy bulkheads front and rear of the cockpit, the rear one having the seat pans as part of the structure. The steel roof structure extends forward from the rear bulkhead, and although 90% is cut away for the door openings, is designed to take some of the body stresses. Sheet steel outriggers extending forward from the front bulkhead carry front suspension mountings, radiator and spare wheel, while similar extensions to the pontoons at the rear pick up a cross member behind the engine which carries the gear box mountings and pivot points for rear suspension. Bodywork front and rear is fibreglass, as are the doors, the rear moulding being hinged to swing up almost vertically to give access to engine, transmission and rear suspension. In the front there is a detachable cover over the spare wheel, which lies flat in a well behind the radiator.

The front suspension uses unequal length tubular A arms angled to provide anti-dive characteristics under braking. Adjustable spring/shock units are basically softer than those in the competition car as a concession to comfort. 11½" Girling discs mounted outboard next to the eight inch rim width Borrani wire wheels carrying 7.00 x 15 Firestones.

The transaxle unit is of ZF manufacture (the DS-25 model), with five all-synchromesh forward speeds, these being first, 2.42; second, 1.47; third, 1.09; fourth, 0.96 and fifth 085:1, with reverse ratio of 3.75:1 and a final drive ratio 4.22:1 (optional 3.33). Drive shafts are large diameter steel tubes with Hooke joints at the

PERFORMANCE TEST

outer ends, and Metalastik bonded rubber-to-metal universals inboard. A ZF limited slip unit is incorporated in the differential, and a Borg and Beck 8½ inch diameter two plate clutch is used, in contrast to the three-plate 7½ inch unit in the racing car.

The engine is a slightly detuned verison of the Shelby-modified 289 unit fitted to the competition car. Compression ratio is reduced from 10 to 9.1, and available bhp drops from 380 at 6,500 rpm to 335 at 6,250. The four 48 mm. Weber carburetors are retained, but hidden by a large pancake-type air cleaner. The tuned exhaust system, with separate pipes for each exhaust port, has the two small expansion boxes replaced, in the interests of legality, by an enormous muffler, which produces an interesting but not obtrusive sound.

Instrumentation is very complete, so much so that the interior resembles an aircraft more than a car, perhaps appropriate in view of the performance available. The instruments are all angled toward the driver, and are both visible and readable at all times. The large diameter tachometer is in front of the driver, redlined at 6,500 and flanked by oil pressure and water temperature gauges, while further inboard there are oil temperature, oil pressure, fuel pressure (supplied by two Stewart Warner electric fuel pumps), ammeter, and a large size speedometer near the centre of the car. Below the gauges are various colored lights, and a row of toggle switches which control such things as windshield heater (electric heating via a grid of fine wires built into the glass), rad fan (auxiliary electric fan for extra cooling at low speed), as well as lights, heater, etc. Horn, indicators and light dipping is controlled by a multi-position lever mounted on the steering column, similar to the Porsche fitment, and there are swivel air vents on the facia, plus a centrally-mounted outlet for the air conditioning system.

Resemblance to aircraft practices comes out in the starting procedure. No less than four steps to go though — switch on master switch (on rear bulkhead to right of driver), switch on fuel pumps, switch on ignition (both on facia), press starter (button on center armrest), and Vroom. When I tried it the first time, I only "vroomed" halfway around the circuit before the motor cut out again — I had forgotten step two, and the fuel was not getting through. The GT40 is still very much a racing car, and you have to work to drive it. At low speeds the steering is heavy, despite the 15 inch wheel (2.8 turns lock to lock), and it needs to be handled firmly at all times, though there is a little kickback. The clutch is heavy, has a short throw and is very definite, being either in or out, while the brakes are tremendous, but again require plenty of pressure as there is no servo-assistance. The accelerator is progressive and light, but the gearshift is the revelation, for the changes can be made with the fingertips, in fact, have to be because force on this progressive type linkage (a la motorcycle, one has to change up or down through all the gears, no short cuts) wrecks the box.

Despite detuning, the V-8 didn't give much apparent power under 3,500 rpm, but after that it really came on. Being conscious of limited experience with a very rare, expensive and powerful automobiles, I was conservative about shift points, keeping around 5,500 which still gave over 130 mph on the back straight. At these speeds the GT went exactly where it was pointed and would tuck in nicely on the corners with power on without getting twitchy. Paul demonstrated on some faster laps that it would stay in hand nearer the limit, albeit with more work from the driver. He was quick to point out having 25% less suspension stiffness than the racing version made life a little busier at those speeds. The softer suspension produced odd shimmying movement on some types of surface but without any effect on directional stability.

It is difficult to imagine where, in Canada, other than on the track, one could use this car to the full. At legal speeds on the highway, the car cruises in top gear at such low revs that it gives over 30 mpg, although the acceleration and braking capacity can be used to work through traffic very quickly, and to stay out of trouble. It is certainly not a car for the inexperienced, and it could be frustrating for the expert, yet maybe just the shape, the potential and the noise it makes doing anything are worth the money. Our hats are doffed to Mr. Ford. It takes courage as well as money to venture into such a specialized field and come out the winner, then make it into a road car. If only a little of the knowledge gained gets back to the passenger car divisions, there could be some exciting developments in that area before too long.

Easy victory

Ford Mk. IV driven by McLaren and Andretti victorious at Sebring

by Dennis Cipnic

The 2-litre Alfa-Romeo 33 in its first race with de Adamich at the wheel streaks away at the start to lead the entire field for the whole of the first lap.

DRIVING a brand new Ford Mk. IV prototype, Bruce McLaren and Mario Andretti won the 1967 Sebring 12-hour endurance race at a record average speed of 102.923 m.p.h. They were alternately chased and led by the winged 2F Chapparal for the first half of the race, but had the second six hours all to themselves and coasted home to an easy victory.

Sebring was different this year. Ferrari, determined to avoid the race, left the upholding of his marque to the North American Racing Team who, faced with a personal injury lawsuit and possible attachment of their cars if they showed up in Florida—all the result of last year's Ferrari-Porsche accident which took the lives of several spectators—decided not to show up.

This left Ferrari's hopes pinned on David Piper's P2, which ran third for several hours but finally dropped out with gearbox trouble. There were, in addition, four privately-entered Dino Ferraris, including one for Pedro Rodriguez and Dan Gurney who, up till now, has been a stalwart Ford driver. However, Gurney did not have a ride for the 12-Hour race, about which more presently, so he and Pedro decided to team up. But at the last minute the Ford Corporation, with whom Dan has a contract, turned thumbs down, whereupon Jean Guichet was flown over from Paris to replace him.

The Dinos proved no match for the Chapparals, Fords, or the pride of Porsches which Stuttgart sent over. There were two 910s and five 906s, plus a 904, three or four 911s and a four-year-old Carrera. The 910s and two 906s were official factory entries. Ford entered only two cars. The Mk. IV was the re-designed J-car, but with conventional transmission. They also entered a Mk. II, with A. J. Foyt and Lloyd Ruby driving. But that was all, which left many of Ford's regular drivers without rides. This is why Gurney decided to seek one with Rodriguez; he was reportedly very unhappy with the Ford decision to forbid it, because he is technically under contract to the Mercury Division, which had no entry at all at Sebring.

Chapparal brought the 2F, with Phil Hill, Mike Spence and Jim Hall listed as drivers, plus the 2D wingless '66 model, with Bob Johnson, Bruce Jennings and an un-named reserve driver. On the eve of the race Hill went down with appendicitis, whereupon Hall replaced him, and Hap Sharp filled the open reserve spot.

The most interesting news of Sebring was actually in two relatively overlooked cars—at least at first. Alfa Romeo sent two of their new Type 33 cars, bearing chassis numbers 004 and 005. Both had 1,996 c.c. V-8 engines, with four overhead camshafts on a 90° design. The frame is a magnesium alloy backbone, and in practice the Alfas instantly drew attention when one of them did well enough to place sixth for the start, ahead of all the other 2-litre cars except for one privately-entered Porsche 906.

Sebring starts *a la* Le Mans, and it is always possible for such a start to come up with a few surprises. This one was positively amazing. The Alfa got away first, followed by a thundering herd; a factory Porsche 910, driven by Hans Herrmann and Jo Siffert, got off several seconds late, and the 2F Chapparal stalled for almost half a minute, finally roaring off well behind the rest.

As the cars came around on lap one the Alfa led, followed by the Fords, several Porsches, the 2D Chapparal and, as the saying goes, many others: 58 others to be exact. The 2F was already 38th, and flying. With Mike Spence at the wheel the car literally tore through the pack, passing three and four competitors at a time, until at the end of the first hour he lay fourth, just behind Piper, who in turn was following the two Fords, with Andretti leading the way by over 30 seconds in the Mk. IV.

Once Piper had gone out the 2F chased the two Fords, and finally overtook the Mk. II model, but could never really pull free of it. This proved to be Hall's downfall. He replaced Spence after two hours plus a few minutes and found himself faced with a difficult situation. He had to chase the Mk. IV if he was to stay in contention, but at the same time he found himself hounded by the Mk. II, which was never more than a minute behind him. Spence had put the car in such a good position, and won the annual sportsman's trophy for doing so, but it was now up to Hall to keep it there.

This meant setting a tremendous pace (the three leaders broke the lap record 20 times in the next two hours), until, as the Fords pitted, the Chapparal finally took over the lead.

But not for long. The Fords came back and chased Hall extremely hard from a lap behind, with McLaren slowly gaining until, at last, Hall had to go into the pits for gas, whereupon both swept by to make it Ford 1-2. Well, Spence jumped into the car, tore off after them, cracked the lap record again and again, finally getting down to 2m. 49s., or 111 m.p.h. which was the same time set by McLaren to win the pole in practice. He got up to the same lap late in the afternoon, but then the pace began to tell. The trans-

The new Mk. IV Ford which Bruce McLaren and Mario Andretti drove to victory laps the Porsche 910 w...

Easy victory

mission case on the Chapparal was getting red hot due to friction overheating from the torque set up by the 427 cu. in. engine fitted for this race. It literally boiled the transmission fluid, cracked open the seals from the adjacent differential, melted the spare which sits just over it and finally cooked the entire back end of the car.

At almost the same moment the other Chapparal, which had been running quite well and was lying fourth, suffered electrical failure. This put the Hall combine completely out of it and, as is their usual practice, they immediately assumed grim faces and vanished into the gathering night.

Now it appeared certain that Ford would win, if only the two team cars did not get involved in a self-defeating intramural dice. So on every pit signal given to either of them for the next six hours there alternately appeared "EZ" or "SLOW". All they had to do was cruise around for the victory.

This put attention back to what was going on behind them, where, as it turned out, an even more interesting pursuit was taking place than the one put on by the Chapparals.

The Porsches were tearing up their opposition. Every Dino went out after suffering legions of difficulties, including, in a brief catalogue: a minor collision, stuck throttle cables, gearbox failure, radiator breaks, broken suspension, leaking gaskets, and much more until, by the sixth hour, only Rodriguez and Guichet were left, and they were far behind. Then, their car literally gave up the ghost. It just quit.

The Alfas had their share of troubles as well; one suffered electrical failure and the other suspension problems so that both of them were out by the halfway mark. This left the Porsches separated from the Ford prototypes by only the privately entered Ford GT40s, of which two were fighting very hard to stay where they were. One was driven by Dick Thompson and Ed Lowther. The other had two experts at distance-racing at the wheel; Nino Vaccarrella and Umberto Maglioli.

Both these cars contested the Porsche *putsch* for over seven hours until Thompson blew a head gasket and, in the 11th. hour, after a pitched battle which had lasted the entire race, the two 910s passed the Maglioli car. The Porsche prototypes had started 7th, 10th, 11th, 13th, 17th, 18th and 19th. They finished 3rd, 4th, 6th and 7th. Three retired. A Porsche 911S, starting 34th, finished 10th. Several Ford mechanics said that if Porsche ever decided to build a 4-litre car it would all be over for everyone else.

There was more than casual good reason for saying this, because after the race was over it was learned that the leading Porsche 910, running at 400 r.p.m. below its potential capability, had finished only eight seconds out of second place and 12 laps behind the winner after 1,237 miles of racing.

The 8-second gap was even more regrettable in view of the fact that, as Sebring's last big surprise, the second place Ford Mk. II, after cruising around for 11½ hours, came in to the pits, topped up its fuel and, upon restarting, suffered ignition failure. It never got started again but was counted a finisher in view of the fact that it had completed 90% of the race. Its final 8-second lead was purely mathematical, based on its calculated total distance covered compared with that of the Porsche.

Twelve hours is a very long time to race, and the fans are often lulled into a state of semi-somnabulance by the boredom. But not this time, and all because of BMC. The redoubtable BMC rally team—virtually unknown to US racing fans—entered a bored-out MGB of 2,004 c.c. for Hopkirk and Hedges, an MGB for Makinen, Rhodes and Baird, and a Sprite prototype for Aaltonen and Baker. They had started 32nd, 45th and 42nd respectively. Then began a demonstration of four-wheel slides, full reverse lock cornering, nose-to-tail driving, rapid fire pit work and incredible twisting, passing techniques rarely seen in road racing.

Despite much derision from more conventional drivers, and a good deal of hooting from the big car fans in the galleries, this technique worked. The big-bore MG finished 11th, and the MGB right behind it 12th (it was also the first overall GT car actually to finish the race. A Corvette not running at the very end was accounted as being ahead of it on the 90% rule). The Sprite came home 13th.

The new layout of the Sebring course proved to be of relatively little account in affecting the overall outcome, though it was apparent that the pace was faster and that small cars have gained a slight advantage. The new portion of the course covers about one third of the total distance of the 5.2-mile airport circuit and eliminates a tight S-turn known as "The Webster" in favour of a faster chicane. However, the slightly more open new turn enables small cars to manoeuvre it quicker than the big machinery which has to brake harder going round the bend.

...hich Mitter and Patrick finished third overall. The new nose and modified tail of the Mk. IV will be noted.

The 4-hour race

The second race of the meeting is usually a sort of thrown-in item; small GTs, sports cars, even Formula Juniors one year. This year, however, it was a 4-hour Trans-Am saloon race and was, from the point of view of American motor sport, even more important than the 12-hour.

The Trans-Am series has caught fire, and Sebring was its proof. There were 71 entries including three factory-sponsored Mercury Cougars (for Parnelli Jones, Dan Gurney and Ed Leslie), 9 Mustangs, 13 Camaros, several Chryslers, Porsches, Alfas, and just about everything else.

At the start Jerry leapt into the lead in his Mustang, closely pursued by Mark Donahue in Roger Penske's Camaro. The Cougars were running slightly behind them along with Dick Thompson in another Mustang. Both Gurney and Jones conked out just past the halfway mark, leaving the win to Titus, and second overall to Thompson, who had started late and made a great dash through the field to catch up. Donahue came in third.

Paddy Hopkirk and Andrew Hedges applied rally driving methods to bring the MGB GT home in 11th place overall and first in its class.

The Chaparral 2F storming out of a corner with wing tilted to apply downward thrust to the smoking rear tyres. Its prolonged battle with the Ford Mk. IV proved too much for the automatic transmission—but it made the fastest lap.

Provisional results

Florida 12-Hour Grand Prix of Endurance, Sebring. April 1, 1967. 1 M. Andretti/B. McLaren (Ford), 1,237.6 miles; **2** A. J. Foyt/L. Ruby (Ford); **3** G. Mitter/S. Patrick (Porsche); **4** H. Herrmann/J. Siffert (Porsche); **5** N. Vaccarella/Maglioli (Ford GT 40); **6** Spoerry/Steinemann (Porsche); **7** J. Buzzetta/P. Gregg (Porsche); **8** Grossman/McNamara (Ford GT 40); **9** Kirby/Johnson (Porsche); **10** Morgan/Guldstrand (Chevy); **11** P. Hopkirk/A. Hedges (MG); **12** T. Makinen/J. Rhodes/Baird (MG B); **13** R. Aaltonen/C. Baker (Austin Healey Sprite).

4-Hour Race. Overall Winner: Titus (Ford Mustang). **Class Winners. Over 2,000 c.c.:** as above. **Under 2,000 c.c.:** Gregg (Porsche). **1,300-1,600 c.c.:** Baker/Richards (Alfa Romeo). **1,000-1,300 c.c.:** Hopkirk/Rhodes (BMC Cooper S). **850-1,000 c.c.:** Consentino (Abarth). **600-850 c.c.:** Wolf (Saab).

CAR LIFE ROAD TEST

FORD GT-40 "SUPER/STREET"

Can a Long-Distance Champion Find Happiness in Everyday Life?

BY DENNIS CIPNIC

GT-40s ON THE street? Daytona, Sebring and Le Mans, maybe, but on the street? When Ford announced last July that some 100 Ford GT-40s were to be built for street use, for sale to private parties, the mind boggled. Could a blood brother to a championship racing car prove docile enough to be driven, without benefit of flags and turn markers, over the same surfaces as Pontiacs, Plymouths and, yes, lesser Fords? It seemed the exciting thing would be to do a touring road test on this most grand of all Grand Touring cars. Only one road car had crossed the Atlantic to the U.S. (delivered to its owner in Seattle by himself, Carroll Shelby), thus it was necessary (and a great lark) to seek GT-40 excitement in England, where GT-40s are assembled.

What better place? In England, the car could be driven over roads ranging from the crooked, narrow country byways of blind and breathless bends to straight, wide freeways, smooth uphill and down, at speeds approaching a gentle 120 mph.

Some may think American roads might have provided the same sort of test. This absolutely is not true. U.S. roads are too well made. There are no American primary highways that are 10 ft. wide, with 6-ft. tall hedgerows on either side, twisting like corkscrews. This type of roadway is the British concept of arterial highway. Fearfully often, on these roads, is encountered a 6-ft. wide Bentley charging rhinoceros-like in the opposite direction at a closing speed of 80 mph and at a distance of about 70 yards.

These conditions proved ideal to test

the controllability of the GT-40 "Super/Street"—if not the heartbeat rate of the driver.

Once the hard facts of performance are recorded, there comes a time when the tester must decide whether, in his opinion, the car handles well, offers an appearance fitting to its role, displays workmanship commensurate with its price and, all else considered, feels right.

Hence, before the start, the conclusion at the end of the test was that the Ford GT-40 in street trim, though it provides brilliant high speed capability and the thrill of ultimate controllability, *as it stands,* lacks the true cast of Gran Turismo—a vital qualification. Why?

First, the GT-40 is not an understated car. It appears as though it will go every bit of its rated true 164 mph. Owners probably never will get offers to drag for beers and every cop on duty will watch the car like a hawk. But, on the other hand, owners will have the satisfaction of knowing that, if necessary, they might be able to beat the highway patrol pursuit to the border.

This certain lack of subtlety extends to the car's outward configuration. It is only 40 in. high, and its doors curve upward into the roof, so that when open, they resemble escape hatches of a Gemini capsule. Every inch of the fiberglass body is as sleek as hand spray painting and polishing can make it. And Ford will paint it any of 150 colors.

THE ROAD car body is identical to that of the racing version. It is just over 14 ft. long and 2 in. under 6 ft. wide. It appears smaller, however. Not until an attempt is made to turn it around in a dead-end street does the rather wide 37-ft. turning circle become apparent. Because of the body's underhang in the front fender wells, it is not possible to use the full turning lock of the steering wheel without rubbing tires against fiberglass, so that 40 ft. would be more nearly correct. This is nearly as great a radius as that of a 17.5-ft. long Toronado.

But this is where the aforesaid *as it stands* qualification comes in for the first time. Ford is now changing the GT body's front panels to provide greater clearance for tight turns, as well as a more stylish "Cobra hump" to the upper fender lines. With these changes, the GT will be able to turn within the originally designed radius. A word of warning to potential purchasers: As far as is known, the GT-40 road car bodies now being made are all of the 40-ft. turning circle type.

Onward and inward, which is quite a trick; the driver must put on a GT-40 like a pair of swim trunks.

The gambit is to put the inside leg on the seat, crouch on the edge of the body, lift the other leg up, slide leg number one down and under the steering wheel while keeping one's toes cocked at a 110° angle to the ankle bone, support the body with the hands while cramming the other leg in, then lower one's self into the seat, remembering to duck as the door is closed or it'll shear off the top of the head.

For a woman it is impossible to get behind the wheel except in slacks, and,

DENNIS CIPNIC PHOTOS

RACE CAR, left, and street machine outwardly are almost indistinguishable one from the other. Giveaways are radio antenna and FORD trademark.

FRONT suspension is short and long A-arms, and ball joints.

FORD GT-40

as a passenger, difficult to enter or exit while wearing a skirt. This means that if the male owner travels with his mate she must have a place to carry her dresses. Well, there isn't one.

The road car has the same minimal FIA luggage space as the race car. Two small overnight cases, two pair of shoes and a folded plastic raincoat use up the entire trunk, which consists of two metal tubs, each measuring 13 x 10 x 15 in., mounted on either side of the gearbox at the very rear of the car. As long as the owner is willing to roll up everything he owns, he could conceivably carry a week's clothing. But if he has a $20,000 car, it is possible he (or his wife) may have some clothes which just aren't made to roll up.

So, ONE EITHER does his Grand Touring in Levis, or uses the car for going to the movies in town, which seems something of a waste, inasmuch as the car's 37-gal. fuel capacity provides a 450-mile cruising range. But here again there is a possibility of change. Ford Advanced Vehicles is toying with three ideas to make the car more GT-ish. They are:

1) Extend the engine compartment deck panel and lower the exhaust system, which now intrudes over the top rear of the engine, leaving more room on top for additional luggage space. The present baffled tube muffler, which uses up 35 bhp, is to be abandoned for a hopefully less wasteful system.

2) Extend the frame 16 in. just behind the seats, leaving the engine in its present position just forward of the rear wheels, and inserting two externally accessible wing doors to luggage space in the body behind the cockpit, thus providing additional sound insulation between the passengers and the engine, and, at the same time, enough luggage space to make the car quite amenable.

3) Extend the frame 2 ft. and put in a jump seat/luggage shelf and make an occasional 2+2 out of the car.

None of these ideas would be terribly expensive to initiate. The GT-40 is built up by hand from a semi-monocoque cockpit tub to which are welded forward and after frame members. Changing the rear frame components to provide for additional length would cost approximately $50 per car. New rear body panels would be necessary, at a master mold price of some $1200. It would then require a few additional man-hours to make the car, but this is what most of that $20,000 already is going for anyway. FAV is bound to undertake one of these ideas, but as yet has made no decision as to which.

The GT-40 enfolds the driver. The seats, which are ventilated leatherette, keep the back from perspiring and cradle the torso as would a G suit. They are excellent, and plans are to make them even better, with built-in headrests.

The steering wheel seems a bit small at first; it is the leather-covered racing

SEMI-RECLINING bucket seats, rigidly mounted to unit chassis, small steering wheel and gear change lever location are pure racing car.

REAR HUB-carrier is located by lower A-arm, single upper link.

SEMI-MONOCOQUE framework forward of the firewall mounts anchorage points for suspension, rack and pinion steering, and oil and coolant plumbing.

wheel, positioned to permit a clear view of the road and of the instruments. The gauges are laid out in aircraft fashion, all framed in leatherette (as is the entire dashboard) across the cockpit, with the tach in front of the driver and the speedometer at the far end, so that it is impossible to read one's speed without taking one's eyes off the road.

Not being able to see the speedometer may be fine for racing, but for a road car to be used in the speed-trapped U.S.A., putting it out of sight is inexcusable. The dash needs to be redesigned.

Another small error lies in the dashboard switchery. All switches are in a row, equally spaced, and look and feel exactly alike, which could (and did) lead to turning on the windshield wiper when what was wanted were the parking lights.

The GT-40 starts with a typical racing machine countdown. Key in and on, master switch on, electric fuel pumps on, then ignition. All are separate controls, and the ignition button is exposed on the front of the center seat divider where a stray knee or angled foot literally could cause havoc. A flip-top cover is to be put over it.

The engine starts with a growl. The de-tuned (from a racing 380 to a street 335 bhp) 289 Ford high-performance powerplant sounds as though it desires to go fast. And when it does over 3000 rpm in any gear, the car doesn't slip silently by the pub. The boys in the back room can hear the GT-40 coming four blocks away, though it is not so loud as to be completely illegal. Authority is audible.

The car literally will leap to 60 mph from a standing start before one can get to the next corner, and still in first gear, though this sort of maximum revving definitely is not recommended. One can cruise at 65 all day in second, pass at 100 in third, and never use fourth or fifth except as cruising overdrives.

The gearbox is the racing ZF progressive 5-speed. It takes a bit of practice to operate, but the progressive action makes fast shifts very positive. Reverse is on a lockout slot, and the gearshift is conveniently located on the outside front corner of the driver's seat where it can catch a trouser leg or render one a cripple.

This, too, is up for change. Ford is designing a crossover system to move the gearshift into the center of the cockpit. And there's muttering about an automatic, which, for road use in this car, probably would work very nicely.

E VEN THAT'S not the end of it. They're going to slip in a new engine. FAV's designers want to offer an optional 325-cu. in. engine with hydraulic tappets and either a 4-barrel Holley or fuel injection, both of which are in the works now. This, they say, will result in a much quieter, smoother machine.

If injectors are used, the cluster of carburetor intakes will disappear from the already too-small rear window so the driver can see what's coming up from behind. From the front, however, things are better. The nearest 4-in. high object visible from the driving position is 14 ft. away. That's better than anything else as fast, or as expensive as the GT-40 and, as far as

DISTANT SPEEDOMETER, left, proved difficult to read. Sameness of toggle switches led to mistakes. Entry to cockpit was training for modern dance.

THE SMALLEST of Ford assembly lines is in Slough, England, where GT-40s are painstakingly assembled by hand and to individual customer's taste.

can be determined, better than the front sightline of any American car.

If it rains, the driver is out of luck. The rear window clouds up, the front does likewise; the defroster doesn't help; and the single windshield wiper covers 80% of the driver's area and only about half the passenger's, leaving the entire right front (for U.S. left-hand drive cars) segment of the window un-wiped—a very large blind spot.

Better cockpit ventilation for slow speed situations would help. The GT-40's windows are for racing not Grand Touring. They don't open. There is a small plexiglass vent screen to shout instructions to the pit crew through, and that's it. And if the driver should want to open the door to get some air while parked, or to get out of the car, he must perform a semi-twist to do it. The door opener is located at the far rear of the panel, behind the person trying to open it.

The GT-40 starts to shine when it starts to move. It is a very easy car in which to go 40 mph over the speed limit without realizing it, because 100 actually seems as slow and easy as 60. It also stops very well, what with the racing rear calipers moved up forward and new double system calipers put on the rear wheels. They're fail-safe disc brakes.

THERE ARE NO wind noises to speak of, and the engine, especially in fifth gear, doesn't sound as loud in the cockpit as the engine sounds in some MG convertibles. The virtually neutral steering is quick. Factory supplied Goodyears hold a line, straight or curved, without wander or quaver, and at speed the forced air system adequately ventilates passenger and pilot spaces. The ride is "sporty," but quite smooth, and the Armstrong shock absorbers are adjustable to whatever degree of softness suits the owner.

The car will accelerate smoothly from 800 rpm in second, from 1000 in third and roar off into the sunset at

1966 FORD GT-40 "SUPER/STREET"

DIMENSIONS
- Wheelbase, in. 95.0
- Track, f/r, in. 54.0/54.0
- Overall length, in. 164.6
- width 70.0
- height 40.5
- Front seat hip room, in. .... 2 x 22
- shoulder room 48.0
- head room 36.0
- pedal-seatback, max. .... adj.
- Rear seat hip room, in. .....
- shoulder room ....
- leg room ....
- head room ....
- Door opening width, in. .... n.a.
- Floor to ground height, in. .. 40.0
- Ground clearance, in. 4.8

PRICES
- List, fob factory $17,120
- Equipped as tested 20,000
- Options included: Am/fm radio, nylon carpeting, foam soundproofing, padded dash, slow-speed fan.

CAPACITIES
- No. of passengers 2
- Luggage space, cu. ft. 2.3
- Fuel tank, gal. 37.0
- Crankcase, qt. 10.0
- Transmission/diff., pt. ...... n.a.
- Radiator coolant, qt. .... n.a.

CHASSIS/SUSPENSION
- Frame type: Stressed semi-monocoque.
- Front suspension type: Short and long A-arms, coil springs, telescopic shock absorbers, link anti-roll stabilizer.
  - ride rate at wheel, lb./in. ... n.a.
  - anti-roll bar dia., in. ...... n.a.
- Rear suspension type: Adjustable lower reverse A-arms, double trailing arms, single upper link, coil springs, telescopic shock absorbers.
  - ride rate at wheel, lb./in. .... n.a.
- Steering system: Rack and pinion.
  - gear ratio .... n.a.
  - overall ratio 14.0
  - turns, lock to lock 2.8
  - turning circle, ft. curb-curb ... 37.0
- Curb weight, lb. 2050
- Test weight 2230
- Weight distribution, % f/r ... 46/54

BRAKES
- Type: Dual line hydraulic, single caliper disc front, dual caliper rear.
- Front disc, dia. x width, in. .. 11.6 x n.a.
- Rear disc, dia. x width ..... 11.6 x n.a.
- total swept area, sq. in. .... n.a.
- Power assist .... none
- line psi @ 100 lb. pedal .... n.a.

WHEELS/TIRES
- Wheel size .... 6.50/15 x 6.50/8.00
- optional size available ... 15 x 9.00
- bolt no./circle dia., in. .... n.a.
- Tires: Goodyear Blue Streak
  - size 5.50-15/7.00-15
  - recommended inflation, psi ... n.a.
  - capacity rating, total lb. ... 3770

ENGINE
- Type, no. cyl. .... V-8, ohv
- Bore x stroke, in. ..... 4.005 x 2.870
- Displacement, cu. in. 289
- Compression ratio 9.1
- Rated bhp @ rpm .... 335 @ 6250
  - equivalent mph 75
- Rated torque @ rpm ..... 329 @ 3200
  - equivalent mph 75
- Carburetion ..... Weber 48 IDA, 4 x 2
  - barrel dia., pri./sec. 1.89/1.89
- Valve operation: Mechanical lifters, pushrods and adjustable rockers.
  - valve dia., int./exh. 1.78/1.45
  - lift, int./exh. .... n.a.
  - timing, deg. .... n.a.
  - duration, int./exh. .... n.a.
  - opening overlap .... n.a.
- Exhaust system: Headers, dual baffle-type mufflers.
  - pipe dia., exh./tail .... n.a.
- Lubrication pump type .... rotor
  - normal press. @ rpm. 50-60 @ 2000
- Electrical supply .... alternator
  - ampere rating .... n.a.
- Battery, plates/amp. rating .. n.a.

DRIVE-TRAIN
- Clutch type: Borg & Beck, 2 plate.
  - dia., in. 8.5
- Transmission type: ZF transaxle.
- Gear ratio 5th (0.85) overall ... 3.59
  - 4th (0.96) 4.05
  - 3rd (1.09) 4.60
  - 2nd (1.47) 6.20
  - 1st (2.42) 10.20
  - synchronous meshing? .... yes
- Shift lever location ... right side sill
- Differential type: ZF transaxle.
  - axle ratio 4.22

6000 rpm without protest. For those who shudder at such figures, or conversely, who desire even greater performance, Ford currently can provide any engine variation on the 289, from the stock Detroit unit to the full race Shelby engine, with Webers or 4-barrel NASCAR-type Holley carburetion. The latter is considered by FAV to be the better choice for a street car.

IF THERE'S one thing the GT isn't short on, it's customization. One may add air conditioning, stereo, am/fm radio, which is nicely mounted in a door panel, heated windshield or Dunlop R-7s in place of the Goodyears. Standard equipment includes nylon carpeting throughout, foam rubber soundproofing, completely padded dash, full shoulder harnesses, slow speed fan for the radiator, electric road horns, wide angle side mirrors, integral rollbar, windshield washer, heater/defroster, and a custom-fitted pedal bar which can be moved to any of five positions in a half-hour to give maximum comfort for various leg lengths.

There's only one thing not obtainable—a self-cancelling turn signal indicator, which is required by law in some parts of the U.S. On the GT-40 the turn signal lever is mounted at right angles to the steering wheel, flips up and down at an odd angle, must be manually re-set and is obviously an afterthought. But, as is everything else, it's being re-worked.

Even the nomenclature of the car is due for an overhaul. Because the GT-40 is a success—Daytona, Sebring and Le Mans—Ford's admen are seeking a name for it. In spite of the fact that the GT-40 is more of a race car than a GT car, then, it might be wise to purchase one now, before it becomes an "Osprey" or "Percheron," because, those who buy 'em now always will be able to say they have original GT-40s. Twenty years hence they'll each be worth $20,000 more than they are now. ■

AS SEEN at Daytona, Sebring and Le Mans, and even in its pre-finished state, the fiberglass nosepiece of the GT-40 appears most formidable.

CAR LIFE ROAD TEST

CALCULATED DATA	
Lb./bhp (test weight)	6.45
Cu. ft./ton mile	198
Mph/1000 rpm (high gear)	23.4
Engine revs/mile (60 mph)	2560
Piston travel, ft./mile	1220
Car Life wear index	31.3
Frontal area, sq. ft.	15.8
Box volume, cu. ft.	275.1

SPEEDOMETER ERROR	
30 mph, actual	
40 mph	
50 mph	
60 mph	
70 mph	
80 mph	
90 mph	

MAINTENANCE INTERVALS	
Oil change, engine, miles	3000
transmission/differential	3000
Oil filter change	3000
Air cleaner service, mo.	none
Chassis lubrication	3000
Wheelbearing re-packing	3000
Universal joint service	3000
Coolant change, mo.	12

TUNE-UP DATA	
Spark plugs	Autolite BF-32
gap, in.	0.032-0.036
Spark setting, deg./idle rpm.	12/1000
cent. max. adv., deg./rpm.	21.5/5000
vac. max. adv., deg./in. Hg.	22/17
Breaker gap, in.	0.018-0.022
cam dwell angle	32-35
arm tension, oz.	27-32
Tappet clear., int./exh.	0.016/0.018
Fuel pump pressure, psi.	n.a.
Radiator cap relief press., psi.	n.a.

PERFORMANCE	
Top speed (7000), mph	164
Shifts (rpm) @ mph	
4th to 5th (7000)	145
3rd to 4th (7000)	128
2nd to 3rd (7000)	95
1st to 2nd (7000)	58

ACCELERATION	
0-40 mph, sec.	3.3
0-50 mph	4.3
0-60 mph	5.3
0-70 mph	6.6
0-80 mph	7.9
0-90 mph	9.7
0-100 mph	11.8
0-120 mph	17.4
Standing ¼-mile, sec.	14.2
speed at end, mph	110
Passing, 30-70 mph, sec.	4.1

BRAKING	
(Maximum deceleration rate achieved from 80 mph)	
1st stop, ft./sec./sec.	
fade evident?	
2nd stop, ft./sec./sec.	
fade evident?	

FUEL CONSUMPTION	
Test conditions, mpg	13.6
Est. normal range, mpg	12-16
Cruising range, miles	444-593

GRADABILITY	
4th, % grade @ mph	
3rd	
2nd	
1st	

DRAG FACTOR	
Total drag @ 60 mph, lb.	

ACCELERATION & COASTING

CAR and DRIVER ROAD TEST

FORD MARK III

The workmanship and most of the hardware in this, the most costly Ford of all, are miserably below the standards of the meanest Falcon.

PHOTOGRAPHY: JOHN HEARST

In theory, the Ford Mk. III should be the world's most desirable enthusiast's car. In theory, the Mk. III is a streetworthy replica of Ford's GT 40—derivatives of which have won Le Mans and the World Sports Car Manufacturers Championship. In theory, this $18,500 car ought to be worth $1500 less than twenty thousand bucks.

In practice, those theories come apart at the seams—like the Mk. III we tested, which was barely 2600 miles old.

To be fair, Ford's representatives assured us that our test car was one of the first Mk. IIIs built and that all our objections would be stilled when the Mk. III program gets rolling. We certainly hope so.

But the fact remains that the workmanship and most of the hardware in this, the most costly Ford of all, are miserably below the standards of the meanest Falcon.

Most of what's wrong with the Mk. III happened in the translation from racer to street machine. We've driven the original GT 40 (*C/D*, November '65) and the big Mk. II (*C/D*, April '67), and we loved them both. The Mk. III is like a wholly different car.

In the first place, it's about as reliable as a two-dollar watch. The electrical system was out to lunch half the time. One driving light didn't work, a parking light had fallen out, the brake-system warning light glowed ominously all the time (the Ford people swore the brakes were okay), and everything except the ignition circuit would cut out at unpredictable moments—then mysteriously cure itself. A control stalk seemed to be connected to the high voltage side of the coil, zapping anybody who tried to use the horn. The shoulder harness inertia reels didn't work, leaving the interior cluttered with yards of useless safety belting. The right-hand door kept flying open. The seat upholstery was coming unglued. The windshield adhesive was smeared all over the dashboard. The transmission and clutch linkages were hope-

> Prior experience with GT 40s and Mk. IIs had prepared us to be enthralled with the street version, but as we got to know the Mk. III...

lessly fouled up. The fuel tank changeover tap was stuck, leaving us with only half of the fuel supply —which, at seven miles per, didn't last very long.

All these are simple quality control problems—and simply unpardonable. At least *we* wouldn't be in a very forgiving mood if we'd just shelled out $18,500 for the car, would *you*?

There are also several design flaws, most of them easily rectified, but we couldn't help wondering why no one had given them much thought before. As a typical example, the fuel line passes so close to the hot engine that vapor lock is never more than a few degrees away. Or: there's so much padding on the floor that the already scarce foot room is even more restricted. And the padding is inadequately secured to the floor, so that it gets all wadded up under the pedals. Enough?

Economy measures are rampant, despite the fact that the Mk. III costs some $2000 more than the GT 40 race cars. The Mk. III's seats are modified British Restall units that retail for about $60, are miserably uncomfortable for anyone much over five-ten, and adjust fore and aft only with considerable difficulty. In the race cars, the seats—marvelously comfortable—are fixed, and the pedals are moveable. The Mk. III's seats contribute nothing; their only virtue is that they're obviously cheaper than the race car's assembly. Many of the other proprietary components are low-cost bits and pieces from British economy sedans, and seem decidedly second-rate when applied to a hyper-expensive Grand Touring machine like this.

Our prior experience with GT 40s and Mk. IIs had prepared us to be enthralled with the street version, but as we got to know the Mk. III, and more and more imperfections reared their shoddy heads, our esteem plummeted. Yet, somehow, the car that the Mk. III was intended to be still shone through and thrilled us. Underneath, it's still a thoroughbred.

The Mk. III is built by J.W. Automotive Engineering, Ltd. The initials stand for ex-team manager (for Ford and Aston Martin) John Wyer, and Ford distributor (in England) John Willment. J.W. Automotive Engineering took over the now-defunct Ford Advanced Vehicles facility at Slough, and sells completed Mk. IIIs to Ford, as well as doing sub-contract work on the racing

... and more and more imperfections reared their shoddy heads, our esteem plummeted. Yet somehow, the car that the Mk. III was intended to be shone through and thrilled us. Underneath, it's still a thoroughbred.

A basically intelligent interior is spoiled by poor seats and hardware.

A quad lighting system replaces the race car's square Cibie units.

Carburetor air is drawn into plenum chamber under the rear window.

cars. The GT 40s and Mk. IIIs are distributed in this country by Carroll Shelby's organization. The Mk. IIIs are sold through Ford High-Performance Dealers, like New York's Gotham Ford, which, through Gotham's Bill Kolb, Jr., is where we borrowed our test car.

There are few basic differences between the race cars and the Mk. III. The sheet steel body/chassis center hull-section is retained, although the spaces between double-skinned sections are filled with a polyurethane foam that absorbs noise, heat, and—for safety—energy. In the race cars, the side pontoons that comprise the main structural members of the chassis are filled with two 18.5-gallon rubber fuel bladders. In the Mk. IIIs, a pair of smaller, 13.8-gallon baffled aluminum tanks are surrounded with a two-inch-thick layer of polyurethane foam to lessen fire hazard in case of a crash.

The front and rear body sections are fiberglass, and are of remarkably good quality. The nose has been restyled to move the headlights up to legal height for street use and to allow the use of sealed beams instead of the generally illegal (in the U.S.) square Cibie headlights. The sealed beams are paired with a set of Marchal driving lights and set under plexiglass fairings, both also illegal in several states. The rear section has been lengthened eight inches to provide a very small (six cubic feet) luggage "locker" over the transaxle and muffler system. The small, lockable front compartment is completely filled by the spare tire. The altered body shape results in a steeper approach angle, but a flatter departure angle, and the tail scrapes on the ground at fairly mild changes of road angle.

The Mk. III's engine is the same high-performance, 306-horsepower, 289 cu. in. V-8 installed in the Shelby American GT 350s (complete with exhaust emission control), not the 385-hp, Weber-carbureted 289s used in the GT 40s that won the World Manufacturers Championship for Ford last year, and not the 427 cu. in. NASCAR-type engines used

FORD GT 40 MK. III

Importer: Shelby American Inc.
6501 West Imperial Highway
Los Angeles, Calif.

Number of dealers in U.S.: 90

Vehicle type: Mid-engine, rear-wheel-drive, 2-passenger GT car, fiberglass body on a stressed steel hull and roof

Price as tested: $18,500.00
(Manufacturer's suggested retail price, plus Federal excise tax, dealer preparation and delivery charges; does not include state and local taxes, license or freight charges)

Options on test car: None

ENGINE
Type: Water-cooled V-8, cast iron block and heads, 5 main bearings
Bore x stroke.................4.00 x 2.87 in, 101.7 x 72.9 mm
Displacement.........289 cu in, 4737 cc
Compression ratio...............10.5 to one
Carburetion..............1 x 4-bbl Holley
Valve gear........Pushrod-operated overhead valves, mechanical lifters
Power (SAE)...........306 bhp @ 6000 rpm
Torque (SAE)........329 lbs/ft @ 4200 rpm
Specific power output......1.06 bhp/cu in, 64.6 bhp/liter
Max. recommended engine speed...6200 rpm

DRIVE TRAIN
Transmission...........5-speed, all-synchro
Clutch diameter...........8.5 in (two-plate)
Final drive ratio................4.22 to one

Gear	Ratio	Mph/1000 rpm	Max. test speed
I	2.42	7.7	48 mph (6200 rpm)
II	1.47	12.9	80 mph (6200 rpm)
III	1.09	17.6	109 mph (6200 rpm)
IV	0.96	20.0	124 mph (6200 rpm)
V/OD	0.85	22.7	136 mph (6000 rpm)

DIMENSIONS AND CAPACITIES
Wheelbase.........................95.3 in
Track..........F: 55.2 in, R: 55.2 in
Length...........................169.0 in
Width.............................70.0 in
Height............................41.0 in
Ground clearance..................5.25 in
Curb weight.....................2340 lbs
Test weight.....................2706 lbs
Weight distribution, F/R..........45/55%
Lbs/bhp (test weight)..............8.85
Battery capacity........12 volts 60 amp/hr
Alternator capacity.............504 watts
Fuel capacity....................27.6 gal
Oil capacity......................9.5 qts

SUSPENSION
F: Ind., unequal length wishbones, coil springs, anti-sway bar
R: Ind., triangulated lower control arm, single strut upper control arm, two trailing arms, coil springs, anti-sway bar

STEERING
Type........................Rack and pinion
Turns lock-to-lock....................2.5
Turning circle....................32.0 ft

BRAKES
F: Girling 11.5-in solid discs
R: Girling 11.2-in solid discs
Swept area....................240 sq in

WHEELS AND TIRES
Wheel size and type
F: 6½L x 15-in, alloy-rim Borrani knock-off wire wheels
R: 8L x 15-in, alloy-rim Borrani knock-off wire wheels
Tire make, size and type
F: Goodyear 5.00/8.90-15 racing (wet weather)
R: Goodyear 7.00-15 racing (wet weather)
Test inflation pressures..F: 28 psi, R: 32 psi
Tire load rating..F: 1100 lbs per tire @ 24 psi
R: 1600 lbs per tire @ 24 psi

PERFORMANCE
Zero to	Seconds
30 mph	1.6
40 mph	2.3
50 mph	3.8
60 mph	5.1
70 mph	6.6
80 mph	8.2
90 mph	10.2
100 mph	12.7

Standing ¼-mile........13.8 sec @ 104.8 mph
80-0 mph....................242 ft (.88 G)
Fuel mileage......7-10 mpg on premium fuel
Cruising range.................193-276 mi

FORD MARK III
Top speed, estimated 140 mph
Temperature 55°F
Wind velocity 1-2 mph
Altitude above sea level 83 ft
In 4 runs, 0 — 60 mph times varied between 4.9 and 5.3 seconds

CHECK LIST

ENGINE
Starting.............................Poor
Response........................Excellent
Vibration........................Very Good
Noise............................Very Good

DRIVE TRAIN
Shift linkage..................Unacceptable
Synchro action..................Very Good
Clutch smoothness..............Unacceptable
Drive train noise...................Good

STEERING
Effort..........................Excellent
Response........................Excellent
Road feel.......................Excellent
Kickback............................Fair

SUSPENSION
Ride comfort........................Good
Roll resistance.................Excellent
Pitch control...................Excellent
Harshness control...................Fair

HANDLING
Directional control.............Excellent
Predictability..................Excellent
Evasive maneuverability.........Excellent
Resistance to sidewinds.........Excellent

BRAKES
Pedal pressure..................Excellent
Response........................Excellent
Fade resistance.................Excellent
Directional stability...............Fair

CONTROLS
Wheel position......................Poor
Pedal position......................Fair
Gearshift position..................Poor
Relationship........................Fair
Small controls......................Poor

INTERIOR
Ease of entry/exit..........Unacceptable
Noise level (cruising)..............Fair
Front seating comfort...............Poor
Front leg room......................Fair
Front head room.....................Poor
Front hip/shoulder room.............Poor
Instrument comprehensiveness...Excellent
Instrument legibility...........Excellent

VISION
Forward.............................Good
Front quarter.......................Good
Side...........................Very Good
Rear quarter........................Poor
Rear................................Fair

WEATHER PROTECTION
Heater/defroster....................Fair
Ventilation.........................Good
Air conditioner......................—
Weather sealing.....................Good

CONSTRUCTION QUALITY
Sheet metal/fiberglass.........Very Good
Paint..........................Very Good
Chrome.........................Very Good
Upholstery..........................Poor
Padding.............................Good
Hardware............................Poor

GENERAL
Headlight illumination..........Excellent
Parking and signal lights...........Good
Wiper effectiveness............Very Good
Service accessibility...............Good
Trunk space.........................Poor
Interior storage space..............Fair
Bumper protection...................Poor

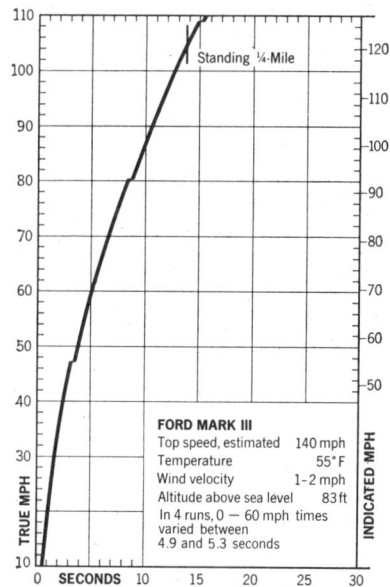

FORD MARK III

in the Mk. IIs and J-cars (C/D, May), although, presumably, the former engine is available on the Mk. III as an option. The Mk. III's transaxle, the German-made ZF 5DS-25 5-speed, and the 8.5-inch Borg & Beck twin-disc clutch are identical to those fitted to the GT 40 race cars.

The suspension is essentially the same as the race cars', although with alterations to the geometry that result in slightly more anti-dive, anti-lift, anti-squat, and ground clearance. The spring, shock, and roll rates are lower, and the roll distribution is changed to suit the new geometry and the slightly less tail-heavy weight distribution. The inboard suspension pick-ups are rubber-bushed instead of Heim-jointed, to isolate road shock, and the hub carriers are aluminum instead of magnesium for better corrosion resistance. Compared with the race cars, the Mk. III has a longer wheelbase (by 0.3 inches) and a narrower track (by 1.9 inches at the front; 2.4 inches at the rear). Overall, the car is the same width as the GT 40, a half-inch taller, and nine inches longer.

The brakes are Girling solid discs, not the Kelsey-Hayes vented discs on the race cars, because the street car doesn't need to repeatedly slow down from top speed to 35 mph. (We estimate our test car's top speed at 144 mph to the race cars' near 200.) The disc diameters of 11.5 and 11.2 inches, front and rear, are close to those of the original Ford GT's, which had 11.5-inch Girling solid discs all around. Twin master cylinders and vacuum boosters are used. Fifteen-inch Borrani wire wheels with knock-off hubs are standard equipment; cast magnesium wheels are optional. Standard rim widths are 6.5 inches front, and eight inches rear; the mag wheels are two inches wider all around.

Other differences are minor, and include a center-mounted (and ungated) transmission shift lever, provision for left- or right-hand drive, and designed installations of such amenities as radio, air conditioning, stereo tape deck, and TV.

We have never driven a car that attracted so much attention. People would stop dead in their tracks, drop their jaws, and stare open-mouthed. Even cops would react at first with astonishment, then do a double take, and—by the time they figured we must be doing something wrong—we were gone. One toll-booth coin collector, however, remained nonplussed. As a staff member followed the Mk. III through the toll station, the collector nodded in the direction of the low-slung racer and shrugged matter-of-factly. "Eh! Batman."

The Batmobile should handle so good. The Mk. III's race-bred suspension is beautiful. It develops an incredible amount of cornering force, with a gentle understeer that can instantly be exchanged for stable oversteer with a jab at the throttle. It rides around corners like a ground-effect machine on the end of a tether. The steering is uncannily responsive, with the precision of—not surprisingly—a good race car. The overall stability of the car makes the driver feel completely safe at speeds upwards of 120 mph.

The Mk. III could reach 120 within the confines of the test facility at New York National Raceway, which includes a drag strip roughly half a mile long (including the run-off area). The Mk. III's acceleration isn't much better than that of a hot Super Car, as its quarter-mile acceleration of 13.8 seconds at 105 mph indicates, but it keeps on pulling long after most Super Cars have quit. Slowing the Mk. III down from exotic speeds, the car displayed excellent braking ability, except in all-out panic stops. The brake balance is biased toward the rear, and under hard braking the rear end would snake around nearly out of control. Losing adhesion under any circumstances tends to get vicious, and, due to the low polar moment of any mid-engined car, damn near instantaneous.

Despite Goodyear's admonition against using racing tires on the street, the Mk. III comes equipped with English Goodyear wet weather racing tires—with bigger ones in back (7.00-15) than in the front (5.00/8.90-15), making the choice of which one is carried as a spare somewhat arbitrary. The ride, considering the inherent harshness of racing tires, is quite smooth—another tribute to the car's excellent suspension design.

Although the gear ratios are beautifully staged (close your eyes as the car disappears into the middle distance and its Ferrari-like ripping-canvas shriek transports you to Le Mans), changing the gears is a cruel joke. As mentioned, the clutch and transmission linkages were hopelessly out of whack. Just as the clutch is about to bite, a return spring goes over center, and ruins any attempt at smooth engagement. Finding any gear was like trying to locate the men's room in the Catacombs, and strongly reminiscent of the scene in "Grand Prix" where James Garner loses a gear at Monaco: "Raaaaza-crunch! Raa-aaaza-graunch! Raaaa-AAAAZA-clunk-blub-blub-blub." Wrong cog. The only way to shift was suddenly . . . and pray.

FORD MK. III VS. FORD MACH 2		
	Mk. III	Mach 2
Wheelbase	95.3 in.	107.3 in.
Overall length	169.0 in.	175.0 in.
Width	70.0 in.	68.0 in.
Height	41.0 in.	47.0 in.
Track: Front	55.2 in.	60.8 in.
Rear	55.2 in.	61.6 in.
Weight	2340 lbs.	2650 lbs.

Getting in and out of the Mk. III is not unlike spelunking, and we are stiff with admiration for anyone who can do it in a Le Mans-type start in less than three minutes. Girls in slacks need not apply; Birds in miniskirts more than welcome. The car is only 41 inches high (comparison: the Corvair coupe's 51 inches), and although the doors wrap over the roof almost to the centerline, getting in is still an athletic event. Step up onto wide door sill (formed by chassis' pontoon section), step onto seat, then start wriggling legs down and around low-mounted steering wheel. With gravity helping you, it's easy, at least compared to getting out.

Once inside, despair at lack of accommodation, lack of workmanship, lack of quality hardware, lack of planning for practical street application. But lay the Mk. III into a turn or see a bystander turn lime-green with envy, and everything's almost okay again.

We doubt if Ford is seriously interested in exploiting the market for the enthusiasts' ultimate street machine—there's little profit in it, and the company's image is made on the race track—but if Ford meant it, we could offer some suggestions.

Last month, we described the Mach 2, a racing-type street car built up from mass production parts. The Mark III is a street-type racing car built up from limited production parts. There should be room for something in the middle. Maybe Ford already has a car on the drawing boards that makes optimum use of both concepts, a car that could acquit itself well at Le Mans and still be almost at home on Skyline Drive. That would be the car the Mk. III should have been, and we hope it's not long in coming. **C/D**

CHALLENGE AT LE MANS
FORD MK. II

"THERE'S NO SUBSTITUTE FOR CUBIC INCHES!" WILL ENZO MAKE HENRY EAT THOSE WORDS?

BY JON McKIBBEN

FERRARI SHOCK troops stole a march on sports racing car armchair experts by complete domination of the vaunted Ford Mk. IIs in this year's Daytona Continental 24-hour road race.

Though the first word of this article is Ferrari, it is the development of the soundly defeated car that is to be treated herein. However, before dismissing the Mk. II as a loser, it is wise to recall the 24-hour race at Le Mans, France, in 1966. There, Ford took the bouquets and Ferrari settled for garlic.

The 1, 2, 3 Ford sweep at Le Mans, 1966, was accomplished by cars that were—and remain—outstanding examples of American automotive engineering as applied to racing machinery. As such, the Ford Mk. IIs deserve a close examination to discover the reasons for their aggressive success, the reasons Mk. IIs are the most impressive sports racing machines ever conceived in Detroit.

Much has been written about the original Ford GT-40 and its subsequent development from the Eric Broadley-built Lola-Ford coupe into an outstanding sports racing car with excellent speed and road-holding capabilities. Unfortunately, the GT-40 lacked the inherent reliability needed for long-distance endurance racing.

The Mark II is a logical continuation of the theme started by the GT-40. Grossly oversimplified, the Mk. II bears out that old American adage, "There's no substitute for cubic inches." The Mk. II has shown itself to be very reliable, and endowed with sheer speed that is probably unmatched in racing today. A notable exception to this statement is, of course, the 1967 Daytona race, where transmission problems eliminated Ford from competition. To the consternation of some automotive pseudo experts, the 427-cu. in. engine has not ruined the handling of the Mk. II. With the minor changes made to the suspension system and body aerodynamics, the Mk. II is more stable and easier to drive than the original GT-40s raced in the 1964 Le Mans event with the 289-cu. in. engines.

Engines of 427-cu. in. displacement in sports racing cars certainly are not a new idea, but have never before achieved appreciable success or general acceptance. Engines of this size normally are very heavy, and require a correspondingly heavier chassis to accommodate this mass. The majority of designers believe that a smaller, lighter engine, in a properly designed light-weight chassis, results in a superior automobile for road racing. While this school of thought is not without merit for sprint races over relatively short road courses typical of the U.S., it must be recalled that Ford was concerned with endurance racing, in particular at Le Mans. With the 3-mile long Mulsanne straight making up a major portion of the Le Mans course and the remainder of the course consisting of extended "dragstrips" connected by fairly slow curves, horsepower is of extreme importance.

TWENTY-FOUR hours is a long time to extract this horsepower from a high-rpm, supertuned engine. The 450 bhp that Ford considered necessary for Le Mans would have been almost impossible to obtain from the 289-cu. in. engine with any degree of reliability. This output was well within the reach of the 427 engine with a level of tuning that permitted very long engine life.

Over the past four years, Ford has developed and produced a number of variations of the 427-cu. in. engine, one of which was a lightweight version contrived for installation in Shelby Cobras. Performance was a known factor, as the 427 had been released in single and dual 4-barrel forms for drag, stock car and road racing. If such becomes necessary, Ford can install engine equipment on the Mk. II which will make the current version resemble a sewing machine motor, but reliability would suffer. With power in the 500 to 550 bhp range, though, the Mk. II would be a fierce machine indeed.

One of the prime considerations in preparing the 427 engine package for the Mk. II was the utilization of as many production components as possible, the Mk. II engine being a lightweight version of the aforementioned Cobra powerplant. Durability of the production components was an unknown quantity for sports racing use, but these engines had an impressive record of reliability in long-distance stock car races on NASCAR and USAC circuits at a much higher level of specific power output than that believed necessary for Mk. II application. To jump ahead, the latest version of the Mk. II engine is, from a performance standpoint, a detuned NASCAR engine with smaller valves and lower compression ratio.

MAJOR MODIFICATIONS to the production 427 engine consisted of changes to reduce weight, improve inherent reliability and incorporate dry sump lubrication. The engine fits in the tiny Mk. II chassis and weighs only 580 lb., less clutch, exhaust manifolds and air cleaner. This is a tribute to the Ford engineering group that supervised the project. The weight of the powerplant is remarkable when compared with similar displacement U.S. production engines. Special components designed primarily to reduce the oppressive mass of the standard 427 include cylinder heads, crankshaft vibration damper, water pump housing and engine front cover, all of aluminum, and a magnesium oil pan. The original cast-magnesium intake manifold has since given way to a production aluminum unit (in spite of the weight penalty) because of problems in obtaining consistently homogeneous magnesium castings.

The aluminum cylinder heads essentially are patterned after the production cast iron heads. Internal ribbing is added and section thickness is increased, as in typical aluminum casting technique. Aluminum-bronze valve guides and stellite valve seat inserts are incorporated, along with steel thread inserts for exhaust manifold attachment. Valve diameters in the aluminum heads are reduced from 2.19 to 2.09 in. for the intakes, and from 1.72 to 1.65 for exhausts, compared with current production 427 engines. Intake and exhaust ports have been revised slightly to compensate for the slightly smaller valves and lower airflow rate.

The oil pan and front cover are designed not merely to save weight, but to form the basis for the dry sump lubrication system. Oil addition restrictions imposed at Le Mans required that the Mk. II engine have an oil capacity greater than production, and space and ground clearance limitations ruled out simply extending a production pan, so a dry sump system with remote mounted reservoir was imperative. To facilitate installation and eliminate external fittings and lines, the system includes two oil scavenger pumps housed in the lower portion of the front cover and a production pressure pump in the normal location in the block. The front cover is a sand casting with bushings installed to carry the front ends of the scavenger pump shafts. The rear ends of these shafts ride in bushings in the scavenger pump cover. Scavenger pump drive is through a single roller chain driven from a sprocket on the nose of the crankshaft. A 3/8 pitch chain transmits the 0.5 bhp required by the scavenger pumps at 6200 rpm. Total scavenger pump capacity is 80 gallons per minute at 6000 rpm. This is approximately four times the capacity of the pressure pump, insuring oil return to the reservoir under all road racing conditions. Oil is routed to the scaven-

SHELBY COBRA 427 engine provides the basis for the Mk. II powerplant, with standard production parts used wherever possible to minimize component development time and insure readily available spares.

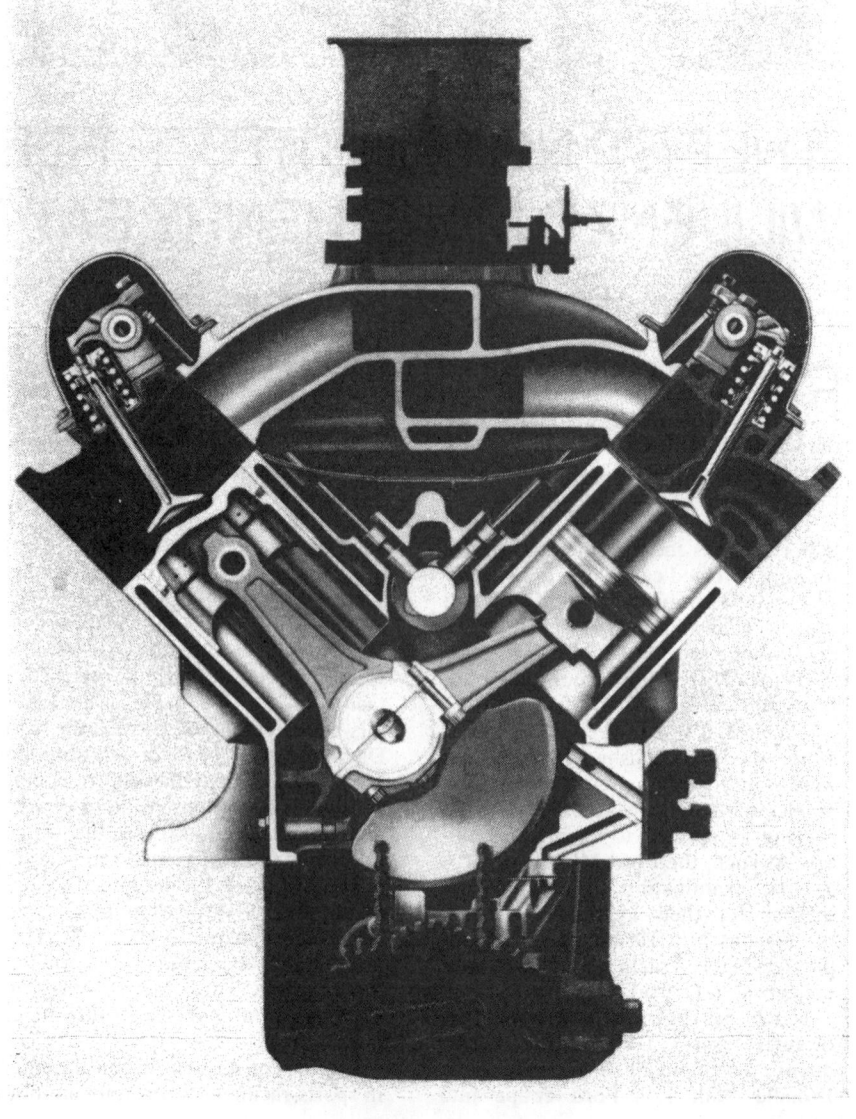

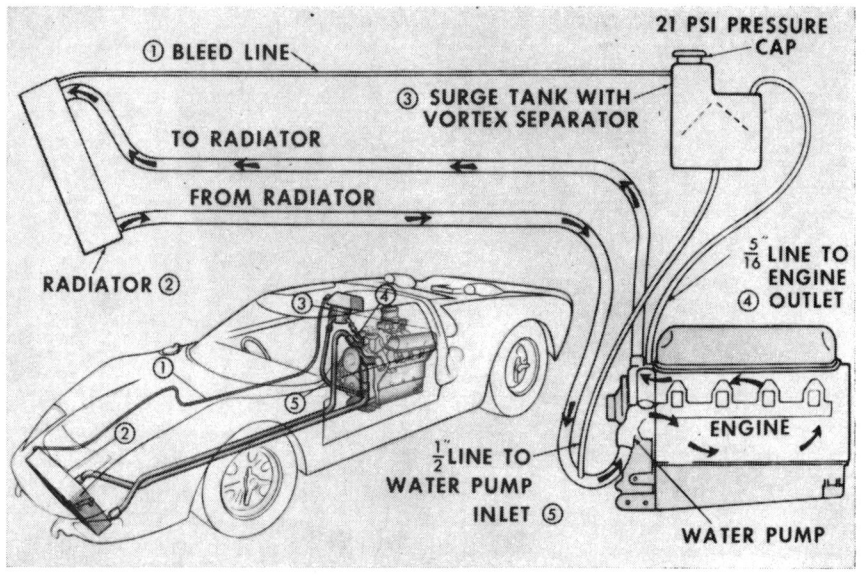

COOLING REQUIREMENTS of the 7-liter engine dictate large, efficient front-mounted radiator nestled in low nose section of the Mk. II. Surge tank with vortex separator is utilized to insure exclusion of air from system at high engine speeds. Water pump modifications are aimed at reducing unit weight and increasing coolant flow.

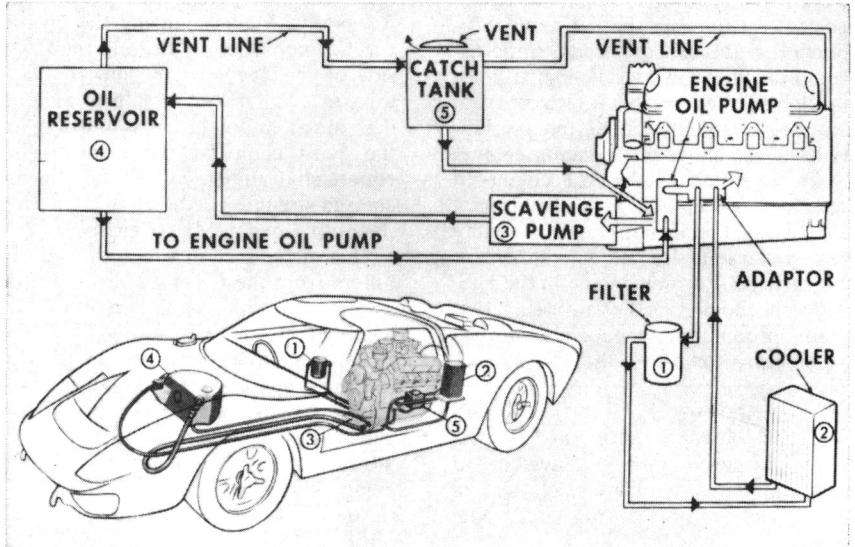

DRY SUMP lubrication system is most notable departure from normal domestic automotive practice in Mk. II. Air is removed from system at high-mounted, vented catch tank, which returns liquid to engine oil pan where scavenger pumps return all lubricant to reservoir.

MK. II

ger pumps through galleries cast into the oil pan and front cover. Fixed scavenger pump pickups are positioned at the front and rear of the pan floor. The accompanying diagram shows location of lubrication system components. Standard racing car practices have been adhered to in oil filtering, cooling and distribution.

While the dry sump lubrication system is the most dramatic departure from domestic automobile practice in the Mk. II powerplant, the remainder of the engine is not without its individual features. The electrical system in particular yields an analysis which reads like a dissertation on component reliability. No other area of vehicle construction is as severely neglected by most racing car builders as the electrical system. Ford was well aware that endurance races often are won or lost by failure of the proverbial 5¢ part, and took all possible precautions against that part being an electrical component. Le Mans race rules place paramount importance on electrical durability. Vehicles must be shut off during all pit stops and restarted with integral self starters. Replacement of the starter, generator or battery is prohibited, as is battery charging by outside means. The windshield wiper, self starter, lighting equipment and all warning devices must remain in working order throughout the race. Obviously, no electrical chances could be taken by Ford. None were. Heavy-gauge wire was utilized throughout the car, with heavy-wall high-temperature insulation. Thermosetting insulation was chosen for all wiring, because it will not melt in the event of circuit overload and damage adjacent wiring. Circuitry was studied to insure that wires would be the minimum length possible consistent with harness location free from hazards of engine heat, suspension movement, and body panel removal. Switches installed were heavy-duty aircraft or premium truck items. A master disconnect switch in the primary circuit was fitted for safety during pit stops and vehicle storage. Wherever possible, component groups and windings were encapsulated in epoxy for increased resistance to vibration.

STARTING AND charging circuits were made up of production units with the above-mentioned modifications. A 52-ampere-capacity alternator supplies all vehicle running requirements. Battery power is needed only for starting. The 53-ampere-hour battery is of multipiece construction, with hard epoxy sealing and hard case. Voltage regulation is provided by a modified production transistorized unit. The starting motor is capable of one function—hot cranking the Mk. II engine. Cranking speed is high enough to purge the engine of excessively rich vapors and permit fast starting. The unit is a production starter modified for vibration resistance and increased strength.

Backyard race car builders probably will feel a bit of empathy with the Ford engineers who constructed the windshield wiper system. Rather than design, develop and produce a custom system, a time-consuming and expensive procedure, a Boeing 707 aircraft assembly was selected. The 28-V. DC motor operates on 12 V. in the Mk. II, reducing wiping speeds to a more suitable rate for automotive use and adding a measure of reliability by operating at well below rated voltage. Wiper drive is transmitted to an oscillating gearbox through a flexible cable. The wiper arm is mounted on the gearbox with a provision for adjusting arm tension. Blade pressure of 30 oz. eliminates windlift at high speeds.

Ignition for the Mk. II engine is provided by the same breakerless transistorized system used on the GT-40. Reliability and performance consistency make a breakerless system the obvious choice. The elimination of contact points and attendant point bounce and rubbing block wear problems insures constant engine timing. The Mk. II distributor uses an 8-fingered variable-reluctance magnetic pickup in place of points, and incorporates centrifugal advance. Mechanical tachometer drive is included in the distributor housing.

The production Holley 780 cfm single 4-barrel carburetor required some modifications to adapt it to sports racing. First, the choke and air horn were removed to reduce restriction. A center-discharge accelerator pump was added to insure equal fuel supply to the four venturis. Delrin baffles were used in the float bowls to prevent fuel being spilled into the venturis on hard acceleration and deceleration, but the center-pivot design of the production Holley carburetor sufficed for cornering force accommodation. Enlarged fuel discharge passages and booster venturi slots for improved fuel flow and distribution completed the carburetor performance modifications.

Development work on various production engines demonstrated that 427s respond to 32-in. tuned length, individual 2.25-in. diameter tube exhaust systems, as employed in Mk. IIs. Eight header pipes join in two tailpipes. Each group of four is made up of the pipes from front and rear cylinders from one bank and the center pair of cylinders from the other bank of the V. Maximum firing interval separation is thus achieved. Ford used this arrangement, with differences in pipe diameters and tuned lengths, in Indianapolis and sports racing cars, such as the GT-40.

Modifications to the production short block assembly are confined mainly to tolerance reduction and detail refinements such as surface finish improvement, oil seal redesign, and controlled bolt torquing procedures.

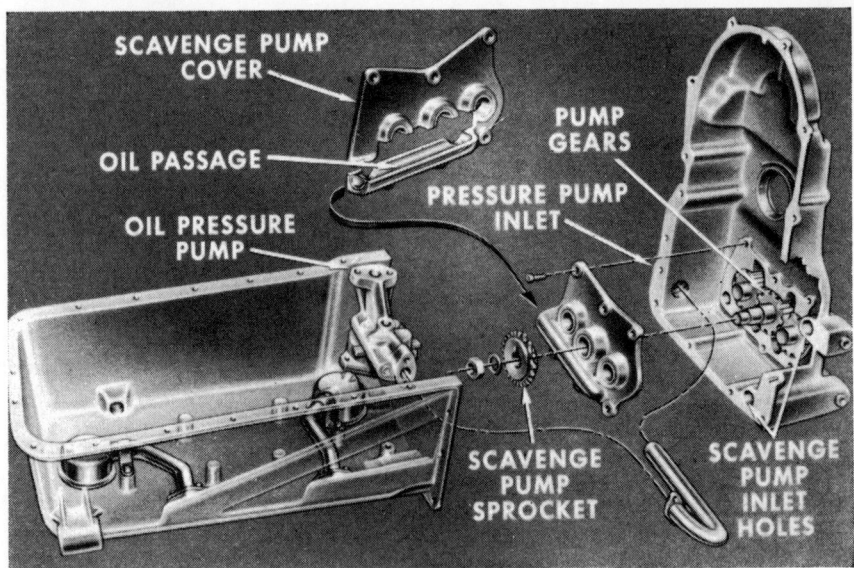

CAST PAN and front cover of the Mk. II engine serve as distribution passages, pump housings and intermediate oil reservoir. Internal mounting of pumps eliminates vulnerability problems inherent in designs with externally located components and exterior plumbing.

Very rigorous inspection is given all parts. Lest the fact that so many production parts are used leads to the assumption that the Mk. II engine is an unsophisticated piece of Detroit iron, one must remember that the production 427 is, above all, a racing engine. Since inception of the 427 engine in 1963, it has been used in drag and stock car racing applications, and probably has undergone as much refinement for racing use as any engine in the U.S. Thus, it should not be surprising that many production components proved satisfactory for use in the Mk. II.

Coupling the 427 to the GT-40 gearbox was accomplished by machining a special cast steel flywheel to accommodate a double disc clutch and a production starter ring gear. The ring gear was pressed on and welded for safety. Mass balancing the engine was accomplished by drilling the front side of the flywheel. In view of Daytona race failures, it is safe to assume that much midnight oil is burning in the Ford camp as the transmission countershaft undergoes redesign for increased strength necessary to cope with the output of the Mk. II engine.

One major area in which the Mk. II differs from the GT-40 is in the brake system. As with the vast majority of components in the automobile, the brakes had to be designed to fit into the same space as the GT-40 system. The problems posed by this restriction can be best appreciated when it is realized that the Mk. II, with its larger engine and chassis strengthening modifications, weighs approximately 2860

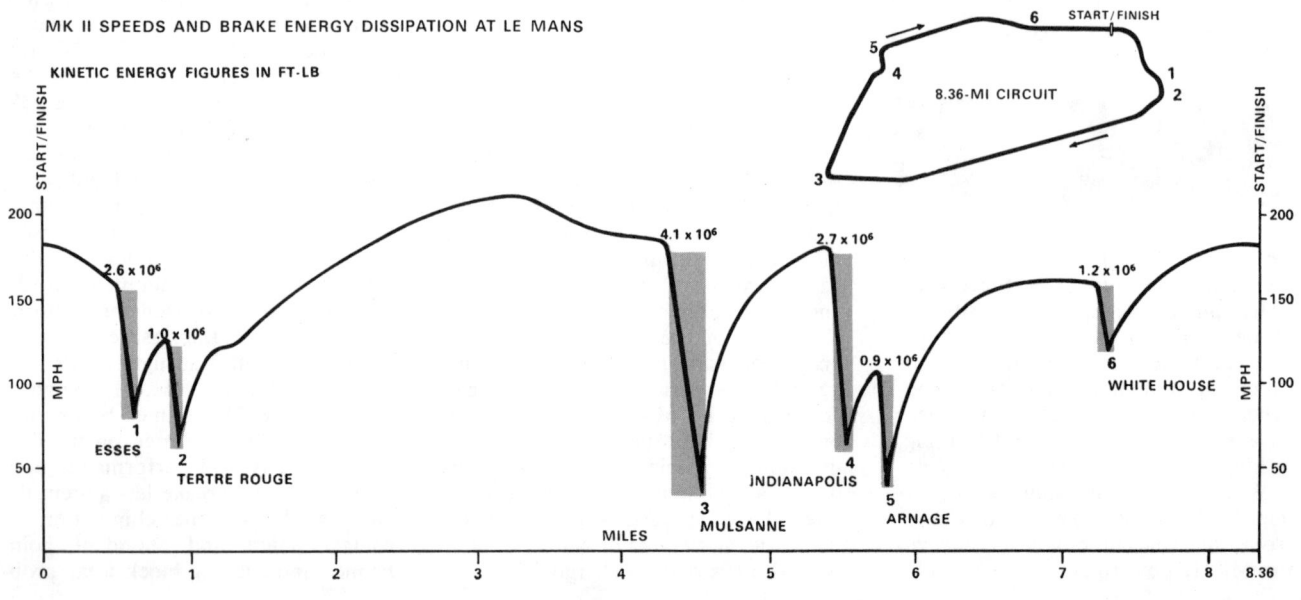

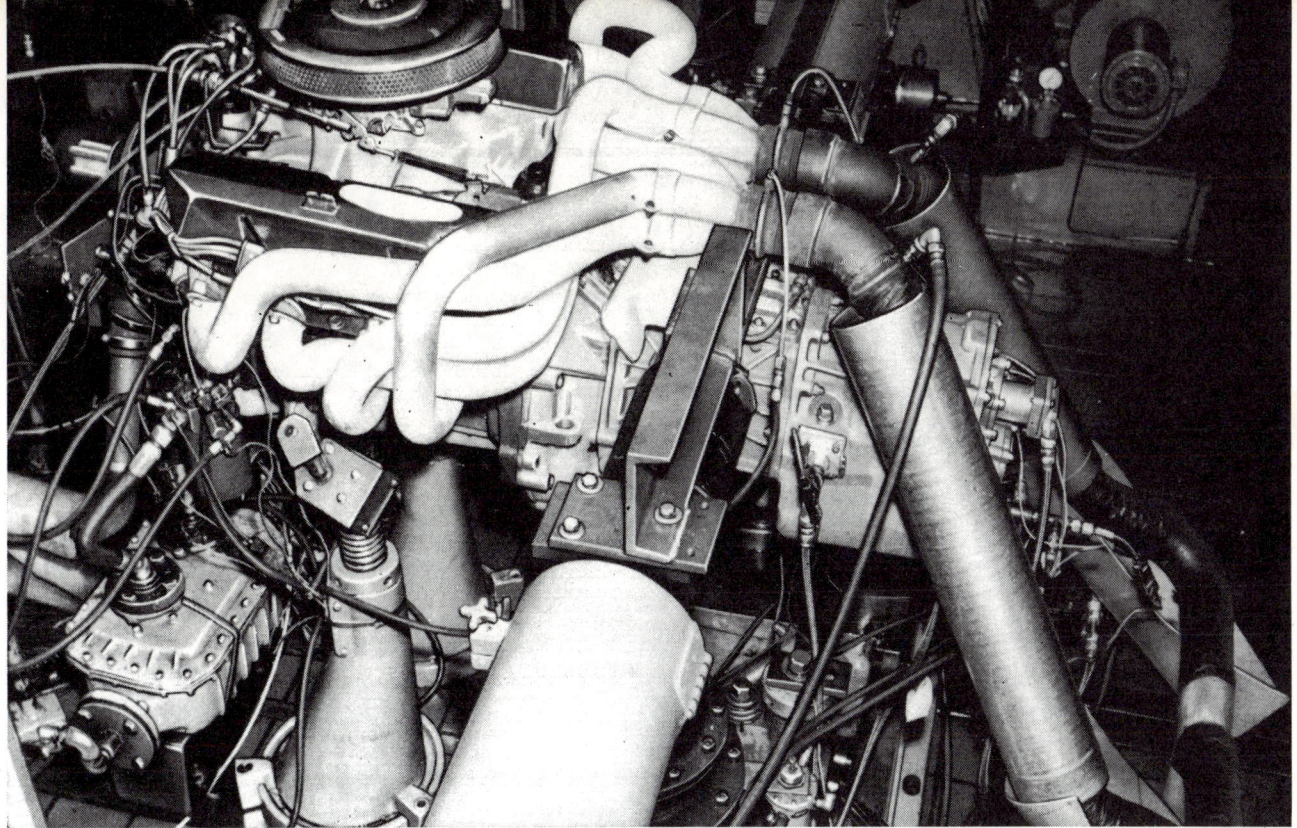

EXTENSIVE DYNAMOMETER simulation program provided Ford engineers with valuable durability information, which yielded answers to many questions concerning the Mk. II design's suitability for endurance racing before competition began.

MK. II

lb., compared with 2400 lb. for the GT-40. Add to this the fact that disc brake assemblies were forced to fit within the confines of the same sized wheels and suspension linkage limitations, and the problem facing the Mk. II brake team becomes evident.

Limiting parameters with significant effect on brake performance included retention of the 11.56-in. rotor diameter and basic fixed caliper assemblies of the GT-40, and a strict policy of minimum vehicle alteration. The weight increase of approximately 17%, coupled with the higher speed potential of the Mk. II resulted in the brakes being forced to absorb 25-30% additional kinetic energy. Heat dissipation became the prime consideration. While disc brakes have achieved a reputation for being fade resistant and virtually invulnerable to failure due to repeated high speed stops, racing sports car performance increases over the past few years have resulted in difficulties which, while not of the same nature as previous drum brake problems, are nonetheless difficult to solve. Rotor damage due to excessive temperatures at the friction surface is a persistent problem in long races. However, the most critical deficiency, from failure to dissipate heat at a sufficient rate, is brake fluid boiling. With normal drum brakes, abuse of the braking system manifests itself in fade, which becomes progressively evident to the driver through increased pedal effort and lack of brake effectiveness. Though fade warns the driver of excessive temperatures, disc brakes continue to provide a substantial amount of retardation until fluid vaporization temperature is reached in caliper assemblies. Then, abruptly and with no particular warning, *all* braking effect is lost in the portion of the system in which the fluid has vaporized. The Mk. II is equipped with a dual master cylinder arrangement to provide partial braking in the event of failure or fluid vaporization at one wheel. Front to rear brake proportioning in the Mk. II is accomplished by an adjustable balancing beam and pushrod arrangement. Thus, front to rear braking may be proportioned to suit driver preference and course variations. On the subject of brake proportioning, the basic weight distribution of the Mk. II is an asset to maximum brake utilization. Mk. II's static weight distribution of 38% front, 62% rear permits very high deceleration rates without the rear wheel lockup that plagues basically nose-heavy automobiles. As rapid deceleration transfers weight to the front of the vehicle, dynamic weight distribution becomes nearly optimum, insuring that all four brakes contribute substantially to achieving minimum stopping distances. Extensive cool air ducting, 0.75-in.-thick ventilated rotors, and regular fluid replenishment to rid the system of accumulated moisture, combined with high temperature seals and linings have given the Mk. II the most effective braking system in racing today.

With the basic automobile package herein developed, Ford embarked on a very intricate program of dynamometer simulation to test the drive train and brake system in the laboratory. Many hours of laboratory testing and detail improvement resulted in a racing automobile that has shown excellent performance and reliability from the start of its competitive career. Ford has expended an astronomical sum of money in its attempt to construct the world's finest endurance racing sports car, but it has achieved this goal in a remarkably brief period of time, and proven the ability of its engineering staff by winning what is considered to be the supreme test, the 24 hours of Le Mans.

NO AUTOMOBILE is invincible in the face of competitors with as much ability as Enzo Ferrari, but the raw potential of the Mk. II certainly seems to foretell many more successful races, at least until Ford decides that international road racing competition has achieved its desired goals. One thing is certain. Ford Motor Co. has raised the American automotive industry status in the eyes of the world's motor sports enthusiasts to a level not attained in many years. For this, and for developing the remarkable Mk. II automobile, Ford Motor Co. deserves the respect of every American. ∎

35th Le Mans 24-hour race

Ford fantastic

Gurney/Foyt car shatters race record by 10 m.p.h. and also wins Index of Thermal Efficiency

Report: Philip Turner with Charles Bulmer and Michael Bowler
Pictures: Maurice Rowe and Paul Skilleter

FOR the second year in succession Ford were victorious at Le Mans but whereas in 1966 the winning car was driven by two New Zealanders (Bruce McLaren and Chris Amon) this time it was an all-American win for sharing the wheel were Californian GP driver Dan Gurney and the 1967 Indianapolis winner from Texas, A. J. Foyt. The winning car led from the second hour onwards except for the re-shuffling caused by fuelling, but it was no run-away victory this year with a Ford-arranged 1, 2, 3 finish. Ferrari fought back bitterly to avenge their 1966 defeat and finished second and third. Michael Parkes and Ludovico Scarfiotti co-driving the second car, and Willy Mairesse—that doyen of Belgian drivers—and "Beurlys" the Equipe Nationale Belge P4 that finished third.

At one time it seemed possible that Ford

Appropriately photographed at the part of the course known as Indianapolis—the American-driven winner.

would repeat their 1, 2, 3 trick for by the ninth hour they held the first three places and the Ferraris seemed unable to match the sheer speed of the big 7-litre cars one of which in Denis Hulme's hands hit a staggering new lap record of 3m. 23.6s., 147.894 m.p.h., no less than seven seconds under the 1966 record of 3m. 30.6s. established by Bruce McLaren in a Ford Mk. II. The new Ford Mk. IVs are certainly very fast and established a new record in the distance covered in winning the race this year.

At 3.30 a.m. on Sunday morning, however, Andretti in second place had a brake lock as he swooped into the Esses out of control, the car cannoned from bank to bank until it came to rest in the middle of the circuit. Following close behind were the Fords of McClusky and Schlesser and both cars hit either Andretti's Ford, the banks, or both varieties of obstacle and all three were eliminated. None of the drivers was seriously injured but the Ford squadron had been drastically reduced.

Provisional results

35th Le Mans 24-hour race. June 10/11. Run on Le Mans 8.14-mile circuit.
Weather: *overcast, windy but dry.*

1 D. Gurney/A. J. Foyt (7-litre Ford Mk. IV), 3,249.630 miles, 135.483 m.p.h.
2 L. Scarfiotti/M. Parkes (4-litre Ferrari P4), 3,217.146 miles, 134.128 m.p.h.
3 W. Mairesse/"Beurlys" (4-litre Ferrari P4), 3,157.306 miles, 131.637 m.p.h.
4 B. McLaren/M. Donohue (7-litre Ford Mk. IV), 3,008.211 miles, 125.418 m.p.h.
5 J. Siffert/H. Herrmann (2-litre Porsche 907), 2,999.772 miles, 125.066 m.p.h.
6 R. Stommelen/J. Neerpasch (2-litre Porsche), 2,940.994 miles, 122.615 m.p.h.
7 V. Elford/B. Pon (2-litre Porsche), 2,738.268 miles, 114.169 m.p.h.
8 G. Koch/C. Poirot (2-litre Porsche), 2,688.116 miles, 112.072 m.p.h.
9 H. Grandsire/J. Rosinski (1.3-litre Alpine Renault), 2,685.197 miles, 111.954 m.p.h.
10 A. de Cortanze/A. le Guellec (1.3-litre Alpine Renault), 2,670.835 miles, 110.903 m.p.h.
11 R. Steinemann/D. Spoerry (3.3-litre Ferrari GT), 2,658.901 miles, 110.837 m.p.h.

Of the other entries the Chaparrals lasted much longer than most people expected, one car driven by Phil Hill and Mike Spence holding second or third place for many

12 R. de Lageneste/J. Cheinisse (1.3-litre Alpine Renault), 2,606.946 miles, 108.688 m.p.h.
13 G. Vinatier/M. Bianchi (1.5-litre Alpine Renault), 2,601.543 miles, 108.463 m.p.h.
14 R. Buchet/H. Linge (2-litre Porsche 911S), 2,582.174 miles, 107.654 m.p.h.
15 C. Baker/A. Hedges (1.3-litre Austin Healey), 2,420.068 miles, 100.896 m.p.h.
16 M. Martin/J. Mesange (1.3-litre Abarth), 2,193.480 miles, 91.433 m.p.h.
Record lap: D. Hulme (7-litre Ford Mk. IV), 3m. 23.6s., 147.894 m.p.h.

Index of Performance: 1 J. Siffert/H. Herrmann (Porsche), 1.386.
    2 L. Scarfiotti/M. Parkes (Ferrari), 1.299.
    3 R. Stommelen/J. Neerpasch (Porsche), 1.281.

Index of Thermal Efficiency: 1 D. Gurney/A. J. Foyt (Ford), 1.49.
    2 J. Siffert/H. Herrmann (Porsche), 1.45.
    3 A. de Cortanze/A. le Guellec (Alpine Renault), 1.44.

'Motor' Trophy (first British car): C. Baker/A. Hedges (Austin Healey).

Le Mans

hours before retiring on Sunday morning. The two Lola-Aston Martins, on the other hand, both went out with engine trouble early on in the race and in fact the only British car among the 16 finishers was the works-entered Austin-Healey Sprite driven by Clive Baker and Andrew Hedges.

Scrutineering and practice

At scrutineering, which began in torrid, pre-thunderstorm heat on the Tuesday before the race at 7 a.m. and continued throughout Wednesday, Ford and Ferrari revealed their hands. The Ford attack would be launched by four of the new Mk. IVs backed up by two works-entered Mk. IIBs, a MK. IIB from Ford France, two Ford GT40s entered by Ford France and the Scuderia Filipinetti and John Wyer's two Mirages, the lighter GT40-based cars which the FIA has ruled are not strictly Fords, so that the points they gained in the Constructors' Championship for their win at Spa go to Mirage and not to Ford.

The Mk. IVs are developments of the lightweight J that first appeared at the 1966 Le Mans Test Days, but not in last year's race. They are notable for the aluminium honeycomb construction of their hulls, a technique borrowed from the aero industry and, by comparison with the Mk. IIs that won at Le Mans last year, they are 8in. longer, 2in. lower and 300lb. lighter, weighing 2,205lb. to the 2,505lb. of the Mk. II. They are powered by the latest version of the 7-litre CID V-8 originally developed for stock car racing but with the power increased since last year from 490 to 530 b.h.p. by modifications to the cylinder block to eliminate the water transfer passages between the block and the cylinder heads and by fitting two Holley four-choke carburetters on a new intake manifold in place of the single Holley four-choke instrument with which the 1966 cars were equipped.

Andretti and McLaren drove a Mk. IV to victory in its first race, the Sebring 12-hours, in March of this year, when there were no Ferrari P4s present. The four cars entered for Le Mans consisted of two prepared by Shelby America and two by Holman and Moody. Dan Gurney and Indianapolis winner A. J. Foyt were to drive a Shelby Mk. IV—with a special bulge in the roof to accommodate lanky Dan's head, and in the second car were Bruce McLaren and Mark Donohue. Drivers of the two Holman and Moody Mk. IVs were Mario Andretti and Lucien Bianchi and Lloyd Ruby and Denis Hulme.

The Mk. IIs had been improved in various respects since finishing first, second and third here last year. The new nose and tail sections were no longer topped by that pair of ship's type ventilator air intakes which were such a distinguishing feature of the 1966 Mk. II. These new Mk. IIBs are powered by the same new 530 b.h.p. engine as the Mk. IVs and the works cars were driven by Frank Gardner and Roger McClusky and Paul Hawkins and Ronnie Bucknum. The Ford France Mark IIB was co-driven by Jo Schlesser and Guy Ligier.

At scrutineering, the commissaires insisted on the fitting of exterior driving mirrors on the Mk. IVs as they did not consider the rear view sufficient through the steeply sloping window past the massive carburetters. Sensibly, the scrutineers did not object to the complicated fire fighting equipment even though it occupied the second passenger's seat which, according to Appendix J, should be free to be occupied at any time during a race. Actuated by two flame sensitive infra-red contacts and by a heat sensitive contact located at strategic positions inside the car, this equipment is designed to fill the interior with an inert gas should fire break out. As the equipment imposes a weight penalty of some 200lb., it is hardly an aid to performance.

Spearhead of the Ferrari counter-attack were four of the latest 4-litre P4 V-12s with three valves per cylinder for their 450 b.h.p. direct injection engines. The three works cars were two coupés for Gunter Klass and Peter Sutcliffe and for Mike Parkes and Ludovico Scarfiotti, and an open spyder for Chris Amon and Nino Vaccarella. The fourth P4 was allocated to the Equipe Nationale Belge to be driven by Willy Mairesse and "Beurlys".

In addition to the works cars there were three independently entered Ferrari P3/4s with carburetters for their two valves per cylinder engines. Jean Guichet and Herbert Muller were driving the Scuderia Filipinetti car, Richard Attwood and Piers Courage the Maranello Concessionaires car and Pedro Rodriguez and Giancarlo Baghetti the North American Racing Team P3/4. The Ferraris went through scrutineering with no great alarms and excursions on Wednesday afternoon and according to the weighbridge they were just under or just over 1,000 kilograms.

Although the race was expected to be a Ford-Ferrari battle it was also confidently predicted that the Chaparrals would lead during the early stages. But would these novel 2Fs with their high-set aerofoils, rear mounted radiators and automatic transmissions stay the distance? In spite of their new 7-litre Chevrolet engines, they were even lighter than the Ferraris at 993 kilos.

The two beautifully prepared Lola-Aston Martins, now with fuel injection for their new V-8 engines, caused some alarm and despondency when it was found that their fuel tanks held 10½-litres more than the permitted maximum. Surtees' car had a new tail with a very Ferrari-like look which, it was hoped, would reduce the drag, although, in fact, it didn't. On the weighbridge the Lola-Astons recorded 1,060 kilos.

The 2-litre class which had been expected to provide a battle of an intensity rivalled only by the fight for all out victory was unfortunately decimated before the race even started. Alfa Romeo decided after the Nürburgring 1,000 kilometres that more development of their V-8 engines and gearboxes was required and so withdrew all their cars. Then another blow—Ferrari withdrew all three Dinos, which left only the Porsches and two Matra-BRMs for neither the 4.7-litre Ford engined Matra nor the Alpine with the new 3-litre Renault-based Gordini V-8 appeared for scrutineering. The works Porsches consisted of two of the long-tailed 907s, for Mitter and Rindt and Siffert and Herrmann, two 910s for Stommelen and Neerpasch and Buzzetta and Schutz and a 906 for Vic Elford and Ben Pon. None of the cars used the flat 8 engines which had been used so successfully at Nürburgring to break up the opposition. The Matra-BRMs were comparatively new cars with the radiators mounted behind the rear wheels and one had completed a 14-hour endurance run on the Bugatti circuit just to find out its fragile points, if any.

As usual, scrutineering produced trouble for some and heartbreak for others. The works Mini-Marcos was found not to comply with the windscreen regulations and Jem Marsh spent a long, long Tuesday night doing drastic modifications to the glass-fibre body. Bizzarini came with two cars, one front engined, the other rear engined, and both obviously hastily prepared on a shoe

Mulsanne Corner with Scarfiotti in the Ferrari and Bianchi squatting behind in the 7-litres-worth of Ford.

Ah well, next year, then? Chaparral (above) came close to putting up a splendid show until an oil seal failure eliminated their remaining runner. Car behind is Siffert's Porsche, which won the Index of Performance.

Will the Dunlop Bridge be rebuilt as a wide-oval? Cars are: 54, Nathan; 12, Irwin's Lola-Aston; 14, Piper's Mirage; 16, in the distance, the Graber/Dumay Ford France car.

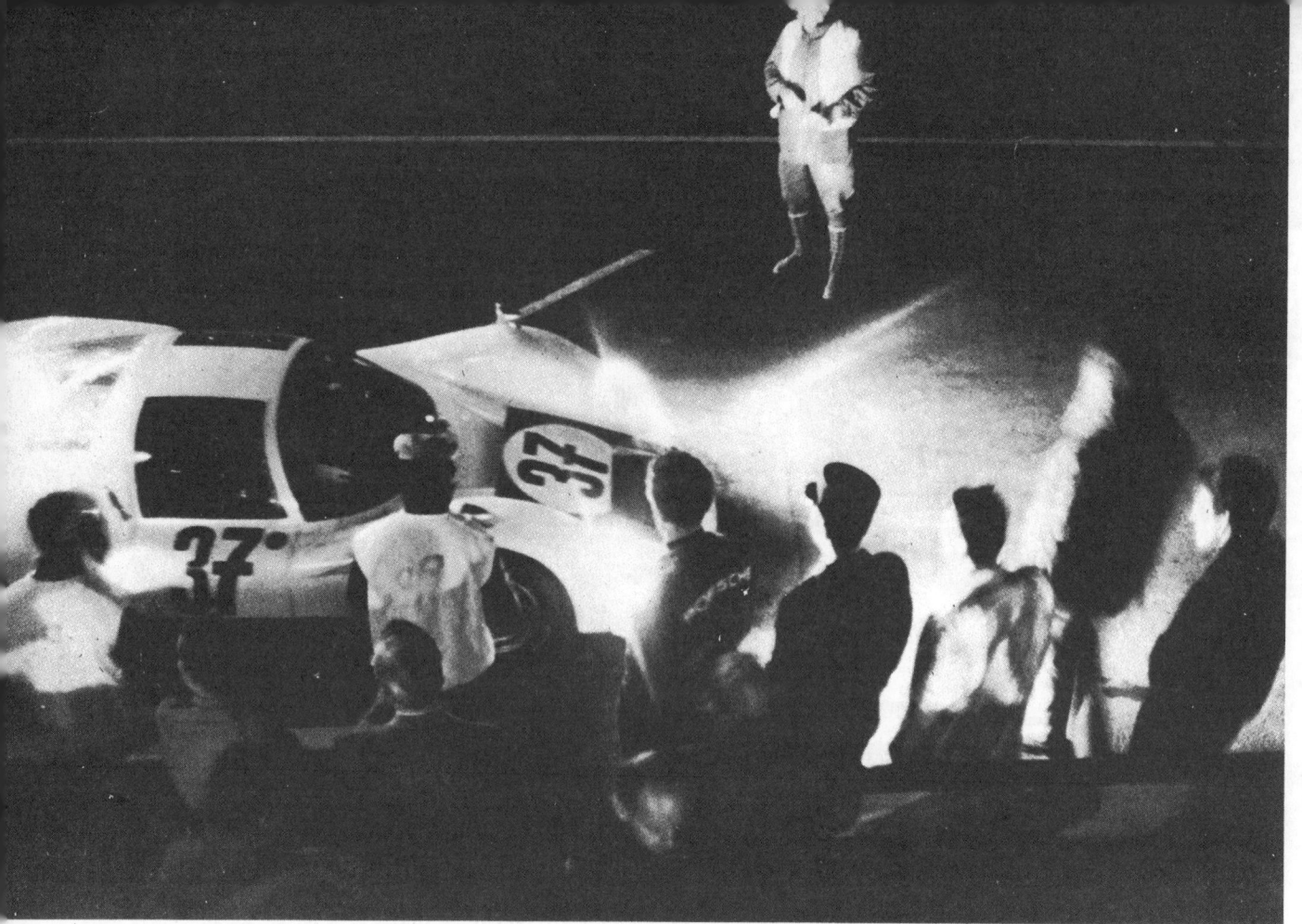

Seventh finisher—the Elford/Pon Porsche pulling away after a swift fuelling stop during the night.

Le Mans

string. The commissaires decided that, really, they could not accept the cars, and the poor Italian who had used up all his slender resources to bring the cars to Le Mans set off for Italy with but 70 francs in his pocket.

Fastest car during the first practising session on Wednesday evening was the Chaparral which, with Phil Hill at the wheel, lapped in 3m. 27.4s. fairly early on in the evening and this speed was not improved on, the second fastest being Willy Mairesse (Ferrari P4) in 3m. 30.9s. On the following evening, the Chaparral went even faster, putting in a lap in 3m. 24.7s., well below not only Dan Gurney's 1966 race record of 3m. 30.6s. but also Bandini's lap of 3m. 25.5s. with a Ferrari during the Test Days in April. Then, at 10.30 p.m., in the dark, Bruce McLaren in the yellow Mk. IV Ford lapped in 3m. 24.4s., an average speed of 147.316 m.p.h. for the lap. McLaren reached around 215 m.p.h. along the Mulsanne Straight. Third fastest was Mario Andretti, 3m. 26.1s., with another Ford Mk. IV followed by Gardner (Mk. II), 3m. 26.4s., Bucknum (Mk. II), 3m. 27.8s. and Ruby (Mk. IV), 3m. 28.1s. Then came the first of the Ferrari P4s with a lap by Scarfiotti in 3m. 28.9s.

But although this meant that Ford would occupy five of the first six positions in the line-up for the start of the race, all was not joy in the Ford team, for the Mk. IVs had been plagued throughout practising by a queer epidemic of windscreen cracking. Hairline cracks would suddenly develop in the big, laminated screens even when the cars were stationary in front of their pits. Various theories were put forward, but the most likely seemed to be that the fault lay in the incorrect tempering of the glass. Urgent messages to Detroit ensured that a further batch of windscreens set off over the Atlantic on Thursday night and they duly reached Le Mans in time to be fitted for the race.

The race

Saturday, 4 p.m. to 10 p.m.

It was about 3.30 p.m. when the cars began to arrange themselves—with human aid—in order of practice times in a long line in front of the pits and for some time confusion reigned fairly supreme. Order was eventually restored and then came the last desperate 15 minutes during which killing time became slow, very slow murder. Not for all teams, however, for the Lola mechanics were hard at work on the gear selection mechanism of the Irwin/de Klerk Lola-Aston Martin, with Eric Broadley himself lending a hand while an anxious Surtees looked on.

Finally, under an overcast sky, the drivers ranged themselves in their little circles on the far side of the road, and the Minister for Youth and Sports, Monsieur Francois Missoffe, raised the big Tricolour in the air and dropped it. Came the patter of feet, the slamming of doors and then, nothing, for what seemed like an age before the first engine burst into life. And even then it was not one of the cars at the head of the column, for several midway down were nosing out into the road before Pedro Rodriguez led the pack away in the white and blue NART Ferrari with the Fords of Bianchi and Gardner close on his tail. Both Chaparrals were very slow away—some said because Jim Hall had given strict instructions that his drivers must fasten their safety belts first.

Then they were all gone save for the Nathan which was last away by a considerable margin. While the dancing bits of paper settled to earth again we waited eagerly for the leaders to come into sight at White House at the end of their first lap. It was the blue Ford Mk. II of Paul Hawkins that swept into view with a considerable lead from Gardner's Ford, the Ferrari of Rodriguez, Schlesser in the white Mk. II of Ford and Gurney in the flaming red Mk. IV. Mike Spence with the first of the Chaparrals was well back in 18th place but, coming up fast with headlamps blazing.

A surprising number of cars swept in to the pits at the end of this first lap. Both Mike Salmon's Ford GT40 and Jaussaud's Matra-BRM had crumpled right doors that had not closed properly, Roger Nathan came in with the Nathan to attend to the clutch and Clive Baker stopped with the Sprite because the red light indicated that the dynamo was not charging.

But the biggest blow to British hopes came on the third lap when Surtees came slowly in to his pit with smoke pouring from the engine of his Lola-Aston Martin. A piston had gone and the car was out already. Hulme, too, came in on this lap with the Ford Mk. IV but rejoined the race again after a four-minute stop. Then on the sixth lap Chris Irwin came in for a long stop with the second Lola-Aston while the mechanical drive to the fuel pump was repaired.

By the end of the first hour the Hawkins/Bucknum Ford Mk. II still led from the Gurney/Foyt Ford Mk. IV, and the McLaren/Donohue Mk. IV. Fourth was now the Phil Hill/Spence Chaparral, and fifth and sixth the Ferrari P4s of Amon and Vaccarella and Rodriguez and Baghetti. But then at the end of the first hour came a flurry of refuelling stops by the Fords which let the Chaparral into the lead until it, too, stopped for petrol. The tactics of this race hinged to quite a large extent on the fact that the Fords had to refuel every hour but the Ferraris every hour and a quarter, while the Chaparrals could last almost as long as the Ferraris. This meant that the Fords would require 24 refuelling stops during the race while the Ferraris would require only 19. Therefore, the Ferraris could well afford to let the Fords charge ahead and make the running.

After two hours and the refuelling stop re-shuffling, the Gurney/Foyt Ford led from the Chaparral, then came the Fords of Andretti and Bianchi and McLaren and Donohue, followed by two works Ferraris. Shortly after 5 p.m. the Salmon/Redman GT40 caught fire on approaching Mulsanne Corner. Mike Salmon drove it into the sand and bailed out with minor burns and the car was extinguished by the pompiers.

In the third hour, the Ickx/Muir Mirage retired with run bearings and the second NART Ferrari of R. Rodriguez (not related) and C. Parson was stuck hopelessly in the sand at Mulsanne.

The second Lola-Aston seemed to have regained its form after its extensive repair session at the pit but, just before 7 p.m., after three hours of racing, it was driven slowly along the pits to retire into the paddock. Before the hour was out it had been followed into retirement by the second Mirage with engine trouble, by the Team Elite's Lotus 47 driven by Wagstaff and Preston, by one of the Peugeot 204-powered CDs, by the Nathan, and by the Jaussaud/Pexscarolo Matra-BRM. Already, the race was taking its toll.

But still up at the front the Gurney/Foyt Ford led from the Hill/Spence Chaparral, with the Ferraris lurking like patient wolves in around fourth and fifth places. And there were still another 18 hours to go.

General Classification after 4 hours

	Drivers	Car	Laps	Speed	
1	Gurney/Foyt	(Ford Mk. IV)	67	140.22	m.p.h.
2	Andretti/Bianchi	(Ford Mk. IV)	66		
3	Hill/Spence	(Chaparral 2F)	66		
4	McLaren/Donohue	(Ford Mk. IV)	66		

Crumpled but unbowed. This is the Hedges/Baker Austin-Healey Sprite which was the only British finisher—and it won the 'Motor' Trophy.

Like a couple of runaway dumplings—front car is the Mairesse/"Beurlys" Ferrari and, following it through Terte Rouge, the Mirage of Piper and Thompson.

| 5 | Parkes/Scarfiotti | (Ferrari P4) | 66 |
| 6 | Amon/Vaccarella | (Ferrari P4) | 65 |

Index of Performance

1	Mitter/Rindt	(Porsche 907)	1.356
2	Audruet/Bouharde	(Alpine)	1.355
3	Parkes/Scarfiotti	(Ferrari)	1.337

Retirements

		Reason
"Franc"/Fischaber	(Porsche)	Clutch cable broken
Surtees/Hobbs	(Lola-Aston Martin)	Piston
Salmon/Redman	(Ford GT 40)	Caught fire
Lawrence/Marsh	(Mini-Marcos)	Broken oil pump
Ickx/Muir	(Mirage)	Bearings
Irwin/de Klerk	(Lola-Aston Martin)	Engine
Wagstaff/Preston	(Lotus 47)	—
Piper/Thompson	(Mirage)	Engine
Ballot-Lena/Dayan	(CD)	Cooling
Nathan/Beckwith	(Nathan)	Electrics
Jaussaud/Pexscarolo		

Saturday/Sunday 10 p.m. to 4 a.m.

As the race entered its second quarter the field had already been depleted to 38 runners; it was the two Shelby Ford GT Mk. IVs and the faster Chaparral on the same lap with two works Ferraris—Amon/Vaccarella and Parkes/Scarfiotti—ahead of two more Fords. The slower Chaparral had been stationary at its pit for some time, unable to restart after a fuelling stop, when Phil Hill brought the sister car alongside for fuel and a check on the automatic transmission; this 9-minute stop cost him a drop from fourth to seventh spread over the hour. Amon's Ferrari dropped out when it caught fire while he was driving back to the pits on a wheelrim after a puncture. About the same time Porsche lost the Rindt/Mitter Porsche streamliner when the former came in after a spirited convoy with team mate Siffert with 2,000 r.p.m. too many on the clock.

At the stroke of the seventh hour, Ferrari had the Parkes/Scarfiotti car in second place but the Fords soon climbed back and by the ninth hour it was cars 1, 2 and 3 lying first, second and third—No. 1, the Gurney/Foyt car, was three laps ahead. The Chaparral had reached fifth despite a further 9-minute pit stop.

Through the shower of champagne you can see Scarfiotti on left, then lady with flowers, Parkes, Gurney with thumb in suitable attitude, and then Foyt.

Le Mans

A spirited performance by Servoz Gavin and Beltoise had pulled their Matra-BRM into a position just behind the fastest two Porsches at one point, but it developed an oil leak, wasted a quarter of an hour at the pits while some more was drained off and then, finally, two hours later, the whole lot drained itself and the Matra was pushed away.

Night is normally a period of consolidation when lap speeds drop by around 5 seconds but still the leading Fords were lapping in around the 3m. 30s. mark with the Chaparral—troubled by its vane sticking in the braking position—some 5-7s. slower and on a par with the Ferraris. The pace was still too hot for the last of the NART Ferraris—Rodriguez and Baghetti—and a cloud of smoke announced a collapsed piston.

At the 10th hour it was still the same Ford 1, 2, 3 order and again at the 11th hour with Nos. 3 and 2 swapped over. Still Parkes and Scarfiotti were fourth and the Chaparral fifth. The Ford France Mk. II Ford of Ligier and Schlesser was sixth. There were still 29 runners of which seven were Alpine Renaults; the sole British survivor was the Clive Baker/Andrew Hedges Manx-tailed Sprite going steadily after earlier electrical troubles.

And then as the race neared mid distance with Ford in a seemingly unassailable position (as near unassailable as one could ever be with so far to go) Bianchi brought No. 3 in, to hand over to Andretti. As Andretti then got under way through the Dunlop bridge and started braking for the Esses, one brake grabbed and the car spun, cannoning off one bank and then the other, before finishing in the middle of the track with bits all around. Roger McCluskey in Ford No. 5, who was running ninth, was next on the scene; he spun in avoidance and shunted another bank. Jo Schlesser in the Ford France car was the next and he too had to spin out to avoid contact with the cars if not the banks. That left three bent Fords and a whole lot of debris for everyone else to avoid which they did successfully, although the Sprite, which was close behind, narrowly avoided a spin of its own. At the same time, Ford's third place car was in the pits having a clutch slave cylinder replaced, so in just half an hour Ford were reduced to an easy first, and a hard pressed sixth with three Ferraris and a Chaparral in between; but it was still only half distance.

General Classification after 8 hours

	Drivers	Car	Laps	Speed
1	Gurney/Foyt	(Ford Mk. IV)	132	138.89 m.p.h.
2	McLaren/Donohue	(Ford Mk. IV)	131	
3	Parkes/Scarfiotti	(Ferrari P4)	130	
4	Andretti/Bianchi	(Ford Mk. IV)	130	
5	Schlesser/Ligier	(Ford Mk. II)	128	
6	Mairesse/Beurlys	(Ferrari P4)	128	

Index of Performance

1	Andretti/Bianchi	(Ford Mk. IV)	1.356
2	Hermann/Siffert	(Porsche 907)	1.356
3	Larrousse/Depailler	(Alpine Renault)	1.340

Retirements during period		Reason
Ruby/Hulme	(Ford Mk. IV)	Accident
Dubois/Tuerlinckx	(Shelby 350 GT)	Gearbox
Amon/Vaccarella	(Ferrari P4)	Burnt out
Guichet/Muller	(Ferrari P3)	Out of oil
Buzzetta/Schutz	(Porsche 910)	—
Bertaut/Guilhaudin	(CD)	Accident
Vidal/Offenstadt	(Alpine Renault)	Lubrication

Sunday 4 a.m. to 8 a.m.

For once dawn broke at Le Mans without the usual early morning mist. Only 24 cars were still running and several of these were showing the strain of 12 hours racing. Gurney and Foyt had built up a commanding lead and were taking things easily to keep the Scarfiotti-Parkes Ferrari six laps behind with the remaining Chaparral holding off the other two P4 Ferraris and the McLaren-Donohue Ford.

General Classification after 12 hours

	Drivers	Car	Laps	Speed
1	Gurney/Foyt	(Ford Mk. IV)	197	137.69 m.p.h.
2	Parkes/Scarfiotti	(Ferrari P4)	192	
3	Hill/Spence	(Chaparral 2F)	191	
4	Mairesse/Beurlys	(Ferrari P4)	190	
5	McLaren/Donohue	(Ford Mk. IV)	189	
6	Klaas/Sutcliffe	(Ferrari P4)	189	

One of a game little band of Alpine-Renaults of which four finished, out of eight starters, in 9th, 10th, 12th and 13th positions.

Le Mans continued

Index of Performance

1 Siffert/Herrmann	(Porsche 907)	1.340
2 Larrousse/Depailler	(Alpine Renault)	1.327
3 Parkes/Scarfiotti	(Ferrari P4)	1.300

Retirements during period

Drivers	Car	Reason
Johnson/Jennings	(Chaparral)	Electrical
Maglioli/Casoni	(Ford GT 40)	
Rodriguez/Baghetti	(Ferrari P3/4)	Collapsed piston
Beltoise/Servoz-Gavin	(Matra-BRM)	Oil loss
Mitter/Rindt	(Porsche 907)	Engine
Wicky/Farjon	(Porsche 911)	—
Greder/Dumay	(Ford GT 40)	Drive shaft

This was a situation which didn't last very long. At 5.30 a.m. Phil Hill brought the Chaparral in to the pits to investigate an oil leak and there it stayed for over three hours while the mechanics removed the gearbox and changed an oil seal. That, in effect, was the end of a challenge which had lasted much longer than most people had anticipated; soon afterwards the Attwood-Courage Maranello Ferrari, which had been circulating very slowly to survive without an oil top-up, was finally pushed away when it became clear that the engine was no longer oil-tight. The Greder-Dumay GT40 retired with a broken universal joint and a noticeable misfire.

That reduced the field to 22 and left the three works Ferraris sandwiched loosely between Gurney and McLaren, who was really hurrying to try and bring his Ford into a position where the team would be less vulnerable. At 6.38 a.m. Mairesse brought his Ferrari in for a major 2,000-mile service which included new brake pads and tyres; "Beurlys" took it over and started to pile on the pressure, lapping considerably faster than the others, who, in turn, increased their speed when they had had similar attention. But these pit stops took quite a long time and the running order remained unchanged at 8 a.m. Meanwhile, the Corvette Stingray which had been running like a train and looking almost as large, retired, and the Poirot/Koch Porsche came in, first with incipient clutch trouble, and later with serious clutch bothers which delayed it for over half an hour.

General Classification after 16 hours

	Drivers	Car	Laps	Speed	
1	Gurney/Foyt	(Ford Mk. IV)	262	137.15	m.p.h.
2	Parkes/Scarfiotti	(Ferrari P4)	255		
3	Mairesse/Beurlys	(Ferrari P4)	253		
4	Klaas/Sutcliffe	(Ferrari P4)	252		
5	McLaren/Donohue	(Ford Mk. IV)	250		
6	Bucknum/Hawkins	(Ford Mk. II)	246		

Index of Performance

1 Larrousse/Depailler	(Alpine Renault)	1.300
2 Herrmann/Siffert	(Porsche 907)	1.299
3 Parkes/Scarfiotti	(Ferrari P4)	1.295

Retirements during period

Drivers	Car	Reason
Andretti/Bianchi	(Ford Mk. IV)	Accident
Gardner/McClusky	(Ford Mk. II)	Accident
Schlesser/Ligier	(Ford Mk. II)	Accident
Bondurant/Guldstrand	(Corvette)	—
Attwood/Courage	(Ferrari P3)	Out of oil
R. Rodriguez/Parson	(Ferrari P2)	Accident

Sunday 8 a.m. to 10 a.m.

At 8 o'clock the Martin/Mesange Abarth 1300, lying last in general classification, slipped further down the scale after a 20-minute investigation into gearbox maladies. One of the 1-litre Alpine Renaults retired and the Audruet/Bouharde 1,300 c.c. car spun at Tertre Rouge and was unable to continue. Clive Baker spun the game little Sprite in the Esses at 8.20 a.m. but Andrew Hedges continued after they had inspected the damage—to the tail only—arranging to make frequent checks that no exhaust fumes should be getting at the driver. In fact, the overcast sky never let go its promised rain, but any circuit just gets more and more slippery as oil and rubber pollute the surface, which might explain the sudden spate of spinning.

Paul Hawkins/Ron Bucknum had worked their Mk.II GT Ford—the original leader—back into sixth place, but the earlier overheating must have left its mark as the engine gave up at 9.40 a.m. and the sump was empty. The first five remained the same as at the 16th. hour. Meanwhile the average speed was considerably higher than last year's; the leading Ford had covered 293 laps instead of 273! On the index of performance, the streamlined Porsche retained the lead it had only lost once since the eighth hour, and at the 18th. was leading from the Parkes/Scarfiotti Ferrari and the Stommelen/Neerpasch Porsche. Curiously, the fastest Ford was also leading the Index of Thermal Efficiency from the more likely Alpine Reanults by a useful margin.

Sunday 10 a.m. to 4 p.m.

After 18 hours of racing the Gurney/Foyt Ford led by five laps from the Parkes/Scarfiotti Ferrari P4, and the Klass/Sutcliffe Ferrari P4 was third, with the Équipe Nationale Belge Ferrari P4 fourth and the McLaren/Donohue Ford Mk.IV fifth. The Chaparral challenge had wilted and died and, soon after resuming racing following its long pit stop to replace an oil seal, the remaining Hill/Spence 2F came in to its pit again, and after a long consultation was driven slowly away to retirement with no oil pressure. Its going drew a round of sympathetic applause from the spectators, for the strange, high-wing cars had gripped the imagination of the French. Next year wings will be worn by many other contestants, we venture to prophesy.

Shortly afterwards the Ford team suffered further setbacks, for the McLaren/Donohue Mk.IV shed its rear engine cover at speed. Bruce McLaren collected it on his next lap and rammed it roughly into place but a long pit stop was then required while it was stuck together with what looked like outsize Sellotape. Just to redress the balance, however, the Klass/Sutcliffe Ferrari P4 stopped out on the circuit with a broken gearbox, so now the score stood at Ford first and fourth and Ferrari second and third. Dan Gurney brought in the leading red Ford which was fitted with new front wheels and new pads for its front discs before Dan handed over the wheel to Foyt.

General Classification after 20 hours

	Drivers	Car	Laps	Speed	
1	Gurney/Foyt	(Ford Mk. IV)	325	136.137	m.p.h.
2	Parkes/Scarfiotti	(Ferrari P4)	320		
3	Mairesse/Beurlys	(Ferrari P4)	315		
4	McLaren/Darohue	(Ford Mk. IV)	300		
5	Siffert/Herrmann	(Porsche 907)	295		
6	Stommelen/Neerpasch	(Porsche 910)	294		

Index of Performance

1 Siffert/Herrmann	(Porsche 907)	1.305
2 Parkes/Scarfiotti	(Ferrari P4)	1.299
3 Stommelen/Neerpasch	(Porsche 910)	1.285

Retirements during period

Drivers	Car	Reason
Andruet/Bouharde	(Alpine Renault)	Spun
Larrousse/Depailler	(Alpine Renault)	—
Bucknum/Hawkins	(Ford Mk. II)	No oil pressure
Therier/Chevalier	(Alpine Renault)	Mechanical trouble
P. Hill/Spence	(Chaparral)	No oil
Klaas/Sutcliffe	(Ferrari P4)	Transmission

The big Ford was lapping at around 3m. 45s. whereas the Ferrari in second place was speeding round at 3m. 35s. Not only was the Ferrari catching the Ford on the road but it also required fewer pit stops. Moreover, when the Ferrari did stop, it was usually for a shorter time than the Ford. The race was by no means a foregone conclusion, therefore, and Ferrari continued to contest for victory.

Soon after 2.30 p.m. the leaders stopped to refuel, first the Ferrari and then the Ford. Neither changed tyres nor drivers, and thereafter the gap between the two cars became steady at around 35 seconds on the road for both were lapping consistently at 3m. 40s. Ferrari had, in fact, conceded the race, knowing the Ford's lead to be too great to be attacked unless trouble should strike at the last minute.

So the race ran to its close. Large numbers of policemen appeared in front of the pits and were whistled at by the crowd. The carpenters again did their lightning construction act of a presentation stage. Half an hour to go, and the leading Ford blinked its right winker as it passed the pits to show it would be in next lap for its final refuelling stop. This took 1m. 17s. and the car rejoined the race to the cheers of the populace with Foyt still at the wheel. Then Ferrari team manager Franco Lini signalled Mike Parkes in also. Mike got out of the car while it was being refuelled and appeared to be having an amiable discussion with Scarfiotti as to who should drive the last stint: it was Parkes who climbed back in again.

While the Ford purred round like a big cat that had sheathed its claws there were sympathetic cheers for the Martin and Mesange Abarth as it set off to crawl round on a final lap after a long re-building session in front of the pits. Finally it was 4 p.m. at last and the Parkes/Scarfiotti Ferrari was the first to see the chequered flag. Then the winning Ford crossed the line. Dan Gurney jumped aboard and sat on the bonnet and was joined by a character clutching a rheoboam of champagne who evaded the police and marshals by running like a hare. Finally came the presentation of the winning crew on the platform and more, much more, champagne for Dan Gurney discovered that if you first give a rheobaom a good shake you can then point it like a cannon and spray all your friends. Joy was in fact unconfined.

M

CARS ROAD TEST

BY MARTYN L. SCHORR

FORD'S GT-40 MARK III COSTS AS MUCH AS SEVEN MUSTANGS, HAS ONLY TWO SEATS AND DOESN'T EVEN HAVE ROLL-DOWN WINDOWS. BUT IT'S

THE ONLY WAY TO FLY!

HAPPINESS is a GT-40 Mark III! For the first time since the days of the Deusenberg and the stock market crash, the jaded automotive performance buff really has a choice of products to choose from in all price ranges. And if the factory doesn't build them exotic enough, Mr. Jaded Buff can always go to Shelby American in Los Angeles, California, for a custom GT-500 Mustang or to Baldwin Chevrolet in Baldwin, New York, for an SS-427 Camaro with stock-type engines to 600 hp. But now, thanks to Ford Motor Company, he doesn't have to settle for a customized and repowered Motor City machine. All he needs is a minimum of $18,500 cash or *mucho* credit and he can drive away in the most exotic high-speed genuine Gran Turismo car ever to carry a domestic car manufacturer's name.

The car we are referring to is the '67 Ford GT-40 Mark III, a *new* street version of the GT-40 that dominated production GT racing in 1966, winning the International Manufacturers'

Championship for Sports Cars. If this car isn't instant happiness, we don't know what is! It's low, sleek, fantastically fast and so functional that it even has room for a passenger and luggage space for lunch!

The GT-40 street machine was first available last year, but Ford and Shelby American (exclusive distributorship in this country) ran into some trouble with the Motor Vehicle people in a few states. The original design had to be modified as the lights were too low and ground clearance was inadequate. The '67 Mark III version reflects these design changes and will pass any state inspection. Shelby American is now taking orders through Cobra dealers at $18,500 per copy.

We were introduced to this unreal piece of machinery by Bill Kolb, Jr., the dynamic young high-performance

In order to lift up the rear to service the engine or reach the stowage locker, the gull-type doors must be opened. Frontal visibility is good, rear is terrible.

Midship-mounted 306-hp Shelby 289 backed up by a five-speed ZF transaxle supplies the punch. Excellent weight distribution (55% on rear wheels) accounts for superb road manners.

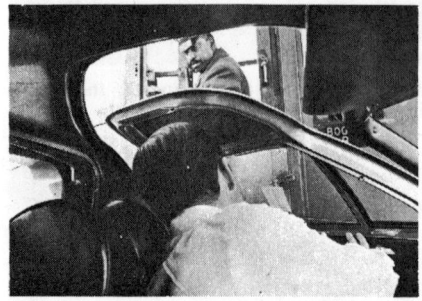

Limited window travel necessitates opening of door to pay bridge tolls, etc.

Well-instrumented dash keeps driver and passenger informed of engine condition.

Stowage compartment is roomy enough for a helmet and a couple of baloney sandwiches!

sales specialist at Gotham Ford in New York City. Because of his experience with race machinery he was entrusted with the care and feeding of the original GT-40 Mark III prototype by the chief executive of the Ford Motor Company. Once he got clearance to release the $70,000 prototype, we loaded up the lunch-box-size trunk with a couple of cameras, a Bell helmet and a tripod and took off. There was barely enough room for a few spare rolls of film in the stowage locker after the tripod was forced in.

While the Mark III retains the basic design and performance of the original GT-40, it has been extensively modified to conform to regulations governing the use of cars on public roads. The most obvious difference in the exterior appearance of the two cars is the use of dual headlights in the Mark III. This has been done to raise the lighting to legal height and to provide superior road lighting at night without blinding approaching motorists.

While the Mark III may be considered a traffic stopper on the road, it does even more of a job in this department when it's parked and being readied for a trip. Since you almost always have to put something in the trunk locker (no room inside for storage) you are insured of gathering a crowd. Before Kolb had the Bell helmet in the trunk on our initial trip, we had already gathered a crowd of at least a dozen spectators—some passersby and some motorists who had pulled to the curb after doing a doubletake when we drove out the front door of Gotham's showroom! Getting to the stowage space means, would you believe, that you have to open both doors to get to the latch controls for the rear section! Then you release the outside locking latches and lift the complete rear section of the body. At this point the Mark III looks like a cross between the Batmobile and the Chapparral! By the time we put the goodies away ans secured all the latches, we had completely goofed traffic on First Ave. and collected at least 20 bug-eyed spectators.

From every angle the Mark III looks as though it belongs on a race track. Even with modern styling trends as advanced as they are, it's hard to conceive of a car that can handle a 6-foot-

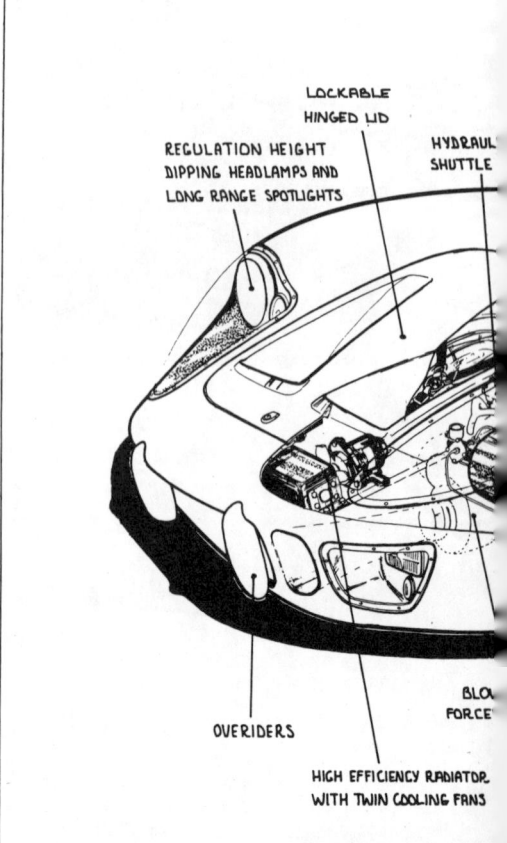

GT-40 Mark III looks right at home on the sidewalk in front of Gotham Ford's showroom. Car is an instant crowd-gatherer. Thanks to the midship engine and the aerodynamic styling, car is stable to 200 mph. Headlights are legal in all states.

With only 5 inches ground clearance much care must be exercised pulling into driveways and running over potholes.

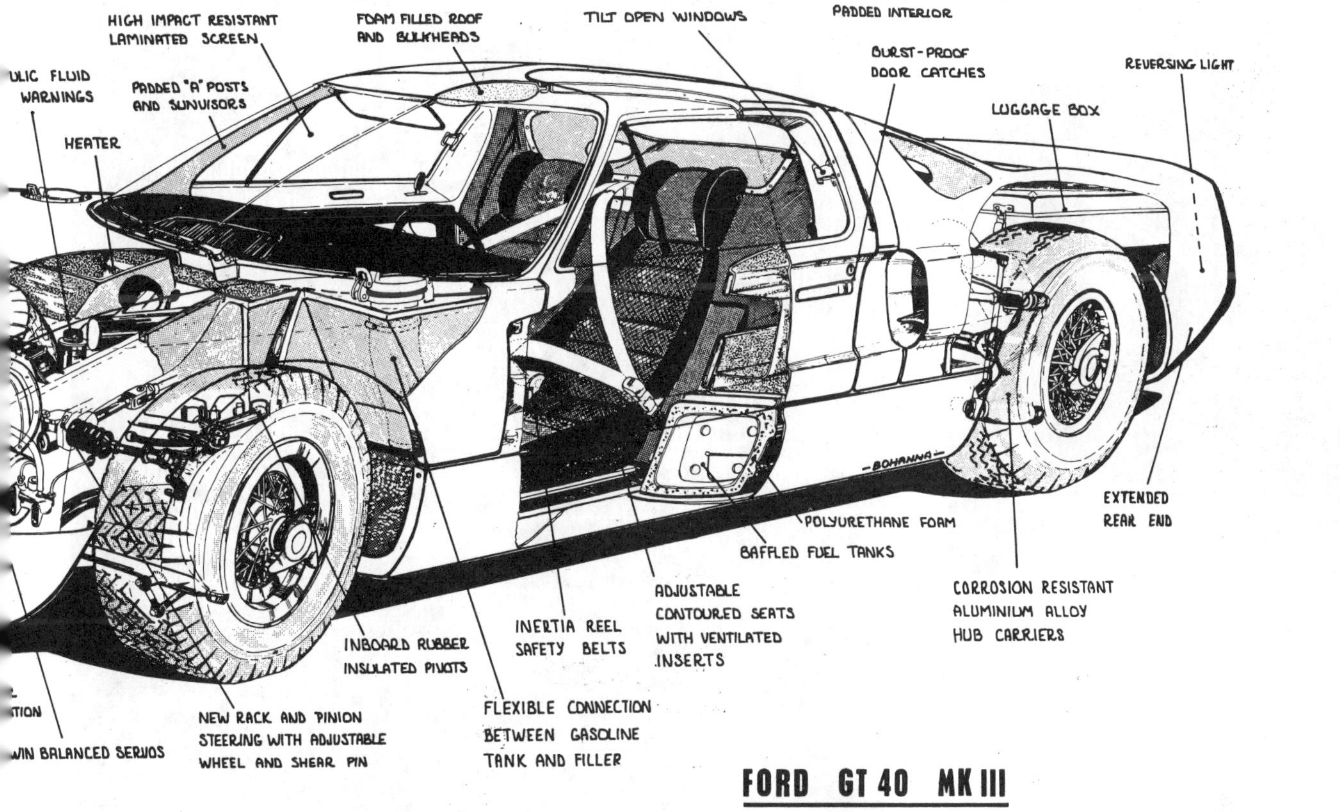

FORD GT 40 MK III

2-inch test driver being only 39.8 inches high. The styling is absolutely unreal. The wide mouth front end and the functional scoops give the Mark III the appearance of a beast on the prowl.

The construction techniques used in the Mark III are certainly worth noting. The chassis is incorporated in the design of the body for maximum flexibility. It's basically a structural foam sandwich chassis and body design with a flat floor pan. The body is high-tensile reinforced fiberglass and features a removable nose and a hinged rear section. By lifting the rear section it's possible to service the engine, complete drivetrain and suspension. The side

The only car we encountered during test that was faster than the Mark III was a six-banger NYC Police car. You can't hardly beat those full-race radios! Scientifically-designed buckets sport built-in headrests.

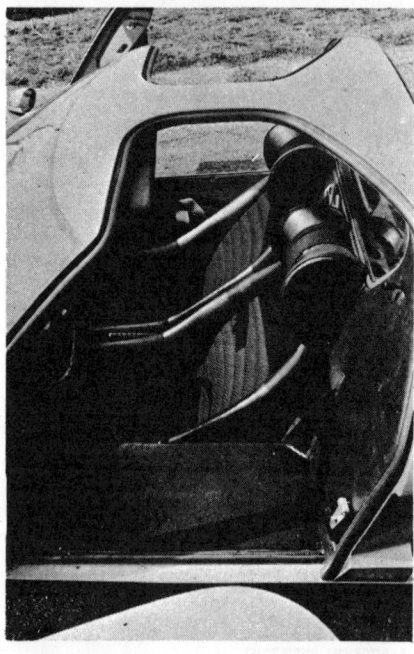

sills form the main structural members and contain built-in specially-baffled fuel tanks. Each fuel tank has an individual flip-top racing filler mounted in the front fenders and holds 13.8 gallons. They are insulated from heat and noise by polyurethane foam. This foam filler

1967 FORD GT-40 MARK III SPECIFICATIONS

ENGINE

Type	OHV V-8
Displacement	289 cubic inches
Compression Ratio	10.50-to-1
Carburetion	Single Holley Quad
Camshaft	Solid, .457-inch lift
Horsepower	306 @ 6000 rpm
Torque	329 foot/pounds @ 4200 rpm
Exhaust	Dual headers, dual pipes
Ignition	Dual point

TRANSMISSION

Make	Five-speed ZF-5DS-25
Control	Floor shift

REAR END

Type	Limited-slip transaxle
Ratio	2.50-to-1

BRAKES

Front	11.50-inch discs
Rear	11.20-inch discs

SUSPENSION

Front	Rubber-isolated HD independent
Rear	HD transaxle, coil spring shocks
Steering	Rack and pinion
Overall Ratio	N/A

GENERAL

List Price	$18,500
Price As Tested	$70,000 (Prototype)
Weight	2200 pounds
Wheelbase	95 inches
Overall Length	169 inches
Tire Size	5.80 x 15/7.00 x 15 Goodyear

PERFORMANCE

0 to 30 mph	3.8 seconds
0 to 60 mph	6.8 seconds
Standing ¼ mile	N/A mph
Elapsed Time	N/A seconds
Top Speed	175 mph (EST)
Fuel Consumption	10-18 mpg

GT40 MARK III continued

material is also used in the hollow cavities in the sills and in the roof section to form sound absorbing beams of great torsional strength.

Once you practice getting in and out of the Mark III you can throw away the shoehorn and play LeMans driver. The doors on the Mark III level off at the top of the sills, which means that you really have to step up into the car, then dive right down. The tops of the doors contain almost the complete roof section. It takes a certain amount of practice, especially if you are over 6-feet tall and weigh more than 200 pounds. Once behind the thickly padded race car wheel you get the feeling that you are about to be pushed out on to the track for a quick warm-up lap. The adjustable, ventilated bucket seats have built-in headrests that really work and place the driver and passenger in a semi-reclining position. Once you are in place you put on the inertia reel belts, reach for the key switch and wait for the electric fuel feeders to stop ticking. Then you make contact and the healthy, snarling Cobra-type 289 roars to life.

The most unusual feature of this exotic machine is the Cobra engine which is midship-mounted and hooked up to a five-speed transaxle. It's hard to believe that a car with Ford on its hood could have so much machinery in its trunk! The standard engine in the Mark III is a Shelby-built 289 Cobra with 10.50-to-1 pistons, a Holley center-pivot-float 715-CFM quad mounted on a Cobra high-riser manifold and a solid-lifter cam. This engine is a duplicate of the ones used in the GT-350 Mustangs and is rated at 306 hp at 6000 rpm. The exhaust system on the Mark III is a complex one, incorporating a crossover transfer pipe to reduce pressure interference caused by uneven firing impulses on each cylinder bank. Small mufflers bring the sound level down to an acceptable roar! Backing up the midship-mounted engine is an imported ZF 5DS-25 five-speed transaxle which provides full synchronization and a wide range of final drive and intermediate ratios. Our test car was fitted with a two-series final drive ratio which enables the Mark III to reach a top end of over 170 mph. Other ratios are available from Shelby American.

Driving the Mark III takes some getting used to even if you have already logged many miles in the hottest domestic iron. With the Bonneville rear gearing, the prototype was no quicker than a good running Ram Air GTO and certainly nowhere near as quick as a 427 435 hp Corvette. However, acceleration is not the Mark III's forte! At 100 mph the 306-hp Shelby 289 just loafs along with the shifter in third or fourth gear. You tend to forget just how fast you are going, as the semi-reclining driving position minimizes the feeling of speed. The pedal area is rather tight and if you wear size 12 shoes you really have problems. Throttle control is rather smooth and precise, but the clutch seems as though it would be better suited for use in one of Ford's drag racing vehicles instead of the Mark III. The clutch is an 8.5-inch Borg and Beck unit of twin plate diaphragm spring design which is either in or out. Slippage in traffic is something you only dream about—it's stallsville once you start playing tag with the taxis in city traffic!

Because of the basic design of the Mark III, visibility is another thing you have to dream about. On the open road we didn't have much trouble with lane changing and that sort, as we just laid into the loud pedal and easily charged away from anything in the next lane! However, it can get kind of nervy when you're limited by thick traffic. Frontal visibility is not bad because of the well-designed impact-resistant laminated windshield. At the rear it's another story, however. The side racing mirrors are poor substitutes for the real thing, and the so-called rear window does little more than let you check the Holley quad. Since the engine is immediately behind the cockpit you have to look around the quad and the air cleaner to see what's happening.

After a while you are so taken by the car's superb road manners that you forget about things like poor visibility and windows which tilt open just a couple of inches for ventilation. Besides the window on the engine that you don't need, Ford has supplied the Mark III with an additional window on the engine compartment. The window we're talking about is the wall-to-wall full-instrumented dash which is set into a non-reflecting recess. Matching black-faced instruments with white numerals are used along with racing toggle switches and well-marked warning lights. There's even a warning light which advises you that it's time to call the dual electric cooling fans into action. Once the temperature goes over a pre-determined redline the light goes on. In traffic we didn't keep them on as the fans draw a fantastic amount of amperage. A super-large tach occupies the position of honor in front of the driver, while the speedometer is at the passenger's end of the dash, angled to face the driver.

Once you are moving along in the Mark III you feel as though you own the road. It's the type of feeling you get when you know the car was designed for speeds to 200 mph and that the brakes and tires are capable of handling any situation that might arise. Because of the geometry designed into the rack and pinion steering, lane changing simply requires the slightest movement of one finger. Steering control is superlative, unlike any other street machine sold in this country. The braking system can handle panic stops from any speed, thanks to 11.5-inch front discs and 11.2-inch rear discs. The Goodyear Wet Weather Racing tires look as though they belong on an Indy car and stick like glue under full throttle takeoffs and panic stop shutdowns. Regardless of what we did, even throwing the car out of control on purpose, the suspension could not be faulted.

We actually hated to give the car back to Gotham Ford, even though it was a bit unnerving being responsible for a $70,000 prototype. With just 2.25 inches of ground clearance, a certain amount of discomfort, the fantastic power potential of a 2200-pound, 306-hp, five-speed missile, and a starting price of $18,500, it's pretty obvious that the Mark III is only for the super-discriminating buff who has everything else. It can be fitted with a radio, stereo tape, an air conditioner and even a TV set right at the factory.

Knowing Bill Kolb, it won't be long before he takes delivery of another one fitted with a five-series rear and a 450-hp drag-type 289 Cobra-type mill. Anyone for Double A Sports dragging?

RACING HISTORY OF THE FORD GT PROTOTYPES

BY JONATHAN THOMPSON

Four years and 244 entries brought nine major international victories, fifteen minor wins and three championships

CUTAWAY DRAWING BY MATI PALK

ENGLISHMEN LIKE to point out that the Ford GT started life as a Lola. It was a direct development of the 1963 Lola GT, a mid-engined, Ford-powered prototype designed by Eric Broadley for Le Mans. The Lola dropped out of the 1963 race but obviously had a lot of potential. Ford, eager to get into international racing quickly, established Ford Advanced Vehicles under Englishman Roy Lunn and retained Broadley and a third Briton, ex-Aston Martin team manager John Wyer, to develop the design as the Ford GT. The new American challenger to Ferrari appeared in April 1964. Thirty-eight months later it ended an up-and-down but eventually fruitful career as the totally changed Mk.4, with almost twice the displacement and a "team" reliability based on multi entries.

There were three basic Ford GTs: the original 4.2/4.7-liter GT-40, which accomplished little as a prototype but later dominated the Sports category with impressive regularity; the 7-liter Mk.2, built on the same chassis, which won Daytona, Sebring and Le Mans and the 1966 Manufacturers Championship; and the much lighter Mk.4, née J-Car, which won Sebring and Le Mans last year after a seemingly endless gestation period but was unable to prevent Ferrari from recapturing the constructor's title. (The Mk.3 was a road-equipped GT-40 built in England for such wealthy sportsmen as would test Mrs. Castle's 70-mph limit to the full—sort of an Anglo-American LM.)

We won't give technical analyses of all the models here (see the June and July 1964, May 1965, April, May and October 1966 and March 1967 issues of R&T); it will take all the available space to cover the Ford's four-year, 69-race competition career and describe briefly the several variations of the three basic models that have appeared.

The first Ford GT was shown to the public in New York. After being completed by FAV at Slough, England, it was rushed across the Atlantic so that its debut could be all-American. English motoring journalists were quick to describe the new car as no more than a glorified Lola; the basic configuration and placement of the 255-cu in. (4.2-liter) pushrod Indianapolis-type engine were very similar to Broadley's original 289-powered car and the center section's wrap-over doors—the design's most distinguishing feature—were identical. Informed American writers conceded the inspiration to Broadley and the overall engineering responsibility to Lunn, but kept in mind the fact that the engine and financing came from this side of the ocean. The car's later successful development was totally American and justified the original billing. Just the same, Ford of Dearborn sent out some ridiculous press material showing, through spurious styling sketches, how the GT was really developed from the V-4 Mustang I project and strongly related to the then new 1965 Mustang production car! Well, the Mustang did have imitation side scoops.

Aside from the multitude of chassis problems that all competition cars must eliminate through continual race testing, the Ford GT had serious aerodynamic faults which could be ascribed to the styling studio's desire to make it look pretty. It *was* a handsome, purposeful car, but in its very first outing, the Spring 1964 Le Mans trials, the clean nose underwent the first of a series of surgical operations that lasted two years before an efficient combination of penetration and radiator ducting was worked out.

Le Mans was always the chief target of the Ford campaign, but the team was smart enough to know that a new design must be run often under varying conditions to become raceworthy. So one GT-40 appeared in the Nürburgring 1000-km race as a warm-up for the French 24-hr event. Three-time Le Mans winner Phil Hill was paired with Bruce McLaren, who had done much of the GT-40's initial test driving; the Ford retired, but not before it had shown itself already competitive to the well-established Ferrari 275P. A three-car entry went to Le Mans, with Richie Ginther/Masten Gregory and Dick Attwood/Jo Schlesser joining the team. The three cars were identical, with 4.2-liter Indy engines and Colotti transaxles, and shared a consistent white-and-blue color scheme. Ginther/Gregory led the race in the beginning and Phil Hill set a new lap record as dawn was breaking, but all three cars retired. The basic problem was the Colotti gearbox, though the 4.2

Prototype for Ford was 1963 Lola GT, raced at Le Mans by Hobbs/Attwood while gearbox lasted.

GT-40 appeared in April 1964. Note similarity of center section to Lola, clean nose (changed for Le Mans, right).

Shelby-developed 4.7 GT-40 won 1965 Daytona 2000-km with Ken Miles/Lloyd Ruby driving.

In April 1965 Le Mans trials this extended nose was tried for better penetration. Slightly shorter form was used on 7-liter cars in race.

GT X1 was entered by McLaren, driven by Amon in fall 1965 Mosport, Riverside, Nassau events. Car was cross between GT-40 roadster and long-nosed 7-liter Le Mans car, but was too heavy for sprint events. Automatic transmission was also tried.

FORD GT PROTOTYPES

engine was also proving unsuitable. Two weeks later the same entry achieved the same results in the Reims 12-hr race; the only difference was that the Attwood/Schlesser car had a different engine: the Shelby-developed 4.7-liter unit. Except for one car which ran unsuccessfully in the Nassau Tourist Trophy in November, the 1964 season was over for Ford.

Carroll Shelby's Cobras had come within a whisker of taking the 1964 GT Manufacturers Championship in their first attempt, so it seemed wise to Ford executives to give Shelby American the primary responsibility for developing and racing the GT-40, while letting FAV continue with several cars and adding Ford France, Rob Walker of England and Scuderia Filipinetti of Switzerland to the program. Shelby started modifying his cars in California; the 4.7-liter engine, heavier but with greater torque, became standard for the GT-40 and the gearbox and brakes underwent thorough redesign. Results seemed to be immediate. The Shelby-blue GT-40s finished first (Ken Miles/Lloyd Ruby) and third in the Daytona 200-km race and only a Chaparral sports/racing car beat the McLaren/Miles Ford at Sebring.

FAV ran one car in the Targa Florio, a green GT-40 roadster entrusted to Bob Bondurant/John Whitmore. The Sicilian circuit has never been kind to large, powerful cars and the Ford retired after various adventures. At the Nürburgring the car

Le Mans 1964: Ginther/Gregory led at start, Hill/McLaren (above) made up ground after delay and set early-morning lap record, but both cars retired with gearbox trouble. Attwood/Schlesser Ford caught fire, burned out. Noses were snipped to aid cooling.

Ford Advanced Vehicles ran green GT-40 roadster in 1965 Targa Florio and Nürburgring 1000-km (above) without success.

Le Mans 1965: McLaren led, Hill again set lap record, both 7-liter cars used up gearboxes.

First outing for revamped Mk.2 was 1966 Daytona 24-hr. Miles/Ruby led easy 1-2-3 sweep of event.

Mk.2 roadster of same pair took 1966 Sebring race, followed by Hansgen/Donohue Mk.2 coupe. Hansgen later died in Le Mans trials.

was joined by two Shelby machines (one a 5.3) and another GT-40 for Ford France. The only one to finish was the Chris Amon/Ronnie Bucknum car in 8th place.

So, again, Le Mans. Someone had decided that 7-liter engines would propel the GT-40s just that much faster down the Mulsanne straight, so the two Shelby-entered cars for McLaren/Miles and Hill/Amon were so equipped. These have been referred to since as Mk.2s, but the designation was not actually applied until the car was redesigned for 1966. The 1965 Le Mans cars had enormously long noses and vertical tailfins and went like blazes. They were backed up by four GT-40s for Walker, FAV, Ford France and Filipinetti. The story of the ensuing debacle has been well told by Henry Manney ("Casey at the Bat," Sept. 1965 R&T); not a single Ford was running at four o'clock on Sunday. Another year had gone by and Ford didn't seem any closer to the intended Le Mans victory. But the decision was made to stick with seven liters for the prototypes and to build 50 of the GT-40s for the 1966 Sports category. To get some more miles on the 7-liter chassis, Ford gave a long-nosed roadster to Bruce McLaren to run in the Fall 1965 North American pro series. Bruce raced his own McLaren-Oldsmobile but put Chris Amon in the Ford, known rather sneakily as the GT X1. An automatic transmission was tried, but automatic or manual, the X1 was too heavy to be competitive with the sports/racing types. Amon drove it at Mosport, Riverside and Nassau, his best placing being a 5th in the Times GP. Peter Sutcliffe gained a second victory for Ford at the end of 1965 when he took the Pietermaritzburg 3-hr race in South Africa in his private GT-40.

Essex Wire GT-40 of Skip Scott/Peter Revson was 3rd overall, 1st in Sports class at 1966 Sebring.

Weird, ugly J-Car made first public appearance in 1966 Le Mans trials, was shelved for a year.

Mk.2's first European event was Spa 1000-km; it went well but couldn't catch latest Ferrari P3.

Le Mans 1966: third time lucky. Mk.2s of Amon/McLaren (leading here), Miles/Hulme, Bucknum/Hutcherson came 1–2–3. Five other Mk.2s failed.

J-Car finally emerged as Mk.4, won 1967 Sebring driven by McLaren/Andretti; Foyt/Ruby Mk.2 was 2nd. Surprisingly, only one of each type had been entered, in contrast to the failure of 5 out of 6 Mk.2s at Daytona. J-Car's angular lines were smoothed out appreciably.

FORD GT PROTOTYPES

For 1966 Ford was well prepared. The Mk.2 had been thoroughly tested and was supplied to Holman-Moody as well as Shelby, while the Essex Wire team received GT-40s to contest the Sports category. The Mk.2s had many detail refinements and were distinguished by new medium-length noses and engine air intakes mounted high on the rear quarter panels. They were 1-2-3-5 at Daytona (now a 24-hr race) and 1-2 at Sebring, with Miles/Ruby winning both events. The Sebring-winning Ford was called the X1 but was actually a Mk.2 with the top cut off; though a roadster, it differed in almost every other detail from the car campaigned by Amon in 1965. At Sebring, Ford began a new practice of painting the team cars different colors (the Sebring winner was a nice Italian red). This probably aided in identifying the cars from the pits but to the casual spectator it also gave the erroneous impression that a half dozen private teams were using Fords to battle one another. Ferrari offered no resistance at Daytona and sent only a token P3 to Sebring.

Meanwhile Ford had been hard at work on the J-Car—a new lighter car that proved to be as ugly as the original GT-40 had been tidy. The J-Car ran in the Le Mans trials in April but was slower than the Mk.2 and much slower than the Ferraris. Its body featured a low, pointed nose, an angular midsection and a severly chopped tail. It didn't handle well and its racing debut was postponed to 1967—probably the wisest decision Ford made.

CONTINUED ON PAGE 140

NEW FORD GT—Ford Motor Company's high-performance lab on wheels!

Wouldn't you think we'd show it hurtling through the straight at Sebring, or winging out of a hairpin turn at Watkins Glen?

Could be. But this 200-mph projectile wasn't built just to win more racing laurels—or for speed alone. Call it a research tool—blueprint to new and exciting machinery for you and your neighbors to drive.

The GT coupe, only 40 inches high, explores a bundle of way-out ideas. The build is semi-monocoque, letting the body share stresses with the chassis. A V-8 engine, displacing 256 cubic inches, is mounted midship between driver's seat and rear axle to put the pounds in the right places. For greater safety, fuel is fed from flexible plastic cells located in car side-members. Ducted ventilation, forced air cooling of seats, unit seat-and-body construction, rear axle-mounted 4-speed manual transmission, disc brakes, low-rate independent springing of all four wheels—all shed new light on car design, on sharper handling and safer driving.

Wheeled laboratories like the GT give us answers *right now* we otherwise might not get for years. What we learn today—about cams and carburetors, comfort and control, suspensions and stressed metals—pays off today, in cars better built because they are Ford-built.

FORD-BUILT MEANS BETTER BUILT  MUSTANG · FALCON · FAIRLANE · FORD · THUNDERBIRD
COMET · MERCURY · LINCOLN CONTINENTAL
MOTOR COMPANY

Ride Walt Disney's Magic Skyway at the Ford Motor Company Wonder Rotunda, New York World's Fair

RACING RECORD

1964

Nürburgring 1000-km, May 31
GT-40: P. Hill/McLaren retired

Le Mans 24-hr, June 20–21
GT-40: P. Hill/McLaren, Ginther/Gregory, Attwood/Schlesser retired.

Reims 12-hr, July 4–5
GT-40: P. Hill/McLaren, Ginther/Gregory, Attwood/Schlesser retired.

Nassau Tourist Trophy, Nov. 29
GT-40: P. Hill retired.

1965

Daytona Continental 2000-km, Mar. 7
GT-40: Miles/Ruby 1st, Ginther/Bondurant 3rd.

Sebring 12-hr, Mar. 27
GT-40: McLaren/Miles 2nd, P. Hill/Ginther retired.

Monza 1000-km, Apr. 25
GT-40: McLaren/Miles 3rd, Amon/Maglioli retired.

Targa Florio, May 9
GT-40: Bondurant/Whitmore retired.

Nürburgring 1000-km, May 23
GT-40: Amon/Bucknum 8th, P. Hill/McLaren, Trintignant/Ligier, Whitmore/Attwood retired.

Guards Trophy, Mallory Park, June 6
GT-40: Attwood 2nd.

Le Mans 24-hr, June 19–20
7-liter: McLaren/Miles, P. Hill/Amon retired. GT-40: Bondurant/Maglioli, Ireland/Whitmore, Trintignant/Ligier, Müller/Bucknum retired.

Canadian GP, Mosport, Aug. 25
GT X1: Amon retired.

Times GP, Riverside, Oct. 31
GT X1: Amon 5th. GT-40: Scott 11th.

Kyalami 9-hr, Nov. 6
GT-40: Sutcliffe/Ireland 2nd.

Nassau Races, Nov. 27–Dec. 6
GT X1: Amon retired two events.

Pietermaritzburg 3-hr, Dec. 27
GT-40: Sutcliffe 1st.

1966

Daytona Continental 24-hr, Feb. 5–6
Mk.2: Miles/Ruby 1st, Gurney/Grant 2nd, Hansgen/Donohue 3rd, McLaren/Amon 5th, Ginther/Bucknum retired. GT-40: Sutcliffe/Grossman 9th, Revson/Gregory/Lowther 17th, Scott/Thompson retired.

Sebring 12-hr, March 26
Mk.2: Miles/Ruby 1st, Hansgen/Donohue 2nd, Foyt/Bucknum 12th, Gurney/Grant retired. GT-40: Revson/Scott 3rd, Grossman/Lowther 10th, Holquist/Jennings/Kovaleski 13th, Payne/Cuomo 15th, Bentley/Byrne 22nd, G. Hill/Stewart, Whitmore/Gardner, Pabst/Gregory, McLean/Oulette, Sutcliffe/Ireland, Wonder/Caldwell retired.

Memorial Trophy Race, Snetterton, Apr. 9
GT-40: Attwood 3rd.

Monza 1000-km, Apr. 25
GT-40: Whitmore/Gregory 2nd, Müller/Mairesse 3rd, Ligier/Greder 6th, Scott/Revson, Ireland/Amon retired.

Tourist Trophy, Apr. 30
GT-40: Sutcliffe 3rd.

Brands Hatch 500, May 7
GT-40: Sutcliffe/Liddell 2nd, Ireland/Amon retired.

Targa Florio, May 8
GT-40: Ligier/Greder retired.

Silverstone, May 14
GT-40: Scott 6th; Sutcliffe, Liddell retired.

Spa 1000-km, May 22
Mk.2: Whitmore/Gardner 2nd. GT-40: Scott/Revson 3rd, Sutcliffe/Redman 4th, Ireland/Amon 5th, Mairesse/Müller, Hobbs/Neerpasch retired.

Mallory Park, May 28
GT-40: Sutcliffe 2nd, Liddell 4th.

Nürburgring 1000-km, June 5
GT-40: Ligier/Schlesser 5th, Sutcliffe/J. Taylor 6th, Bond/Spence 12th, Whitmore/Neerpasch, Scott/Revson, Ireland/Salmon retired.

Le Mans 24-hr, June 18–19
Mk.2: Amon/McLaren 1st, Miles/Hulme 2nd, Bucknum/Hutcherson 3rd, Hawkins/Donohue, Whitmore/Gardner, Bianchi/Andretti, Gurney/Grant, G. Hill/Muir retired. GT-40: Ireland/Rindt, Ickx/Neerpasch, Grossman/Ligier, Scott/Revson, Sutcliffe/Shoerup retired.

Crystal Palace, July 2
GT-40: Sutcliffe 1st, Liddell 2nd, Redman 3rd.

Martini Trophy, Silverstone, July 9
GT-40: Sutcliffe 6th, Liddell 7th, Bond 8th, Salmon retired.

Wills Trophy, Croft, Aug. 15
GT-40: Liddell 1st, Cussons 3rd.

Surfer's Paradise 12-hr, Australia, Aug. 21
GT-40: Sutcliffe/Matich 2nd.

Eagle Trophy, Brands Hatch, Aug. 29
GT-40: Salmon 2nd, Ireland 4th, Liddell 5th.

Austrian GP, Zeltweg, Sept. 11
GT-40: Salmon 4th, Casoni 7th, Rindt 9th, Ireland 10th.

Zolder, Belgium, Sept. 11
GT-40: "Beurlys" 1st.

Ford France GT-40 of Greder/Giorgi went well in 1967 Targa Florio, placed 5th behind much nimbler Porsches.

Le Mans 1967: Gurney/Foyt Mk.4 won at record 135.48-mph pace. This car is the subject of our cutaway on pages 86–87.

PROTOTYPES
FORD GT

Only the GT-40s showed up for the Monza 1000-km race, won by a lone Ferrari P3. Whitmore/Gregory (the latter back on Ford's side after winning Le Mans for Ferrari in 1965) came 2nd overall to win the Sports category. At Spa a Mk.2 made its European debut, entered by Alan Mann Racing for Whitmore/Frank Gardner. It was outclassed on the sweeping Belgian circuit by the Mike Parkes/Lodovico Scarfiotti P3 but took 2nd place ahead of three GT-40s, which by now weren't getting much opposition from the Ferrari LMs.

And again Le Mans. There was a lot of bad-mouthing when Ford entered no less than eight Mk.2s, backed up by five GT-40s, but Ford had learned about Le Mans attrition and wanted insurance. As it turned out, only three of the 13 Fords went 24 hours, but they were 1st, 2nd and 3rd. A cute finishing strategy prevented the race-long leaders, Ken Miles/Denis Hulme, from taking a deserved victory; this seemed especially sad later in the year when Miles lost his life testing the J-Car at Riverside. No one had done more to make Fords race winners than Miles. Ford won the 1966 Manufacturers Championship with the three wins at Daytona, Sebring and Le Mans and the 2nd at Spa.

In addition to the GT-40s raced by the major Ford exponents in the international Sports category, a number were campaigned by true private owners, primarily in England. Three minor wins were scored in GT-40s at Crystal Palace (Peter Sutcliffe), Croft (Eric Liddell) and a repeat in the Pietermaritzburg 3-hr (Mike Hailwood/David Hobbs).

The 1967 season is recent enough not to require much comment. Transmission failures knocked one Mk.2 after another out of the Daytona 24-hr race, the best-placed Ford being the

Coupe de Paris, Montlhéry, Sept. 25
GT-40: Ireland **1st**.

Dixon Trophy, Silverstone, Oct. 8
GT-40: Fry **2nd**.

Paris 1000-km, Montlhéry, Oct. 16
GT-40: Attwood/Schlesser, "Beurlys"/Mairesse, Vaccarella/Casoni retired.

Kyalami 9-hr, Nov. 5
GT-40: Sutcliffe/Love, Nelson/Crabbe, Hobbs/Spence retired.

Cape International 3-hr, Nov. 26
GT-40: Hobbs/Hailwood, Nelson/Crabbe retired.

Pietermaritzburg 3-hr, Dec. 27
GT-40: Hailwood/Hobbs **1st**, Nelson/Crabbe **7th**.

1st, International Prototype Trophy 1966
1st, International Sports Car Championship 1966

1967

Daytona Continental 24-hr, Feb. 4–5
Mk.2: McLaren/Bianchi/Gurney **7th**, Foyt/Gurney, Andretti/Ginther, Ruby/Hulme, Donohue/Revson, Bucknum/Gardner retired. GT-40: Ickx/Thompson **6th**, Wonder/Caldwell **8th**, Casoni/Maglioli retired.

Autosport Trophy, Snetterton, Mar. 23
GT-40: Hawkins **1st**, Hulme **2nd**, Salmon **3rd**, Harris **5th**, Nelson **7th**.

Autosport Trophy, Silverstone, Mar. 27
GT-40: Hulme **1st**, Hawkins **2nd**, Salmon **5th**, Harris **6th**.

Sebring 12-hr, Apr. 1
Mk.4: McLaren/Andretti **1st**. Mk.2: Foyt/Ruby **2nd**. GT-40: Maglioli/Vaccarella **5th**, McNamara/Grossman **8th**, Thompson/Lowther, Wonder/Caldwell retired.

Snetterton GT race, Apr. 8
GT-40: Crabbe **1st**.

Silverstone GT race, Apr. 15
GT-40: Fry **1st**.

Monza 1000-km, Apr. 25
Mirage: Piper/Thompson **9th**, Ickx/Rees retired. GT-40: Schlesser/Ligier **6th**, Nelson/Liddell **11th**, Greder/Giorgi, Borel/Ballot-Lena, Drury/Oliver retired.

Spa 1000-km, May 1
Mirage: Ickx/Thompson **1st**, Piper/Thompson retired. GT-40: Sutcliffe/Redman **6th**, Salmon/Oliver **8th**, Schlesser/Ligier, retired.

Targa Florio, May 14
GT-40: Greder/Giorgi **5th**.

Martini Trophy, Silverstone, May 20
GT-40: Hawkins **1st**, Salmon **2nd**, Liddell **4th**, Sutcliffe **7th**, Gardner retired.

Nurburgring 1000-km, May 28
GT-40: Greder/Giorgi **7th**, Crabbe/Pierpoint **8th**, Schlesser/Ligier **10th**, Nelson/De Klerk retired.

Crystal Palace Group 4 race, May 29
GT-40: Hawkins **1st**, Gardner **4th**, Liddell **5th**, Harris **8th**, Sutcliffe retired.

Le Mans 24-hr, June 10–11
Mk.4: Gurney/Foyt **1st**, McLaren/Donohue **4th**, Andretti/Bianchi, Hulme/Ruby retired. Mk.2: Hawkins/Bucknum, Gardner/McCluskey, Ligier/Schlesser retired. Mirage: Ickx/Muir, Piper/Thompson retired. GT-40: Casoni/Maglioli, Salmon/Redman, Dumay/Greder retired.

Auvergne Trophy, Clermont-Ferrand, June 18
GT-40: Hawkins **1st**, Sutcliffe **2nd**, Schlesser **3rd**.

Reims 12-hr, June 24–25
Mk.2: Schlesser/Ligier **1st**. GT-40: Bond/Sutcliffe **7th**, Pierpoint/Crabbe **8th**, Nelson/Liddell **12th**, Maglioli/Vaccarella, Greder/Giorgi retired.

Silverstone Group 4 race, July 15
GT-40: Liddell **2nd**, Crabbe **5th**, Drury **6th**, Fry **7th**, Hawkins, Lucas retired.

Circuito de Mugello, July 23
Mk.2: Schlesser/Ligier **4th**. GT-40: Nelson **13th**.

BOAC 500, Brands Hatch, July 30
Mirage: Rodriguez/Thompson retired. GT-40: Liddell/Gethin **12th**, Drury/Holland **14th**, Sutton/Bond **16th**, Lucas/Pike, Crabbe/Charlton retired.

Wills Trophy, Croft, Aug. 13
GT-40: Liddell **4th**, Drury **5th**, De Klerk **6th**, Sutcliffe retired.

Austrian GP, Zeltweg, Aug. 20
GT-40: Hawkins **1st**, Vaccarella/Maglioli **3rd**, Nelson **5th**, Neerparsch/Crabbe, Hulme/Lucas ret.

Brands Hatch Group 4 race, Aug. 28
GT-40: Hawkins **2nd**, Liddell **5th**, Sutcliffe **6th**, Prophet **7th**, Lucas retired.

Holts Trophy, Crystal Palace, Sept. 9
GT-40: Drury **6th**.

Oulton Park Group 4 race, Sept. 16
GT-40: Hawkins **1st**, Bond **5th**, Hobbs, Corner, Humble retired.

Mallory Park GT race, Sept. 24
GT-40: Nelson **2nd**.

Skarpnack Group 4 & 6 race, Sept. 30
Mirage: Bonnier **1st**, Hawkins **2nd**.

Paris 1000-km, Montlhéry, Oct. 15
Mirage: Ickx/Hawkins **1st**. Mk.2: Schlesser/Ligier **4th**. GT-40: Giorgi/Jabouille, Vaccarella/Maglioli, Corner/Blades retired.

Kyalami 9-hr, Nov. 4
Mirage: Ickx/Redman **1st**. GT-40: Hailwood/Nelson **3rd**.

1st, International Sports Car Championship 1967

John Wyer's Mirage (shown here at Le Mans in front of winning Mk.4) was a lighter, more aerodynamic version of GT-40 with 5.7-liter engine. Jacky Ickx won 1967 Spa 1000-km, Paris 1000-km and Kyalami 9-hr, with Thompson, Hawkins and Redman.

Jacky Ickx/Dick Thompson GT-40, entered by John Wyer under his new firm, J.W. Automotive Engineering. Sebring saw a triumphant debut for the J-Car, now better streamlined and finally respectable enough to join the official line-up as the Mk.4.

Wyer was out to show Ford what could have been done to the original GT-40 design; the resulting Mirage prototype won convincingly at Spa from the Chaparral and the Ferraris. The Mirage was a much-lightened, better streamlined car which used 5.1 and 5.7-liter Holman-Moody prepared versions of the 4.7-liter Cobra engine. Sponsored by Gulf Oil and painted a striking light blue with orange trim, the Mirage benefitted from the virtuoso driving of Belgian *comingman* Jacky Ickx. Later in the season Mirages won the Paris 1000-km race at Montlhéry and two minor events at Skarpnack, Sweden and Kyalami, South Africa.

Once more, Le Mans. Twelve Fords (four Mk.4s, three Mk.2s, three GT-40s and two Mirages) were deemed sufficient, but ten would have been too few—only two finished. The surprise was that the two winning drivers were Dan Gurney/A.J. Foyt, a pair not thought to be of long-distance race temperament.

As far as Dearborn was concerned, the GT campaign ended last June with the second Le Mans victory. Ford announced its withdrawal from prototype racing to concentrate on stock cars and Group 7 machinery, a decision prompted by the 3-liter limit on prototypes for 1968 but probably one that had already been considered. Ford France continued to race a Mk.2 after Le Mans, winning the Reims 12-hr race, while Paul Hawkins won five minor races in his private GT-40.

The GT-40 will probably be a strong competitor for overall victories in 1968 races (5-liter Sports Cars are allowed). Ford's entry into Group 7 racing has been conspicuously unsuccessful, but it took three years to win Indianapolis and three years to win at Le Mans, so 1969 may be Ford's big year in the Canadian-American Challenge Cup.

A STREETCAR NAMED DESIRE

An afternoon with a road-going Ford GT40

BY SIMON TAYLOR

AUTOSPORT get a lot of offers to try second-hand cars, but a phone call last week from Rodney Lyons of the Epping Motor Co. sounded a bit different. "We've got three road-going GT40s in stock—like to borrow one for an afternoon?"

Although our Overseas Editor, who has owned and raced GT40s, might not have been too excited by this, the next available afternoon—a drizzly Thursday—found me sneaking out of the office and making for Ilford, where I found the three machines— one fiery red, one brilliant yellow, one a rather nice medium green—lurking incongruously in the yard of Rodney Lyons' dry-cleaning business.

All three cars are competition models, rather than the heavier, lushly upholstered road cars, but they have comparatively cooking engines and the interiors are very civilized with carpeting and neatly labelled switches. They were built originally for an American film commercial, and have each done around 4000 road miles; with four-choke Holley carburetter and mild cam, but the usual GT40 crossover exhaust system with brief straight-through silencing, power is probably around the 305 bhp mark. All have Borrani wheels with the odd mixture of racing Goodyears (5.50-15s) on the front and R7 Dunlops (7.00L-15s) at the back.

Climbing aboard is mainly learning the knack of squeezing each leg between the fairly large diameter leather-covered wheel and slithering down until one's feet reach the adjustable pedals, but once one is settled in and has tightened the full harness the ventilated hammock-type seats are phenomenally comfortable. Visibility forward is first-class, visibility to the rear perfectly adequate, and the only major blind spots are caused by the big air intakes on the rear panels. The steering wheel is at a comfortable arm's length away, and the docile clutch and ruthlessly firm, servoless brake pedals are adjustable. Just under the right hand is the lever for the ZF all-synchro five-speed gearbox, with a hinged guard for reverse.

A touch of the starter button (no ignition key) and the engine is burbling away behind you at a smooth 900 rpm. A whiff of throttle and there's a sort of civilized shriek, like a gramophone record of a Formula 1 car with the volume turned down; on with the high-speed wiper, which rushes back and forth across the screen at a frantic rate, and we are pointing the GT40's snub nose towards the derestriction signs.

This is not a road test, for that is the province of John Bolster, and no attempt was made to take any acceleration figures —on such a greasy day, they wouldn't have meant anything. Moreover, to assess the GT40 fully would take a lot of miles, a lot of equipment, and a better driver than me. But my hour or so of GT40 motoring did serve to give an idea of what it's like to drive around in perhaps the most exciting looking road car anywhere. People stand stock-still on zebra crossings and stare in open-mouthed amazement; lorry drivers lean down from their towering cabs and offer a swap (which you drown with a blip of throttle); schoolboys jump off the kerb with delight and wave. While one is sitting patiently in the fast lane at 45 mph waiting for a queue to clear, the driver of the family saloon in front will suddenly see this red blob crouching in the bottom of his mirror and his resulting swerve to the left nearly sends him off the road.

And when a gap in the traffic appears and the right foot opens all the chokes of the Holley, the car weaves as the rear wheels spin and the car bounds forward with stomach-tightening force. The needle swings round the rev counter as though the car were in neutral, but it's in bottom and by the time it says 6500 the speedo says 60 mph. Across the gate to second, the rev counter needle's going round just as fast, and at 95 the gearlever is pulled back an inch and a half and we're in third.

The acceleration in third gear is perhaps the most impressive of all. The car is going quickly now, the road streaming under the nose and the car feeling relaxed and absolutely secure as the engine note rises and rises. Maximum in third is almost 130, but by then we've reached some more traffic and the brakes pull us down to 40 again. We're still in third gear; in fact, so flexible is the car with its mild cam and Holley carb that one can trickle down to 20 mph in top and pull away. After a few minutes' familiarization the car feels quite compact, and driving it through shopping crowds is uneventful and unfussy. Maximum speed in fourth, I'm told, is 145, which is when you change into top! Absolute top speed, allowing for tyre growth, is probably knocking on 170.

The suspension is firm by road standards, and the racing tyres transmit every catseye and ridge in the road; their mixture of patterns, perhaps, is responsible for a slight wandering tendency when going fast on a damp, bumpy road, but this feels more insecure than it actually is and is cured by respect for the throttle pedal and a light touch of the wheel.

Noise is certainly not excessive—and who wouldn't put up with a little mechanical music for performance like this?—and above the note of the engine one can clearly hear the clatter of the floating brake calipers and the gobble of the fuel pumps (although with this engine in a car weighing 17 cwt, with the performance limited by British roads, a fuel consumption of over 17 mpg is perfectly possible). There is a fair amount of wind noise at speed, too, but over the fairly short period that I drove the car it did not feel at all tiring. If you don't carry luggage, and if your passenger has short legs (the battery box lives on the passenger's side), this GT40 is certainly a usable road car.

Every so often one drives a car which is so exceptional that the memory of how it sounds and feels remains at one's fingertips and in one's ears for a long time. The tenth commandment—Thou shalt not covet thy neighbour's roadgoing GT40—is taking a lot of beating from me.

CONTINUED FROM PAGE 89

sophistication and engineering of a European car. These people have never looked closely at a GT40, for it would be difficult to find anything less American or less crude. The only "iron" thing about it is the basic block and heads of the Detroit-built V8 engine, for the rest it is pure Grand Prix and the detail workmanship and mechanical finish is such that R.A.C. Scrutineers enthuse over it. The chassis is of sheet steel .024 inches thick and welded into a semi-monocoque structure including the central part of the roof. The nose piece is a single hinged panel of reinforced fibreglass, as are the doors, which form part of the roof, and the hinged tail section.

When the Ford empire set up its small specialised factory at Slough and called it Ford Advanced Vehicles I thought it was a bit of a joke. After a week of motoring in a GT40 I can now appreciate that not only have they produced an Advanced Vehicle, but it is here with us today and is a new conception in GT motoring that must soon become common-place. Ferrari and Lamborghini are still experimenting with the conception, while Lola is starting with us, and Lotus are turning to it, but Ford are now well advanced, as the name board outside the factory in Banbury Avenue, Slough, Buckinghamshire, tells us. The selling price of a road-equipped GT40 is £5,900 plus £1,353 purchase tax (total £7,253) which is just over three-and-a-half E-type Jaguars! Is it worth that much? If you have the money to buy a new conception in road motoring you will not be disappointed; if a Jaguar, Ferrari or Aston Martin satisfy you then the unbelievable qualities of a Ford GT40 will probably be beyond your appreciation. In the publicity material John Wyer says the engine of the GT40 is detuned for road use, but "will give a more than average performance"—the understatement of the year, I feel.—D.S.J.

OVERTAKEN VIEW.—This is the view that many other road users must have had of the Ford GT40 during the test week. While not being a pretty car, the GT40 is impressively functional looking. Some people have described it as beautifully ugly.

LE MANS:
Lone JW Ford outlasts Porsches
Rodriguez/Bianchi win 24 Heures du Mans — Porsches unreliable but survivors are second and third — Alfas and V12 Matra impress

By SIMON TAYLOR and PATRICK McNALLY   **Photography by PETER BURN**

PEDRO RODRIGUEZ, Lucien Bianchi, Gulf and JW Automotive won the 1968 Le Mans 24 Hours last weekend, and in so doing clinched the 1968 FIA Manufacturers' Championship for Ford. This was Ford's third Le Mans win running. The fearsome 3-litre Porsche challenge faded with mechanical and electrical troubles during the first half of the race, but the 2.2-litre Rico Steinemann/Dieter Spoerry Porsche took second place from the sole surviving 3-litre Porsche of Rolf Stommelen/Jochen Neerpasch.

The next three places were taken by the fast, reliable and impressive 2-litre Alfa Romeo T33s. David Piper/Richard Attwood were a fine seventh in Piper's Ferrari LM, and another car to impress was the V12 Matra of Servoz-Gavin/Pescarolo, which only lost second place in the closing stages due to a couple of punctures and an accident.

ENTRY

LE MANS 1968 was dealt two heavy blows before it even started. One was at the hands of the CSI last year, when the introduction of the 3-litre Group 6 regulations killed off in one swoop the great Ford Mk 2 versus Ferrari P4 battles, reducing the serious works participation and opening the field to much more humble private entrants. The second was the result of the French strikes last summer which caused the postponement of the race to the last weekend in September, bringing forebodings of uncertain weather conditions, heavy tolls on electrical systems in the longer hours of darkness, and above all fog.

However, what did give the race some sorely-needed prestige was the fact that, as the final round in the FIA World Championship of Manufacturers, it was bound to decide the title between Ford and Porsche. Porsche led Ford by two points, but both *marques* had scored points in more races than they were allowed to count, so that the situation was basically that if a Ford won, the championship was Ford's, and if Porsche won, the title went to Stuttgart. Thus naturally full fields came from Porsche System Engineering, hungry for their first outright Le Mans win, and JW Automotive.

Officially there were four works 3-litre Porsche 908s, and the 2.2-litre 907s were private entries, but Porsche, with their usual dedication to the job in hand, built no less than seven new cars for the race; the "private" 907s were all very much works cars.

The 3-litre 908s—of which 16 have now been built (Group 4 next year?)—had long-tailed bodies with twin fixed vertical fins and also a fixed aerofoil and adjustable flaps which, as at Watkins Glen and Zeltweg, are operated optimistically by suspension travel, so that when the cars dip under braking, or roll in a corner, the appropriate flaps rise. The larger wheel bearings packed with specially-developed grease were as at Zeltweg, and the brake pad area had not been increased in size—surprising for a 24-hour race with a high-speed straight and two very sharp corners. A notable modification to the internals of the six-speed gearboxes concerned the use of different alloys on the selector fork sleeves, which gave cause for worry during practice as the different metals had different heat expansion rates. Weight was around 812 kilos; the reliable flat-eight engines were unchanged, and the cars still

Pedro Rodriguez tweaks the winning JW Automotive Ford GT40, which he shared with Lucien Bianchi, through Mulsanne. Their win clinched the manufacturers' championship for Ford.

ran on 15-ins wheels, unlike their 2.2-litre sisters which were on 13-ins higher-profile tyres.

Driver pairings were intelligently thought out, with Jo Siffert sharing the lead car with his old partner Hans Herrmann; Gerhard Mitter was driving with quick Vic Elford, while in the third car was the smooth, fast pair of Jochen Neerpasch and Rolf Stommelen. The fourth car flew the American flag, being entrusted to Joe Buzzetta and Scooter Patrick.

The three 2.2-litre cars were officially entered by Spaniard Alex Soler-Roig, by the Swiss team Squadra Tartaruga—under whose colours faithful Porsche privateer and Swiss motoring journalist Rico Steinemann has driven for years—and by French Porsche enthusiast and entrant Philippe Farjon. Basically unchanged, the 907s were without doubt potentially the most reliable cars entered and very light (713 kilos), and were obviously Stuttgart's insurance against total failure among the 908s. They had long-tailed bodies with fixed aerofoils and fins but no flaps, but to the layman's eye they were almost indistinguishable from the 908s apart from the smaller wheels and the horizontal fan visible under the rear window. The power output was around 260 bhp, to the heavier 908s' 330, and the smaller cars were using five-speed gearboxes.

Soler-Roig was sharing his car with Rudi Lins, and in the Tartaruga car was Steinemann's habitual team-mate Dieter Spoerry. Philippe Farjon's entry was being driven by veterans Robert Buchet and Herbert Linge, who has been a Porsche test driver for many years and was having his last Le Mans—in the fastest car he had ever raced.

No better representative

Although Ford of America were not at Le Mans this year, they could not have asked for a better representative to take on the fearsome all-white seven-car works Porsche challenge than John Wyer's meticulously organised JW Automotive team. Gulf rather than Ford are responsible for the backing of the team, and with team manager David Yorke's unparalleled driver control, the three-car team was easily Porsche's biggest problem. A brand-new GT40 joined the pair that have flown Ford's flag in the Championship rounds this year, but through no fault of their own JW were without their best driver pair, Brian Redman—still recovering from his broken arm at Spa in June—and poor Jacky Ickx, who has broken his leg in the Canadian GP only a week earlier and is out of racing for three months. Robin Widdows, due to take the wheel of the third car with Brian Muir, was still recovering after his crash at Snetterton test-

ing JW's car for next year, the Mirage-BRM Group 6 prototype, although he was on hand as a reserve, and Derek Bell, who was due to replace him, had to refuse at the last minute due to his Formula 1 contractual ties with Ferrari and Shell.

Nevertheless, Yorke and Wyer assembled a very strong team of drivers particularly experienced in long-distance events. That familiar pair Paul Hawkins and David Hobbs were joined by Pedro Rodriguez (released from his Goodyear contract for the occasion); Pedro was partnered by Lucien Bianchi, who has driven for JW with Ickx since Redman's accident, and was having his 13th Le Mans. In the third car were Brian Muir and the Formula 1 surprise of the season, Jackie Oliver, who had already been approached for this race to share Ulf Norinder's Lola. Two of the GT40 trio were powered by stroked 5-litre dry-deck engines on carburetters with Gurney-Weslake heads and Sullivan profile flat-tappet camshafts, but the Hawkins/Hobbs car used a conventionally gasketed motor. These engines were said to have run the full race distance on the test bed with simulated braking and gear-changing patterns, and output was quoted at 415 bhp, but the fact remained that the GT40 had yet to prove itself capable of 24 trouble-free racing hours. Changes for this race included 10-ins front rims for more braking stability, and larger wet sumps which had been baffled against surge under braking and acceleration as well as under cornering by using four traps instead of the usual two; sump capacity was now two gallons, and the pump was mounted on the back of the gearbox. The orange and blue Gulf colour scheme varied cleverly from car to car for identification purposes. Average weight of the three cars was 1008 kilos.

Backing up the JW onslaught were two private GT40s, both prepared by the works at Slough. The Strathaven car was having its first outing since it was inverted by Michael Salmon at Spa, and Salmoné was sharing the green car with Scots GT40 man Eric Liddell, while in the car of Belgian Ford dealer Claude Dubois was that hairy old fox Willy Mairesse, having his first race for many a long day. Down to share the car was "Beurlys" (Jean Blaton), with the aristocratic Hughes de Fierlandt on hand to take over if Blaton's arm injury proved troublesome. Both cars had Gurney heads but were running 4.7 blocks.

Only two Lola T70 coupés had been accepted (although other experienced Lola pilots, including Mike de Udy, had entered as early as any, and big cars were in pretty short supply). One was the blue and yellow Sports Cars Unlimited car of Ulf Norinder which went so well at Brands Hatch on Bank Holiday Monday; Sten Axelsson was

Long distance experts Rico Steinemann and Dieter Spoerry drove a well-judged race with the 2.2-litre Hart Ski Porsche 907 and claimed second place. Here they lead the eighth-placed 3-litre Alpine-Renault of André de Cortanze/Jean Vinatier.

co-driving, with Richard Bröström as team manager. Jackie Epstein's car was shared with ever-reliable Edward Nelson, and featured an Alan Smith-prepared 5-litre Chevrolet mill with dry sump, while the Norinder car had a Traco 5-litre; both were on carburetters.

Five 3-litre prototypes carried France's hopes of outright victory—the first time she has been able to entertain such hopes with any confidence for many years. In the lone V12 Matra Group 6 car, at 917 kilos the heaviest 3-litre, were Johnny Servoz-Gavin and Henri Pescarolo; contrary to common belief, the engine was just as it is used in Formula 1, and had not been endowed with detuning modifications. Power output was given as "between 380 and 400 bhp" according to Gérard Ducarouge; the new tail section was much neater than on the previous V8 Ford-powered machines, and shows how quickly Matra are learning from their Grand Prix programme. The space-frame chassis is basically similar to the original Type 630, the V12 engine and its five-speed ZF gearbox nestling neatly in the back.

For Automobiles Alpine, the complete season's effort was concentrated on this race, and their four A220s were the lightest 3-litre cars (797 kilos) in the race, although the Gordini-designed V8 engine produces a scant 300 bhp despite recamming which has increased torque. Lessons learnt from their lone entry at Zeltweg had resulted in rerouting oil piping, and the plumbing for the rear-mounted radiators had been revised. A full range of Michelin racing tyres for all weather conditions was being used, and the cars' handling was said to be their strong point, thanks to modified suspension geometry giving vastly improved stability. A ZF box is used, and ATE ventilated disc brakes.

Driver pairings were Mauro Bianchi and Patrick Depailler in the first car, backed up by Henri Grandsire/Gérard Larrousse/André de Cortanze/Jean Vinatier and Jean Guichet/Jean-Pierre Jabouille. The Bianchi/Depailler car was in fact entered by Ecurie Savin-Calberson, who were also running one of the smaller cars, but again this was only in name.

Three other entries completed the big Group 6 category. One was John Woolfe's Chevron-Repco, familiar to British racegoers, but yet to prove itself in a long-distance event, although basically very well designed and with enormous potential. The first man to make a Chevron GT go, Digby Martland, was sharing the car with Woolfe. From the United States came the other two, the very professional turbine team from the Howmet Corporation, who brought both their McKee-chassised cars for Dick Thompson/Ray Heppenstall and Bob Tullius/Hugh "Double Dibble" Dibley. The preparation of these cars was superb, and although the power was only equivalent to 330 bhp, and their single-speed transmissions had trouble with the two tight corners when geared for the long straight, their roadholding and reliability were in their favour, and somewhat surprisingly the team were expecting to go for 12 hours before changing brake pads. However, the thirsty turbines were expected to need a drink of paraffin every 50 minutes—28 stops in the complete distance—and without the high pressure refuelling equipment that Howmet are used to having in the USA, each stop could cost them a full minute. The turbines weighed in at 808 kilos, which was surprisingly light.

Prancing Horse is lame

It is a long time since Ferrari's representation at Le Mans has been of such a low standard. With no form of works cars or support, the Prancing Horse was a little lame. By far the most professional entry was the familiar light green 275LM of David Piper, with its lightweight fibreglass body and wide Campagnolo wheels; co-driver was Richard Attwood. The other English LM was Paul Vestey's purple car, codriven by Roy Pike. By contrast, the North American Racing Team's original entry of three 4-litre cars turned out to be a vintage 275LM for Americans Masten Gregory and Charlie Kolb, apparently the same car with which Gregory and Jochen Rindt won in 1965 (and looking as if it hadn't had a spanner laid on it since, apart from the adoption of Campagnolo wheels); their familiar and well-campaigned Dino, which, as the result of a competition for French drivers called the Trophée Chinetti, was to be driven by François Chevalier and Bernard Lagier; and a Ferrari GTB *Competizione* for Bob Grossman and Edgar Berney.

Scuderia Filipinetti entered two Ferraris: a 275LM and the GTB *Competizione* with which Steinemann and Spoerry won the GT class last year. Originally the LM was to be driven by Herbert Müller and Claude Haldi, but Jonathan Williams, after the Serenissima was withdrawn, decided he was not keen on driving one of the Corvettes, and took over Haldi's place for his first-ever LM drive. The LM, although your original bog-standard wire-wheeled 1964 example, was turned out to Filipinetti's usual high standard. In the GTB were Jacques Rey and Haldi.

Filipinetti had also entered the largest cars in the race, two massive 7-litre Chevrolet Corvette Stingrays, which showed signs of works preparation, even to an American GM mechanic conveniently taking his holidays in Switzerland to cast an eye over the work. In charge of one of these Group 3 monsters were Umberto Maglioli, who first raced at Le Mans in 1952, and rally man Henri Greder, with Sylvain Garant and Jean-Michel Giorgi in the other. Ski hero Jean-Claude Killy was to have driven one, but General Motors decided not to release him, as an accident would have been bad for their non-racing image. With their huge mag wheels and ground-shaking outside exhausts, these big red machines were very impressive and very heavy (1485 kilos), if not particularly Group 3.

The third biggest car in the race was a 5.3-litre Chevrolet-powered Iso Rivolta saloon, straight off the showroom floor, for Giorgio Pianta and Enrico Pinto; before it was returned to the showroom to be sold as a one careful owner car, never raced or rallied, Pianta convincingly rolled it at Terte Rouge during Thursday's practice.

Wisely, Autodelta SpA decided to concentrate on the 2-litre category where the works Porsches were absent, and fielded four of the now extremely fast Tipo 33 V8s. All had long tails, fins, six-speed gearboxes, and automatic fire extinguishing systems, and claimed power output was an optimistic 260 bhp. Driver pairings were Carlo Facetti/Spartaco Dini, Nanni Galli/Ignazio Giunti, Mario Casoni/Giampero Biscaldi and Nino Vaccarella/Giancarlo Baghetti. The total T33 challenge was boosted to six cars by a pair of T33s from the Belgian van der Straaten team, which were identical to the works cars and had been prepared at Milan. Driving these were Teddy Pilette/Rob Slotemaker and Serge Trosch/Karl von Wendt.

Surprisingly, only two 2-litre Porsches were on hand, Jean-Pierre Hanrioud/André Wicky in Hanrioud's 910 and Christian Poirot's Carrera 6, the sole 2-litre Group 4 car, which he was sharing with French hillclimb king Pierre Maublanc. Other Group 6 2-litres were a near-standard Fiat Dino for Marcel Martin/Jean Mesange, Jem Marsh's club racing Marcos-Volvo which replaced his original Mantis-Repco entry, shared with John Quick, and the long awaited all-British effort, the Healey SR with 240 bhp V8 2-litre Climax engine and Clive Baker and Andrew Hedges as drivers. The car was well turned out, but looked big and heavy (928 kilos) beside its Alfa (780 kilos) and Porsche (680 kilos) opposition.

Most purposeful among the smaller-capacity machinery was the Alpine armada, with five cars of various capacities. Officially only one 1300 and two 1000 cc Alpines were works entries, for Bernard Tramont/Jean-Luc Therier, Jean-Claude, Andruet/Jean Pierre Nicholas and Jean-Louis Marnat/Jean-François Gerbault. In a 1470 version were Alain Leguellec/Alain Serpaggi, with local men Christian Ethuin/Bob Wollek in the Trophée le Mans car. Other small Group 6 entries were Chris Lawrence's Cortina-powered Deep Sanderson shared with John Wingfield, the Donald Healey Sprite of Roger Enever and Alec Poole, the well-prepared Simca-powered Moynet of Jean Max/René Ligonnet, based on a Costin-Nathin, and

The Virage Ford was in use for the first time in a race here; here, as Jean Max struggles to push the Moynet to its pit, the Greder/Maglioli Stingray leads the Maublanc/Poirot Carrera 6 and a 911.

the eccentric Hrubon of Philippe Marchesi/Patrick Champin, which failed to qualify.

Apart from the GTBs, the Stingrays and the ill-fated Iso Rivolta, the Group 3 entry was confined to four Porsche 911s (Jean-Pierre Gaban/Roger van der Schrick, Guy Chasseuil/Claude Ballot-Lena, Meier/de Mortemart and Claude Laurent/Jean-Claude Ogier) and a brace of Alpines (Bernard Collomb/Georges Heligoin and Joseph Bourdon/Nusbaumer).

PRACTICE

SCRUTINEERING was on Monday and Tuesday, and was carried out with the usual attention to unimportant detail and a scant regard for CSI regulations. The Howmet team had a bit of trouble because the rear vision on the two TXs was at first not considered sufficient, but eventually the cars were accepted. The Chevron-Repco's ground clearance was only just sufficient, while the NART GTB arrived too late for official scrutineering after being held up at Orly Airport.

Practice began on Wednesday with full five-hour session from 5 pm to 10 pm, with virtually everybody present and correct. From the very start it was obvious that the Porsche-Ford battle was on in earnest. Each team vigilantly checked the other's times, with Jacky Ickx's time in the JW GT40 of 3 m 35.4 s at the test weekend last April as the target. Despite the fact that the new Ford corner has been eased since then following complaints from drivers that it was dangerously tight, for a long time no-one approached that time of 3 m 35.4 s. Eventually Jo Siffert did it; he had started out at 3 m 46.2 s, chiselled his way down to 41.6, and then did a 37.8. Then with only a hour of daylight left, a smile on the face of Porsche development chief Pietsch indicated that at last Ickx's time had been equalled—but not beaten. The outright lap record before the Ford corner was built was 3 m 23.6 s to Denny Hulme in the 7-litre Ford, and with the new chicane it will be a long time before that is beaten.

Less happy with Ford corner were, ironically, the Fords, which were losing to the Porsches on acceleration out of the corner, and lost the advantage they had previously had round the fast curve past the pits, where their high-speed roadholding had told. Fastest Ford driver was David Hobbs, who posted a 3 m 41.8 s, a time equalled, to the astonishment of some and the delight of the French, by Johnny Servoz-Gavin in the V12 Matra. Hobbs' team-mate Hawkins was lapping equally impressively, with two more 3-litre Porsches next up, Mitter/Elford (3 m 42.6 s) and Neerpasch/Stommelen (3 m 43.5 s).

French hopes had a further boost when Mauro Bianchi got the 3-litre Alpine round in 3 m 46.9 s, faster than the other two JW GT40s of Oliver (3 m 47.5 s) and Rodriguez (3 m 47.8 s). The fourth 3-litre Porsche of the American pair achieved 3 m 49.7 s, while Norinder's Lola, despite an alternator failure which curtailed his practice, wheeled round in 3 m 52 s. Alex Soler-Roig was only 2.5 sec slower than the Buzzetta/Patrick 3-litre in his 2.2-litre Porsche, showing how well he can go in a Group 6 car. Jabouille was another to go well in a 3-litre Alpine, posting 3 m 57.2 s, and fastest 2-litre was the T33 Alfa of Vaccarella, who was 2.4 secs under the 4 mins barrier, with Casoni only 1.5 secs slower. Dick Thompson achieved the best Howmet time in 3 m 57.7 s, with Dibley (who ran out of fuel) and Tullius slightly slower. The Howmet team decided to change ratios overnight so that the cars could achieve maximum revs on the straight, and the lower ratio was intended to help low-speed acceleration.

No one else broke 4 mins, though Müller and Greder bravely controlled the big Stingrays and got down to 4 m 2.2 s. Jonathan Williams was very unhappy with the insensitive steering of the big cars and he and Müller gratefully opted for the Filipinetti 275LM.

The yellow Dubois GT40 was one of the first cars in trouble; the sump plug had not been properly tightened and Mairesse trundled round liberally coating the course before he realised the oil pressure was zero and came in to the accompaniment of applause from the big ends. A replacement 4.7 engine was arranged via Wyer. Salmon and Liddell were just getting in the groove with the Strathaven GT40 when a rumbling from a rear wheel told of bearing failure, and when a mechanic tried to remove the wheel the ears broke off the hot knock-on hub cap, which kept the car in the paddock for the rest of the session.

David Piper had frightful luck with the Ferrari; a carburetter trumpet came loose, and the retaining nut and washer were gobbled up by the engine. Surprisingly enough damage was confined to two bent valves, although the combustion chamber needed a little fettling. There were no real indications of any serious weak points in the Fords or the Porsches, although the gearbox on the Buzzetta/Patrick 908 was removed from the car and carefully dismantled for internal inspection.

Thursday

Once again Porsche dominated the second and final practice session, again a five-hour stint starting at 5 pm. On this occasion it was Neerpasch who was quickest, getting down to within 0.4 sec of Siffert's Wednesday best. Seppe didn't bother to get within 3 secs of his previous time but was still second fastest; then came Elford with a 39.3. With two hours of practice still to go, the Porsches were confidently wheeled away, having secured the first three places in the start line-up. The Fords were going quicker than before, with Rodriguez doing a 39.8, 2 secs faster than Hawkins who equalled Hobbs' time of the previous day. For most of the session Fords ran only two cars, as the third was being fitted with the new sump, but towards the end of practice reserve driver Robin Widdows had his first drive since his accident, scrubbing in some new tyres and then running out of fuel just as he was getting warmed up.

Servoz-Gavin, driving with his usual panache, was still faster than his team-mate Pescarolo, but did not equal his Wednesday time in the Matra, but Mauro Bianchi got the V8 Alpine wound up even tighter and recorded 3 m 43.7 s, although he complained that he was 500 rpm down on the straight. Buzzetta's 3-litre Porsche was also going faster, beating Bianchi's time by 0.5 sec. Oliver got the third JW car down to 44.6 s. 5.2 secs quicker than Mairesse in the re-engined Dubois GT40.

The Strathaven GT40 was again in trouble, the oil pressure dropping lap by lap until the engine finally seized as he accelerated out of the hairpin, and it was thought that Liddell might not have done enough laps to qualify as co-driver. The same applied to Richard Attwood, for the Piper Ferrari, its cylinder head and valvegear repaired, now had electrical bothers and was parked out on the circuit while helpful marshals tried to rewire it. Norinder got down to 3 m 52 s again, but then the Lola dropped a valve when co-driver Sten Axelsson was driving, and arrangements were made to borrow a replacement from Lolas and fly it out.

John Wyer lent Michael Salmon one of their full dry-deck 5-litre spare engines, and the Strathaven car was also given a higher fifth gear to avoid over-revving. Jem Marsh and John Quick failed to qualify their Marcos-Volvo because it was short of steam on the straight, and they went home, while the NART GTB was deemed to have unhomologated wheels for Group 3; as it was over 3 litres it could not go into Group 6 and was withdrawn. The Hurbon was also too slow to qualify. Apart from the Rivolta's roll, the only incident on the second day was when Jacques Rey, bedding in new brake pads in the Filipinetti GTB, shunted the back of his Stingray team-mate Henri Greder under braking after getting a tow from the big American car.

The Healey-Climax had gearbox trouble, and new ring gears were flown out; they were only fitted on Saturday morning because the customs man at Orly thought ring gears were some sort of jewellery and held them up.

After practice times from the two days had been amalgamated, the official starting order was announced as follows. The starting driver is given first.

1. Siffert/Herrmann (3.0 908), 3 m 35.4 s.
2. Stommelen/Neerpasch (3.0 908), 3 m 35.8 s.
3. Mitter/Elford (3.0 908), 3 m 39.3 s.
4. Rodriguez/L. Bianchi (5.0 GT40), 3 m 39.8 s.
5. Servoz-Gavin/Pescarolo (3.0 Matra), 3 m 41.8 s.
6. Hawkins/Hobbs (5.0 GT40), 3 m 41.8 s.
7. Buzzetta/Patrick (3.0 908), 3 m 43.2 s.
8. M. Bianchi/Depailler (3.0 Alpine), 3 m 43.4 s.
9. Muir/Oliver (5.0 GT40), 3 m 44.6 s.
10. Mairesse/Beurlys (4.7 GT40), 3 m 49.8 s.
11. Grandsire/Larrousse (3.0 Alpine), 3 m 50.4 s.
12. Norinder/Axelsson (5.0 Lola), 3 m 52 s.
13. Soler-Roig/Lins (2.2 907), 3 m 52.6 s.
14. Vaccarella/Baghetti (2.0 T33), 3 m 53.6 s.
15. de Cortanze/Vinatier (3.0 Alpine), 3 m 53.7 s.
16. Epstein/Nelson (5.0 Lola), 3 m 54 s.
17. Giunti/Galli (2.0 T33), 3 m 54.1 s.
18. Guichet/Jabouille (3.0 Alpine), 3 m 54.9 s.
19. Linge/Buchet (2.2 907), 3 m 55 s.
20. Thompson/Heppenstall (Howmet), 3 m 56 s.
21. Facetti/Dini (2.0 T33), 3 m 57 s.
22. Steinemann/Spoerry (2.2 907), 3 m 57.4 s.
23. Casoni/Biscaldi (2.0 T33), 3 m 57.4 s.
24. Dibley/Tullius (Howmet), 3 m 58 s.
25. Salmon/Liddell (5.0 GT40), 3 m 58.1 s.
26. Greder/Maglioli (7.0 Stingray), 3 m 59.8 s.
27. Müller/Williams (3.3 275LM), 4 m 1.8 s.
28. Piper/Attwood (3.3 275LM), 4 m 2.9 s.
29. Gregory/Kolb (3.3 275LM), 4 m 2.9 s.
30. Garant/Giorgi (7.0 Stingray), 4 m 8.2 s.
31. Woolfe/Martland (3.0 Chevron), 4 m 9.3 s.
32. Vestey/Pike (3.3 275LM), 4 m 11.2 s.
33. Pilette/Slotemaker (2.0 T33), 4 m 11.6 s.
34. Wicky/Hanrioud (2.0 910), 4 m 13.8 s.
35. Trosch/von Wendt (2.0 T33), 4 m 15.2 s.
36. Poirot/Maublanc (2.0 Carrera 6), 4 m 18.6 s.
37. Baker/Hedges (2.0 Healey), 4 m 22.1 s.
38. Haldi/Rey (3.3 GTB), 4 m 22.6 s.
39. Leguellec/Serpaggi (1.5 Alpine), 4 m 23.2 s.
40. Chevalier/Lagier (2.0 Dino), 4 m 25.1 s.
41. Therier/Tramont (1.3 Alpine), 4 m 34.2 s.
42. Wollek/Ethuin (1.3 Alpine), 4 m 34.7 s.
43. Gaban/van der Schrick (2.0 911), 4 m 35.2 s.
44. Ballot-Lena/Chasseuil (2.0 911), 4 m 37.4 s.
45. Martin/Mesange (2.0 Fiat-Dino), 4 m 42.8 s.
46. Lawrence/Wingfield (1.6 Deep Sanderson), 4 m 47.3 s.
47. Max/Ligonnet (1.2 Moynet), 4 m 48.7 s.
48. Laurent/Ogier (2.0 911), 4 m 49 s.
49. Enever/Poole (1.3 Sprite), 4 m 53.7 s.
50. Nicolas/Andruet (1.0 Alpine), 4 m 55.7 s.
51. Marnat/Gerbault (1.0 Alpine), 4 m 56.7 s.
52. Nusbaumer/Bourdon (1.3 Alpine), 4 m 58.8 s.
53. Collomb/Heligoin (1.3 Alpine), 5 m 1.4 s.

RACE

AFTER completely dry practice sessions, hearts sank about two hours before the 3 pm start when grey clouds covered the Sarthe circuit and there was a heavy shower. Since 7 am the crowds had been converging on the circuit, and now the tribunes and enclosures were almost as crowded as they usually are in June.

All the usual pomp and bull was rapidly dispensed, with national anthems and presentations; blue and white were predominant at the head of the line-up, with the three Porsche 908s, the two JW GT40s, the V12 Matra, and then the fourth 908, the fastest Alpine and the third JW car. The rain came and went, and came again, and the wretched mechanics were kept trotting up and down the pit road with wet tyres, dry tyres and jacks, to the light-hearted applause of the masses above the pits. The shrill bark of the Porsches and the roar of the GT40s as they warmed up was split by the whistle of the two Howmets, and then all was silent as the drivers took their positions opposite their mounts on the other side of the road, with the road damp but the rain holding off for the occasion.

Suddenly it was 3 pm and the flag fell. The drivers scampered across the road and leapt aboard their mounts; first to move was the Alfa T33 of Casoni, but at the head of the queue the three 908 Porsches pulled out as one, their long tails sliding wildly on the still wet track, and under the Dunlop bridge it was just Stommelen from Siffert and Mitter. Much slower away were the JW GT40s, whose drivers wisely deemed it worthwhile to put their seat harness on at the start of a 24 hour race, and the Howmets, which took a few seconds to come to the boil and whistle away at the tail of the field.

Well up in the rush away from the line was the Belgian Claude Dubois Ford, but unfortunately Willy Mairesse had not shut his door properly in his haste; as the front runners thundered down the long Mulsanne Straight Mairesse's door flew open at over 150 mph, and as he fought to shut it the car went off the road into the trees and completely destroyed itself. Mairesse was rescued from the horrifying-looking wreckage with injuries that were surprisingly confined to cuts, bruises and shock.

Through the Ford corner and past the pits came the Porsches to complete their first lap, starting as they meant to go on. Stommelen still led, with Siffert in his slipstream and Mitter already dropping back; next up was Buzzetta to make the 908s 1-2-3-4, followed by Giunti's Alfa T33, Bianchi's 3-litre Alpine, Müller in the Filipinetti Ferrari LM and the first of the JW GT40s, Muir's, which was rapidly gobbling its way through, chased by team-mate Rodriguez, Guichet's 3-litre Alpine, Norinder's Lola and Hawkins in the third JW car. Straight into the pits came the V12 Matra for rapid attention to its windscreen wiper motor; the road was obviously still wet enough for wipers in traffic.

Lap 2 and the four Porsches and the lone T33 of Giunti were still in front, but the JW cars were now lining up in sixth, seventh and eighth places. They soon disposed of the Alfa, but Buzzetta proved more of a problem. Meanwhile Seppe Siffert had inevitable taken the lead on lap 4; Muir, after trying furiously to take fourth place from Buzzetta, dropped to the tail of the JW trio, and on lap 7 a determined Rodriguez squeezed past the American Porsche driver and immediately pulled well away. The second retirement came on this lap when Serge Trosch's VDS Alfa went bang at White House and came to rest with a ventilated block. De Cortanze's Alpine had, like the Matra, needed attention to its screen wiper, and Dick Thompson didn't think his Howmet was quite right, and handed over to designer-codriver Ray Heppenstall after only three laps; Clive Baker found that the Healey-Climax was already misfiring due to water on the ignition and came in for a looksee.

On lap 8 the Ford supporters received their first blow when Hawkins brought the fourth-placed car in with a badly chunked

The Alfa Romeo T33s were impressively fas lay second for a while and finally finished

Brian Muir struggles to dig the JW GT40 o 1-litre Alpine of Nicolas/Andruet and its te

The Matra V12 was the darling of the crow motoring by Henri Pescarolo (seen here) and stages.

reliable; this is the Giunti/Galli car, which

the Mulsanne bank while the Index-winning mate go through.

orking up to second place thanks to press-on ny Servoz-Gavin before retiring in the closing

rear tyre; all four wet-weather tyres were replaced with dry compound boots—the circuit was now almost completely dry, as Siffert's rapidly descending lap times bore witness—and two laps later David Yorke called Rodriguez in for a complete tyre change, to be on the safe side. This left only Muir on the same lap as the leader, in fourth place—but on lap 12 Yogi had a big moment under braking for Mulsanne which ended deep in the sand bank. He tore up advertisement hoardings and pushed them under the rear wheels, but the car was stuck fast, so with encouragement from the spectators and soft drinks from the marshals, poor Brian set to work to dig the car out—a job which took him almost exactly three hours, as of course the rules forbid any outside help.

A similar single-handed effort was put in by Jean Max who pushed the Moynet, which had suffered oil pump trouble, in from the country and was almost exhausted as he toiled up the slope to his pit, to enthusiastic applause from the French crowd. His work was in vain, however, for after much work his pit never got the car going again.

As Siffert reeled off his 16th lap the first hour was completed; Guichet's 3-litre Alpine had passed Giunti's Alfa and, with the Fords' troubles, lay fifth a lap behind the leading Porsche quartet. Masten Gregory was going tremendously well in the ancient NART LM just behind Giunti and ahead of Norinder's Lola, while Müller's Filipinetti LM was ninth. Rodriguez had lost little time with his wheel change and was now tenth, followed by the 2.2-litre Porsches of Steinemann and Linge, Bianchi's Alpine, Piper's Ferrari and Soler-Roig's 2.2 Porsche. The Matra was 16th after its pitstop, just ahead of Hawkins.

Norinder and Gregory were enjoying a tremendous ten-tenths dice for seventh place, the Lola driver perhaps incensed by an ill-informed official report that he had spun; this probably referred to Garant's big Stingray, which had done so. Dibley had brought the Howmet in with a rear wheel bearing gone, and the mechanics started a three-hour repair job which included removing the wishbones and the upright. The trouble with the Thompson/Heppenstall Howmet turned out to be a faulty fuel control unit, which limited the car to 70 per cent power and kept it down to little more than 100 mph on the straight, but had the advantage of making the car's fuel stops more infrequent.

At about 4.30 the routine stops started, temporarily shuffling the order, and for some the stops were longer to sort out the wear and tear of 90 mins' motoring. The Müller Ferrari LM had a leaking oil tank, and the resultant mess had to be cleaned up before Jonathan Williams took over, while Britain's Group 6 hopes took a knock when the clutch on the Healey-Climax jammed on its splines out on the circuit and Clive Baker had to abandon it, then John Woolfe brought in the Chevron-Repco, which had been running smoothly about halfway down the field, after just two hours' racing with steam curling ominously from one exhaust pipe. A head gasket had gone, and the car was pushed away. Paul Vestey spun his LM at Arnage, crumpling the back of the car against the bank, and the car was in the pits for almost 50 mins before Pike took it back into the race.

Whereas the two remaining JW Fords were now going strongly and had gradually chiselled their way up to third and fourth places, the Porsche team were not without their troubles. The Siffert/Herrmann car was still singing round well in the lead—by 5 pm, one-twelfth distance, it had lapped the entire field—and Mitter/Elford were second, but a longer than scheduled routine stop had dropped the Buzzetta/Patrick 908 behind Rodriguez/Bianchi and Hawkins/Hobbs. The other 908 of Stommelen/Neerpasch had lost over two laps when they had trouble with the engine fan, and the pitstop to sort it out dropped the car to 13th place.

The 3-litre Alpines of Guichet/Jabouille and Mauro Bianchi/Depailler lay sixth and seventh, two laps behind the leader but going well; next up were the Giunti/Galli T33, the V12 Matra and the Piper/Attwood Ferrari LM, which had got ahead of the Steinemann/Spoerry and Linge/Buchet Porsches. Further down, the Lolas of Norinder/Axelsson and Epstein/Nelson were running 20th and 21st, the Norinder car having been delayed by a faulty fuel feed which would not pick up the last three gallons in the tanks. The little Sprite of Enever and Poole was circulating happily, by no means at the tail of the field.

The next hour was fairly uneventful, apart from the Porsche 911 of Meier/Demortemart spinning heavily into the barrier at the Esses and damaging itself too seriously to continue. Still the Siffert/Herrmann 908 piled up its lead, so that by 6 pm it was two laps ahead of the second car, which was then the Buzzetta/Patrick 908; routine stops had dropped the JW Fords to third and fourth. The Mitter/Elford car had lost an alternator drive belt and was now fourth. The quickest 3-litre Alpine, the Guichet/Jabouille car, had been unable to restart after a routine stop, and a 50 mins stop had dropped it to the tail of the field, but the Bianchi/Depailler car was still there in sixth place ahead of Servoz-Gavin and Pescarolo in the V12 Matra. Giunti and Galli were now easily the first 2-litre drivers, their T33 still eighth.

It was towards the end of the fourth hour that Porsche received their toughest setback. With 59 laps completed and Siffert again at the wheel, the leading 908 Porsche suddenly went missing, and news filtered through that he had stopped out on the circuit. Eventually Seppe regained his pit to tell the Porsche team that either the clutch or the gearbox had failed, and an anxious Pietch sent a mechanic out to the abandoned car to find out, and see if it could warn of possible weak points on the cars still running. It proved to be the clutch.

At 6.55 pm Brian Muir finished his long dig and drove the deditched GT40 to his pit, but there was now no hope of the car qualifying under the minimum distance rule, and although Oliver took the car out for a few laps, there was little clutch left after all its reversing and it soon retired. At almost the same time the rear suspension on the crippled Howmet was completed and it rejoined, the team deciding to keep the car running until they were actually disqualified. Its team-mate was still going reliably, if slowly, on its reduced power, and managed to spin at Tertre Rouge.

By 7 pm it was quite dark, under a clear, cold moonlit sky, and the real Le Mans atmosphere took over as the lights were turned on in the pit area and the Village behind the paddock. The two JW GT40s, after their undemonstrative start, now lay first and second; then came the two remaining healthy 908s, the cars of Buzzetta/Patrick and Mitter/Elford, while to the delight of the crowd the V12 Matra, which with its superb exhaust note sounded in very rude health, was now fifth from the Bianchi/Depailler Alpine and the Giunti/Galli Alfa. The Stommelen/Neerpasch 908 was again in trouble with its engine fan, but two of the backup 2.2-litre 907s, Steinemann/Spoerry and Soler-Roig/Lins, were running reliably in ninth and tenth places.

The Norinder/Axelsson Lola had been disqualified on a technicality: Axelsson ran out of petrol due to the car's previous starvation problems, got out of the car and walked further away from the car than the 50 metres the rules allow. The two Stingrays had been rumbling happily round,

149

Sole survivor of the Porsche 908s was the Rolf Stommelen/Jochen Neerpasch car which, after dropping to 21st place with fan problems, made a spectacular climb up through the field to third.

but now Maglioli's went sick; fuel starvation had blown a head gasket, and the car was retired. The Deep Sanderson threw an injection drive belt at Indianapolis; Wingfield got out to pick it up, strayed more than 50 metres from his car and was disqualified. The Tullius/Dibley Howmet, already three hours in arrears, lost a further 25 mins when a fuel pump belt was replaced. Earlier Gérard Larrousse had spun his 3-litre Alpine and clouted the bank at Mulsanne; now his co-driver Henri Grandsire had a horrific moment when the brakes failed at Mulsanne and he left the road. Fortunately the car slotted sideways neatly between two trees, and Grandsire was unhurt, although the car was an instant retirement. The NART Dino, after sounding sick for several hours, stopped with no oil pressure and radical internal grumblings.

A 8 pm the Hawkins/Hobbs GT40 had gone into the lead; both it and its Rodriguez/Bianchi sister had completed 75 laps, as had the third-place Porsche 908 of Mitter/Elford, with Buzzetta/Patrick a lap in arrears. Fifth and sixth came the French hopes, the Matra V12 and the Bianchi/Depailler Alpine, while the Soler-Roig/Lins 2.2-litre Porsche was now seventh ahead of the Giunti-Galli Alfa. The Steinemann/Spoerry 2.2 Porsche was ninth, with the T33s of Vaccarella/Baghetti and Facetti/Dini close behind. The NART 275 LM was still going strong in 12th place, chased by the Salmon-Liddell GT40 and the Casoni/Biscaldi Alfa; next up were the Ferrari LMs of Müller/Williams and Piper/Attwood.

Jacques Rey crashed the Filipinetti Ferrari GTB at Indianapolis, damaging it front and back, and then a tyre punctured on the Epstein Lola while Nelson was driving, and he had to limp back to the pits from the Mulsanne Straight on the wheelrim. The puncture damaged the rear bodywork and a rear light, and by the time Nelson crept into the pits the car was overheating badly; the wheel was quickly changed—the Lola was fitted with huge octagonal centre-lock wheel nuts—and a replacement lamp rigged, and Epstein did a quick lap to cool the water before stopping for more next time round. Eric Liddell put the Strathaven GT40 in the sand at Mulsanne and dug it out again, and then suddenly the leading JW Ford, with Hobbs at the wheel, was in the pits with clutch trouble. Without more ado the mechanics set to removing the gearbox, and in an astonishing 80 mins the clutch had been replaced—needing removal of rear cross-member, exhausts and subframe—and the car was back in the race.

So by 9 pm, with the Rodriguez/Bianchi GT40 just out from a pitstop, a Porsche 908 was once more in the lead, the Buzzetta/Patrick car; both this and the third-place 908 of Mitter/Elford had had stops to adjust their headlights, and the Mitter/Elford machine was still throwing alternator belts. The V12 Matra sounded as fruity as ever and was fourth, but the Bianchi/Depailler Alpine had dropped to 16th after a 17-mins stop to sort out troubles with the doors and exhaust system.

Although the Howmet that was so far behind had not yet been disqualified, this was bound to come, and so the turbine team's hopes rested on the Thompson/Heppenstall car; however, at 9.45 Dick Thompson got into trouble at Indianapolis and the car rolled, resulting in severe car damage but none to the driver. Once the six-hour point had been passed the other Howmet's laps were numbered, and when it came in for its next routine stop it had to retire.

Von Hanstein's protestations

The Elford/Mitter Porsche was still plagued with alternator troubles, despite the fact that two alternators are fitted to the 908s; eventually an alternator was changed, but the regulations forbid this and the stewards, despite Von Hanstein's protestations, ruled that the car should be disqualified. A similar fate befell the 2.2-litre Buchet/Linge 907, which had had starter solenoid bothers earlier; the solenoid was on the starter and the whole unit had to be changed, but this too is not allowed, so both cars were driven into the paddock.

At 10 pm the Rodriguez/Bianchi Ford was a lap ahead of the Buzzetta/Patrick 908, which was still healthy; the Matra was now third and the Soler-Roig/Lins 907 fourth, while the consistent Giunti/Galli T33 Alfa was still first 2-litre and leading the Steinemann/Spoerry 907. At 10.30 the newly-clutched Hawkins/Hobbs car rejoined the race and, to help their morale, just before 11 pm the second-place Porsche hit trouble. Once again it was the 908's Achilles heel, for this one had had started to throw alternator belts, and after a 40-min stop the car was pushed away.

Higher and higher soared French hopes, for this put the Matra into second place at 11 pm despite hourly stops for fuel, so that it was now three laps behind the JW car. The Steinemann/Spoerry 907 was going very well, and had passed the similar Soler-Roig/Lins machine; behind them the four works Alfa T33s were holding fifth, sixth, seventh and eighth places and dominating the 2-litre class in a fast and reliable display—just like the 2-litre Porsches of seasons past. Giunti/Galli were still ahead, followed by Vaccarella/Baghetti, Facetti/Dini and Casoni/Biscaldi.

Behind the Alfas, and going as fast as in the early stages, was the sole surviving 3-litre Porsche of Stommelen/Neerpasch, its fan troubles now apparently over. The 3-litre Alpine of Bianchi/Depailler was now back in front of de Cortanze/Vinatier's identical car, and then came three 275LM Ferraris, the Filipinetti Müller/Williams car leading Piper/Attwood and Gregory/Kolb. The Carrera 6 of Maublanc/Poirot was next, with the VDS Alfa T33 of Pilette/Slotemaker 18th—until a half-shaft broke on the Mulsanne Straight and the car was out. The second-place Matra had lost one of its rear lights, had a hasty stop to fix it at 11.40, and continued on its way still only three laps down on the leader, and one tour ahead of the Soler-Roig Porsche; a routine stop had dropped the Steinemann/Spoerry car back temporarily so that at midnight it split two of the Alfas.

Should after midnight the Hawkins/Hobbs GT40, which had been going as well as ever with its new clutch although 27 laps behind its team-mate, went missing. It had stopped at the Mulsanne signalling pits with a major engine blow-up, and so now only one JW car was left. Also in trouble was the NART Ferrari 275LM of Gregory/Kolb, which came in to have the front suspension and steering checked; half an hour later it was in again suffering from lack of brakes and the mechanics wasted valuable minutes extracting a badly-fitted pad. Another Ferrari having problems was the Piper/Attwood car; Attwood thought the front suspension was collapsing, but in fact somehow a stone had got caught between a front brake caliper and the wheel, and in four minutes the car was on its way, although he stopped a lap later for a further check. The Vestey/Pike LM was also in difficulty, and retired just before 1 am when it lost second gear. Others in trouble as the night wore on included the Epstein Lola, which had lost two teeth from its final drive pinion, probably as a delayed result of its half-lap with a punctured rear wheel locking the limited slip and over-loading the pinion. The Epstein mechanics decided to try to change the crownwheel and pinion with the gearbox in situ.

Still the Ford droned round, now a further lap ahead of the Matra at 1 am; the Steinemann-Spoerry 907 was back in third spot, with Giunti/Galli still up there fourth ahead of the Soler-Roig/Lins 907, which was beginning to sound a little rough. On the same lap, having picked up three more places, was the Stommelen-Neerpasch 3-litre Porsche, with the other three Alfas strung out behind. Behind tenth man Bianchi in the first 3-litre Alpine was the Piper/Attwood Ferrari LM, which had passed the Vinatier/de Cortanze 3-litre Alpine and the Gregory-Kolb LM after the latter's troubles.

At 1.45 am the sky clouded over and there was a heavy shower of rain, which gave way to a steady drizzle that seemed to go on for hours. One of the first to fall foul of the change of conditions was Bianchi, who spun the leading car right under David Yorke's beady eye coming out of the Ford corner, but he was able to carry on without damaging anything but his dignity.

Just when it looked as though the Steinemann/Spoerry 907 was Porsche's main hope, the car came in for a routine stop and a brake disc was discovered to be radially cracked; the tired Porsche mechanics spent 15 mins discussing the situation, finally sending the car back into the race without changing the disc. To top up Porsche's cup of sorrow, the Soler-Roig/Lins 907, which had been well-placed throughout the race, went right off song and came in with a broken cam follower. After desultory attempts to mend it, the car was out of the race. The Guichet-Jabouille 3-litre Alpine lost further time when, after scraping its exhaust on the track in showers of sparks, it had a long stop to fix it.

The result of all this was that by 2 am the Giunti-Galli Alfa was third and into a fourth place came the 3-litre Porsche, gradually planing away the deficit. A quarter of an hour later the incredibly reliable Autodelta Alfa team lost a car when the Baghetti/Vaccarella T33 stopped on the Mulsanne Straight with fuel pump trouble. The Facetti/Dini car had a 10-mins stop to dry its electrics.

As the rain continued to fall the race reached its halfway point. With 177 laps completed, Pedro Rodriguez and Lucien Bianchi still held their four-lap lead over the musical Matra V12 of Johnny Servoz-Gavin and Henri Pescarolo; a further three laps behind, with 170 tours completed, were the Giunti/Galli Alfa Romeo, the 3-litre Stommelen/Neerpasch Porsche and the Steinemann/Spoerry Porsche. The Bianchi/Depailler Alpine 3-litre was one more lap behind in sixth place, followed by the Facetti/Dini and Casoni/Biscaldi T33 Alfas and then, several laps back, the de Cortanze-Vinatier 3-litre Alpine, and the Ferrari LMs of Piper/Attwood, Gregory/Kolb and Müller/Williams. The Guichet-Jabouille 3-litre Alpine was next up, 22 laps behind, chased by the Carrera 6 of Poirot/Maublanc, the 910 of Wicky/Hanrioud, and the Garant/Giorgi Stingray. Among the welter of smaller Alpines and Group 3 Porsches still running came the Salmon/Liddell GT40 in 24th place after changing an electrical transistor ignition control box; the Ford had just passed the clockwork Sprite of Enever and Poole, both having completed 141 laps, 36 less than the leader. And in the pits the Epstein mechanics worked on in the rain on the Lola's transmission.

Dirt, fibreglass and Detroit iron

The first serious consequence of rain, darkness and a circuit over 13 hrs racing came when Sylvain Garant, in the Group 3-leading Corvette Stingray, went wide on the uphill curve past the pits and under the Dunlop Bridge, and slammed into the bank. Dirt, fibreglass and Detroit iron were strewn all over the track, which was virtually blocked as the car rebounded and came to rest against the opposite bank; Garant was not seriously hurt, but furious torch signals and flashing lights reduced the traffic to walking pace as cars threaded warily through the marshals bustling excitedly about in the wet darkness. Matra wisely seized the opportunity to have a pitstop to change the V12 onto wet tyres, as did Porsche with the 908.

This accident gave the overall Group 3 lead to the 911 of Chasseuil/Ballot-Lena, and the Gaban/Van der Schrick 911 which was close behind lost time with a spin out of the Virage Ford. From then on there was little change for over an hour, except that the rain increased in intensity, and the Piper/Attwood Ferrari gradually slipped back, being nursed along as its battery was being over-charged due to a faulty regulator. The Guichet-Jabouille Alpine had its alt-

The Grandsire/Larrousse 3-litre Alpine-Renault leads Paul Vestey's 275LM Ferrari round Mulsanne. Both cars were out of the race by 1 am.

ernator belt tightened, and the Vinatier-de Cortanze Alpine had its rear lights mended. The presence of the rain may have meant that the much-dreaded fog was absent, but it lost the V12 Matra its second place at around 4.25 am when further screenwiper bothers manifested themselves, and after attempts at running repairs the French car spent three laps in the pits being fitted with a new wiper motor, losing its second place to the incredible Giunti/Galli Alfa and putting the JW Ford even further into the lead.

At 5 am, with no sign of dawn or dry weather, Rodriguez/Bianchi had seven laps in hand over the Alfa, and the 3-litre Porsche was only a lap behind the Matra; 28 of the 54 starters were still running, and among them was the Epstein/Nelson Lola, 70 laps behind the leaders but now running again with a new crownwheel and pinion after over three hours' work in the rain and darkness by the Epstein mechanics. The Matra had a couple of brief stops, one to check the screenwiper again, while the Biscaldi/Casoni Alfa got a new wiper blade. The Steinemann/Spoerry car looked the fastest car on the circuit, and the 3-litre Neerpasch/Stommelen 908 dropped a place behind it to fourth when the clutch would not free, but a pitstop just after 5 am seemed to cure the trouble. Piper was going quickly again, his over-charging now sorted out by the hours of headlight racing.

Guichet/Jabouille finally retired their 3-litre Alpine at around 6.30 am when its electrical troubles came to a head in complete failure on the Mulsanne Straight. The Filipinetti Ferrari 275LM of Herbert Muller/Jonathan Williams had been going very well despite having lost first and second gears during the night and having headlights that only worked on dip. Jonathan was negotiating the Mulsanne kink at 170 plus by lining up with a luminous marker board, and by the time his headlights picked up the curve he was more or less round it. However, having passed the Gregory-Kolb LM into ninth place overall, the car ran a rear wheel bearing and retired in time for breakfast. The NART car didn't last much longer, for no sooner had Gregory handed over to Kolb after a long, brave night stint than the Floridan buried it in the bank at the Esses and damaged it too badly to make it worthwhile digging it out.

At 7 am the Ford had completed 212 laps to the Alfa's 205; then came the Matra, the 2.2-litre Porsche, the 3-litre Porsche, the Bianchi/Depailler Alpine and the other two T33 Alfas, both going happily but sounding a little damp, and making occasional stops to dry their electrics. The Matra's screenwiper had packed up yet again, but now a grey dawn was breaking and the rain had almost completely stopped, and at 7.15 it retook second place from the Alfa. Fifteen mins later the leading car, now being driven by Bianchi, came in with a puncture, but no damage had been done and the JW GT40 was soon on its way—unlike the Epstein Lola which, after all the work, got another puncture out on the circuit and had to limp in again, this time to retire. The Salmon-Liddell GT40 was another dawn casualty: the gearbox, which had until then been working perfectly, suddenly started to shriek as Salmon came down the box for Mulsanne, and no ratios at all could be selected; eventually the car struggled round to the pits, but it did not go out again.

The sole remaining Porsche 3-litre had a routine stop for new brake pads, but then came in again with a repetition of its earlier clutch trouble for a much longer stop. When the 8 am positions were announced, the Matra was back to third again after Pescarolo made a brief refuelling stop about 20 secs behind Giunti and Galli—and this time the Alfa held the gap. The Maublanc/Poirot Carrera 6 had been disqualified for allegedly keeping its engine running during a pitstop, despite Poirot's protestations of innocence. The Alfas were noticeably the hairiest on the still wet track, according to the other drivers who had to sit behind and watch, but three of their four-car works team were still running among the 24 survivors. The sixth place Alpine had more trouble with its exhaust falling off, and the Vinatier/de Cortanze 3-litre had a long stop during which all brake pads were changed. A similar job was done by the JW mechanics in 4 mins at 8.30, and Rodriguez took over the wheel of the leading car. After another stop to repair its exhaust system, the Bianchi Alpine now needed clutch adjustment, but it still held sixth place.

With six hours to go the Ford led by six laps, with the Matra second once more, on the same lap as the Alfa of Giunti/Galli; the 2.2-litre Porsche, the 3-litre Porsche and the Alpine filled the next three places ahead of the other two Alfa T33s and Piper/Attwood, whose Ferrari was now ninth. The dice for second place was kept exciting by the fact that the Matra had to make more frequent pitstops than the Alfa, but usually managed to catch it before stopping again. At every Matra pitstop the crowd applauded, and once when it repassed the Alfa in front of the pits they shouted themselves hoarse. It also passed the leading Ford to unlap itself by one lap, and from the cheering from the stands one would have thought it was taking the lead, but Pedro Rodriguez was driving to team orders and David Yorke didn't want a five-lap lead thrown away. In fact the 3-litre Porsche was now going faster than any other car, its clutch now functioning properly, and was gradually catching up again. but the 10th place Porsche 910 of Wicky/Hanrioud made several lengthy stops to replace broken rockers and dropped way down the field, eventually retiring with less than two hours left. The

Flashing down the Mulsanne Straight is the Thompson/Tullius Howmet, which later rolled.

Bianchi/Depailler 3-litre Alpine dropped from sixth place with a long stop to rebuild the exhaust again and sort out a temperamental starter, but eventually rejoined.

The whole scene changed soon after 11 am, when the second-place T33 came in with a broken rear shock absorber mounting. This took 35 minutes to replace; then suddenly the V12 Matra and the Bianchi/Depailler Alpine were both missing, and a huge pall of black smoke rose skywards above Mulsanne. The loudspeakers were ominously silent, but then the Matra mechanics heaved sighs of relief when their car came limping in with a punctured front tyre. The Alpine had gone off at the Esses when the brakes failed; the car had spun into the bank and virtually exploded. Mauro Bianchi's overalls were alight when he got out, but happily his injuries were not serious. The banks, bales and hoardings caught fire and the road was completely blocked; traffic queued up to go through the holocaust, and the Matra had collected its puncture here.

All this drama meant that at noon, with three hours to go, second to the JW GT40 was the Spoerry/Steinemann 2.2-litre Porsche 910, with the Matra now third; the Alfa was fourth with the 3-litre Porsche on the same lap and closing fast. Twenty mins later this eventful race showed that it was not over yet when the Matra went missing again: another puncture had caused the car to go off the road, and a small electrical fire had damaged the wiring, and after being near the front of the field for so long (and with its Formula 1 engine still on all 12) it was out. Inexorably the 3-litre Porsche closed on the Alfa, and when it went by Porsches were second and third—obviously willing a gremlin to get to work on the Ford's innards.

Imperturbable

But with two hours left, still the Ford burbled round on its imperturbable way, six laps ahead of the Steinemann/Spoerry car. The Alfas held the next three places, the gallant Galli/Giunti pair still leading Facetti/Dini and Casoni/Biscaldi, and the Piper/Attwood Ferrari, still with its lights blazing to use up unwanted electricity, was seventh from the remaining 3-litre Alpine, which was chased by three of its smaller brethren and then the three Porsche 911s. An hour to go and the position had not changed; Piper took over the green LM to finish the race, and all the Ford supporters sat tight and hoped that some quirk of fate would not intervene in the closing minutes.

With 15 mins left the enormous and traditional posse of gendarmes appeared dead on time in front of the pits and lined up to prepare for the onslaught of the crowd, to the accompaniment of equally traditional derisive whistles from the masses. Incredibly the Alpine Renault GT of Bernard Collomb, which had been stationery and silent in its pit for 6½ hours, chugged out to try to do a final lap and finish the race, but it failed to make it and expired out on the circuit.

With six mins to go a carpenter appeared and built a winner's rostrum with incredible speed, and then suddenly there was the man with the chequered flag and the 36th Grand Prix d'Endurance was over. First to get the flag was the GT class-winning Porsche of Jean-Pierre Gaban and Roger Van der Schrick, and then in a flurry of orange overalls in the pit road the Gulf JW mechanics expressed their delight as Lucien Bianchi brought the winning car over the line to win Ford's third Le Mans in a row, and clinch for Ford the 1968 World Championship of Manufacturers.

The two remaining Porsches took second and third places to sweeten Porsche's bitter pill a little, although it was the "private" 2.2-litre car in second place. Despite its long pitstop near the end—which lost it a certain second place—the Giunti-Galli Alfa was still fourth, with its team-mates in fifth and sixth positions to score a clean sweep in the 2-litre class. To emphasise this the red cars lined up in formation and cruised round together for the last couple of laps.

A Ford, two Porsches, three Alfas, and then the lone Ferrari of David Piper, who once again had shown that he knows what long-distance racing is all about. Although only one of the 3-litre Alpines finished, it was followed home by three of its smaller sisters, and the French firm also had the Indices of Performance and Thermal Efficiency under their belts.

Unluckiest team of all were Chasseuil/Ballot-Lena, whose Porsche 911 seemed assured of 14th place and third in the GT category; it dropped a valve two laps from the end and, although this did not affect its overall placing, it did not qualify as a finisher as it couldn't cross the line under its own steam. The Fiat Dino of the local French drivers Martin/Mesange had a pretty reliable race, but they did not cover enough laps to qualify as finishers, a fate which also befell the other Group 3 Alpine of Bourdon/Nusbaumer, making the Enever/Poole Sprite the last of the 15 official finishers.

This was the first Le Mans win for both Rodriguez and Bianchi, although they have long experience of the race, but John Wyer must have had memories of nine years ago when he was Aston Martin team manager as he mounted the winners' rostrum. For Steinemann and Spoerry it was the pinnacle of a successful partnership in long-distance racing by the Swiss pair, justifying the interest Porsche show in them. In contrast with the works Porsches, both the Autodelta Alfa-Romeo 133s and the smaller Alpines had shown tremendous reliability, and the Alfas showed great speed as well —a far cry from when the early T33s first appeared and they were slow and unreliable, too. Three of the four works Alfas finished, and four of the five small-capacity works Alpines. All credit, too, to the Sprite of Enever and Poole, which had put up a splendidly consistent performance.

34th Grand Prix d'Endurance et de Rendement de 24 Heures du Mans, September 28-29
FIA Groups 4 and 6 Championship for Manufacturers, final round

1. Pedro Rodriguez/Lucien Bianchi (5.0 Ford GT40), 330 laps, 2727.02 miles, 115.2 mph.*
2. Rico Steinemann/Dieter Spoerry (2.2 Porsche 907), 325 laps.*
3. Rolf Stommelen/Jochen Neerpasch (3.0 Porsche 908), 324.
4. Ignazio Giunti/Giovanni Galli (2.0 Alfa Romeo T33), 321.*
5. Carlo Facetti/Spartaco Dini (2.0 Alfa Romeo T33), 314.
6. Mario Casoni/Giampero Biscaldi (2.0 Alfa Romeo T33), 304.
7. David Piper/Richard Attwood (3.3 Ferrari 275LM), 301.
8. André de Cortanze/Jean Vinatier (3.0 Alpine A220), 296.
9. Alain le Guellec/Alain Serpaggi (1.5 Alpine A210), 288.
10. Jean-Louis Therier/Guy Tramont (1.3 Alpine A210), 287.*
11. Bob Wollek/Charles Ethuin (1.3 Alpine A210), 281.
12. Jean-Pierre Gaban/Roger Van der Schrick (2.0 Porsche 911), 280.*
13. Claude Laurent/Jean-Claude Ogier (2.0 Porsche 911), 275.
14. Jean-Pierre Nicolas/Jean-Claude Andruet (1.0 Alpine A210), 272.
15. Roger Enever/Alec Poole (1.3 Austin-Healey Sprite), 271.

Index of Performance: 1, Nicolas/Andruet; 2, Giunti/Galli; 3, Steinemann/Spoerry; 4, Therier/Tramont; 5, Facetti/Dini; 6, Wollek/Ethuin.
Index of Thermal Efficiency: 1, Therier/Tramont; 2, le Guellec/Serpaggi; 3, Wollek/Ethuin; 4, Rodriguez/Bianchi; 5, Nicolas/Andruet; 6, Enever/Poole and Laurent/Ogier.

* Class winners.

Fastest lap: Rolf Stommelen/Jochen Neerpasch, 3 m 38.1 s, 222.321 kph (record for modified circuit).

Did not qualify: Michel Martin/Jean Mesange (2.0 Fiat Dino), 253 laps; Joseph Bourdon/Nusbaumer (1.3 Alpine-Renault GT), 215 laps; Bernard Collomb/Georges Heligoin (1.3 Alpine-Renault GT), 167 laps.

Retirements
First hour: Willy Mairesse/"Beurlys" (4.7 Ford GT40), accident; Serge Trosch/Karl von Wendt (2.0 Alfa Romeo T33), thrown rod. **Second hour:** Jean Max/René Ligonnet (1.2 Moynet-Simca), oil pump; Clive Baker/Andrew Hedges (2.0 Healey-Climax SR), clutch; John Woolfe/Digby Martland (3.0 Chevron-Repco), head gasket. **Third hour:** Meier/de Mortemart (2.0 Porsche 911), accident. **Fourth hour:** Ulf Norinder/Sten Axelsson (5.0 Lola-Chevrolet T70 Mk 3), left car, disqualified; Jo Siffert/Hans Herrman (3.0 Porsche 908), clutch. **Fifth hour:** Brian Muir/Jackie Oliver (5.0 Ford GT40), clutch; Umberto Maglioli/Henri Greder (7.0 Chevrolet Corvette Stingray), head gasket; Chris Lawrence/Jon Wingfield (1.6 Deep Sanderson-Ford), left car, disqualified; Henri Grandsire/Gérard Larrousse (3.0 Alpine-Renault), loss of brakes, accident; François Chevalier/Bernard Lagier (2.0 Dino-Ferrari), blown engine. **Sixth hour:** Jacques Rey/Claude Haldi (3.3 Ferrari 275GTB), accident. **Seventh hour:** Gerhard Mitter/Vic Elford (3.0 Porsche 908), changed alternator, disqualified; Herbert Linge/Robert Buchet (2.2 Porsche 907), changed starter, disqualified; Hugh Dibley/Bob Tullius (Howmet TV turbine), insufficient distance covered, disqualified; Dick Thompson/Ray Heppenstall (Howmet TV turbine), accident. **Eighth hour:** no retirements. **Ninth hour:** Joe Buzzetta/Scooter Patrick (3.0 Porsche 908), alternator; Teddy Pilette/Rob Slotemaker (2.0 Alfa Romeo T33), half-shaft; Jean-Louis Marnat/Jean-François Gerbault (1.0 Alpine-Renault A210), electrics. **Tenth hour:** Paul Hawkins/David Hobbs (5.0 Ford GT40), blown engine. **11th hour:** Paul Vestey/Roy Pike (3.3 Ferrari 275LM), lost second gear. **12th hour:** Giancarlo Baghetti/Nino Vaccarella (2.0 Alfa Romeo T33), blown engine. **13th hour:** Alex Soler-Roig/Rudi Lins (2.2 Porsche 907), broken cam follower. **14th hour:** Sylvain Garant/Jean-Michel Giorgi (7.0 Chevrolet Corvette Stingray), accident. **15th hour:** no retirements. **16th hour:** Jean Guichet/Jean-Pierre Jabouille (3.0 Alpine-Renault), electrics. **17th hour:** Jackie Epstein/Edward Nelson (5.0 Lola-Chevrolet T70 Mk 3), final drive and puncture; Herbert Müller/Jonathan Williams (3.3 Ferrari 275LM), rear wheel bearing; Masten Gregory/Charlie Kolb (3.3 Ferrari 275LM), accident. **18th hour:** Michael Salmon/Eric Liddell (5.0 Ford GT40), gearbox failure; Pierre Maublanc/Christian Poirot (2.0 Porsche Carrera 6), disqualified. **19th and 20th hours:** no retirements. **21st hour:** Mauro Bianchi/Patrick Depailler (3.0 Alpine-Renault), loss of brakes, accident. **22nd hour:** Johnny Servoz-Gavin/Henri Pescarolo (3.0 Matra V12), puncture, accident, electrical fire. **23rd hour:** Jean-Pierre Hanrioud/André Wicky (2.0 Porsche 910), broken rockers. **24th hour:** Guy Chasseuil/Claude Ballot-Lena (2.0 Porsche 911), engine failure.

'This magnificent machine...'
Driving the Ford GT40

IT WAS Ford of America (who else?) who invented the disposable racing car. "Hey boy, fetch another GT40 from the van; this one's smoking...." You might well scorn the transatlantic technique of crush 'em with dollars—but wait. Consider not the miserable fate of Ford's opposition struggling by at Le Mans on a paltry budget of a few hundred thousand. Better to reflect that the world is now richer by around one hundred gems of

by Roger Bell

pedigree racing machinery which, without an almost bottomless racing purse, Ford would never have built. Future generations will look back at Henry F II as a charitable sportsman, not a ruthless tycoon, when they jostle with open cheques for a Vintage GT40.

Mind you, it must have been reassuring for the hired hands who drove these remarkable *bolides* at Le Mans and elsewhere to think that if a missed gear sent all eight pistons through the plastic roof in a mushroom cloud of blue smoke, Mr. Ford

Continued on the next page

'This magnificent machine...'

would foot the bill and wheel out another car. Unfortunately, we were not driving one of Mr. Ford's GT40s when it erupted into a smoke bomb at 125 m.p.h. Not only did it belong to a private customer but, worse still, it was the only one he had. Conscientiously, our thoughts turned not so much to baling out (instinctive reactions were already preparing for that emergency) but how to break the news of a charred shell to its proud owner. This dramatic little incident luckily fizzled out to nothing; investigation once we had stopped revealed that a glob of oil had centrifuged out of the filler on the long MIRA banking and dribbled on to the exhaust pipe. Hence the smoke screen.

The episode in itself meant nothing yet it served to emphasise that this fabulous machine provided the most exciting and memorable three days test driving we have had.

The car was kindly loaned to us by Peter Sheen, an erudite enthusiast who seems to absorb more encyclopedic facts about cars than all the motoring mags can provide (he once won a *Motor* quiz) and backs this knowledge with extravagant, specialist machinery of which the GT40 is the latest. Basically, it is a Mk. 1 racer with a standard high performance 4.7 engine of the sort that, for a few extra dollars, anyone can have in their stock Mustang. Most of the GT40 road cars are in this de-tuned racer form, the rare Mk. 3s being the only ones specially designed (well, orientated anyway) for road use.

It seems unlikely that the total number of GT40s will much exceed the hundred mark when the line finally ends (which it hasn't yet). When we last checked, John Wyer's Slough works had built 81 "production" closed cars (remember that 50 had to be built to homologate the car in Group 4), seven prototypes, four open cars and three (of the planned seven) Mk. 3 roadsters which, for the record, have softer springs, rubber bushed suspension, better heat and sound insulation (one even has refrigeration) and a more refined cockpit among other things. The Mk. 4 7-litre cars that won at Le Mans last year were wholly American made by Shelby and Ford so they hardly qualify as Slough GT40s at all—unlike the Mk. 2 '66 7-litre Le Mans winner which did hail from the Trading Estate, Bucks.

But back to Peter Sheen's highly bulled Mk. 1 which, though it has a lowly chassis number, actually left the works as a new car fairly late on in the GT40 history. (The chassis was held as an on-the-shelf reserve, hence the delay in completion.)

All undone: the guillotine doors, massive fuel tank fillers, single wiper blade, spare wheel "boot", and outstanding engine room accessibility can all be seen in this aerial shot.

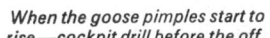

"... the shape is not of this world to folk who have never seen a modern sports racing car..."

Mêlée of plumbing (right) is Shelby's tuned exhaust system. Flush flip-up handles (far right) minimise external protrusions. The shovel nose (below right) "peppered with more air holes than a kilo of Gruyere". No splash back from this massive filler (right corner).

When the goose pimples start to rise—cockpit drill before the off.

'This magnificent machine...' continued

The car is part of the natural scenery in a circuit paddock, attracting attention but not necessarily a crowd. Drive one down the High Street—especially a bright yellow one—and Lady Godiva on a matching pink elephant would not command a bigger audience. With its great shovel nose sneering from a giant plastic bubble peppered with more air holes than a kilo of Gruyère, the shape is not of this world to folk who have never seen a modern sports-racing car.

Getting in (or out) for the first time is best done in privacy since to scramble into the footwells over the side plateaux calls for gymnastic contortions. Get it wrong and you finish up with the gear lever hooked up your left trouser leg and your right foot wedged behind the steering wheel in an idiotic and almost irreversible position. Even when installed you can still make a fool of yourself by slamming the guillotine door on your head, leaving a shock of hair on the outside, if not a slice of scalp. That one gets a good laugh.

But, oh boy, once you are hermetically sealed inside, lying back in the magnificent enveloping hammock with a panoramic forward view over the low drooping nose, the stage is yours, the audience goggle-eyed and the goose pimples rising. Cockpit drill before firing up is odd but easy. You twist-on the battery master switch by your left shin and then throw a couple of toggle levers on the dash for the ignition (there is no key) and the two Stewart Warner electric fuel pumps which momentarily patter like a football rattle and then settle down to a rythmic clop, clop, clop behind your left thigh somewhere. You stab the central starter button with a pensive finger which instinctively recoils as the engine blips instantly with a hysterical WHANG on just a dash of throttle. A couple more whang, whangs to clear its throat and the big V-8 settles into a busy tickover, the smooth throb of eight idling pistons, 16 chattering valves and a sighing hiss from the air intake six inches behind your neck being broken by that pulsing clop, clop of the fuel pumps, like a heart beat suddenly reviving a dormant beast.

It is only a short drop for your right hand from the rather large, leather-rimmed steering wheel to the wooden-topped gearlever on which an exploratory waggle reveals only that there seems an impossibly small lateral movement to accommodate the necessary five prongs of the ZF box's five-gear gate. The secret is virtually to forget lateral crossovers altogether and merely snick the light, short-travel lever to and fro—back into first, forward for second, back for third and so on. A latch mechanism prevents wrong slotting so just a quick stab in the right direction will find the next gear.

It needs to be fast, too, because the engine, with practically no flywheel inertia to keep it spinning, blips up and down like a Tyrolean yodeller. (Switch off and it doesn't just slow down and stop so much as cut dead, like a light bulb going out). Moreover, the upper four ratios are so close that the engine note barely alters pitch when you change gear. On most big-torque gearboxes, instant gear-changing is marred by a heavy long-travel clutch but in complete contrast the GT40's is so light and short that it might have come from a Hillman Imp. It also takes up the drive as smoothly as a fluid coupling. Just occasionally, we got lost in the gear lever maze, invariably through trying to over-rule the latch mechanism by leap-frogging a gear. In a change from fifth to first, you must visit fourth, third and second on the way. If you do get lost the answer is not feverishly to stir the lever but leave it in the first slot that engages and GO for the engine is so incredibly tractable that really any gear will do—as the top gear acceleration figures vividly confirm. At any speed below 120 m.p.h. you can notch up another 20 m.p.h. in under 5 seconds by flexing your big toe (no need to change out of top) emphasizing, at the bottom end, the engine's colossal torque from idling speed upwards and, at the other, the very low drag of the body. You can actually start off from rest in top after a few yards of gentle clutch slip and still have sufficient urge to out-drag practically anything else from the lights.

Basically, the engine is a standard high-performance 4.7-litre Ford V-8 with a Holley four-barrel carburetter (not the four Webers of some Mk.1s) and Shelby's bunch-of-eight high-riser exhausts some of which cross over in a melee of plumbing to the opposite tail pipe. A by-product of this free-flow tuning system is that the engine does not have the characteristic twin-beat warble of most production double-plane V-8s but a smooth, crisp siren, like a muffled Formula 1 engine where a single plane crankshaft allows the exhaust pipes to emerge between the cylinder banks, not below

Performance comparison

	GT40	4.2 E-type
Maximum speed	160 m.p.h.	150 m.p.h.
Acceleration		
0-40	3.2 sec	3.7 sec.
0-60	5.3	7.0
0-80	7.7	11.0
0-100	11.8	17.2
0-120	15.9	25.2
¼ mile	13.1	14.9
In top gear		
20-40	4.1 sec.	5.5 sec.
40-60	4.1	5.3
60-80	4.2	6.6
80-100	4.3	7.3
100-120	4.8	7.8

them. The current racing engine with its Gurney-Weslake heads and stronger bottom end is a far wilder machine developing over 400 b.h.p. but even the stock version (rated at around 330 b.h.p. but probably nearer an honest 290 according to Inside Information) gives this 17 cwt. car a formidable power/weight ratio and a tremendous performance. Peter Sheen has covered the standing quarter mile in 12.3 seconds at Santa Pod—a time we could not quite match (with two up) in a couple of all-out runs on MIRA's concrete ribbon. Well, not quite all out because the brand new clutch wanted to slip more than the wheels would spin so we nursed it off the line quite gently before booting hard. Even so, the car would rocket up to 120 m.p.h. and beyond faster than any other we have tested. Even John Woolfe's famous 7-litre Cobra, fractionally quicker to 100 m.p.h., could not live with it above 2 miles a minute when the Ford's streamlining (or perhaps the Cobra's lack of it) really starts to pay off. On MIRA's relatively short 2.8 mile outer circuit, the GT40 would surge up to 6,500 r.p.m. in top which, on 6.50 × 15 Dunlop Yellow Spot R7 tyres, corresponds to around 160 m.p.h. (170 m.p.h. on the optimistic speedometer which had been tuned to different tyres). This is far and away the highest speed we have recorded at MIRA yet apart from the deafening noise and the wind pressure which suddenly unlatched the door (we hadn't secured it properly) these all-out runs were notable only for the ease and stability with which the car made them. Just as well when you consider that the big-gun 7-litre machines ran out of push at something in excess of 220 m.p.h. down the Mulsanne straight.

We had experienced Formula 1 acceleration on the road before and, in the Rover BRM gas turbine, Grand Prix handling too. Combine them both, as the GT40 does, and the result is sensational, completely shattering any pre-conceived ideas about what is possible in terms of acceleration, adhesion and cornering power. There is not the slightest hint of anything quite so rude as roll, lurch or understeer when you will some pressure onto the steering wheel. The car merely changes direction and thrusts you hard in the side with g forces that would fling even an Elan off the road, at the same time delivering stronger self-centring through the otherwise light and very direct rack and pinion steering. Along with quite strong kick-back that makes the wheel writhe in your hand like a captive snake comes super-sensitive feel, too.

Obviously, there is enough surplus torque in first and second gear to unstick the tail if you power a corner too hard but it is astonishing just how viciously the car will accelerate from the apex without getting out of line. And novel, too, in that you can change down three times into second for a 70 m.p.h. corner.

Being firmly sprung, the car is at its best on good roads which it seems to skim along with uncanny smoothness. On the rough, speed is restricted not so much by lack of adhesion as jitterbugs in the steering and Rose-jointed suspension which can rattle like a laden tea trolley on cobbles. Yet underlying this inevitable vibration over sharp disturbances, the suspension feels unexpectedly resilient and practically floats the car over long wavelength humps and depressions. One thing's for sure: those supermen bombing down Mulsanne at 200 plus are relaxing in far greater comfort that you are on a wooden bench in the stands. That is, provided that they have ear plugs because at maximum speed it sounds as though you're sitting in the tail pipe of a Lightning with the afterburners on. Come to think of it, there wouldn't be much time for relaxation near the end of Mulsanne because the unservoed brakes demand an almighty heave on the pedal. Drivers who can't ring the bell with a 200 lb. kick need not apply.

As road transport, there are other shortcomings, too. Although the car is absurdly easy to drive and will idle happily in a traffic jam (thermo-static fans keep the water temperature constant) a GT40 is hardly at its best in the High Street. The over-your-shoulder blindspot is so bad that you can lose a bus in it. Worse still, without any ram pressure to force cooling air through the facia vents, the cockpit simmers like the dry heat room of a Turkish bath—hence the extra insulation and even refrigeration in the Mk 3 cars. It is not much good for shopping expeditions, either, since with two up there is hardly room for a folded string bag, let alone the goodies. Parking manoeuvres are to be avoided, too; apart from the restricted rearward view, the turning circle is large and when you're squeezing through gaps the car feels as manageable as a channel ferry hovercraft from your low-down vantage point practically in the middle of the turtle shell body. It *is* wide, too, and the wheel arches bulge just where they cannot be seen. And then there is the loving ritual of the oil can; like a cherished steam loco, the GT40 ought to have a squirt of lubricant (on its Rose joints) before each long run. Couple these irritations with the small problem of getting in and out and you can understand the reluctance of the Metropolitan police to issue the GT40 with a Hackney carriage licence. Not that the police aren't interested—like bluebottles in the marmalade, lawmen find a GT40 irresistible!

24 HEURES DU MANS 1969

Ford's 4th Straight

BY CYRIL POSTHUMUS

"THE TUMULT AND the shouting dies, the captains and the kings depart . . ." Le Mans is long over now, and you all know about Ford's fantastic fourth win and Porsche's desperately narrow defeat. But what a great race it was, what a turn-up for the book, what an incredible finish. There have now been 37 Le Mans 24-hr races, each and every one with its dramas, heartbreaks and tedium, but you'll have to go back a long time to find one matching Le Mans for sheer sensation and sustained interest.

It's hard to love Le Mans, all the same. Many pros in racing, and most journalists and photographers hate the place. It's smelly, dirty and overcrowded; the French officials, "men, vain men, dressed in a little brief authority," delight in being awkward; there are far, far too many interfering police around (on British circuits they control traffic, that's all), while the all-pervading air of crude commercialism taints the very real excitement of the battle between great marques like Porsche, Ford, Ferrari and Matra.

One wonders how paying spectators endure it in their noisy, dusty enclosures, with the dubious amenities of stinking 18th-century latrines and the added insult of having to stand in line *and* pay for them; the eternal grubby sand to flounder through: the hot, sickening wafts from the hamburger and hotdog stalls, and the hot, sickening prices the vendors have the nerve to charge for everything. There has to be some huge counter-attraction at Le Mans to fill the enclosures to bursting point with half a million spectators or so each year, and of course there is—the race itself, the savage pace, the harsh, thrilling music of multi-cylinder engines at work, going on and on through the day, the night, and through the day again to the climax and relief of the finish.

Of course it all began long before the traditional Saturday start on the traditional second weekend in June. This year the all-important national elections *(Pompidou ou Poher pour Président?)* mucked up the status quo and nearly shifted the whole race to another weekend, but eventually they settled for a 2 p.m. start instead of the usual 4 p.m. Then Porsche looked like wrecking the status quo even more thoroughly by withdrawing all their cars, and as they were fielding about 25 percent of the entry that mattered this would have been calamity from all angles. Smoldering over the FIA's cavalier ban on airfoils and "separate aerodynamic surfaces," the Germans demanded the right to use the suspension-controlled flaps on their big 4.5-liter flat-12 917s, declaring that the car was designed around them and demonstrating very forcibly before some splendidly frightened officialdom that they were unsafe without them.

Having clinched the Manufacturers Championship anyway, Porsche could play "san fairy ann" and tell the organizing AC de l'Ouest to go *étoffe* themselves, even though they badly wanted to win Le Mans and had seven very well prepared cars entered to try to do that very thing. In contrast, the ACO, already confronted with the withdrawal of four works Alfa Romeo 33s, three works Lolas, two Lancias and two Abarths, obviously wouldn't let such animators of the course as seven factory Porsches go without a struggle, even if it helped Matra's and Alpine's chances. A fine old *brouhaha* it was, with petitions and special meetings thrown in, ending in a climb-down compromise and permission for Porsche to race their 917s with the moveable flaps in operation, though the 908s had to wear theirs in a fixed position.

That settled, how did the field look? On paper, outright victory lay between Porsche, Ferrari, Matra and Ford, with inevitable qualifications on strength of entry, know-how, determination, resources, reliability and optimism. Porsche looked truly formidable. Four big 917s in all were listed, three works cars of which one served as reserve and nonstarted, and one private one, the first to be sold, for a big, cheery English lover of big hairy cars, amateur John Woolfe. And three 3-liter, flat-8 908s, two closed, one open, all of which put odds heavily on the first German victory at Le Mans since 1952, reinforced by staggering practice times in which, despite the Ford chicane just before the pits, Rolf Stommelen in a 917 lapped the 8.35-mile Sarthe circuit in 3 min 22.9 sec, which is 148.49 mph and faster than Denny Hulme's 3:23.6 record of 1967, set without the chicane in the 7-liter Mk 4 Ford. They say the 917 was doing almost 240 mph down the Mulsanne Straight. Some Group 4 car!

In face of such opposition, it was comforting to see Ferrari, the old hands at Le Mans, back again, although only two 312Ps, beautiful creations though they are, was cutting things a bit lean. Both had coupe tops, and one was all-new, though 420 bhp of 3-liter V-12 engine paled somewhat before the 585 bhp of Stommelen's Porsche. Matra put in four cars *pour la France,* all 3-liter prototypes with F1-based V-12 engines; they'd had a lot of trouble with crashes and injured drivers beforehand but were very determined about Le Mans. Three were open, one an all-new 650 for Jean-Pierre Beltoise/Piers Courage, two were older 630s for Johnny Servoz-Gavin/Herbert Muller and Nanni-Galli/Robin Widdows, and the fourth car was last year's 630 coupe for Jean Guichet/Nino Vaccarella—a fine international assortment of talent.

Two of the Fords were, of course, our old friends the Gulf-sponsored JW Automotive GT40s, with Jacky Ickx/Jackie Oliver in last year's winning car, and David Hobbs/Mike Hailwood in the second. There were also four privately-entered GT40s—one Alan Mann-prepared for owner Malcolm Guthrie and Frank Gardner, one for Peter Sadler/Paul Vestey, one a German entry for Kelleners/Jost, sponsored by the *Deutsche Auto Zeitung,* and one a French entry for the ASA-Esca organization. All Fords had full 5-liter engines—you can't give anything away in Group 4 these days.

With the Lola works withdrawal, the Daytona winners were represented only by the Scuderia Filipinetti's Traco Chevy-powered T70 GT Mk 3b for Jo Bonnier and that Kansas City character Masten Gregory—a formidably experienced pair. As it happened, the very same Ferrari 275-LM with which Masten won Le Mans with Jochen Rindt in 1965 was again running, again entered by NART (North American Racing Team, as if you didn't know) and driven by unemployed Alfa man Zeccoli and American Sam Posey. NART entered two other cars, a brand new Ferrari GTB4 Daytona and a 2-liter Dino, but alas and alack, Ricardo (no relation) Rodriguez in the Dino spun in front of Bob Grossman in the GTB4 on the Mulsanne brow, the pair inscribing their fate most legibly in black rubber as they bounced and rebounded off the new Armco barrier which has been erected along the entire straight. Neither Ferrari was deemed raceable after this drastic encounter, so Sam Posey transferred to the old 275LM, Bob Grossman just watched, and Le

The winning Ickx/Oliver Ford GT40 comes down the home stretch, finishing just this far ahead of the Herrmann/Larrousse Porsche.

The 12-cyl Porsche 917 led for hours and hours, set fastest lap, but faltered before the finish to hand the victory to Ford.

LE MANS 1969

Mans old hand Luigi Chinetti found himself with one car to team-manage instead of three.

Apart from the Lola, Filipinetti had two other charges—a real rumbleguts 7-liter Chevrolet Corvette Stingray coupe for Frenchman Henri Greder and Swiss up-and-comer Reine Wisell and a 275GTB Ferrari for Rey/Haldi. Then there were four Alpine-Renault 3-liter prototypes with rather gutless Gordini-developed V-8 engines. A twin-cam version, promised for months, was not ready so they had to rely on 310 meager horsepower, plus mild enterprises such as rear-mounted radiators and electronic stabilizers which restricted suspension travel at high speed. The drivers would have preferred 100 more hp.

Below the 3-liter mark there were Porsche 910s and 911s galore, two Belgian-entered Alfa Romeo 33s, hordes of blue Alpines in 1.5-, 1.3- and 1.0-liter sizes to guarantee at least one French victory, an Abarth, and the mighty British effort —one 2-liter Climax-engined Healey, one 2-liter BMW-engined Chevron, one 2-liter BRM-engined Nomad, a 1.3 Ford-engined Piper and a 1.3 Unipower. Neither the pretty Piper nor the homely Unipower, both unready and trouble-dogged, could qualify, which left the Healey, Chevron and Nomad, plucky efforts each, to represent the country whence came the winning Bentleys, Jaguars and Aston Martins of yesterday. Never mind, we've got Harold Wilson...

Practice, held in close, heavy weather, revealed several things, Porsches, their tendency to leak oil, the disastrous effects of getting 1st gear instead of 3rd, after which Woolfe's car needed an engine change; wheel and ventilation troubles *chez* Matra, engine worries *chez* Chevron; run bearings and withdrawal by the French-entered GT40; manifest unreadiness of the Piper—but what a looker; front spoiler troubles *chez* Ferrari, cured by throwing them away; bird trouble for Bonnier, sprayed with a largesse of feathers and gore when one jammed in a cockpit ventilator; a cracked bellhousing on the Hobbs/Hailwood GT40 which ruffled JW serenity; and the fact that superb ability on skis does not make an instant racing driver, as demonstrated by Jean-Claude Killy when he rolled his 1.5 Alpine at "Indianapolis" on his second lap...

So, AT LAST, The Day, sunless but hot, with air as thick as the gendarmes. Two hours before starting time the place was packed to bursting point with public and police, while over the public address system, in between much Gallic ado about nothing, they were playing that damnable song *"Les Vingt-Quatre Heures du Mans..."* Now came the finest hour for the gendarmes and petty officials with *carte blanche* to boss everyone around, to motion innocently and often prettily hanging legs back onto the pit counter, to check passes, and generally be unpleasant, while the public opposite whistled its customary derision.

Then engines started one by one, and soon the air vibrated with revving engines. The phalanx of silver-white Porsches at the front end of the long line of cars growled angrily in unison, the lovely red Ferraris joined in, while simultaneously by signal, the four blue Matras broke into a superbly bestial paeon of V-12 noises, causing all nearby to clap fingers hastily to ears. Rodriguez rolled up late and got a warm cheer, Frank Gardner chatted cheerily to Guthrie, Beltoise talked busily with his hands, Alpine mechanics ran hither and thither, and the *flics* gaped stupidly. Then came the order, *"Arrêtez moteurs"* and silence—apart from the excited chatter of the multitude—as the drivers took up their places on the road opposite for the running start so traditional to Le Mans yet soon, perhaps, to change because of safety harness problems.

Two o'clock, the *tricouleur,* and the *départ.* Forty-four drivers sprinted, and one ambled, across to their cars. The ambler was Jacky Ickx ("the last lap counts, not the first"), who was to win the race by bare yards yet who squandered that distance and much more by his leisurely getaway. His GT40, in similar mood, took its time to fire, joining in long after Stommelen had stormed away in a fine 45 degree slide to head a long string of Porsches on the first, perilous round. Past the pits he slammed, Elford's 917 at his tail, three 908s, the Lola, another Porsche and Hobbs' GT40 following and then, while an Alfa, two Matras and an Alpine also blatted through, back towards White House there came in a terrible flash, a tower of flame—and no more cars.

John Woolfe had lost his fierce Porsche 917 at White House; the car went off the road into a bank, bounced back upside down and exploded. Right behind, Chris Amon's Ferrari 312P charged into the blazing fuel tank; frantically pressing the Ferrari's extinguisher apparatus he baled out, getting away with a bad fright and slight burns. Other cars stopped at all angles behind the holocaust until firemen got it under control, and then trickled through, chastened at this first lap calamity. Poor Woolfe—whose co-driver, veteran Herbert Linge, had offered to take first stint—died almost at once.

Frank Gardner's GT40, sprayed in passing with blazing fuel, stopped at the pits; Jabouille's Alpine, too, was slightly damaged by flying debris; the rest went on with the race, Stommelen and Elford setting the pace in the big snarling 917s at around 139 mph. Before the first hour was up the Porsche armada held the first six places. Came the usual Le Mans phases; the first pit stops for driver-change, fuel, oil, water and maybe tires according to the cars' appetites; and the first retirements. A Porsche 910 and the pretty little Abarth spider were first to go, the boxy little Healey was dead unlucky, got a bolt through the radiator during the Woolfe accident, cooked its plugs and boiled away its water

Fourth went to France's big hope, the Beltoise/Courage Matra.

and its chances. Gardner's GT40 needed a radiator change and, more significantly, Stommelen's flying 917 developed an oil leak and a smoke screen, losing time and the lead in efforts to remedy same.

That gave the sleek open 908 of Siffert/Redman a turn at leading, though Elford/Attwood soon thrust their bigger 12 ahead, manfully keeping the revs down to 8000, and pegging it at a mere 218 or so mph down Mulsanne. But the Stommelen/Ahrens sister car was really in trouble; a gearbox oil seal had gone, and its smoke trail was getting thicker, so that the battery of 908s in reserve must have comforted ex- and present team managers Huschke von Hanstein and Rico Steinemann, both Teutonically deadpan in the pits. Yet it was the Siffert/Redman 908, one of their big hopes, which went next, contracting a seized gearbox just before the fourth hour. *Zut alors* . . . Behind, the Gulf Fords lay 7th and 8th, traveling nice and steadily, straining nothing.

Elsewhere attrition was making hay. The blaring red Ferrari 312P of Rodriguez/Piper, depressingly way back after the lap 1 fracas, lost more time investigating gearbox trouble, though the engine sounded as if it would go on forever. The mechanics on the Gardner/Guthrie GT40, having a harder time than the drivers, now changed a driveshaft; Grandsire's 3-liter Alpine overheated, then blew its top, leaving room at the pits for other ailing Alpines. Slotemaker's 2.5 Alfa 33 broke its tail, then an oilpipe, and went out; Lanfranchi's Nomad-BRM went out with oil in the wrong places; Wicky's Porsche 911 threw a rod; the Filipinetti Ferrari 275GTB took an oil too early and was disqualified, and Gosselin's 2-liter Alfa 33 had braking trouble at the Ford chicane, went straight through it, and was wrecked. The 45-car starting list was beginning to look sick.

By the sixth hour, quarter distance, the leaders were Elford/Attwood (Porsche 917), averaging 136.1 mph, two laps ahead of Mitter/Schutz (Porsche 908), and third, *mes amis,* lay the Beltoise/Courage Matra; fourth were Lins/Kauhsen (Porsche 908) and fifth Nanni-Galli/Widdows (Matra), with the Gulf GT40s of Hobbs/Hailwood and Ickx/Oliver dogging their tracks. The other 908s were having their troubles, Herrmann/Larrousse losing 31 minutes changing a front hub, while Mitter rolled a tire off at Mulsanne—it all costs time and helps the opposition—as instanced when Beltoise enjoyed second place for a short time, only to drop to fourth with a long pitstop.

So the pattern of the race developed. Porsches out in front, nursing as much as they dared; the slower Matras trying hard; the GT40s just sitting, for this was Le Mans and did not the Book of Wyer counsel wait-and-see, even when the Sage himself was absent by his sick wife's bedside? The attrition continued, tidying up the lap charts of those who had to try and keep one. Gardner/Guthrie packed it in. So did the yellow Chevron of Brown/Enever (gearbox); the Bonnier/Gregory Lola needed new gaskets; Widdows' Matra dropped from the first six with fuel injection trouble; the Sadley/Vestey GT40 departed with electrical maladies, and the Stommelen/Ahrens Porsche was an ominously long time at the pits, its fine pace broken. Someone must have smashed that *"Vingt quatre heures du Mans"* record, bless him, for we hadn't heard it since the start. By now the lights were on and it was Le Mans *allumé*. The gaily-lit restaurants, *le village,* the fair, and the woods beyond offered varied diversions to the continuous boom of the cars; the race was young and there's still tomorrow, so hell . . . Yr hmble svt., I regret to record, simply went to bed.

One of the interesting things about Le Mans is to return on Sunday morning, fresh and defiantly shamefaced before the stalwarts who stayed all night, and wonder at the remarkable changes which the long run through the dark and the cold, misty morning can wreak on the race. The 24 cars left at midnight had been reduced by several important runners—the Stommelen/Ahrens Porsche had gone (clutch, etc.); the Servoz-Gavin Matra had gone (steering), the Greder/Wisell Corvette had gone (lack of gears); Masten Gregory in the rebuilt Lola had a rod go at full chat along Mulsanne; Alpine, having a terrible Le Mans, had lost all their V-8s one by one and also two 1500s so far; Udo Schutz touched the rail in the Mulsanne kink and practically wrote off his 908 but not himself (Hobbs punctured on the debris); and the Ferrari, alas, had gone too (transmission, etc.) after consuming pailfuls of oil.

But the surviving Porsche 917 of Elford/Attwood was still bombing around in front, averaging 132.123 mph by 10 a.m. Sunday and four laps up on the Lins/Kauhsen 908. Porsche still 1-2, but the Fords were there behind them, loping like patient wolves waiting for the travelers to tire. Ickx/Oliver lay third, 4 laps back, Herrmann/Larrousse (908) were fourth, Hailwood/Hobbs (GT40) fifth and Beltoise/Courage (Matra) sixth, each separated by a lap. Then Fate resumed its cruel game with Porsche. First it picked on the leading 917, bringing Attwood to the pits just after 10 with severe clutch slip. They doused it with gasoline and off he went again, hesitantly and trailing a dismal stream of smoke next time around.

The crowd buzzed, sleepy newshawks in the press stand perked up, and Gulf-JW team manager David Yorke's eyes

Pit action for the 3rd-place finisher, the Ford driven by Hobbs and Hailwood.

LE MANS 1969

gleamed. Small wonder, for a lap or two later Rudi Lins in the second place 908 stopped and handed over to Willi Kauhsen—who returned after a mere lap for urgent work on *his* clutch, then resumed racing very gingerly. He never reappeared, for the transmission seized at Mulsanne and one more Porsche had gone. Now Ickx/Oliver were second and gaining swiftly; by 11 o'clock they were leading, just as the Elford/Attwood 917 pulled in crestfallen to its pits. *Kaput* was the bitter verdict, and the once proud Porsche, now grimed, oily and broken, was pushed slowly and sadly away. The crowd clapped, cheered and whistled, and one would like to think they did it in sympathy for a magnificent effort, cruelly ended.

What next? Ten minutes later Ickx brought the Ford in for water and brake pads, and while halted Hans Herrmann in the 908 whipped past to retrieve the lead for Porsche. By the time Ickx was back racing, the Porsche was 47 sec ahead until it, too, stopped for fuel. Frenchman Larrousse took over and began a grim duel with the Ford, holding it off by bare yards until 12:30 and the last pit stops. Ickx shot in for fuel and out again, co-driver Oliver having to sit out the final drama, while Larrousse led until his pit stop two laps later. Then the ever youthful veteran Hans Herrmann set off, the full load of Porsche responsibility on his shoulders, just as Ickx tore through. The crowd could scarcely contain themselves at the excitement.

Next lap the Porsche and the Ford were nose to tail; 15 yards apart the lap after; shuttling back and forth as the last laps unreeled. With under an hour left, Herrmann came through ahead; next round Ickx repassed; the round after that Herrmann led again; then it was Ickx again as the warring pair came up on Hailwood in the 3rd-place GT40. Mike moved up beind his teammate and kept off Herrmann and then, in the middle of this desperate last-hour Grand Prix, a long, thin blue line of police moved in on the pit area and the grandstand crowd broke into derisive whistles and catcalls. Then Hailwood dashed suddenly to the pits—he was running out of fuel and was nearly rammed at 180 mph or so by an agitated Herrmann—bringing the Porsche back on to Ickx's tail.

A mere 15 sec before 2 p.m. and the finish, the pair fled past the pits, thereby having to cover another desperately tense lap while the flag, going out at 2 p.m. precisely, ended the race. At last they came into sight, blue 100 yards ahead of white, and it was Ford the victors from Porsche—just! After all that terrific tension it was light relief to watch the police form walls each side of the presentation dais, unattainable by Ickx and the winning car on one side and by co-driver Oliver and the jubilant Gulf-JW pit crew on the other. Oliver solved it by charging straight through the legs of the police, and the two triumphant Jackies met on the roof of their gallant GT40.

The results herewith tell the rest of the tale. Of how the ancient GT40s took 1st, 3rd and 6th places *and* won the Index of Thermal Efficiency, really gilding their place in the Hall of Fame; of how Matra covered themselves in glory in their second Le Mans with three cars out of four finishing. Of how a Ferrari *did* finish, the grand old 275LM ably driven by Zeccoli and Sam Posey, the first and only U.S. driver home. Of how Alpine saved the shreds of self-respect by winning their umpteenth Index of Performance with their last surviving car . . . But whew, what a race!

24 HEURES DU MANS 1969

Le Mans, France—June 14-15, 1969

Driver/Driver	Car	Gr.	Miles
1 Ickx/Oliver	5.0 Ford GT40	4	3104.35
2 Herrmann/Larrousse	3.0 Porsche 908	6	3104.28
3 Hobbs/Hailwood	5.0 Ford GT40	4	3077.04
4 Beltoise/Courage	3.0 Matra 650	6	3071.76
5 Guichet/Vaccarella	3.0 Matra 630	6	3002.69
6 Kelleners/Jost	5.0 Ford GT40	4	2852.53
7 Galli/Widdows	3.0 Matra 630	6	2760.24
8 Zeccoli/Posey	3.3 Ferrari 275LM	4	2747.86
9 Poirot/Maublanc	2.0 Porsche 910	6	2604.54
10 Gaban/Deprez	2.0 Porsche 911S	3	2560.47
11 Lena/Chasseuil	2.0 Porsche 911T	3	2518.27
12 Serpaggi/Ethuin	1.0 Alpine	6	2443.21
13 Laurent/Marche	2.0 Porsche 911T	3	2401.10
14 Farjon/Dechaumel	2.0 Porsche 911S	3	2389.57

Distance: 372 laps of 8.35-mi circuit, 3104.35 mi. (Record: 3249.6 mi, Dan Gurney/A.J. Foyt, 7.0 Ford Mk 4, 1967.)

Avg speed: 129.39 mph. (Record: 135.483 mph, Gurney/Foyt, 1967.)

Fastest lap: 3:27.2, 145.419 mph, Elford, 4.5 Porsche 917. (Record: 3:23.6, 147.89 mph, Denis Hulme, 7.0 Ford Mk 4, 1967.)

Index of Thermal Efficiency: 1 Ickx/Oliver, 2 Hobbs/Hailwood, 3 Kelleners/Jost, 4 Serpaggi/Ethuin, 5 Beltoise/Courage.

Index of Performance: 1 Serpaggi/Ethuin, 2 Herrmann/Larrousse, 3 Beltoise/Courage, 4 Guichet/Vaccarella, 5 Ickx/Oliver.

Last Year's Winners: Pedro Rodriguez/Lucien Bianchi, Ford GT40, 2764.2 mi, 114.9 mph.

AUSTRALIA'S ROARING FORDY

PICS: PETER BARR

THE FORD GT40 IS NOT REALLY everyone's idea of what a car should be —but then young man about town, owner Colin Hyams, is not exactly everyone.

Since he achieved his driving licence, Mr. Hyams has at one time or another owned pretty near everything worthwhile owning—Ferraris, Lancias, Jaguars, Aston Martins, and vehicles of similar ilk, have all passed through his hands—some quickly, others not so quickly. To widen the list you could add an immaculate XK SS, a Pontiac Bonneville convertible (purchased I imagine in a more impressionable moment), a Land Rover (painted gold), and even a 250F Maserati —oh yes, naturally there **was** a Rolls-Royce.

Mr. Hyams is a rather rich young man and indulges his motoring whims much as you or I would change our shirts—often.

Now he has the GT40—and this is quite a piece of motor car.

Painted bright red, it is only produced on days when the skies are clear and the sun is shining, a 280SE Mercedes currently fills the bill for inclement weather.

Being the only Ford GT40 in Australia—and probably the fastest registered road car in the world—certainly in this country, we had more than a moderate amount of trouble placing ourselves within the confined quarters of the missile as Mr. Hyams was not all that keen on publicity.

But persistent effort eventually paid off—and our efforts proved worthwhile.

First off—the car is quick—would you believe indecently so.

Mind you, as a half-brother to the car that won at Le Mans one should expect it to be quick but 12.5 seconds through the standing quarter mile?

That is definitely **very** quick.

What's more the damn thing has that sort of performance all the way up through its five speed ZF gearbox to the theoretical maximum of 209 mph.

Apart from that maximum speed—which I am quite prepared to accept as factual without actually proving it for myself—the car is a charger all the way down the line.

It's a sobering thought to realise that it is capable of breaking the 50 mph speed limit—in first gear even yet.

In fact first eventually wound out at 65 mph with second topping 98 mph—and we were just getting down to business.

Third is capable of producing 135 mph, fourth runs out at something in the region of 160—and you still have top gear to go!

A brief history of the car is interesting.

It is **not** a normal road-going GT40 but rather a circuit car modified for road use. It originally served as a team spare but has never been actually raced; Colin purchased the car by "devious means" through the auspices of Paul Hawkins and the late Mike Spence and

200mph GT40

200 mph GT40

although he's giving away no secrets about its landed cost in this country a figure of $40,000 might not be all that far out.

It was shown at the 1967 New York Motor Show and in consequence is somewhat better finished than the run-of-the-mill GT40.

It has the racing lightweight chassis, a five litre fully modded engine, ZF gearbox—and weighs out at 1800 lbs; the later 7 litre versions weighed out at 2800 lbs. and although faster in outright speed were not as good in handling or brakes.

The engine will pull comfortably to 7000 rpm through the gears and puts out an estimated 400 bhp plus—which is a largish lump of power in an 1800 lb. car.

Yet it is amazingly tractable.

We had the car trickling along at speeds of 25-35 mph in top and although we don't recommend it—at least the car will do it.

In Europe, Colin claims to have regularly covered distances such as 300 miles in two hours and in these sort of conditions the water temp. never rose above 70 degrees—with oil temp. much the same.

Forty gallons of fuel are carried in sponsons on either side of the cramped cockpit with a fuel transfer switch located beside the passenger's seat. Quick filler caps are fitted to either side of the flush mounted windscreen and the engine uses 110 octane fuel—with a fair degree of thirst.

Instrumentation and controls are naturally extensive; the speedometer (on the passenger's side) is inclined towards the driver with the tachometer directly ahead of him. There is no ignition key —only an ignition switch operated in conjunction with the fuel pump switch— instruments include oil temp. and oil pressure, interior temp. (it gets pretty hot inside), stop watch, tacho. and fuel pressure gauge; controls cover headlights (quartz iodine), wipers, washers, headlight dip and flash, fuel pump and ignition—and there is a master switch which turns off the lot if you are about to a have nasty moment.

The seats are fully ventilated and very close together and the driver sits almost centrally in the car; foot controls are fully adjustable to driver but interior conditions can only be described as cramped—you wear the car rather than sit in it.

Entering and exiting the car are skills acquired over a long period of ownership and the driver almost invariably finishes up with the gearstick up his trouser-leg; once in, the seats are very, very comfortable and a full race harness adds to a sense of security.

The GT40 cannot be likened to any other car I have ever been in on the road. It is patently built for competition—and fast competition—and the fact that it is capable of being driven on the road with a high degree of comfort (for such a car) is something of an anomaly.

Prior to our run Colin had not started the car in a fortnight but at the first turn of the starter motor there was a dull "whump" and it ticked over like a Customline—"starts almost as well as the Mercedes", commented Colin.

Performance, as indicated by the figures, is of the neck-snapping type and handling (it wears Firestone Indy racing tyres) could only be bettered by a few top-line out and out circuit cars.

However the car does not see many road miles.

During the past four months Colin estimates that he has covered less than 1000 miles—reasons being (a) it leaks like a sieve in wet weather; (b) he's petrified of bending the panelling and (c) he is invariably followed by coveys of gendarmes who figure he's just got to do something terribly illegal and wouldn't it be great to book a GT40 and make local history.

I have read some immense "cans" on the GT40 in overseas mags. and, if judged as purely a road car, they are probably quite apt. This instance however is entirely different as this particular vehicle must come very close to being the enthusiast's ultimate—it goes, it stops, and it looks—like a million dollars.

It's hardly ideal transport for the weekend shopping and if you planned an interstate trip you would need to send everything other than a toothbrush over by separate transport.

But don't take my word for it all— read the comments of Tim Britten who, after both trepidation and lengthy deliberation—came along as passenger.

TIM BRITTEN COMMENTS (Quietly)

IT'S HAPPENED.

At last I've got to ride in a car with enough acceleration to genuinely frighten me. Honest to God slap-in-the-back acceleration.

The type that pins you terrified to your seat as the scenery rushes towards you at an ever-increasing rate. Neck muscles are powerless against the tremendous forward thrust that forces your head deep into the upholstery.

The car hurtles around corners as if it were connected by chains to the curve centre. It builds up lateral forces that make you wish you'd tightened the safety belt a little further and when it stops it throws you against the harness and lifts you off the seat.

And while your reflexes are flat out trying to catch up with what happened twenty yards back, the car is streaking into another corner with the speedometer indicating a ridiculous 111 mph.

Ridiculous because the fastest you'd ever been around that corner before was a hair raising 75 mph.

And of course the GT40 is not at any time approaching its limit—no signs of drifting or hanging the tail, it just follows the selected line and responds instantly to any alteration in lock.

On the exit of a corner, there is a boom of power and before you know it you are into the next and negotiating it at a dizzy speed.

Stepping on the brake pedal brings the car to an instant, dead-straight stop and you cannot suppress a sigh of relief because you figure it's all over.

But in a final demonstration of how effectively the GT40 puts its 400 bhp onto the road, you once again find yourself helplessly thrown back against the seat, watching the speedometer soar towards the 100 mph mark. Brakes are applied, and suddenly everything is peaceful, the only sound being the audible thumping of your heart. Yes, it was everything you expected.

Extricating your shaking frame from the car, you look down and ask yourself whether you would do it again.

If you're completely honest with yourself, I'm sure your decision would be the same as mine.

Every inch built for 200 mph GO — fully modified engine is amazingly tractable and ticks over like a limousine — instrument panel is obviously competition orientated — entry to car usually involves a gearstick up the trouser leg.

Ford's greatest racer reborn

The real thing is outside most people's price range but kit versions of the famous GT40 are now available. Andrew Kirk has been driving one of the latest models on the road. Pictures by Ron Easton.

The prototype replica GT40 poses at Shelsley Walsh hill climb circuit, resplendent in Gulf livery

TODAY it is impossible to put a price tag on a genuine Ford GT40 but, back in 1971, cars regularly changed hands for the paltry sum of £3,500. Just imagine! For this short period of time a GT40 was just about affordable exotica; by 1972 the typical price had soared to a less appealing £10,000. Now the sky's the limit.

For between £6,500 and £7,000, Phoenix Automotive of Goole claims it is possible to put together a KVA GT40 replica, similar in looks to the one pictured, using second-hand components. Phoenix is now the agent for Ken Attwell's beautifully authentic looking MkI, and those acquainted with his work may well remember the remarkable Ford XR3-engined MkIII that made its debut a year or so ago. This latest version is based on perhaps the most familiar and best loved body style of which it is an exceptional copy. To all but the ardent GT40 spotter, the short bodied KVA MkI is a deceptive illusion.

The body is strengthened in all the right areas for road use, each fibreglass panel is a quality moulding and this is reflected in the £3,350 (plus VAT) price of the basic kit. Besides the 19 separate bolt-on body pieces, which include bonnet, double-skinned doors and moulded dashboard, is a tubular steel chassis fitted with rear wishbones and a rollover bar in the centre section. The replica appears over-engineered, perhaps a little agricultural compared with the original racer, but it has been designed with safety in mind and consequently is extremely sturdy with its additional side bracing and gusseting.

The centre body section comes ready-fitted to the chassis with the doors hung, rear section hinged and a strengthened zinc-plated floorpan in situ. Various other small items are included, such as headlight covers and sealing strips, but otherwise all specialised parts are purchased separately from either Phoenix or KVA.

The KVA GT40 by Phoenix (to give the car its proper title) is designed so that anyone with a reasonable engineering background can finish the car if so desired. To quote from the manufacturer's information leaflet, "the GT40 Replica has been developed by Phoenix with ease of construction in mind. Few people have specialist knowledge or access to specialist equipment. For this reason the kit has been developed so that it can be built by a person of average intelligence using a good tool kit".

If, on the other hand, an owner decided — through lack of time or space — to commission someone else to do the building, then Phoenix would be happy to oblige, though a fully-assembled car such as the one pictured which uses new components throughout is a touch expensive at £18,000. The £6,500 to £7,000 figure is for a car using second-hand components but there is no reason why the overall results should be any less appealing.

For simplicity and cheapness, the suspension components are all Ford-based. Cortina Mk3 or Mk4 double wishbones are used at the front together with Granada hubs and ventilated discs, while at the rear, the wishbones supplied operate in conjunction with coil-over shock absorber units and Granada hubs and brakes. Other systems could be adapted to fit but Phoenix prefer this low-cost option. Steering is via Cortina rack and pinion and ancillary equipment is similarly of Ford origin.

The choice of power unit is left entirely to the owner's discretion, but the chassis will take anything from a Ford V6 — as featured here — to a small block Ford V8 engine of either 302 or 289 cu in. The V6 is a cheaper alternative which can be easily picked up for reasonable cost secondhand and according to Phoenix, gives the car acceptable acceleration (0-60 in 9 sec) and a top speed around 135mph.

They are also looking into fitting a Rover V8 unit which could well prove the best alternative of the three with its light weight, good power output and reasonable cost.

The American V8 options also require the most expensive trans/axle arrangement to cope with the large power outputs and then things begin to get a little bit expensive. The ZF five-speed

Like a grown up Dinky toy, all the doors and boot open on this real racer

gearbox as used in various racing versions is an obvious choice and, providing the budget will allow for this £3,000 unit, there is nothing better. It is a full synchromesh box and therefore also ideal for road use. The Hewland unit is a slightly cheaper alternative, though its straight cut gears are not really suited to town driving.

Citroen transaxle

Phoenix recommend the much cheaper Citroen SM trans/axle arrangement — which is also used on the Lotus Esprit — for the medium power units, but the Renault V6 arrangement fitted to this example, is another option that appears to work well. Cooling is handled by a forward mounted radiator equipped with twin electric fans and the water supply ducted through the body. The windscreen is a genuine GT40 item that is still in production; it costs over £200 and, again, is available through Phoenix.

If there is one area where the car falls short in appearance it is in the width of the rear wheels and tyres. Phoenix have tried to make the car as practical as possible by fitting similar sized tyres all round, thus necessitating only one spare, but they have not done the car any favours in the looks department. Even the 205/60 VR 15in Avons on 7in rims look skinny under those gaping wheel arches and are a fair amount slimmer than the 12in wide rims that were normally fitted with equally massive tyres to racing versions. The wheels themselves are fairly authentic looking. The Compomotive split rims painted black and finished with chrome spinners are passable copies of the original Hallibrand magnesium design.

The Phoenix car, resplendent in Gulf livery is the first KVA MkI to be built and consequently is very much a prototype with one or two areas that still require attention, such as lowering the front suspension to get the nose down and fitting suitably improved ventilation.

The interior layout is typical GT40 and climbing in over the wide sill and lowering yourself carefully through the deeply cut-away door you get the immediate impression that this is no run-of-the-mill car. Once the door has been carefully shut over your head, the surroundings begin to register. Facing the driver is a very simple dashboard which Phoenix have made sure is a faithful reproduction of the original, dominated by a rev counter and ancillary gauges. The 170mph speedometer appears almost an afterthought, perched on the far side of the dashboard in front of the presumably terrified passenger, while a lengthy row of toggle switches ranged along the bottom of the instrument cluster control ancillary functions.

Seating on this car is looked after by a pair of Corbeau buckets while the steering wheel is a Mota-Lita item. Those are the details. The overall effect, it must be said, is one that would not be particularly appealing to either claustrophobics or — due to the small footwell of this prototype — those who are tall in stature.

Cramped interior

The cramped and uncomfortable feeling is made worse by the fact that only small eyeball type vents are responsible for fresh air ventilation. Air conditioning therefore would be welcome and is something that Phoenix are well aware of. The logistics of fitting a Granada system is currently under evaluation. As with almost all other racers of 1960s vintage, the interior is uncompromisingly black and, combined with the steeply raked, beetle-browed windscreen and low roofline, gives the occupants the impression that they are inside a very special motor car.

First impressions once on the move are of the forward seating position, the heavy steering — the wide, 205 section Avon Turbospeed radials mean that it is considerably heavier than the standard Cortina from which it is derived — the Ford V6 rumbling away in the back and the delightfully balanced handling. The gear change of the Renault unit is quite smooth and reasonably precise, although obviously somewhat different in feel from the ZF gearbox.

Acceleration of the V6 powered car, even with the standard specification 2.8-litre Ford Granada non-injection engine is impressive enough; it makes one wonder what the Rover V8 might be like! That engine would certainly make the car *sound* more authentic, the only real area in which the test car arguably falls down, for there is no denying that visually it looks the part.

The only slight hiccup with our car was a marked vibration around 2,500-3,000 rpm when accelerating from rest and a shudder from the rear discs under anything like hard braking, suggesting that there is some sort of wind-up effect taking place in the suspension which could perhaps be eradicated by a slight modification to the angle of the rear trailing arms. Of one thing though there is no doubt, the KVA GT40 by Phoenix is otherwise a very well engineered and finished kit. There is need for detail improvement as one would expect from any prototype built in five weeks — a good deal of sound proofing between engine and driver, and air conditioning, would help — but it is indisputably eyecatching transportation from which ever way you look at it. I for one have been converted.

Narrow tyres give away the game from the rear

Cost breakdown of specialised components

MkI Kit including body panels and chassis	£3,350.00
Windscreen	£230.00
Adhesive for above	£43.00
Side and rear window (plastic)	£97.00
Fuel tank	£98.00
Quartz halogen headlamps	£49.45 each
Headlamp fixing kit	£12.50 each
Rear lamp cluster	£13.50 each
Pedal box assembly	£79.50
Front coil springs	£28.00 each
Rear coil springs	£24.50 each
Front shock absorbers (adjustable)	£24.50 each
Rear shock absorbers (adjustable)	£39.50 each

All prices are subject to VAT
KVA Limited, 70 Hendrefoilan Road, Tycoch, Swansea SA2 9LU. Tel: 0792 203118 (KVA can supply kits)
Phoenix Automotive Limited, The Grange Industrial Estate, Rawcliffe, Goole, North Humberside. Tel: 0405 69901 (Phoenix can supply kits and ready built cars)
For further details contact:
Philip Porter on 058 479 336

GT40 MK V

PHOTOGRAPHY BY VIC HUBER

Brand-new and twenty years old: a racing legend you can buy.

BY KEVIN SMITH

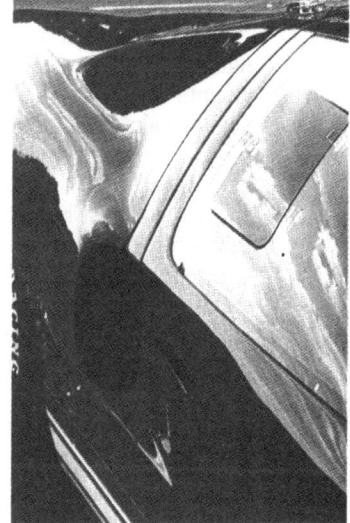

Fort Myers, Florida—Sometimes passion just won't listen to reason, and thank God for that. Look at this car, will you? Utterly impractical as a road vehicle and twenty years outdated as a racer. No one even knows what to call it: Replica? Continuation? Rerun?

So how does somebody feel after paying over $75,000 to put this hopeless beast into his garage? "Ah, it's fantastic," beams Lamont Johnson, of Fort Myers, Florida. "Something I dreamed about."

And fantastic it is, this JW Automotive Engineering GT40 Mk V.

Oh, some people would struggle over the wide sill of the monocoque toward the right-side driver's seat, get the little shift lever up a trouser leg while trying to snake down around the steering wheel, finally get situated only to find each shoe sole covering a pedal and a half, and pronounce the whole exercise totally unacceptable.

Let them.

Other people, the *right* people, will settle into that semi-recline and feel oddly at home. They will look out the sharply raked windscreen over the downturned nose and see the Dunlop Bridge approaching at 170. They will breathe in the unmistakable English sports car aromas and catch a dewy hint of French countryside at sunup. They will grip the quick-acting, leather-covered wheel and sense the awesome responsibility of piloting a machine of such capabilities.

That's what the Mk V is for—to recall memories, conjure visions, and tighten guts. It couldn't do that if it delivered reasonable 1980s transportation—if it were a Cadillac or a Honda or something. But a Cadillac or a Honda didn't win Le Mans four times straight, 1966 through 1969. Ford GT40s did. And some of them weren't so very different from Lamont Johnson's brand-new Mk V.

Half a dozen pairs of hands create the reborn GT40. JW Automotive Engineering (the principals were John Wyer and John Willment) built GT40 Mk Is for Ford and customers in the late Sixties, and some of the very people who worked on the cars then are part of this project. Today they are using the same plans and identical components, and even continue chassis numbers from where they left off in 1969, at number 1086.

JWA starts with a sheet-steel monocoque tub that's mildly redesigned, to substitute hand-fabricated pieces for a few specialized stampings. Fully adjustable spherical-jointed wishbones hang from each corner, where we also find coil-over shocks and twelve-inch ventilated disc brakes with four-piston calipers. The nose, tail, and doors are fiberglass out of original molds. Workmanship throughout is absolutely first-rate—much better than any racer got twenty years ago.

Power can be whatever a customer likes, using the small-block Ford V-8 as a base. JWA mates the engine to a ZF five-speed transaxle (the one from BMW's M1 is close to the original but tough to find—a Pantera box

GT40 MK V

flipped upside down also works). The gears engage with metallic precision, though the lever throws are long; a big, two-handed reverse lockout tang on the shift gate shouts "Racer!" as surely as do the clanky four-point belts and the fire extinguisher between the seats.

Lamont Johnson wanted his car—number 1098—to be fast. His 302 mounts the big-valve aluminum Gurney-Weslake heads like those on the '68 and '69 Gulf-Wyer Le Mans winner. Weber 48IDA carbs, "bundle of snakes" exhaust headers, and a cam that's too fitful for street use combine for over 400 hp at 6500 rpm and stumbling and overheating under 70 mph. (Hey, it's a race car, right? Anyone who wanted cleaner road running could build a nice 300-hp single four-barrel engine—and *still* get this 2300-pound car down the road smartly.)

What does somebody do with a beast like this? The motoring enthusiasm that brought this new GT40 Mk V to the Johnsons' twenty-three acres on the Caloosahatchee River is a family affair. Lamont and his wife, Donnie (her granddaddy had the first auto in Lee County, Florida, a 1903 Curved Dash Olds), roll out "the 40"

BY PHIL LLEWELLIN

Byfleet, England—The wheel has turned full circle for Jim Rose, a cheerful Londoner who specializes in stitching together the sort of cars that don't come rattling off production lines like so many cans of baked beans. Jim's credentials include working on the epochal Lotus 25 driven by Jim Clark, and on the Flying Scot's Lotus 29 Indy car.

Twenty years ago he was building GT40s for the Alan Mann and Carroll Shelby race teams. Then came a spell with Holman Moody. Right now, back home in England, it's 1966 all over again. Jim Rose is building GT40s. That's right. Building new cars from the ground up, not rebuilding or restoring yesterday's retired heroes.

Ford's waist-high winner didn't cease to exist when production stopped in 1969. It just did a Sleeping Beauty act for twelve years before being revived by a gallant prince. That role was played by Peter Thorp of Safir Engineering. He worked out an agreement with JW Automotive Engineering, which had obtained all GT40 design and production rights from Ford in 1967. JWA's John Wyer had been the managing director of Ford Advanced Vehicles for the previous four years.

Thorp finalized his agreement with Wyer's partner, John Willment, toward the end of 1979. The package's contents ranged from engineering drawings to molds for the fiberglass bodywork. JWA also endorsed the pedigree of what is now known as the GT40 Mk V by granting the car its name and the right to continue the chassis number sequence used during the original program.

Until then, Safir had been involved in things like building Formula 3 single-seaters and converting Range Rovers for oil-rich Arabs: "That was all about six-wheel drive and a perch for the falcons," Thorp chuckles.

Picking up the threads dropped by JWA in 1969 was a little easier than sucking Stilton cheese through a drinking straw. The original monocoque tub was stamped out by Abbey Panels of Coventry in 80,000-pound presses, but the dies had been scrapped long since. Jim Rose, representing one-sixth of Safir's workshop employees, had to work out how to fabricate the tub by welding pieces of hand-formed, zinc-coated steel.

"It's completely different—and absolutely identical," he points out. "In other words, only an engineer with an intimate knowledge of the original tub could spot the changes.

"Build quality is one thing that has changed quite a bit. In the old days, the tubs were really just another job on the assembly line at Abbey Panels. Lots of people were involved. Now we have to get *everything* exactly right, otherwise the blokes in final assembly moan like hell. We make sure all the little details are correct. That's the difference between a component supplier and a very small, close-knit team dedicated to building complete cars."

Len Bailey, the original program's

---

in the cool of an occasional dusk for a quick eighty-mile cruise up I-75. "I don't like the bugs, but ya gotta take something," says Lamont, who believes such cars should get used.

This one feels much as you might expect an endurance racing coupe to feel: stiff and stable (though not particularly harsh), quick on its feet, very loud inside and out, and completely untaxed at street speeds—even grossly illegal ones. The cockpit ventilates, sort of, if you maintain enough air speed. You might not want to do Portland, Oregon, to Portland, Maine, in this car, but don't forget that Bruce McLaren and Chris Amon lived happily in one like it for 3002.72 miles in June of 1966.

If you must weigh the alternatives to this kind of purchase, understand that an original GT40 with little race history will hit you for six figures and need lots of fix-up (back then, long life meant twenty-four hours; the tubs corrode horribly). And you'd still not benefit from the quality and upgrading of the Mk V.

Lamont Johnson has Florida license plate "GT40" on order. But his right-looking (if bogus) GT40 British number plate fits the car just too neatly.

"Hey, Lamont. Where you gonna put that Florida plate anyway?" we inquire.

He grins and shrugs. "In the door pocket."

REVIVAL

project engineer, helped redesign the tub. He also provided nitty-gritty details about the modified front suspension used by Alan Mann's cars (it worked better than JWA's in the GT40's halcyon days, according to no less an authority than John Willment) and went on to incorporate some upgrades he'd had in mind to try back in '69.

Other changes have also been evolutionary rather than revolutionary, resulting in the sort of car the GT40 might well have become had it remained in production between 1969 and 1981, when the first Mk V was completed. The fuel tanks are aluminum, not rubber, constant-velocity joints have replaced rubber donuts, and there has been a switch from solid Girling disc brakes to a four-pot, vented-rotor AP system.

"The original brakes were fine on the track, but a little dodgy for road use," Peter Thorp explains with a grin. "Not a lot happened the first few times you pressed the pedal. Apart from your heartbeat accelerating."

Today's GT40s come together at Brooklands Garage, two adjoining workshops located behind what appears to be just another automobile dealership in Oyster Lane, Byfleet, Surrey. Byfleet is a short drive from London, and within just a few minutes of the old Brooklands racetrack, where aero-engined monsters raced between the World Wars. Hidden away behind the dealership showroom is sufficient space for a batch of six cars to progress, step by handcrafted step, from sheetmetal to this middle-aged kid's idea of the perfect birthday present.

Each Mk V takes six months and about 2000 man-hours to complete, which helps to explain why prices range from 40,000 pounds sterling (27,000 dollars) for a rolling chassis to nearly 60,000 pounds sterling (40,000 dollars) for the whole kit and caboodle with a 4.7-liter Ford V-8 engine bubbling out a healthy 320 horsepower. Most of the Mk Vs go as rollers to the United States, where the typical customer then has an appropriate engine installed.

Bosomy maidens wearing nothing but saucy smiles share workshop walls with posters of gung-ho race and rally cars. That's pretty well the only thing this operation has in common with bread-and-butter car production.

Computers, welding robots, and other high-tech stuff? No sir. The GT40 Mk V's birthplace relies on the traditional skills of the craftsmen; on snippers, spanners, screwdrivers, and deft thwacks with a hammer. Jim Rose and his five colleagues come from the same mold as the old-time artisans who created magnificently ornate and enduring wrought-iron gates for the stately homes of England.

Peter Thorp, an enthusiast who has owned more Ferraris than I've had hot dinners, revived the GT40 because it was just about the last big-time race winner that also made at least a modicum of sense as a road car. He calls himself an accountant by nature, if not by qualification: "Despite that, I must admit there's no way I could describe this as a sensible thing to do. There have been times when giving potential customers money to go away would have made more sense than building automobiles.

"That's the penalty you pay for being a perfectionist."

FORD'S ROADGOING GTs

Ford GT40s have been loosed on the streets before. The run of some eighty "production" Mk Is, necessary for homologation as a GT car, included thirty-one cars sold in road trim. "Road trim" involved little more than a milder 289 and softer springs, but the market for pure racers just wasn't big enough. Licensing of these machines was the responsibility of the buyers.

A more serious if short-lived effort was the GT40 Mk III, an attempt to make a viable, streetable sports car out of the Ford GT. Externally, front fender lines were changed to get legal headlamps up to regulation height, the tail was extended to accommodate a modest luggage bin, and tiny chromed bumperettes were added. In the interests of civility, the change list included upgraded heating and ventilation systems, adjustable seats with inertia-reel safety belts, flip-open side windows, a better-finished interior, and rubber bushings for some suspension pivots. The 306-horsepower 289 from Carroll Shelby's GT350 was bolted to the five-speed.

Ford contracted with JW Automotive Engineering to build Mk IIIs in both right- and left-hand-drive configurations (Mk Is were all right-hand drive), though the shift linkage got obstinate when the lever moved from the right-side doorsill to the center tunnel. The car was announced at $18,500 in 1967, $2000 more than the Mk I racers, and the most costly Ford street offering of the day. It came under fire for cheap detailing and poor quality control, but it was a thrilling car at heart.

Federal safety standards (which killed lots of interesting cars in 1968 because of excessive costs to redesign) ended what promise the Ford Mk III may have had. Only seven were ever completed. —KS

Top photo: A young Carroll Shelby (left), who distributed GT40s in the U.S., sends off the lucky buyer of a Mk I road coupe.

Bottom photo: Stirring in concept but hasty in execution, the GT40 Mk III street car is now among the rarest of Ford GT models.

REPLICA RACER

ERA presents a more affordable GT40.

BY KEVIN SMITH

New Britain, Connecticut—You may not have heard of this town, but it used to be the Hardware Capital of the World. The old American Hardware Corporation, among others, lived here—offices, production, everything. (The Corbin Motor Vehicle Company, which built the Corbin car of 1903–12 right here, became American's Corbin Lock division).

Today there's not much manufacturing left in New Britain (there's not much *New Britain* left in New Britain), thanks to industry's general southward migration. But that doesn't mean nobody's making anything here. In fact, the town even has an automotive industry, of sorts.

Over the past couple of years, some 150 of the nicest Cobra replica kits have been shipped out of a humble clump of brick and concrete block structures on the corner of Dewey and East Main. You don't see any "ERA Replica Automobiles" signs until you've found the place.

The blood-stirring Cobra that has been ERA's mainstay is getting a stablemate. And they couldn't have picked a better one. Back in 1965, when the original 427 Cobra was showing its already antiquated heels to almost everything on the street and track, another Ford-powered beast was shaking the pillars of international endurance racing—with the full faith and credit of the Ford Motor Company and absolutely modern, ground-breaking technology driving it forward. It was the awesome GT40, a car related to the Cobra by history, but utterly different from it in every meaningful way.

With the GT40, ERA takes on a vastly more complex car for emulation than it had in the Cobra. But these guys don't just put GT40 fiberglass over a tube frame and a transverse V-6. They build their own sheet-steel semi-monocoque tub, with tubular steel suspension arms, all like the original car's. And they fill the engine bay with a small-block Ford V-8 (in the prototype I drove, a 289 with the proper Weber carbs and

PHOTOGRAPHY BY GREG JAREM

"bundle of snakes" exhaust headers).

A Pantera ZF transaxle is the current gearbox of choice, though ERA's president, Phil Gaudette (he's also the fiberglass man), is working on alternatives from Porsche and Renault. ERA's own cast-aluminum hub carriers will mount Corvette disc brakes. Rack-and-pinion steering comes from Porsche or MG. The customer chooses road wheels and tires; the prototype used lightweight Center Line wheels (15.0-by-8.5 and 15.0-by-10.0), with ERA's Halibrand-style inserts, carrying 225/60 and 255/60 Eagle VR tires.

The ERA GT had barely turned a wheel when I sampled it, and no one pretended it was ready to be tested

and evaluated seriously. (Refinement of the car's road manners, balance, and control feel had not even begun.) But the project showed promise: The car looks spectacular—and indistinguishable from an original GT40 until you hunker down to examine details. Also, speed and acceleration are not a problem, with 200 to 300 bhp—depending on engine tune—propelling 2600 pounds.

ERA will offer a Mk I replica in both race and road trim, plus a Mk III street car replica. Right-hand drive might also be an option. The basic kit will list at $21,500; add engine, gearbox, tires and wheels, brakes, paint, and other odd bits, and you can have a nice car on the road for about $30,000. First deliveries are planned for early this summer.

No kit car is easy to recommend, because so much depends on the individual who ultimately screws the thing together. But given a reasonably adept owner/builder, plus a successful development program by ERA, this GT40 replica will wind up an exciting and thoroughly entertaining automobile. To find out more about it, contact ERA Replica Automobiles, 608–612 East Main Street, New Britain, Connecticut 06051; 203-229-7968.

GT FORTÉ

Of all the GT40-type cars now being made, the Safir – being an official continuation of the original Ford run – is streets ahead of the copies. Doug Nye reports

Brooklands Garage, opposite Byfleet village green in Oyster Lane, stands within a few hundred yards of the old Locke-King estate and Motor Course from which it takes its name. Follow Oyster Lane back towards the main Waterloo-Portsmouth railway line and you will see the dark concrete retaining walls backing the old track's Byfleet Banking, topped by the iron railings which once used to buzz to the exhaust notes of cars tearing round the concrete speedbowl over that lip among the bushes.

Some Fords ran there between the wars. One Ford variant under another name, for example, was driven by a dentist named Alfred Moss who would have a son named Stirling. But at Brooklands, Ford never became a name with which to conjure. Far from it...

Perhaps it's ironic, therefore, that long after the Brooklands Motor Course had died, and the modern industrial estate grew on the site of the old Flying Village within the loop of the Byfleet Banking, that various Fords should quite literally begin re-production on this site. Brian Angliss has been building his Cobras there for several years, and in 1981 I met Peter Thorp, whose neighbouring Safir Engineering company had just revived production of what many saw as the late, lamented Ford GT40. Before taking on Safir, Peter had done well in the air-freight business. He was an enthusiastic private motorist and lover of good cars, Ferrari foremost, BMW close behind. Safir was heavily into the umpteen-wheel Range Rover conversion business, selling largely, it seemed, to aristocratic gents of Middle

Opposite top: Safir Engineering's famous yellow roadster – chassis number 1090, and their prototype. Far left: Like all GT40s, the tub is all steel. Whereas older GT40s may now be rotting, Safir's rustproofing is more substantial. Note the impressive four-pot aluminium calipers and vented disc brakes. Top left: Very impressive – 350bhp of 289ci Ford V8 as prepared by Mathwall Engineering lurks in the prototype. Top right: The BRM six-spoke wheels are from the original Kent Automotive castings. Above: Desirable line-up – customer's coupé (red), Gulf car for Canada (centre) and Thorp's own lightweight Kevlar, SVO-engined model. Left: An exacting copy, beautifully built. Photos by Geoff Goddard

Eastern persuasion and intent upon obliterating their desert homelands' wildlife.

As far back as 1975 Peter had bought the Token-Cosworth RJ02 Formula 1 car, renamed it the Safir and ran it twice on a shoestring for Tony Trimmer. They finished last in both the Race of Champions and the non-championship Silverstone meeting that year, but in retrospect at least this brief dabble with Formula 1 was fun while it lasted…

Then, in 1980, Peter began the project which revived production of the Ford GT40 at Safir's Brooklands plant. Impetus for the idea came from Safir's workforce, already including four former GT40 racing mechanics, headed by Jim Rose; he had worked variously for the original Ford Advanced Vehicles outfit, JW Automotive Engineering, Alan Mann Racing and the US-based Holman & Moody satellite concern.

FAV had been set up to originate the entire Ford GT Le Mans car project in 1963-64. JW had combined the experience of ex-FAV chief John Wyer with the funding of Ford main dealer and team patron John Willment to inherit GT40 manufacturing rights and 'works team' racing after FAV's closure. Mann's was a leading independent Ford team which pursued its own independent development, while Holman & Moody were Stateside specialists charged by Ford with getting results from the mid-sixties GT programme when the Brits seemed unable to hack it…

With this encouragement, Peter Thorp had tried to buy an original-series GT40 in decent condition, planning to enter and race it in the growing number of European historic events for which it would be eligible. But he could not find a GT40 in decent condition for what he regarded as a sensible price…

The original FAV and JW Automotive-manufactured cars used monocoque chassis welded up from rolled and pressed sheet steel panels. This was unusual in the racing world where most monocoques were riveted and sometimes bonded from aluminium. There were advantages and disadvantages to both steel and aluminium structures. Certainly, for racing purposes a steel tub is almost capriciously overweight compared to an aluminium one, and steel rusts easily where aluminium does not. The steel-tub GT40s became time-bombs, ticking away to corrosive auto-destruction unless they were very well cared for, which quite often was not the case.

Conversely, the welded-steel GT40 tubs, if well maintained, have proved extremely durable, several sustaining the kind of mileages which would have long-since demolished a racing-style riveted alumin-

He could not find a GT40 in decent condition for what he regarded as a sensible price…

ium chassis. Although considerably lighter, and rust-resistant, the riveted aluminium monocoque ages rapidly as its rivet-holes become oval, seams spread, rivets chatter and chafe and without constant re-zipping – and in many cases complete panel replacement – they go through a Lotus Elite style process of spontaneous disassembly… To re-skin and re-rivet an 'ali' tub is to give it a *real* treat.

In Safir's case, Peter Thorp's search for an affordable original GT40 in decent condition drew a blank. At that time prices were rocketing, and what he considered to be a fortune was being asked, "for some awful old rot-boxes". Then by chance he met John Willment, of JW Automotive fame, who still held the GT40 manufacturing rights. They discussed GT40s in general, and with Jim Rose and his colleagues' experience concentrated at Safir the conversation came round naturally to restarting production after its 11 year break.

In effect, Safir would build a revised and modernised version of the standard GT40 Mark I production model, which would then be sold through JW Automotive Engineering Ltd although that company had effectively lain dormant for several years. JW would draw a royalty on every car sold. Production would be restricted, an initial batch of 25 being visualised, to maintain the model's exclusivity.

The new Safir-built cars' design would be updated by original chassis engineer Len Bailey, and they would be marketed as 'GT40 MkVs'. They would carry '*JW Automotive Engineering Ltd*' chassis plates, no Ford identity being attached. The Ford Motor Company tacitly approved the project, but to protect themselves from any potential product liability problems should a high-rolling customer do just that in his new MkV, they felt unable to allow their name to be used formally.

Thorp and Willment reached agreement for Safir to base its MkV run on the original designs, drawings, patterns and spares still held by dormant JW Automotive. New Safir-built chassis would be numbered on from the original 1000-series system, which had ended effectively at '1089' with the final three serials reserved for unassembled cars existing in component form. Thus Safir's prototype would become JWA's number '1090'. This itself created a minor paperwork problem once the first 11 MkVs had been completed, for original chassis numbers '1101' to '1107' were allocated to the long-tailed, four-headlamp, road-going GT40 Mark IIIs built by JW during the original run. Consequently the MkV run would break at this point, further skip numbers '1108' to '1114' which went onto the left-over original-series tubs obtained and completed by other people, and then take up again at '1115'.

Just what kind of a house in the home counties can you buy for £60,000 nowadays anyway? First-time buyers may be more happily tempted by the Safir GT40…

Roadster GT40s – like the first Safir – were rare, but Ken Miles and Lloyd Ruby won in one at Sebring in 1966

The Mark V specification would be as close to the original GT40 Mark I as possible without being strait-jacketed by it. Where sensible advantages were available from improved modern technology, they would be incorporated. This detail redesign to absorb such improvements, and to suit Safir's production facilities and funding, landed on Len Bailey's freelance drawing board. Ultimately Ford would be sufficiently impressed by these revived GT40 MkVs to allow Safir/JW to apply 'Powered by Ford' decals, but still no marque badging…

The main changes from original Mark I spec involved alterations to adapt the welded-steel monocoque to hand fabrication. This was necessary because some of the vital original press tools had been lost. In fact, fabrication saved a little weight without compromising any of the original tub's vaunted strength and integrity. Visually the differences between a Mark I Ford tub and a Mark V Safir are obvious, as the Mark I outer-sill panels were curved pressings while the MkV's are angular, with two flat panels seamed together along a crisp bottom edge.

Len's redesign also incorporated some suspension geometry improvements which had once featured on the ultimate Alan Mann team cars and which were apparently in advance of JW's own spec. Other changes were necessary to accommodate modern AP ventilated disc brakes, while the original rubber bungee driveshaft UJ doughnuts were replaced by Hookes type. The ZF five-speed 5DS25/2 transaxle was adapted from modern BMW M1 stock, but its 'innards' were in any case near-identical to the original GT40's, only the top of the casing's output housing and the clutch throw-out arrangements having been materially updated since then.

The original GT40's bag-type fuel cells had been dogged by various troubles – not least sourcing and pattern costs – so Safir adopted instead twin alloy tanks with a cross-feed system, mounting as before in the monocoque sills beneath each door.

Their prototype Mark V was laid down in 1980, destined for Peter Thorp himself, and since he prefers open-air motoring it was to be an open-topped roadster with a detachable fabric tonneau cover. Its lack of a rigid roof section demanded a reinforced tub to compensate. The problem was how to stabilise the rear cockpit bulkhead and screen-and-scuttle framework without the standard roof panel – which is deeply indented for the door wrap-overs on each side – linking them fore and aft. Jim Rose's fabricators added a second transverse rear baffle or bulkhead panel within the sills on each side to stiffen the rear bulkhead foundation, and so prevent it flexing fore and aft. Up front, extra fillets were welded into the A-posts (supporting the door hinges) at the foot of the screen. These amendments were unnecessary in the normal roofed-in cars whose standard monocoque was already so well proven and understood, irrespective of those changed sill-sections in MkV form.

It was decided that the 289cu ins Ford V8 engine would be offered as standard, with iron heads and a single four-barrel Holley carburettor for sensible public road use. Stuart Mathieson's Mathwall Engineering company would assemble, supply and tune the engines in Britain, but since considerable interest was expected from North America and the basic

> **Smiths Industries were cajoled into supplying GT40 instruments including 0-200mph speedos with the appropriate sexy red illumination**

purchase price would inevitably be quite high, any customer preference could be entertained. It was logical for Safir/JW to offer the MkV in rolling chassis form, less engine, in that market … where Ford V8 lumps and parts were more readily and more cheaply available than over here.

Initial progress was painfully slow on the prototype as it became apparent that most of the pattern equipment and jigs had been discarded or scrapped during the years of inactivity. Great help in locating original parts and resourcing others came from Brian Wingfield of the British GT40 Owners' Club (manufacturer in his own right of the superb, live-axled DeeType Jaguar replicas) and from Brian Angliss who loaned his original GT40 and supplied some important key components.

Safir invested both time and money quite heavily in creating all-new patterns and jigs, necessary for items like the new front uprights required by ventilated disc brakes. They found that one of JW's old suppliers had preserved an original set of body moulds, which were pressed back into service for the MkV, while Kent Automotive still had the original BRM six-spoke wheel casting patterns used in later Mark Is and were willing and able to supply mag wheels in the appropriate sizes. The original complex cross-over exhaust jig was also unearthed, while Jim Rose's team produced from original drawings components like wishbones, pedal assemblies, gear linkage and steering column, plus numerous sub-assemblies where proprietary components were unobtainable.

As deliberate policy, the appearance of the MkV, both external and interior, was kept as close as possible to original Mark I. Even Smiths Industries were cajoled into supplying original style GT40 instruments including 0-200mph speedos with the appropriate sexy red illumination …

Peter's prototype roadster was completed at last in March 1981, and while still gleaming in its original bright yellow Safir showed it off to one or two journalists. Peter had it fitted with 302CID Ford V8 engine equipped with Gurney-Weslake free-flow heads and a four-barrel Holley carburettor. Power output ex-Mathwall was around 350bhp. As I discovered when I drove it, this engine provided very smooth, flexible and undramatic motoring even in heavy traffic, while also giving enough sheer 'grunt' to set the adrenalin pumping well and truly on the open road! The MkV, of course, was a car you 'put on' rather than 'sit on', and it was certainly an exciting projectile in all departments. A real GT40 updated, just as intended …

AP provided a progressive and light new twin dry-plate clutch to replace the original rather heavy, competition-tailored three-plate type. The Jack Knight rack and pinion steering was extremely positive and full of feel although the turning circle in original form was rather large and would be reduced. The 12ins diameter ventilated disc brakes were as powerful as predicted, and progressive despite the pedal demanding heavy pressures. The first customer car was subsequently fitted with two-servo assistance.

Like the original GT40 roadster, Safir's prototype MkV had no real top frame panel above its windscreen, but one was added later to this car, and to the subsequent second roadster which replaced it as Peter Thorp's own car. The original was sold to a

Original roadgoing GT40 Mk3 had quad headlamps, quarter-light windows and a longer tail for luggage capacity

Sandwiched between Ford GT40 and Safir GT40 in Ford chronology is GT70, three examples of which were made

German customer, sprayed red, and is now back at Safir's new Brooklands Garage premises looking pristine and ready for resale.

Peter's replacement roadster now uses one of two special lightweight MkV tubs, the other yet to be assembled into a complete car as I write. Weight has been saved by a combination of finer-gauge skins in certain areas and extensive drilling and perforation, and further weight has been saved on the roadster by using an exotic Kevlar body instead of the standard GRP.

Where the lightest standard MkV weighs around 980kgs (2160lbs) the boss's latest roadster scales 900kgs (1984lbs) and that's a difference one can feel and demonstrate on the stopwatch. It is fitted with a Ford SVO V8 engine with alloy heads as developed for TransAm and NASCAR racing in the USA. This unit stands taller than normal, which makes clearances beneath the tail body-panelling tighter and exaggerates heat build-up there.

Obviously the MkV was going to be an expensive car to build and even more expensive to buy. Unfortunately, the project rather got off on the wrong foot in the important US market where an early and unfortunately influential press misprint quoted a fabulously outrageous price. Once such an impression has been inflicted upon Americans it seems terribly difficult to persuade them otherwise. Funny people. In this high-rolling market another problem has been the limited attention-span of some attracted by the GT40 mystique and able to afford such a fun car. Buying a brand new £60,000 car which looks as good and should go better than a £125,000 old one seems to attract wealthy impulse buyers who might even take two if they could only wrap them up and take them away right *now*. But having instead to order the car, discuss their preferred detail spec and then wait months while it is completed is too much for their limited patience – impulse enthusiasm evaporates quickly.

MkV prices evolved into 1986 at £59,250 (excluding taxes) for a complete car to standard spec fitted with a rebuilt Ford 289CID hipo V8, or £49,950 as a complete rolling chassis without engine and ancillaries. A less complete rolling chassis option reduced the price to £36,225, while providing one took a chassis as well, a complete body panel set was also available at £3675. No! Safir would not sell you one of these panel sets to fit your KVA or other GT40 replica.

Obviously such a price for the complete car would bring you everything that an original-series GT40 could offer apart from its individual history, its almost inevitably worn-out componentry and its flakes of internal tub rust...

For just under 60 grand the wealthy enthusiast could arm himself with a brand spanking new road or race GT40 as good as anything JW Automotive ever provided, indeed more so, in view of the the modernity offered by the MkV's updated braking and suspension systems. What is more, for that kind of money prospective customers could specify their individual requirements. The final price would have to be adjusted to accommodate such customising, but it should all have worked well...

However, looking at it objectively, the Safir/JW set-up seemed perfectly capable of building the cars very nicely to high standards, but they were certainly never adequately geared to promoting their cars effectively within the right market. As with so many British projects, there was precious little wrong with the engineering and the heart behind it, but the sales drive was lacking.

Between 1981-87 several modifications were made to Safir's MkV run, such as the adoption of AP four-pot alloy brake calipers in place of the original iron ones, larger radiator, a new stainless steel exhaust system, a rear-mounted oil cooler to save the additional heat source of oil piping through the cockpit, wider use of expensive Aeroquip hosing in the engine bay, improved quality body panel mouldings, and the substitution of low-baked Glasurit two-pack paint finishes which maintain their shine much better than the original cellulose.

The later MkV tubs have been welded up from Zintac zinc-coated corrosion-resistant steel sheet, and as the stainless exhaust systems eject heat to atmosphere far more rapidly than the older pipework extra cooling louvres are moulded into the rear screen transparency.

> **As with so many British projects, there was precious little wrong with the engineering and the heart behind it, but the sales drive was lacking**

The right-hand gear-change and all-synchro transaxle also saw development, ZF themselves modifying the basic M1-series 'boxes on Safir's behalf to come closer to original GT40 configuration, clutch throw-out for example swapping sides. Early cars used 8ins-wide BRM rims all round, later numbers 8ins fronts, 10ins rears. Proper GT40s always ran treaded tyres as standard – pre-slick days you see – and the MkVs used Goodyear NCTs originally, more recently superseded by BF Goodrich Comp T/As, 215/60 VR15 and 255/60 VR15 sections, which have proved very effective on the road.

Spax adjustable dampers have always been used although one would look at alloy Konis for serious competition. Crucially, four Spax dampers cost about the same as one Koni, while there's little substantial difference in individual damper weight.

The original Mark Is used Stewart-Warner fuel pumps, the MkVs set out with Bendix but have more recently been rigged with Japanese Mitsuba twin pumps which look more like the original S-Ws than the Bendix ever did. One Mitsuba easily delivers sufficient fuel-flow for road use but two are required to sustain adequate high rpm feed in competition.

Sixteen of the originally-projected batch of 25 GT40 MkV have now been produced, including two as yet uncompleted chassis – one the second lightweight unit – which are yet to complete final assembly at Brooklands Garage.

Of the 16 sold thus far, one went to Norway (of all places!), five to Britain (including the original '1090' roadster which has since been to Germany and back), and 10 to North America where they have been accepted for what the colonials choose to describe as 'vintage' racing.

Currently, in the wake of the oil price recession cutting off demand for their exotic Range-Rover conversions, Safir is running down MkV production to concentrate instead upon the growing high-performance conversion of quality saloon cars like Mercedes and BMWs.

So there is now at least one MkV tub ready-built and available to order, plus – on paper – eight more chassis numbers to complete the originally projected batch. Three things seem certain. First, any future MkV customer will have to pay considerably more for his new car, in line not only with Safir's escalating production cost but also with the car's re-sale value relative to the spiralling prices recognised for old original Mark Is. Secondly, the sheer quality of construction and specification flexibility offered by Safir/JW is absolutely in the best traditions of the

Spot the difference – this is a Safir at Goodwood

original-series customer GT40s, as Ford's tacit approval for the project surely proves. Thirdly, Safir seem to have done themselves few favours by playing their MkV cards as close to their chest as they have, for the MkV has been relatively unpublicised for such an impressive car of that collectable calibre.

It remains to be seen whether or not the full projected MkV run of 25 will be completed, but if you should be in the market for a GT40 and a six-figure price for a clapped out and probably spurious old one is *just* beyond you ... don't give up. You could still have a brand new one for a five-figure sum, and how's this for a public service announcement? The telephone number is 09323 45132 and, *no*, I am not on a percentage ...

It's a curiously disappointing thing to have to say, but one more thing is certain. Try a GT40 MkV against a GT40 MkI and you probably *would* be able to tell the difference, because the MkV would be much better ... All it would lack is that often intangible, if not fraudulent, thing called history.

John Willment (left) and John Wyer inspected the Safir